E-Learning and Digital Education in the Twenty-First Century

Edited by M. Mahruf C. Shohel

Published in London, United Kingdom

IntechOpen

Supporting open minds since 2005

E-Learning and Digital Education in the Twenty-First Century
http://dx.doi.org/10.5772/intechopen.87797
Edited by M. Mahruf C. Shohel

Contributors
Igor Balaban, Miran Zlatović, Željko Hutinski, Jowati Juhary, Dominique Verpoorten, Pascal Detroz, Françoise Jérôme, Johanne Huart, Charanjit Kaur Swaran Singh, Eng Tek Ong, Noor Alhusna Madzlan, Tarsame Singh Masa Singh, Mazura Mastura Muhammad, Revathi Gopal, Siti Shuhaida Shukor, Nor Azmi Mostafa, Mahendran Maniam, Emad Farouk Saleh, Monika Hattinger, Maria Spante, Glenda H.E. Gay, Eugenia Kovatcheva, Milena Koleva, Mildred Atieno Ayere, Khaled Hamdan, Abid Amorri, M. Mahruf C. Shohel, Dev Raj Acharya, Mohammad Mojibur Rahman, Muhammad Naveed Anwar, Arif Mahmud, Munira Azhar Urmee, Md. Ashrafuzzaman, Atm Shafiul Alam, Ling Ma, Andy Watson, Michael Chai, Vindya Wijeratne, Alessandro Leite Cavalcanti, Isla Camilla Carvalho Laureano, Alidianne Fábia Cabral Cavalcanti, Jucier Gonçalves Junior, Beatriz De Castro Magalhães, Adriana Vieira Nobre, Rachel Cardoso De Almeida, Laís Barreto De Brito Gonçalves, Liz Marjorie Batista De Freitas Leite, Evanira Rodrigues Maia, Maria Do Socorro Vieira Lopes, Grayce Alencar Albuquerque

First published in London, United Kingdom, 2022 by IntechOpen
IntechOpen is the global imprint of INTECHOPEN LIMITED, registered in England and Wales, registration number: 11086078, 5 Princes Gate Court, London, SW7 2QJ, United Kingdom
Printed in Croatia

British Library Cataloguing-in-Publication Data
A catalogue record for this book is available from the British Library

Additional hard and PDF copies can be obtained from orders@intechopen.com

E-Learning and Digital Education in the Twenty-First Century
Edited by M. Mahruf C. Shohel
p. cm.
Print ISBN 978-1-83962-589-3
Online ISBN 978-1-83962-590-9
eBook (PDF) ISBN 978-1-83962-591-6

For EU product safety concerns:
IN TECH d.o.o., Prolaz Marije Krucifikse Kozulić 3, 51000 Rijeka, Croatia, info@intechopen.com or visit our website at intechopen.com.

Meet the editor

Dr. M. Mahruf C. Shohel is currently working at the Doctoral College, University of Surrey, United Kingdom. Prior to his current role, Dr. Shohel worked for several British universities since completing his doctoral studies at the University of Manchester. He is an academic researcher with special interests in education, childhood studies, international development, teachers' professional development, technology-enhanced learning, and social science research methods. Most recently, he has taught "Digital Learning in Emergencies" for postgraduates at the University of Geneva, Switzerland. He has written extensively on development issues in the Global South and conducted research on disadvantaged children including socioeconomically deprived children, street children, sex workers' children, and displaced refugee children. Currently, Dr. Shohel is engaged in the fields of education in emergencies, education for sustainable development and global citizenship, emerging technologies in education, students' learning journeys and their engagement, and teaching and learning in higher education.

Contents

Preface

Over time, e-learning has evolved and changed the landscape of teaching and learning at all levels of education. Emerging learning technologies have made e-learning very diverse in its forms and applications in education, training, and life-long learning. It has created indispensable opportunities to support face-to-face, blended, hybrid, or online courses. Due to the digital transformation of everyday practice, the process of education has become more complicated yet still accessible for diverse groups of learners. The role of teachers has become more complex, as teachers are no longer the only sources of information and knowledge for their students. Formally or informally, educators need to help learners develop new competencies and prepare them for the unknown future in the fast-growing and evolving labour market. The new generations of digital natives are growing up with a set of skills in engaging with the digital world. Blended learning and open and distance learning (ODL) approaches are increasingly being used and becoming the norm in formal, nonformal, and informal educational programmes across the globe. Therefore, to facilitate continuous improvements, flexibility, and accessibility in e-learning and digital education, it is essential to understand the challenges and opportunities by exploring current theories, policies, and practices.

Though this book was planned before the unprecedented COVID-19 pandemic, the effects and impacts of this global crisis on the global education system is reflected in different chapters. During the pandemic, the education sector worldwide has faced unprecedented disruption, which has created a situation in which addressing learning loss and inequality has become paramount. This is affecting the rapidly changing landscape of education and digital transformation. Emergency remote education has forced educators and learners to adopt blended, distance, and hybrid teaching and learning approaches as the "new normal" practice. Therefore, in the context of emergency remote education, teaching and learning constitute a serious challenge for both educators and learners to adopt new teaching and learning strategies to attain effective educational outcomes. Different chapters in this book reflect on the challenges educators and learners face during their transition to the next "new normal."

This book includes fourteen chapters written by academics from different parts of the world based on their own practice and research. It consists of four sections: "E-Learning,"; "Blended Learning"; "Education in Emergencies"; and "Impact of the COVID-19 Pandemic."

Section 1: E-Learning

Chapter 1, "Knotworking as an Analytical Tool for Designing E-Learning While Targeting Industry Competence Needs," outlines challenges and opportunities for teachers in higher education in designing e-learning courses targeting practitioners' development of competency in production technology knowledge. Teachers are challenged to develop up-to-date learning material and digitize learning tasks such as virtual labs and machine-related cases that align with workplace knowledge needs. Design work used for campus-based education is argued to be insufficient to meet online education while targeting industry competence requirements. Teachers and practitioners are in a transformative process when they engage in mutual design work that encompasses a new blended learning situation. In this process, a new target group of experienced practitioners and workplace demands within smart manufacturing. The theoretical concept of knotworking is applied to shed light on the complexity of designing courses for work-integrated e-learning, aiming to enhance professional competence. Based on a longitudinal competence development project, this chapter analyzes the design practice of an e-learning course through the knotworking concept for understanding learning and practices across professional boundaries.

Chapter 2, "Using E-Learning Platform for Enhancing Teaching and Learning in the Field of Social Work at Sultan Qaboos University, Oman," explores the issue of e-learning as a helpful method in higher education institutes in general, and specifically, in the field of social work education in Oman. Based on a study carried out at Sultan Qaboos University, it presents the knowledge and attitudes of students towards reliance on the e-learning platforms, such as Moodle, as a helpful educational tool. It highlights that Moodle as an e-learning platform enhances communication between teachers and students, and among students themselves. Findings illustrate the usefulness of Moodle and the different challenges social work students face using Moodle in their learning. Finally, it offers recommendations to deal with the challenges and highlights implications of the study beyond social work education.

Chapter 3, "The Impact of Online Learning Strategies on Students' Academic Performance," shows how the COVID-19 pandemic has imposed a virtual learning world that involves students in engaging and participating in online lectures and information. It also forced teachers to adopt a new teaching approach to deliver the curriculum content and new means of evaluating students' personal skills and learning experience. This chapter explores and assesses online teaching and learning approaches and their impact on students' academic achievement, as well as students' research strategies with a focus on students' main source of information viz. library online consultation, and the collaboration with their peers. Descriptive and parametric analyses are conducted to identify the impact of these new factors on students' academic performance. It shows to what extent the students' online learning has or has not led to any remarkable improvements in their academic achievements and, whether, to any substantial changes in their e-learning competence.

Chapter 4, "A Model of the Continual Adaptive Online Knowledge Assessment System," presents a model of a novel adaptive online knowledge assessment system and tests the efficiency of its implementation. The system enables continual and cumulative knowledge assessment, comprised of a sequence of at least two interconnected assessments, carried out over a reasonably long period of time. Important characteristics of the system are: (a) introduction of new course topics in every subsequent assessment, (b) re-assessment of earlier course topics in every subsequent assessment iteration, and (c) an adaptive manner based on student's achievements during previous assessments. Personalized post-assessment feedback guides each student in preparations for upcoming assessments. The efficiency of the program was tested on a sample of 78 students and the results show that the proposed adaptive system is efficient on an individual learning goal level.

Section 2: Blended Learning

Chapter 5, "Blended Learning in Higher Education: Faculty Perspective through the Lens of the Planned Behaviour Theory," illustrates how a particular university tried to implement blended learning approaches. The theory of Planned Behaviour has been used to develop a sound conceptual framework for probing faculty members' intentions and their antecedents. In the responses of 114 faculty members, multiple regression analyses detected that attitude toward blended learning, subjective norm, and perceived control explained 73% of the intention to use blended designs for teaching purposes in the near future. The chapter also establishes that pre-lockdown e-learning practices remained rather basic. It concludes that a better knowledge of what can facilitate or impair the diffusion of blended learning is of importance for higher-education institutions and their staff training efforts.

Chapter 6, "Mainstreaming Blended Learning in a Low-Income University," shows how Manseno University (MU), Kenya, adapted a blended learning approach to provide emergency remote education. The university was able to draw from its experience with adapted flexible and blended learning (FBL) approaches for common high-enrollment courses already offered to students on the Learning Management System (LMS). The university sought assistance from schools and departments that already had parts of their programmes running on the LMS. They were able to tap into their expertise and gain access to a valuable collection of resources about online distance teaching and learning (ODTL). That, in turn, assisted the university to develop online or blended versions of its regular face-to-face (F2F) courses that far surpassed expectations, judging from how well their courses performed, and prepare for emergencies such as the COVID-19 pandemic.

Chapter 7, "Using Synchronous vs. Asynchronous Methods during the COVID-19 Pandemic in Malaysia: Preservice and In-Service Teachers' Perspectives," describes the perspectives of teachers about synchronous and asynchronous methods of teaching during the pandemic. It presents preservice and in-service teachers' views on using synchronous versus asynchronous teaching and learning methods during the COVID-19 pandemic in Malaysia. It presents data collected from three groups of preservice teachers and one group of in-service teachers from three different courses in one teacher education university in Malaysia. Implementation of the e-learning approaches including synchronous and asynchronous sessions was planned carefully based on the course learning outcomes. Important elements such as identification of the learning platform, delivering and conveying information to preservice teachers about the e-learning activities, assessment strategies, attendance, and students' reflection were taken into consideration.

Chapter 8, "STEAME Model in Action: Challenges and Solutions in Mastering the Digital Culture," discusses how the STEAME Model could be used. An essential part of the new digital competencies lies in the interconnected fields of Science, Technology, Engineering, and Mathematics (STEM). For students to obtain them, a variety of learning approaches must be applied in an interdisciplinary educational environment and digital culture. Furthermore, to provide students with more holistic understanding, the concepts of Arts are integrated with STEM to become STEAM education. This chapter presents an extended education model taking STEM and STEAM to the next level and bringing the Entrepreneurship discipline into the mix to create an integrated STEAME curriculum. This chapter presents an integrated STEAME curriculum model, methodology for its implementation, and STEAME classroom and environment design as a new education approach to tackle the challenges of the development of skills for the 21st century.

Section 3: Education in Emergencies

Chapter 9, "Education in Emergencies, Mental Wellbeing and E-Learning," highlights the importance of education in emergencies and how a situation like the COVID-19 pandemic creates challenges alongside opportunities to learn for personal and professional development as well as to ensure the mental wellbeing of individuals through e-learning. By exploring the literature, it draws on different perspectives regarding the issues related to effectiveness in handling education and learning in an emergency in addition to preparedness for post and future emergencies. It also reflects on educational professionals' work with students during this pandemic, that is, how educational professionals report on their adaptation journey and how the pandemic impacted the ability to serve and engage learners. From the professionals' best practices to assist students in being successful to online education or hybrid teaching and learning formats, many opportunities arose to shape and reform education for a better future and transform the process of lifelong learning. This chapter also outlines strategies, in general, for the education sector, and in particular, institutions and individuals to be better prepared for future emergencies through the opportunities e-learning offers.

Chapter 10, "Emergency Remote Teaching during COVID-19 Pandemic: Roles of Educators in Malaysia," investigates the roles of educators in one public higher learning institution in Malaysia during emergency remote teaching during the COVID-19 outbreak. It shows that educators were ready to embark on transformative emergency remote teaching. However, they were not sure of the differences between emergency remote teaching and online teaching; these two have different pedagogical approaches. This chapter also shows that educators were able to use appropriate platforms and applications during the pandemic; however, they did not have ample time to study other platforms and applications. It was assumed that some educators have various options to choose from but may lack the knowledge and understanding of how these options work best. The chapter concludes that in accepting the new normal in teaching and learning, educators must be open to new and creative strategies to engage students during emergency remote teaching and learning.

Chapter 11, "Developing Professionals: Experience from a Distance Learning Short Course during the COVID-19 Pandemic," discusses the development and delivery of distance education (DE) courses "stricto sensu" in nursing to strengthen training processes in this area to sensitize critical and reflective professional performance. It highlights the experience of master's students of the Academic Master's Course in Nursing at the Regional University of Cariri, Ceará, Brazil, in the construction and tutoring of a course in the DE modality. Findings show that the experience was positive in the sense of teaching practices, which emerged collectively through discussions and the exchange of knowledge between professors and students in a planned and organized way.

Section 4: Impact of the COVID-19 Pandemic

Chapter 12, "Impact of COVID-19 on Dental Education," focuses on the impact of the pandemic on dental education. People who are in close contact with COVID-19 patients, including dental students and teaching staff, are at increased risk of contamination, as they work close to the oral cavity of patients and have direct contact with salivary fluids in closed environments. As such, social isolation and distancing measures have been adopted by governments, with severe restrictions on dental education. This chapter discusses the impact of COVID-19 on dental education and the role of emergency remote education in the continuity of face-to-face classes and preclinical and clinical education. It also recommends how to address the challenges and the Brazilian reality of teaching-service-community activities.

Chapter 13, "Together Apart during the COVID-19 Pandemic: Assessing Students' Readiness for Online Assessments Using an E-Learning System," focuses on students' readiness for online assessment. This chapter evaluates students' level of e-learning readiness (e-readiness) and whether it had any effect on their performance in the final assessment. Findings show two-thirds of the cohort preferred the online modality, while only one-third had acceptable levels of e-learning readiness. E-learning–ready students felt the disruption in their study routine most, while those who were not e-ready found more time to study after the curfew restrictions were in place. E-learning–ready students attempted their final online assessment earlier than those who were not yet e-ready, but the two groups had similar assessment grades. This chapter concludes that evaluating students' level of e-readiness is vital in providing support for those who have challenges with online learning.

Chapter 14, "Transnational Education and E-Learning during a Pandemic: Challenges, Opportunities, and Future," explores the challenges of transnational education (TNE). While TNE is becoming increasingly popular as a provision for internationally recognised education at the doorstep of students, the temporary shift from the traditional classroom to remote online teaching and learning caused by the COVID-19 pandemic has been challenging for all stakeholders. This shift has also raised significant challenges of both equity and pedagogy. However, given the current crisis in higher education, TNE can be a cornerstone in rebuilding the post–COVID-19 international education system. Based on a systematic literature review and information gathered informally from various stakeholders, this chapter explores the challenges faced by the TNE programmes and discusses the opportunities and future impacts in teaching, learning, and student support as the post–COVID-19 educational landscape emerges. It also provides insight into how a sustainable transnational learning community can be developed for the quality and sustainability of international higher education in the post–COVID-19 era.

All the chapters included in this book are the works of academics who carried out research related to e-learning and digital education. Technological innovations and digital transformation have enhanced practitioners' experiences of teaching and learning practices and created new spaces for learning in the 21st century.

M. Mahruf C. Shohel
Doctoral College,
University of Surrey,
Guildford, United Kingdom

Section 1

E-Learning

Chapter 1

Knotworking as an Analytical Tool for Designing E-Learning While Targeting Industry Competence Needs

Monika Hattinger and Maria Spante

Abstract

This chapter outlines challenges and opportunities for teachers in higher education in their design work of e-learning courses targeting practitioner's competence development of production technology knowledge. Teachers are challenged to develop up-to-date learning material and digitize learning tasks such as virtual labs and machine-related cases that align to workplace knowledge needs. Design work used for campus education is argued to be insufficient to meet e-learning education while targeting industry competence requirements. Teachers and practitioners are in a transformative process when they engage in mutual design work that both encompass a new e-learning situation, and a new target group of experienced practitioners and workplace demands within smart manufacturing. The theoretical concept knotworking, is applied to shed light on the complexity of designing courses for work-integrated e-learning aiming to enhance professional competences. Knotworking refers to tying, untying, and retying together seemingly separate threads of activity. Based on a longitudinal competence development project, this chapter analyzes considerations of an e-learning design practice through the knotworking concept for understanding learning and practices across professional boundaries.

Keywords: e-learning design, professional competence, work-integrated learning, knotworking, manufacturing industry

1. Introduction

University teachers' efforts and activities of developing blended e-learning courses for professional competence development in manufacturing industry pose potentials but causes also challenges for the university, the teaching practice, and the practitioners. In this chapter these transformative efforts have been defined as design work. The complexity of planning and designing of e-learning courses has been discussed from the university teacher's perspective for meeting experienced industry practitioners need of work-integrated learning.

The potential of blended e-learning is claimed to support learning that is more active, participatory, personalized, flexible, and inclusive towards today's diverse learning needs [1–3]. Blended e-learning courses offer a formal system for arranging and constructing new collaborations and learning between teachers and practitioners in which they can integrate organizational, social and individual perspectives for mutual knowledge development [4]. However, designing for new modes of e-learning targeting industry knowledge needs are forcing teachers' work into a changed pedagogical and didactical practice that pushes them into unfolding new learning strategies and to find an applicable course blend of digitized learning material and new communicative strategies outside the class room [5–8]. Arranging for such learning events includes challenges to define a qualitative mix of on-line time combined with spaces of physical effective meetings and defining knowledge content that matches the workplace demands. Altogether these challenges impact the university traditional routines and teacher's knowledge mediation and hence design work and implementation, hence their design practice [2, 9].

The manufacturing industry is constantly challenged by the digital transformation of the engineering work [10] with an increased need of industrial automation and robotics [11, 12], interconnected machines and big data analytics [13], and new production systems [14] put future professionals under continuous reconstruction [15, 16]. Industry professionals need to be competitive and keep up to industry companies efficiency paradigm, and pressured to strengthen and update their knowledge and skills to meet a globalized production [12]. Consequently, learning to become and stay as a competent expert for an entire working life tends to be harder for professionals [16–18].

Given this situation, engineering professionals continuously seek for new knowledge and learning as an integrated part of work, here described as work-integrated e-learning labelled e-WIL [19]. This means knowledge that will further strengthening their industry experiences combined with new theoretical knowledge. Given these potentials and challenges of long-term transformations call for universities to plan, implement and evaluate competence efforts that meet the industry practice in a whole new way. Earlier studies have emphasized the need to further investigate e-learning across professional boundaries in manufacturing organizational domains and communities [20]. Furthermore, it has been shown that designing for learning across such boundaries is hard, therefore it is here argued for a more close and detailed analysis of how to design to actually plan and implement courses for work-integrated e-learning. Professionals are continuously balancing between individual and mutual goals pressured of their obligations to achieve organizational purposeful objectives and results.

To shed light on the professionals (teachers and practitioners) design work, the theoretical concept knotworking [21] was used as an analytical tool to rethink the design work towards more collaborative activities of professionals temporal teamwork. Knotworking refers to tying, untying, and retying together seemingly separate threads of activity. Hence, the purpose of knotworking is to address professionals innovative and creative ideas and to grasp their inner thoughts and actions in a process of e-learning design. This chapter aims to explore professionals' knowledge discussions in forms of knotworking through the cultural historical activity theory, CHAT [22, 23].

To grasp professionals' involvement and interaction in the design work of e-learning courses, an effort has been made to analyze professionals' specific experiences, their identification, and coordination activities towards transformative efforts. Two studies were carried out within the ProdEx, a longitudinal competence development project, with duration between the year 2013 until 2020 [20]. The project was focusing on competence development within production technology knowledge targeting practitioners in manufacturing industry. In this chapter, a re-analysis of the teachers' and practitioners' experiences has been done by applying the knotworking concept following these two research questions:

RQ1: How can knotworking expand a new e-learning design practice for work-integrated learning?

RQ2: What can be learnt on a systemic level from e-learning design work when applying knotworking as an analytical concept?

2. The context of the research

2.1 The ProdEx project

The ProdEx project (Expert in Production Technology) was initiated as a collaboration between one university in West Sweden together with regional manufacturing industry companies in 2013. It has been ongoing for seven years and will formally end in December 2020. ProdEx will however continue as a regular competence program at the university with courses designed targeting industry knowledge needs. The overall project aim is co-production of competence activities for university-industry stakeholders to strengthen industry practitioner's expert competences. Today the project comprises a network of about 40 different industry companies within the automotive and aerospace sector. ProdEx runs by a project group that is situated at a Production Technology Centre (PTC), which is a well-equipped research laboratory with an automation laboratory, multi-task CNC machines, a material laboratory, etc. PTC is affiliated to the university engineering department.

The university project group consists of action researchers, information and communication pedagogues, IT technicians, administrators, and program managers. Representatives from the project group continuously participate in meetings and co-production activities with the industry stakeholders, around competence mapping of knowledge needs and definition of learning content. Cross-boundary activities topics also concern the design practice of evaluating e-learning design technologies and learning forms towards developing professional skills for a future digitalized industrial work practice.

The teachers are also conducting research projects together with many of the industry companies that takes part within the project. The initial courses in 2014, were designed in action design research cycles on an academic master's degree level [24]. Besides, these teachers are regularly teaching campus courses of 7.5 European Credits (ECTS) within the engineering areas such as robotics and automation, cutting processes, sheet metal forming, welding, additive manufacturing, and smart manufacturing etc. With the support of the project they are responsible for the design work of modifying and slicing courses into shorter modules of 2.5 ECTS targeting the industrial instant knowledge needs. Today, in 2020 within the mentioned subject areas, a total of 30 different five-week flexible e-learning courses, each offering 2.5 European Credits (ECTS), have been designed. At the end of the project in 2020, 82 occasions of the courses will have been completed.

2.2 University and industry perspectives on e-learning

Designing courses for competence development on an academic level encompass a dual situation with the industry effectiveness pressure on the one hand, and the blended competence development opportunities offered by the university, on the other [25]. There may be different motives from the two stakeholders' perspectives of the cross-organizational collaboration that presume a productive development. The university aims to strengthening the individual student to learn more, meanwhile the industry aims to increase the efficiency and competitiveness [11].

Colliding interests and conflicts on different systemic levels may occur, rather than foster energetic changes for learning [26]. Hence, cross-organizational collaborations may not per se cause benefits and learning [27] rather needs to be analyzed through its inner activities as power for change [22]. Learning activities with various inner contradictions are however systemic, embedded in history, developing over time, and cannot be studied directly. They rather need to be understood over time and through close collaborations with the actors [28]. How teachers are using learning technologies has been researched in recent years, however essential questions such as teachers' approaches to use learning technologies in course design that integrate practitioners' experiences and the workplace knowledge needs into the design work is relatively scarce [9]. Studies of teachers' professional identities and coordination activities are affecting their e-learning design plans and pedagogical approaches when including practitioners' experience-based and workplace knowledge needs [29]. Industry practitioners need to learn and develop their competences in a constantly changed work practice. For such needs, blended e-learning courses in higher education (HE) offer a flexible way of learning which is adjusted to and integrated in work practice.

Hence, teachers are shifting identities in their professional role when they approach a new target group [30]. Their perceived design challenges, how they identify and frame earlier experiences of e-learning and/or distance education, or maybe lack of experiences affect how their future pedagogical and technological design will be accomplished. Teachers individual's beliefs and ideas have implications on the professional teaching role and in the design work of e-learning courses that aim to involve active participation from the learners (here the practitioners).

Also, practitioners can feel resistance of meeting the academic culture. Teachers are subject matter experts through an academic degree, but now they need to situate and mediate engineering knowledge, targeting a new group of skilled practitioners with workplace experiences. However, if these differences are used wisely, both actors can, despite their differences, can contribute with valuable knowledge in a learning situation. Industry practitioners and engineers traditionally have long experience-based knowledge of handling machines, tools, and systems, rather than theorizing on practical knowledge. They are knowledgeable and often problem-solving oriented. Therefore, it is argued that constructing knowledge together between teachers and researchers, early in the design process [31] will create valuable insights, higher relevance and flexibility in the design of e-WIL courses [24].

2.3 Work-integrated e-learning and engineering knowledge

In the learning literature, there is limited research on learning that includes engineering workplace knowledge built on participant's experiences as knowledge resources, which can be used in blended e-learning courses [32, 33]. Teachers' need to find a learning approach that is more integrative and relational between themselves and the practitioners, which also can be viewed as 'sideways learning' [34]. Other researchers highlight work-integrated learning (WIL) [19, 35], meaning that work and learning is integrated in everyday practices. WIL can be defined as *"an umbrella term for a range of approaches and strategies that integrate theory with the practice of work within a purposefully designed curriculum"* ([19] p. 4). Designing curricula built on 'ways of experiencing' [36] calls for an approach that incorporates expertise from the practitioners' and their workplaces.

However, what is an engineering practice? [37]. In the engineering work environment, products and processes are constantly changing due to increased digitalization, automation, and robotization. There is a continuous need to improve the capabilities in the working process in manufacturing plants [38]. Operators and engineers therefore must both have operational experience and to be up to date on advanced manufacturing knowledge [14, 39]. The continuous reformation of the manufacturing processes requires employees to regularly assess new engineering knowledge and adapt to changes that imply short-term flexibility, instead of long-term perspectives [18]. Besides short-term perspectives, it is hard to find time for education due to time limits (work vs. time to study), and personnel sometimes have limited experiences of e-learning technologies and low management tolerance for taking time off work for studies, etc. [40, 41].

As argued before, teachers need to establish a close collaboration with practitioners in their design work and to incorporate engineering workplace know-how built on practitioners' experiences. However, such activities presume multiple roles of both theoretical depth and practice-based engineering work. They move from a campus situation into a whole new situation of on-line flexible modes with design of for instance practical cases. Practitioners expertise bonds to diverse tasks such as problem solving and everyday hands-on operations of manufacturing systems. Such know-how relates to procedural knowledge and is different from declarative knowledge [42].

Accordingly, teachers' will have to rethink the learning conditions in advance in their design work of e-WIL courses competence development [43]. Hence, to recognize and comprehend the company organization's knowledge base including their culture, traditions, and practical know-how in such design initiatives [44].

3. Knotworking for tying and untying learning activities

Recent year's research on knotworking have emerged as a response to traditional teamwork [21, 45–47]. According to Engeström [21] teams' traditionally means several people gathered to approach a mutual goal and to accomplish a certain work task, however such teams usually lack both context and history. Today, teams are best understood and replaced by forms of fluctuating work in knots, and through knotworking, as a part of a certain context or activities. The notion of knot refers to distributed activities and partially improvised arrangements of collaboration with otherwise loosely connected actors across organizational boundaries.

"It is horizontal and dialogical learning that creates knowledge and transforms the activity by crossing boundaries and tying knots between activity systems operating in divided multi-organizational terrains". ([48], p. 385).

A movement of tying, untying, and retying together seemingly separate threads of activity characterize knotworking ([21], p. 194). Collaborative knotworking shapes and reshapes to local settings and the center is not fixed and coordinated, rather the unstable knot itself needs to be made the focus of analysis [21]. The *knot* of collaborative work is not reducible to any specific individual or organizational entity as the center of control because the *locus of initiative changes* from moment to moment within a knotworking sequence.

Knotworking, and specifically *negotiated knotworking*, can be used to understand the social processes in inter-organizational collaboration of the learning activities [21, 47]. However, knotworking differs from traditional teamwork in the sense that *continuity is connected to the object*, not to the professionals, because the teachers, the practitioners and the initiators of knots can change. Hence, knots can be considered teams because of their changing memberships and the limited time of their existence.

Engeström [23] has defined the first principal of knotworking, meaning the object orientation of an activity. Through knotworking new object orientation might evolve into a new directionality of purposeful meaning ([23] p. 66).

The second principle of knotworking concerns the tool-mediation of human action and activity. For instance, how e-learning technologies tools (video, LMS-systems etc.) are re-meditating information and knowledge between humans. The third principle concerns the mutual constitution of actions and activity. This applies to collective activities, group actions and to the level of co-constructed mutual activities. The fourth principle of knotworking directs to study changes through contradictions. Contradictions are historically accumulated tensions between opposing forces in an activity [34]. Through revisiting historical layered routines in for instance past e-learning design failures and its contradictions, it was possible to re-construct new ways of designing with new technological tools on a systemic level. Applying the knotworking model requires a long-term effort to study and establish new practices across organizational boundaries. It is through temporary groups that tasks are completing in a longitudinal process where the deadline is not fixed, in which mutual co-construction of future solutions are developing into new practices and further challenges.

4. Methodology

During the years 2014–2016 data collection of two research studies took place within the ProdEx project. Study I was conducted from a teacher perspective [30], and the other Study II, was conducted from a practitioner perspective. The data collection of respondents and specific focus from these two studies are outlined in Section 4.1. Section 4.2 is a re-analysis of excerpts from those two studies through the lens of knotworking.

4.1 Studies and data collection

Of the six included research studies conducted within the ProdEx project [20, 49], two studies were selected that in particular take the perspective of the teachers, Study I, and the practitioners, Study II. The original data collection of the two studies are described below. Study I was conducted through teacher interviews during spring 2014 and targeting the five teachers assigned to develop the first e-WIL courses [30]. **Table 1** describes the teachers positions, course subject area and expertise.

The interviews were performed through a thematic interview guide and lasted about one to one and a half hours in duration. They were audio recorded

Position	Subject area (courses)
Associate professor, PhD Industrial Automation	Industrial automation, robotics, programming (PLC, C++), and flexible and virtual manufacturing.
Senior lecturer, PhD Industrial Automation	Industrial automation, electronics, control systems, robotics, and flexible and virtual manufacturing.
Professor Machining, PhD Mechanical Engineering	Manufacturing technology, machining, metal cutting and forming, simulation, and operations management.
Senior lecturer, PhD Mechanical Engineering	Logistics, quality and design, operations management, negotiation skills, robot systems.
Senior lecturer, PhD Mechanical Engineering	Manufacturing technology, electrical engineering, machining, and cutting.

Table 1.
Overview of the five respondents' positions and expertise.

and afterwards transcribed verbatim. Two interviewers were discussing with the respondents (the teachers) in an open dialogue in which alternative knowledge claims were debated throughout the session [50]. There was also a conversational tone and an open-minded approach guided our interest to understand the teachers' interpretations on alignment and representations of an engineering learning practice. The teachers explored how they perceive design challenges, and how they identified and framed earlier experiences of e-learning and/or distance education, or maybe a lack of experiences. They defined their conceptions on design plans for blended e-learning courses targeting industry practitioner's knowledge needs. Also, a focus was on their perceived ideas on work-integrated learning, meaning how to include practitioners' everyday practice into the course situation and how such inclusion could affect the design of real cases, tasks, examinations and blended forms. A content analysis with open coding was conducted and grounded in the data material of the teachers' narratives about their teaching practice. Individual transcripts were compared to find patterns between statements and thereafter categorized (p. 243 [30]).

The practitioner Study II was conducted during 2014–2016 through continuous focus group interview sessions, which were conducted at the end of each course unit. Data from focus group sessions were collected, audio recorded, and participants were taking part in informed consent. Each session took from one hour to one hour and 15 minutes' to perform [20]. The focus group sessions were performed to capture practitioners' course experiences through their ongoing negotiations, methodologically considered as formative interventions [51]. Each session gathered a unique ensemble of practitioners and teachers with the overarching object of strengthening industry knowledge within specific engineering areas. In total 119 participants (practitioners) and 12 focus group sessions were included, see **Table 2**.

The data collection of the study was ongoing for three years and explored the practitioners' perspectives on knowledge construction through the learning activities within the courses. Mainly their reflections, knowledge views and learning trajectory were studied in order to delineate forms and content of mutual knowledge construction on both knowledge content and e-learning design forms. The data analysis focused individuals' expression of their knowledge experiences and the ongoing social interaction between the participants collectively. For this matter, a content analysis was conducted with concepts, unit of analysis, codes, categories, and themes [52]. During the analysis, codes such as learning technologies, pedagogical strategies, web conferencing use, with corresponding sub-codes such as login problems, communication, and interaction, and so on, developed. Furthermore, the analysis captured patterns and traces of new ideas around practitioners' various negotiations that not only concerned e-learning design and technology use, i.e., the cultural tools, but also motives for knowledge development and new learning

Knowledge subjects	Courses	Nr of sessions	Nr of partici-pants
Automation and Robotics	Industrial automation (4) and Machine security in Robotics (1)	5	44
HR and Businesses	Negotiations Skills (3)	3	34
Mechanical Engineering	Machining (3) and Machining with Tribology (1)	4	41
Summary		**12**	**119**

Table 2.
Overview of the focus group sessions, related courses, and number of respondents'.

Actors	Untying	Tying
Teacher perspective	Campus mode versus on-line mode Issues of new e-learning technologies	Designing together with practitioners Designing digitized cases and labs Digitizing learning content Work-integrated learning
Practitioner perspective	Time and routines for e-learning studies as part of work is affecting the work situation Negotiating obstacles to achieve an academic degree	Time and place for qualitative e-learning towards new practices Incorporating business issues for becoming a competent professional in forms of work-integrated learning

Table 3.
Teacher and practitioner perspectives of untying and tying learning activities.

related to their own workplace. In sum, practitioners' different motives for competence development, the overall university support and the company support became an overall categorization.

4.2 Analysis through knotworking

This chapter first asks how knotworking can expand an e-learning design practice for work-integrated learning. Thereafter, it is asked what can be learnt on a systemic level of e-learning design work when applying the knotworking concept on such design practice. Given this, the re-analyzed excerpts from Study I and Study II through the analytical tool knotworking [21] is applied to earlier learning activities to make open problematic solutions, and more readily grasp fluid forms of knowledge exchange and learning between teachers and practitioners.

In particular, these re-interpretations are presented and organized in relation to the knotworking concept to capture the complexity of the identified issues from a teacher perspective (Study I) and a practitioner perspective (Study II), see **Table 3**. First, excerpts from the previous coding processes was re-coded as examples of untying and tying processes. The coding scheme was further developed to categorize interpretations of oral manifestations of untying and tying processes linked to specific demanding situations. Thus, the analysis was both driven by theory-based categories and new categories that emerged from re-interpretations of the transcribed interview materials following the process of systematic combining [53]. The developed coding scheme is presented in **Table 3**.

The analysis in **Table 3**, will further be explored in the result Section 5, in accordance with the coding scheme that developed during the iterative re-analysis.

5. Knotworking as analytical concept in a collaborative design practice

From a learning perspective, knotworking represents an ongoing process that involves the participation of different groups and stakeholders (university and industry). The mix of contributors bring about gaps and de-stabilization of knowledge, practices, and relationships to normal instruction of cross-boundary collaboration to understand and develop both practices [26]. The professional actors must struggle to make sense of identities, coordination activities and creative ideas in unfamiliar situations in colliding activities, as well as in each other expectations. With an activity theory perspective, learning takes place when subjects encounter dilemmas, tensions, and context-bound contradictions in their activity, in this case, the e-learning design work between teachers and practitioners.

The challenges previously presented in the Introduction (Section 1) and in the Research context and background (Section 2), are issues that teachers and practitioners are confronting, summarized as:

1. targeting relevant engineering knowledge through continuous mapping of industry competence needs

2. developing a case-based methodology that stimulate knowledge construction between practitioners and teachers

3. choosing relevant learning technologies and decide on e-learning forms such as number of physical meetings, use of web-conferencing systems, learning management system (LMS) functionalities, etc.

4. meeting experienced industry practitioners need of work-integrated learning, hence intertwining theory with relevant practice for workplace demands of new knowledge

5. understanding how design work is developing over a period of time for meeting both universities and industry needs of competence development

In the results below, tying and untying knots within the e-learning design activities are analyzed from both a teacher and a practitioner perspective. The excerpts are examples of knotworking processes that are negotiated from various levels. For examples problems and solutions regarding decisions on e-learning content for on-line tasks and examinations, experiences of performing such tasks, validity for practitioners to learn and enhance their own (practitioners) everyday knowledge and skills. The object orientation, the tool-mediation, the co-constituted activities and the contradictions [21] are principles of knotworking, which are analyzed in the activities through untying and tying on various levels (micro and mezzo) in which teachers and practitioners actually manifesting their experiences and thoughts.

5.1 Untying: teachers perspectives

Negotiating certain learning situations within the design work is a process of untying identified and experienced issues and to find a new objective.

5.1.1 Campus mode versus on-line mode

One teacher emphasizes physical meetings for interaction: "*... we can push for having at least three meetings here at PTC for discussions and labs with real equipment ....*"

This teacher is untying a problem by departure from habits of a traditional campus teaching mode, towards transformation to an on-line situation. Teachers earlier identities on how to conduct physical labs and to redefine their classroom context into an e-learning context is about finding a balance from one context to another.

5.1.2 Issues of new e-learning technologies

Another teacher within automation, with high software skills, are trying to unfold software issues: "*There is much software, and I think the challenge is how to present the content of the course in a new way.*"

A third teacher argues: "*... technology problems to get connected with industries because of firewalls. Also, we cannot do everything online, we need to meet and discuss according to my experience.*"

Both teachers are explaining their anxiety of handling new technologies and the problems are untyed into certain micro-level issues concerning lack of skills and organizational restrictions. These hindrances make them anxious about how to perform qualitative e-learning solutions.

5.2 Tying: teachers perspectives

Processes of how to solve problems, to find models and new content delivery and also combining resources in new way in order to achieve new goals (both student goals and accomplished exams) are processes of tying together separate threads into future solutions.

5.2.1 Designing together with practitioners

This teacher claim that it is important to include practitioners' knowledge: "*... look after what experiences they bring in with their background and if they have examples connected to the course ... based on that, we arrange the assignments.*"

Another teacher on the same topic: To find ways of explicate and include tacit knowledge is hard: "*There is not a physical explanation on everything they observe. Therefore, we cannot explain everything. So, there is still a phenomenon what a person does that we can't really explain.*"

Both excerpts refer to considerations on how to design for or with practitioners in order to grasp their workplace experiences into an e-learning format. This knotworking process of tying suggests that understanding each other practices (university vs. industry) across boundaries are fruitful.

5.2.2 Designing digitized cases and labs

Actual problem solving (during a course task) is trained through authentic labs, earlier referred to as a process of untying in which labs should be conducted in a physical space. Such activities are strongly bound to hands-on actions and therefore become hard to mediate as digital learning content. However, one teachers says, there is a need for a qualified system for 3D graphics: "*So, I think it's good to create a virtual lab ... it requires a very high graphic quality ... then you can do your experiments online. However, we are not even close to that yet.*"

In the tying process the teacher is suggesting new solutions into an unknown practice with high-quality graphics systems etc. An innovative solution that will generate satisfied practitioners conducting the course. It is a matter of continuously redefining and thereby shaping boundaries of the teaching role as they come to act in both worlds simultaneously.

5.2.3 Digitizing learning content

One teacher says: "*I think the greatest challenge is to choose which content that must be interactive and to do the separation of other learning material... we do not believe in 45 minutes movies.*"

By learning from bad experiences of long video material including all learning material, new ideas are tied into producing short video films and to decide on other tool-mediations for the rest of the learning material in other forms. This is a process of coordination in order to maintain the workflow through intertwining various technologies and pedagogics.

5.2.4 Work-integrated learning

One teacher describes WIL as: "*WIL is two-folded; first to motivate it to the management that knowledge is good, giving specific demands on knowledge that makes you go to business tomorrow. However, for this type of WIL we are planning, when the companies actually buy a course from us, I think they should have a very clear vision, what they should do with the knowledge, and what they want to achieve by educating their staff.*"

This teacher is arguing for how WIL also needs to be included in e-learning, hence designing for e-WIL courses. Tying together the university vision of WIL with blended e-learning targeting and involving industry practitioner's knowledge requirements, is a way of having innovative ideas on how to perform high qualitative design work.

Untying and tying is an on-going process of resolving tensions and dilemmas into tying new solutions and finding good examples to go further with. The old mental models of campus education traditionally do not fit into this new type of practice. The professional teacher identity is grounded in historical traditions of the classroom metaphor in which the teacher also is the expert, and the learner should follow. However, the excerpts above illustrate that such practice is no longer valid in an on-line environment in which involvement of industry professional's know-how needs to be co-constructed.

5.3 Untying: practitioners perspectives

Untying is a process of unfolding problems to further delineate solutions which is illustrated below from the industry practitioners' perspectives with their experiences of conducting e-WIL courses and participating in focus group sessions as part the ProdEx project. They are actively contributing to the design work incorporating their home company requirements together with their individual experience-based know-how of the broad subject area of engineering knowledge.

5.3.1 Time and routines for e-learning studies as part of work is affecting the work situation

This negotiated knotworking of untying concerns the problematic dilemma of the company's dissimilar conditions to allow practitioners to compensate time for studies versus working hours.

Interviewer: *Do you need to compensate with work time for this course day?*
Operator 1: *No, it is more a feeling one has.*
Operator 2: *What I did not do at work today, I must catch up later.*
Operator 3: *I need to clock in at the factory every morning...*

The operators have different issues for not having time to conduct the studies as they wish. Such dilemmas need to be considered for the teachers when they design how and when certain tasks and examinations could be performed and how it will affect the outcome of a course.

Other untying issues regard how the companies businesses objectives of increased business values are interfering the practitioners when the companies rather view them "as investments" and not emphasize and support their individual learning progress.

Operator 3:...will my company earn money after I participated in this course?
Interviewer: Hmm, the payoff may not occur instantly, what do you mean?

Operator 4: Through a single course, no, but maybe with a series of courses.

Operator 2: But this competence initiative was not intended due to the company to earn money on us, we should increase our knowledge in case of foretoken, or?

Operator 1: Do not say so to me, the purpose was to earn money!

Operator 5: XX, the HR manager said that we should increase our knowledge to develop from operators into service clerks (engineers), we are sitting loose in case of foretoken, and need to broaden our knowledge and get academic degrees.

Operator 6: Of course, the company wants to earn money on us, like with everything else...

The discussion is heating up and everybody is chatting in each other's mouths. This untying of a problematic situation in which various obstacles are negotiated as alleged assumptions are not common to consider in the e-learning design work. The ethical dilemmas encountered here, are mostly uncommon when educating students in traditional campus courses.

5.3.2 Negotiating obstacles to achieve an academic degree

Furthermore, in the same session as above, the operators clearly describe problems of getting an academic degree meanwhile fear to not lose the job.

Operator 1: Yes, but that is also a question of study full-time or not. This course will give you some breadth.

Operator 2: But if the company was really interested of, hell yes, let's get Marcus an education so that he will flourish into being as qualified as possible...?

Operator 1: If such case I would study half time right away, but such time is not even possible...

These two operators are eager to achieve personal development but clearly lack any opportunities to find a possible solution. By untying such dilemmas, they also manifest their fearfulness of not being able to hold on to their job if they don't perform competence development. They are time pressured and hence the course content needs to be up-to-date and designed in a flexible form adjusted to full-time work hours.

5.4 Tying: practitioners perspectives

These excerpts refer to the course design regarding breaking up old teaching routines with less talking's and doings in real life. How are such tying of new solutions and routines developing?

5.4.1 Time and place for qualitative e-learning towards new practices

In this session practitioners suggest using the latest technology of modern equipment to learn for new practices.

Operator M1: But we like to have more meetings here [PTC], so we can run the robots down the machine hall.

Technician 2: More web-based tasks and when we are here [at PTC], we like to run more labs, like those we did today on the final exams. Very nice!

5.4.2 Incorporating business issues for becoming a competent professional in forms of work-integrated learning

The skilled expert operators, liked to help out, and felt they had superior skills in relation to those with an academic degree. The university lacked enough preparations to support those with low experience of practical factory work.

Operator 2: You must have your own machine, the material, and also tools to test. These are the prerequisites, otherwise you cannot solve the task.

Operator 6: However, the benefit was to take an example from the own factory.

Technician 1: But you cannot just walk into the factory and start during ongoing manufacturing...

Again, the real case issues return due to lack of possibilities for all practitioners to perform the real case task. Hence, in this process of tying and re-tying, was emerging by pointing to the industry organizations values of high knowledge and how such knowledge could contribute to others. This was possible through finding own solutions in the real-tasks and to unfold experience-based know-how. Finding well-formulated tasks for real cases within the courses became important input to the teachers.

To summarize. The object of activity was fluent in the knots and the professionals brought in new knowledge through historical experiences and responses to their own doings and organizational culture (university and industry). Negotiations were conducted throughout the mutual design work before and during course implementation, which was captured during teaching and learning activities. Results show how negotiated knotworking *on the boundaries* between university and industry need to be accomplished, because crossing boundaries is not enough. It gives an understanding on how to go further with solutions or best practice for future innovative objectives. By applying the concept of knotworking it was possible to grasp explanations and innovations for a new design practice.

6. Discussion

In this research approach, knotworking was applied to the *teacher study* and the *practitioner study* that connected temporary groups of teachers, practitioners, tasks, and tools across organizational boundaries, to improve learning and knowledge development within production technology. The tying and untying of problems and suggested solutions were knotworking that took part during the course activities and hence described during the sessions. Knotworking that was negotiated in conversations and communicated, were studied from both the teacher and practitioner perspectives and in different time scales. Consequently, grasping such expressed knowledge, was used to give implications for the overall e-learning design process towards a qualitative design practice of e-WIL courses. The illustrated analysis show that knotworking, and specifically negotiated knotworking is prerequisite inter-organizational collaborative activities towards new modes of expanded object of activities. This means to find new forms, content, and constructions for strengthening expert knowledge between theory and practice, in order to open up respective expert knowledge area.

The negotiated knotworking analysis showed how habits and routines (structures) are not working anymore. Rather, the study shows the importance of not transfer old habits into a new on-line community situation that asks for a transformative process to act in a whole new way. By setting aside old structures and rather focus on a more creative e-learning mode of new technologies and content production the professionals are pushed to design differently.

Practitioners actively contributed to the creation of work-integrated e-learning through their own expertise and knowledge into the courses as valuable subject resources. Through negotiated knotworking of untying and tying, co-construction of new e-WIL solutions in various forms emerged.

Recommendations are to design in short cycles of learning activities including planning and implementation of both new e-learning technologies, real-case tasks, interactive pedagogy etc. towards qualitative e-WIL courses.

7. Conclusion

The analysis of the two studies explored a broad variation to further understand the e-learning practices in the design and implementation work of e-WIL courses. Given this, the concept of negotiated knotworking emphasized immediate actions of shared objects of interest as well as longitudinal processes of learning activities.

The chapter argues that knotworking is a concept for capturing creativity and innovation in temporary groups that meet around common challenges, in which everyone needs quick and creative input of both the joint work and the own areas of responsibility. To summarize, the following lessons learnt are outlined:

- Knotworking stimulates *direct uptake* on short-term responses to changing objects of activity through tying, untying, and retying together seemingly separate threads of activity

- Organizing for temporarily teams in order to stimulate shared motives, and sharing knowledge and learning insights outside traditional organizational boundaries are crucial

- Decision making and engagement in new learning practices require stakeholders' (industry-university) abilities of inter-organizational boundary crossing activities

- Actors' (practitioners, teachers) willingness to problem-orientation and curiosity of new technology and knowledge sharing need to be supported

- Universities openness to new learning strategies of theory-practical intertwining, stimulating mutual learning through innovative pedagogy, e.g. case-based and work-integrated cases and tasks should be a priority.

Acknowledgements

Acknowledgement to the project management in the ProdEx project at University West, for participation and contribution to the research results. Thank you, all industry partners, involved in the studies during meetings and interviews. The original studies and data collection were funded by the Swedish Knowledge Foundation and this chapter is funded by the Sweden's innovation agency.

Author details

Monika Hattinger[1]* and Maria Spante[2]

1 Department of Engineering Science, University West, Trollhättan, Sweden

2 School of Business, Economics and IT, University West, Trollhättan, Sweden

*Address all correspondence to: monika.hattinger@hv.se

References

[1] Beetham H, Sharpe R. Rethinking pedagogy for a digital age: Designing for 21st century learning: Routledge. 711 Third Avenue, New York, NY 10017.; 2013.

[2] Laurillard D. E-learning in higher education. Changing higher education: The development of learning and teaching. 2006:71-84. Routledge, London and New York.

[3] Lai K-W. Digital technology and the culture of teaching and learning in higher education. Australasian Journal of Educational Technology 2011;27(8):1263-75.

[4] Wang M. Integrating organizational, social, and individual perspectives in Web 2.0-based workplace e-learning. Information Systems Frontiers. 2011;13(2):191-205.

[5] Bennett L. Learning from the early adopters: developing the digital practitioner. Research in Learning Technology. 2014;22:21453.

[6] Buchanan T, Sainter P, Saunders G. Factors affecting faculty use of learning technologies: Implications for models of technology adoption. Journal of Computing in Higher Education. 2013;25(1):1-11.

[7] Osborne R, Dunne E, Farrand P. Integrating technologies into “authentic”assessment design: an affordances approach. Research in Learning Technology. 2013;21 (21986 - http://dx.doi.org/10.3402/rlt.v21i0.21986).

[8] Murray MC, Pérez J. Informing and performing: A study comparing adaptive learning to traditional learning. International Journal of an Emerging Transdiscipline, vol 18, p 111-125, http://wwwinformnu/Articles/Vol18/ISJv18p111-125Murray1572pdf. 2015.

[9] Kirkwood A, Price L. Technology-enhanced learning and teaching in higher education: what is ‘enhanced’and how do we know? A critical literature review. Learning, media and technology. 2014;39(1):6-36.

[10] De Carolis A, Macchi M, Negri E, Terzi S, editors. Guiding manufacturing companies towards digitalization a methodology for supporting manufacturing companies in defining their digitalization roadmap. 2017 International Conference on Engineering, Technology and Innovation (ICE/ITMC); 2017: IEEE.

[11] Ford M. Rise of the Robots: Technology and the Threat of a Jobless Future: Basic Books, London, England; 2015.

[12] Koren Y. The global manufacturing revolution: product-process-business integration and reconfigurable systems: John Wiley & Sons, Hoboken, New Jersey.; 2010.

[13] Günther WA, Mehrizi MHR, Huysman M, Feldberg F. Debating big data: A literature review on realizing value from big data. The Journal of Strategic Information Systems. 2017;26(3):191-209.

[14] Henriksen B, Rolstadås A. Knowledge and manufacturing strategy–how different manufacturing paradigms have different requirements to knowledge. Examples from the automotive industry. International Journal of Production Research 2010;48(8):2413-30.

[15] Susskind R. How technology will transform the work of human experts. Brief. 2016;43(3):22-3.

[16] Susskind R, Susskind D. The future of the professions: How technology will transform the work of human experts: Oxford University Press, USA; 2015.

[17] Belski I, Adunka R, Mayer O. Educating a creative engineer: learning from engineering professionals. Procedia CIRP. 2016;39:79-84.

[18] Schmiede R, Will-Zocholl MC. Engineers' work on the move: challenges in automobile engineering in a globalized world. Engineering Studies 2011;3(2):101-21.

[19] Patrick C-j, Peach D, Pocknee C, Webb F, Fletcher M, Pretto G. The WIL (Work Integrated Learning) report: a national scoping study [Final Report]: Queensland University of Technology; 2008.

[20] Hattinger M. Co-constructing Expertise: Competence Development through Work-Integrated e-Learning in joint Industry-University Collaboration. Trollhättan: University West; 2018a.

[21] Engeström Y. From teams to knots: Activity-theoretical studies of collaboration and learning at work: Cambridge University Press; 2008.

[22] Engeström Y. Learning by expanding: An activity-theoretical approach to developmental research. 2 ed: Cambridge University Press, United States.; 2015.

[23] Engeström Y. Enriching activity theory without shortcuts. Interacting with Computers. 2008;20(2):256-9.

[24] Hattinger M, Eriksson K, editors. Action Design Research: Design of e-WIL for the Manufacturing Industry. In proceedings of the Americas Conference on Information Systems, AMCIS 2015, Puerto Rico August 13-15, 2015; 2015.

[25] Servage L. Strategizing for workplace e-learning: some critical considerations. Journal of Workplace Learning. 2005;17(5/6):304-17.

[26] Fenwick T. Organisational learning in the "knots" Discursive capacities emerging in a school-university collaboration. Journal of Educational Administration. 2007;45(2):138-53.

[27] Yamazumi K. Human agency and educational research: A new problem in activity theory. An International Journal of Human Activity Theory 1: 19-39. 2007.

[28] Engeström Y, Sannino A. Discursive manifestations of contradictions in organizational change efforts: A methodological framework. Journal of Organizational Change Management. 2011;24(3):368-87.

[29] Akkerman SF, Bakker A. Boundary crossing and boundary objects. Review of educational research. 2011a;81(2):132-69.

[30] Hattinger M. Researchers design conceptions of e-learning courses targeting industry practitioners' competence needs. International Journal of Continuing Engineering Education and Life-Long Learning. 2018b;28(3-4):235-53.

[31] Hattinger M, Eriksson K. Co-construction of Knowledge in Work-Integrated E-learning Courses in Joint Industry-University Collaboration. International Journal of Advanced Corporate Learning (iJAC). 2018;11(1): 10-6.

[32] Nicolini D, Gherardi S, Yanow D. Knowing in organizations: A practice-based approach. New York, USA.: ME Sharpe; 2003.

[33] Tynjälä P. Perspectives into learning at the workplace. Educational research review. 2008;3(2):130-54.

[34] Engeström Y. Expansive learning at work: Toward an activity theoretical reconceptualization. Journal of education and work. 2001;14(1):133-56.

[35] Trede F. Role of work-integrated learning in developing professionalism and professional identity. Asia-Pacific Journal of Cooperative Education. 2012;13(3):159-67.

[36] Case J. Education Theories on Learning: an informal guide for the engineering education scholar. © Higher Education Academy Engineering Subject Centre, Loughborough University; 2008.

[37] Sheppard S, Colby A, Macatangay K, Sullivan W. What is engineering practice? International Journal of Engineering Education. 2007;22(3):429.

[38] Downey GL. What is engineering studies for? Dominant practices and scalable scholarship. Engineering Studies 2009;1(1):55-76.

[39] Johri A, Olds BM. Situated engineering learning: Bridging engineering education research and the learning sciences. Journal of Engineering Education. 2011;100(1):151-85.

[40] Bourne J, Harris D, Mayadas F. Online engineering education: Learning anywhere, anytime. Journal of Engineering Education. 2005;94(1):131-46.

[41] Taras DG, Bennett JT, Townsend AM. Information technology and the world of work. News Brunswick, New Jersey: Transaction Pub; 2004.

[42] Corbett AT, Anderson JR. Knowledge tracing: Modeling the acquisition of procedural knowledge. User modeling and user-adapted interaction. 1994;4(4):253-78.

[43] Deimann M, Bastiaens T. Competency-based education in an electronic-supported environment: an example from a distance teaching university. International Journal of Continuing Engineering Education and Life Long Learning. 2010;20(3-5):278-89.

[44] Kunda G. Engineering culture: Control and commitment in a high-tech corporation: Temple University Press, Philadelphia, USA.; 2009.

[45] Engeström Y, Engeström R, Vähäaho T. When the center does not hold: The importance of knotworking. Activity theory and social practice: Cultural-historical approaches. 1999:345-74.

[46] Kangasoja J, editor Complex design problems: An impetus for learning and knotworking. Keeping learning complex: The proceedings of the fifth international conference on the learning sciences (ICLS); 2002: Erlbaum Mahwah, NJ.

[47] Kerosuo H, Mäki T, Korpela J. Knotworking and the visibilization of learning in building design. Journal of Workplace Learning. 2015;27(2):128-41.

[48] Engeström Y. Innovative learning in work teams: Analyzing cycles of knowledge creation in practice. Perspectives on activity theory. 1999;377.

[49] Hattinger M, Eriksson K. Mind the Gap: a Collaborative Competence e-Learning Model between University and Industry. Proceedings of the 53rd Hawaii International Conference on System Sciences; 2020.

[50] Steinar K. InterViews: An introduction to qualitative research interviewing. Studentlitteratur, Lund. 1996;8.

[51] Sannino A, Engeström Y, Lemos M. Formative interventions for expansive learning and transformative agency. Journal of the Learning Sciences. 2016;25(4):599-633.

[52] Graneheim UH, Lundman B. Qualitative content analysis in nursing research: concepts, procedures and measures to achieve trustworthiness. Nurse Education Today 2004;24(2):105-12.

[53] Dubois A, Gadde L-E. Systematic combining: an abductive approach to case research. Journal of business research. 2002;55(7):553-60. https://doi.org/10.1016/S0148-2963(00)00195-8

Chapter 2

Using E-Learning Platform for Enhancing Teaching and Learning in the Field of Social Work at Sultan Qaboos University, Oman

Emad Saleh

Abstract

This chapter explores the issue of e-learning as a helpful method in higher education institutes and universities in general, and specifically, in the field of social work education. It is based on a study carried out at Sultan Qaboos University, Oman and presents knowledge and attitudes of students towards reliance on the e-learning platforms, such as Moodle, as a helpful educational tool. It highlights that Moodle as an e-learning platform enhances communication between teachers and students, and among students themselves. The chapter presents the findings about the usefulness of Moodle, as an e-learning platform as well as challenges of social work students face during using e-learning platform in their learning. Finally, it offers recommendations to deal with the challenges and highlights implication of the study beyond social work education.

Keywords: e-learning platform, higher education, Moodle, social work education, student perspectives

1. Introduction

The world today experiences the strongest era of revolutionary transformation in knowledge and information seeking behavior. This is due to enormous progress based on the technological revolution, especially in the field of information and communication technology (ICT) with all its patterns. The emergence of computer technologies late in the twentieth century, and consequently, the world wide web (the Internet) have had a great impact on the speed of information transference among people since the world has become a global village. The emergence of Web 2.0 has transformed the web into a more dynamic and interactive environment, offering a set of tools that enhance contact and collaboration between users. Several applications, such as online social networks, wikis and blogs, support such Web vision [1].

Most fields of contemporary life have benefited from the enormous evolution of communication and information exchange technology. Accordingly, this evolution reflection to various fields has affected all aspects of life and changed its patterns and styles. The educational sector has never been an exception. The educational process was gradually affected by technology until reaching now to "e-learning" [2].

Mastering the basic skills necessary for using ICT is a requirement in the learning process in all fields of education since these skills play an important role in facilitating communication, getting information and preparing research and studies. The lack of these skills limits the interaction between teachers and their students and getting knowledge resources necessary for teaching.

Using computers and network has become the main prerequisite for education, including teaching and research. Ability to access these resources and using it have become a factor that contributes to the development, progress, and improving the quality of education. It becomes necessary for teachers and students at higher educational institutes to master the skills necessary for extracting and using information quickly and easily [3].

The author, in the following paragraphs, presents a summary of a previous study that he has already conducted. The study was titled: "*The Moodle Application Constraints among Students in Social Work at Sultan Qaboos University*" [4]. It was an attempt to identify the constraints against Social Work students when they were using e-learning applications in their education, specifically, Moodle application.

2. Key concepts

Defining the key concepts is a cornerstone and important task in scientific research. It prevents overlapping between concepts, and it draws a boundary for understanding meaning of a concept in that particular context. The concepts of e-learning and Moodle are the most important key concepts for this chapter. In order for this chapter to achieve its goal, both concepts should be explored so that the readers can understand the intended meanings in the context of this study.

3. e-Learning

People use different words when talking about teaching and learning. Sometimes the same word will mean different things to different people, and sometimes different words will carry the same meaning [5]. The term "learning", according to Webster Dictionary, refers to The act or experience of one that learns, knowledge or skill acquired by instruction or study and modification of a behavioral tendency by experience (such as exposure to conditioning) [6]. More recent theories of learning view it as an active, constructive process. Individuals attempt to make sense of incoming information by interpreting it in terms of their prior knowledge, by questioning its meaning, and by exploring its uses [7]. In the light of the above definition of learning, it can be said that learning as a process can be done through a larger and wider process of education. Hence, the term e-learning can be tackled as a process that is done in terms of the larger and wider process of e-education. Accordingly, the author thinks that the concept specified and intended in this chapter is e-learning, not e-Education, since the current chapter sheds light on a specific part of a larger process called e-Education that includes policies, goals, plans, programs, methods, and techniques.

Recently, e-learning has become a vital word in the field of education and one of the main issues of translation, which was added to the knowledge society. e-Learning – or electronic learning – has been referred to as "technology-enhanced learning," and more recently as "digital learning." e-Learning describes a set of technology-mediated methods that can be applied to support student learning and can include many elements [8]. e-learning can be perceived as a wide concept covering a wide group of applications and processes included computer-based learning, using networks, virtual classes, digital cooperation, and internet-based learning. e-learning can be defined as "communicating the content/material through electronic media: internet/intranet, internal/external networks, transmission by satellite, audio and video tapes, and CDs. e-learning is perceived as a narrower concept than distant learning- that includes learning based on text and courses delivered through written correspondences [9].

e-learning has rapidly grown since two decades after the wide availability of internet services provided to the public, especially in the industrial field since the 1990s. It became an accepted and commonly used component in tertiary education [10]. Currently, activities of e-learning are various and multiple, such as typing the content, training, communicating through the internet and intranet of a school or a university. It also provides students with electronic media, such as, audio and video media, CD ROMs, TV, and finally mobile phones that can facilitate a sound environment for e-learning and support communication wherever the learner is [11]. In addition, e-learning is perceived as a method of teaching using technology and internet with all sections of the course's content. It helps students be more effective learners and provide them with more knowledge through the internet and mutual interaction among students and teachers. It is also appropriate for the design of "virtual reality" that helps students to solve real-world issues. Since technology is merely a vehicle, the e-learning requires well-developed teaching practices with these new instruments.

E-learning, an instructional strategy for imparting needed knowledge, skills, and attitudes in organizations, is here to stay. Its viability, effectiveness, and potential to return tangible benefits to organizations depend largely on how it is designed, delivered, and evaluated [12]. In the recent years, this term was limited to tracks provided by the web or direct electronic lines, using e-mails, visual conferences, focus groups, chat rooms, e-whiteboards on the internet [13]. To avoid overlapping between e-learning and other learning or teaching related concepts, the author provides readers with an operational definition of the term: A joint process between a learner and a teacher, where the learner is the core of the process.

It is a process complementary to the traditional education, that is, university blended learning which uses modern technology in teaching without abandoning the typical educational reality and attendances in classrooms. It starts from certain principles: principles of educational democracy, educational programming and individualization, self-motivation, and developing and continuing education. It depends on the accessibility of learning materials through electronic media related to the internet, an intranet, or direct electronic lines; and a specialized application such as Moodle, Blackboard, Web CT, or any other relative accredited application.

The role of communication media plays a considerable role in the realization of skills necessary for learning. These media can be the internet or intranet with their developed features. It includes all forms of electronically supported education that is based on a set of teaching and learning tools: computers, smartphones, and iPads, etc. It uses emails, visual conferences, discussion groups, chat rooms, and electronic whiteboards on the internet, and supports exchanging audio and video files, pictures, texts supported by such programs as a word, PDF, PowerPoint, and Excel. These applications provide various opportunities or the acquisition of the scientific material and retrieving it, and for mutual dialog among learners, and between the learners and their teacher whenever they agree to do this dialog, through virtual spaces.

The learner, with easier ways, is able to search and get knowledge from e-libraries and different websites. The learner is allowed to do evaluations, tests, and reviews of reports and research, and to correct them electronically before sending them back immediately with the least efforts and the greatest benefits, and precisely.

4. Moodle

Moodle is a learning platform designed to provide educators, administrators and learners with a **single robust, secure and integrated system** to create personalized learning environments [14]. Also we can describe Moodle as a Web application used to manage online courses. It provides the ability to develop courses in an integrated manner. It is one of the open source software packages to provide an electronic environment to manage academic courses. It is a relatively modern system developed in 1999 to by Marti Daugiamas to manage educational activities. "Moodle" is an acronym for "Modular Object-Oriented Dynamic Learning Environment". In this context, Moodle is a dynamic educational media in the learning environment. It is also:

- Course Management System (GMS)
- Learning Management System (LMS)
- Learning Content Management System (LCMS)
- E-learning Platform

This application is distributed under GNU license, which means that it can be downloaded at no cost from the link (http://www.moodle.org). It works without any modifications on any computer using PHP, UNIX, and Windows. It also supports many databases, especially (My SOL). The application is available with various languages and supports the Arabic language in a simple way. This application also supports Word, PDF, PowerPoint and Excel files, in addition, audio/video files, pictures, and external links.

Across the globe, the spread of novel coronavirus COVID-19 has led to profound changes in social interaction and organization, and the education sector has not been immune [15]. Therefore, most of universities and academic institutions relied on many types of e-Learning applications to provide lessons and training to their students, one of these applications is Moodle. It helps us to upload our academic programs, either in undergraduate or graduate stages. Also, through Moodle, we can submit training courses and life-long learning workshops.

Moodle has the superiority over a lot of similar application concerning feedback, its variety of tools for monitoring students' activities, ease of use, quick update that is compatible with learning software developments- according to a comparative study conducted by the German University of Humboldt between Moodle and Blackboard applications. The study found out that Moodle is superior because of ease of use, multiple social interaction tools, and many other accessories.

5. University education and necessity for relying on e-learning applications

The university education is one of the fields benefiting from progress made in Information-Communication Technology. Due to this progress, many methods help in presenting the study material to students easily, quickly, and clearly. This progress has added a new pattern of learning, so-called e-learning [16]. The e-learning is based on an educational philosophy focusing on self-learning: converting the teaching into learning with highly self-dependent students. Accordingly, the communicative media have an increasingly considerable role in realizing skills necessary or learning process. These media can be the internet or intranet with their progressive features. This means that the educational virtual reality, in its philosophy, is based on a number of principles that conceptually differs from the principles on which the traditional education is based: principles of democracy of learning, programming and uniqueness of learning, self-motivation, and developing the continuing learning [17].

Benefiting from computers and WWW in e-learning has not been limited to certain disciplines than others since all disciplines gradually have begun to rely on this new type one way or another. The Higher Education institutions have provided many offers of e-learning, where the traditional methods of learning have improved. The traditional teaching methodology often includes presenting the study material containing the formally assigned texts through lectures, forums or workshops. In this respect, many academic studies have asserted that students learn more effectively when they have the opportunity to discuss the academic material with others and to deal with learning as a cooperative process.

As to applying the e-learning in the Arab universities, a study showed how the Arab universities go along with modern technological developments concerning E-learning management systems, distant education, to what extent they use these developments, and in what courses they use them; where the researcher checked 517 websites of Arab universities, faculties, and institutions. The findings showed that only about 15% of Arab universities have e-learning management systems. They included open universities, virtual universities, and some universities of science and technology in Arab countries and Gulf countries, except the religious universities. In addition, a number of electronic courses were relatively low. Since using the electronic courses management systems will lead to quantitative and qualitative shift in education, and non-use of these systems may lead to technological and scientific backwardness, the researcher presented a set of recommendations for activating the electronic courses and distant education in Arab universities in a simple, quick and affordable way [18]. Although this study showed that weak adoption of E-learning management systems by Arab universities, it asserts the adoption of this pattern of education would lead to the quantitative and qualitative shift in the university education in Arab countries.

The academics have different preferences of teaching methods. Some of them prefer traditional methods that depend on face-to-face lectures and traditional lessons. Others prefer using technology to support their teaching practices. The first group of academics thinks that the traditional methods enable their personal communication with students and that using technology takes students away from teachers, and consequently teachers feel themselves away from their students. This traditional perspective focuses on the role of the lecturer as a source of leadership in the learned subject or material. They think that personal communication between lecturers and students is an empowering thing, where more opportunities for receiving feedback in homogeneous groups support these traditional methods.

The other perspective assumes that using technology enables academics to play the role of facilitator who helps students achieve high progress in the study subject when available and when needed [19]. In this context, one of the applied studies, which included all faculty members in various scientific departments, including the Department of Sociology and Social Work, recommended the integration of the faculty member in the teaching method between the traditional method of teaching in the classroom and contacting students face to face and electronic method through application electronic content management “Moodle” [20].

6. e-Learning as a helpful method in social work education

The specialization of Social Work is one of the recent fields that attempt to depend on this type of learning to complete the professional preparation of its students. The literature or previous studies in this field, in the Arab world, are hardly available. One of these studies assessed the benefits of professional intervention based on using Moodle as one of the e-learning applications. The study found that using this application though developing an e-course has led social work students to acquire efficient knowledge and experiences; they also managed to gain the capacity to solve problems during their study of the course. One of the most important recommendations of this study is to implement research on constraints against social work students' use of e-learning and how to overcome them [21].

Ahmed F. Saleh [22] carried out a descriptive analytical study "trainers and students' attitudes towards using e-learning in Social Work". He assessed the current level of e-learning related knowledge, attitudes, and practice of students and trainers in the field of Social Work education. The findings asserted the high average of attitude component, taking the first in order, the knowledge in the second place, then the third component of practice in the third place [22].

In a study titled "E-learning in Social Work; a Case Study of Assiut university"- a descriptive study applied in the Faculty of Social Work, Assiut University- the study showed that there were no significant differences between student's type and their perspectives on possible constraints when applying the e-learning in Social Work. It asserted that there are significant differences between students' place of residence and their perspectives on the possible constraints in applying the e-learning in Social Work. In other words, it was shown that rural students tend to describe e-learning as more difficult, unlike their counterparts who live in cities [23]. This study directed attention towards the possibility of the existence of some constraints that students may face when applying the e-learning in Social Work Education.

A study by José Albors-Garigos showed students' satisfaction of using e-learning methods. It found that satisfaction rates of learners increase by using e-learning, as compared to the reliance on traditional methods of leaning [24].

Elizabeth Johnson presented a paper on strategies for establishing Management Information Systems (MIS) and technology to improve social work practice and research. She showed the possible role of Management Information System (MIS) to result in the integration of information, management, and monitoring through a single program or special information network of the organization; and that this will improve management, services provided, and the assessment of professional practice. The paper included three strategies for directing and developing MIS programs. The paper showed some lessons produced and implemented by MIS programs to work as administrative and evaluative tools for policy followed at the national level.

The model of MIS presented by Elizabeth Johnson sheds light on possibilities of social workers for integrating technology into social work practice and formulation of creative policies. In addition, these strategies can be used for improving and developing the formulations of concepts and developing various technological creations within social work practice [25, 26]. Accordingly, the paper mentioned above pointed out the positive results achieved by using the MIS in social work practice. Hence, these positive results can also be achieved if the e-learning is used as a complementary type of learning with the traditional learning in both field and theoretical aspects; since the e-learning can be utilized in field training of social work students as well as in-service social workers or before their job assignment.

The above theoretical reviews assert the importance of learning patterns and methods; and that this development is related the developments of the teaching methods used as a response to the enormous evolution in technological methods, communication, and networks...etc. On the other hand, the accelerated increase of information to the so called the knowledge explosion; the growing numbers of students and researchers in the field of social work; their crowdedness within academic rooms; or in the light of far distance between students' residence and academic places, all this makes seeking new methods for communicating information and knowledge to students a very important matter.

Accordingly, reliance on e-learning methods and application and developing them have become inevitable necessity in the field of higher education including social work education; since a lot of developed countries have been depending on it one way or another as a method complementary to traditional education. To make sure how successful any developments in teaching and learning processes are, we should conduct extended studies on all related issues, trying to answer or related questions [27].

The urgent imperative to "move online" caused by the recent Covid-19 pandemic [28]. and It has become necessary to conduct studies and research on e-learning issue, as it is one of the modern issues in our contemporary society in general, and specifically in social work education. In the light of the author's modest experience in the field of e-learning in Social Work Education, and his introduction of some e-learning in the recent years, He observed how students of social work avoid participating in or benefiting from e-learning courses presented through the Web and based on Moodle application. Accordingly, the author believes in the importance of submitting this topic for scientific discussion and research.

7. Methodology

Methodology is generally a guideline for solving a problem, with specific components such as phases, tasks, methods, techniques and tools [28]. In that study, the author adopted the descriptive approach by using the social comprehensive survey method, applied to students of social work as a separate specialization at Sultan Qaboos University's Department of Sociology and Social Work. Data-collection was based on an assessment tool designed by the researcher. The tool's reliability and validity were tested on the basis that it would assess students' preparation and attitudes towards using Moodle and define constraints against using and benefiting from it. The researcher applied content analysis for focus group discussion reports, as one of qualitative research type. The groups consisted of well-selected individuals aiming at benefiting from them through group discussions on a certain topic [29]. Two sessions for two groups of specialized students were held to discuss with them the main subjects of the research.

8. Benefits and advantages of e-learning

Although many people still consider traditional universities as the best way to achieve knowledge and get a diploma, online learning proves to be a great alternative. Students have the chance to study in their own time and especially for free. It represents a great way to study many fields and to boost the level of self-motivation. Online learning is so effective because students can finish their homework quickly, and there is more time left for hobbies or for finding a job [30].

E-learning is characterized by depending on the internet as a medium to present the study materials and submitting them to students without stop and twenty-four seven. This educational pattern views a student as the main element in the learning process, where a student can determine the way and time of his/her learning. In addition, there is the possibility of using multiple learning methods through e-learning, such as virtual class, simulation, cooperative learning, and discussion group. e-learning follows the steps of the traditional learning, e.g., study, tests, and certificates. Registration, management, fee payment and monitoring are done through the Internet in educational institutions or universities that depends on such learning pattern.

In addition, e-learning has many other characteristics reflecting on both student and instructor, on the development and respectable management of courses. Thus, E-learning leads to improve student-learning opportunity for exchanging knowledge and skills. The Web community as an e-learning environment is a comfortable way for communication and more practical for Part-time students, or those who cannot attend in regular classrooms because of distance or for other reasons [31].

E-learning has many features and benefits, starting from the scientific concept of e-learning and instruction and its role in distance education and virtual university learning. They can be summed as:

a. It is beyond time and spatial constraints of education,

b. Increasing communication among students on one hand, and between students and the university on the other,

c. Providing educational opportunities for those who had had no access to education, besides saving much efforts, costs and time,

d. Lessening the managerial burden on teachers,

e. Teachers are accessible anytime.

f. Enhancing students' feeling of equal opportunities in learning, breaking blocks of fear and anxiety, and empowering students to express their thoughts, and

g. Providing considerable accessibility of various resources of information with different kinds [32].

9. Findings

The most important results found by the study included students' enough preparation for using Moodle: students have the basics of using the computer, exploring the internet, and English language skills that enable them to use Moodle. This was due also to the availability of university facilities that help them use Moodle. The following figure shows the arrangement of the sub-dimensions that make up the scale according to the relative strength of each dimension, and the relative strength of the four dimensions combined are: readiness, knowledge, attitude and actual use of Moodle (**Figure 1**).

It shows that the preparation rates reached 77%. Despite this high degree of preparation, it reflects some shortcomings, since the final degree of preparation is supposed to be 100%. Accordingly, it reflects shortcomings with the rate of 23%. The researcher thinks that there is a possibility of overcoming this shortage by

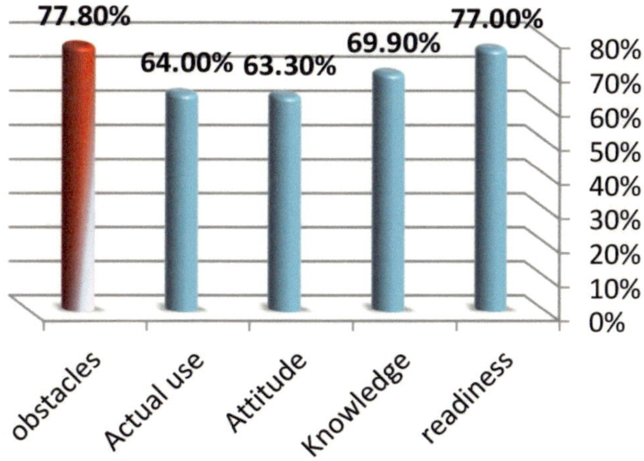

Figure 1.
Results of measuring the sub-dimensions that make up the scale used in the study [33].

helping students increase their computer skills, language skills, and facilitating their internet accessibility from any place wherever they are. On another side, the university should pay more attention to internet services by increasing its speed and efficiency, and continuous development of computer labs. Concerning the cognitive aspect of students, the results of the study showed that they have a good knowledge of Moodle, where the knowledge degree shown by the assessment tool was 69.9%, but it decreases with the total degree of the whole assessment. This means that it reflects the shortage of 30.1, which can be treated by providing students with more learning and training opportunities. As to the relative strength of students' attitudes towards using Moodle, according to the assessment tool, it reached 63.3%. Accordingly, this degree implies shortage in attitudes with 36.7%. The researcher thinks that this shortage can be overcome by getting teachers encourage students to understand this application to achieve the expected great benefits. The research thinks also that showing degrees of shortage in every dimension would serve to clarify the priority of attention needed for dealing with the dimension in question, so that students can get help in avoiding shortcomings, to improve their real usage of this application, and to make use of its all accessories

10. Constraints and recommendations

Concerning the constraints on social work students' usage of Moodle, their point of views came with the following order: insufficient training; few teachers use Moodle in some courses; no incentives from the teachers to encourage using the application; recurrent failures of the internet; the nature of courses does not require using Moodle; insufficient time for using it; and finally, insufficient equipped labs. Thus, the students' suggestions for overcoming these constraints are:

a. To provide training on Moodle beginning from joining the university, especially in the foundation year. This is done through changing the content of computer courses. This course should contain training he students in how to use e-learning applications available in the university.

b. To impose using Moodle on teachers as a means complementary to traditional education, at least in one academic course every academic season. This would affect students' interaction and using of Moodle.

c. To dedicate a time agreed upon by the teachers and students to interact through Moodle, which can be counted as a part of the accredited study time.

d. To pay more attention for developing computer labs and to increase speed and efficiency of computers.

e. The importance of improving the quality of the university's internet services.

f. To provide internet services at students' home through a national communication company to be socially responsible for providing educational support to students: through low costs of getting the internet services by students.

In the light of the constraints on students' utilization of Moodle, their suggestions for dealing with these constraints, and data-analysis, the study recommended the following:

a. To provide continuous training by the university to students on using e-learning applications, or changing computer courses content to guarantee the availability of training in e-learning applications.

b. To oblige social work professors and teachers to publish some E-learning course to encourage students to benefit e-learning applications. In addition, they should have more attention to the continuous activation of each application accessories so that students can achieve the most benefits they could gain.

c. The university and professors should apply mechanisms encouraging students unwilling to use e-learning to use it. This can be done by eliminating the related constraints.

d. To provide the training necessary for developing students' linguistic and electronic capacities, in order to enhance their preparation, knowledge and positive attitudes towards e-learning.

e. It is important to eliminate shortcomings of individual capacities of students and to enhance university possibilities that prevent them from enabling them to absorb, use, or benefit from e-learning applications.

11. Conclusion

Social Work is a recently emergent humanist profession since less than 100 years; since acknowledging its first professional method of Social Casework Method in the period 1917-1919. Thus, this imposed on those who belong to it- academics and practitioners over the past decades- for the continuous development of its professional strategies, methods, and techniques, by which they facilitate an interactive educational environment able to attract social work students' attention. In addition, more efforts have been exerted to provide a better educational environment that helps students to easily exchange knowledge, opinions, attitudes, skills, and experiences. In addition, there have been attempts to facilitate communication among students themselves, and between students and lecturers easily through a safe, guaranteed, and affordable educational environment, and without any inconvenience to any of communication partners. All these can be provided through the appropriate use of e-learning with its multiple applications.

Hence, the astonishing evolution in sciences of computer, internet and communication technology, and its resulting communicative media has led to providing successful and safe educational environments that help learners and teachers perform their roles successfully. Through using e-learning application, students are able to develop their knowledge, attitudes, and opinions through communication with their colleagues who are sharing them the same e-courses; in addition to communication between lecturers and experts responsible for building and teaching these courses.

Students' use of the internet-related applications can develop and enhance their learning-related skills, such as skills of the computer, linguistic, writing skills, and internet skills.

The accessories that characterize e-learning provides lecturers with wider opportunities for benefiting from techniques of communication on the World Wide Web (WWW), and reaching educational experiences, experiments and methods that have never been achieved without the internet, and consequently, enabling students to benefit from such opportunities. Student relying on using e-learning applications provide save their time and efforts in gaining the learning material and exchanging it with any known electronic format (Word, Excel, PowerPoint, Video, Audio and other types of files). Through the next lines, we will shed light on some accessories of Moodle.

The Moodle application has many extensions that enable the user- student or Instructor- to select an activity or resource to perform or play his/her role as instructor. Activities can be: Active Quiz, assignment, Attendance, Booklist, Chat, Checklist, Choice, Crossword, Cryptex, database, External tool, face to Face, Forum, Glossary, Hangman, Hidden picture, hot pot, lesson, Media Collection, Millionaire, Questionnaire, Quiz, Quiz venture, Scheduler, SCORM Package, Snakes and Ladders, Sudoku, Survey, Turn it in, Assignment2 and workshop. All or some of these activities will support the instructor to empower students to practice many types of works through Moodle Application wherever and whenever he/she wants.

The sources used by the instructor can be a book, file, folder, IMS content package, label, webpage, and URL. In addition, Moodle helps users to utilize and use some functions, such as Search forums, Latest announcements, Upcoming events, recent activity...etc.

Finally, the study recommends instructors and students in the field of Social Work Education to depend on using e-learning applications, to develop their abilities, skills, and experiences, in order to enhance their academic and learning performance. It does not matter which application of e-learning, but what is important is to use an advanced application that is easily accessible and usable by students with medium or good potential.

Author details

Emad Saleh[1,2]

1 Fayoum University, Egypt

2 Sultan Qaboos University, Muscat, Oman Sultanate

*Address all correspondence to: dremadfarouk14@gmail.com

References

[1] J.J.P.C. Rodrigues, F.M.R. Sabino & L. Zhou, 2011. Enhancing e-learning experience with online social networks. *IET Communications*, 20 May, 5(8), pp. 1147 - 1154.

[2] Abo-El-Nasr, M. M. (2010). *Recent trends in the management of social work institutions, quality electronic.* Saudi Arabia: Al-araby organization Abdel Meguid, H. M. (2008). *Developing and evaluating the interactive e-learning system for engineering and computer subjects.* Denmark: Arab Academy.

[3] Constande, S. (2007). Modern styles in higher education, multimedia e-learning. *Sixth Conference of the Deans of the Faculties of Arts in universities members of the Federation of Arab Universities Seminar Education Quality Assurance and Academic Accreditation.* University of Jinan, P4.

[4] Saleh, E. F. (2015). The Moodle Application Constraints among Students in Social Work at Sultan Qaboos University. *2015 Fifth International Conference on e-Learning (econf)* (pp. 514-533). Manama, Bahrain: IEEE. doi:10.1109/ECONF.2015.14

[5] Prozesky D. R. (2000). Teaching and learning. *Community eye health*, *13*(34), 30-31.6-

[6] Merriam-Webester. (2017, October 28). *Merriam-Webster Dictionary*. Retrieved from https://www.merriam-webster.com/dictionary/learning.

[7] Wilson, S. M., Penelope, & Peterson, P. L. (2006, July). Theories of Learning and Teaching: What Do They Mean for Educators. doi:http://www.gpsnetwork.org/assets/docs/HE/mf_ltbrief.pdf

[8] *Wheeler S. (2012) e-Learning and Digital Learning. In: Seel N.M. (eds) Encyclopedia of the Sciences of Learning. Springer, Boston, MA. https://doi.org/10.1007/978-1-4419-1428-6_431*

[9] Bachman, K. (1989). *E-learning "Corporate E-Learning A New Frontier"* (Vol. 8). (E. Hoffer, Ed.) Vanguard Management. Retrieved from http://www internettime.com/Learning/articles/hambrecht.pdf.

[10] Lee, K.-T., & Duncan-Howell, J. (2007). How Do We Know E-Learning Works? Or Does it? E-Learning and Digital Media, 4(4), 482-496. https://doi.org/10.2304/elea.2007.4.4.482

[11] Sultan, N., Van De Bunt, S., Davidson, C., & Sentin, D. (2012). *E-Learning in the Arab Gulf: Responding to the Changing World of Education.* (M. Ramady, Ed.) E-Learning in the Arab Gulf: Responding to the Changing World of Education: Springer Science and Business Media.

[12] Derouin, R. E., Fritzsche, B. A., & Salas, E. (2005, 1 December). E-Learning in Organizations. *Journal of Management, 31*(6), pp. 920-940. doi:https://doi.org/10.1177/0149206305279815

[13] Al-Shunaq , Q. M., & Bani Dumi, H. A. (2010). Teachers and students' attitudes towards the use of e-learning in secondary schools Jordan. *Journal of Damascus University, 26*(1), p 237.

[14] Moodle doces, 2020. *About Moodle.* [Online] Available at: https://docs.moodle.org/39/en/About_Moodle [Accessed 30 July 2020].

[15] Michael P. A. Murphy (2020) COVID-19 and emergency eLearning: Consequences of the securitization of higher education for post-pandemic pedagogy, Contemporary Security Policy, 41:3, 492-505, DOI: 10.1080/13523260.2020.1761749

[16] Abdel Meguid, H. M. (2008). *Developing and evaluating the interactive e-learning system for engineering and computer subjects.* Denmark: Arab Academy.

[17] Roy, S. (2011). distance learning around the world. *educational development through utilization of technology* (p. 321). , UAE: UNESCO.

[18] Al-Garf, R. (2008, 1 12). *E-learning and distance education in Arab universities*. (King Saud University, Riyadh) Retrieved 2014, from http://www.gulfup.com/?IsBHJZ

[19] Wells, M., & Brook, P. (2003). Learning about Knowledge Management through Enforced Collaboration using Web-Based Repositories. In K. S. Ang J (Ed.), *4th International We-b Conference (We-b 2003).* Perth Austr alia: Edith Cowan University.

[20] Salim, N. E. (2012). The difficulties faced by the faculty member at Sultan Qaboos University: A Case Study, in the "contemporary societal changes in the Arab world: dimensions and impacts". *The Second International Scientific Conference of Arts and Social Sciences college* (p. 27). Muscat - Sultanate of Oman: Sultan Qaboos university.

[21] Sayed, M. F. (2007). Evaluate the intervention impact by using the moodle program. *Knowledge Society: Social, Cultural and Linguistic Challenges in the Arab World Present and Future, First Scientific Conference, Arts and Social SciencesCollege , Sultan Qaboos University. 1*, pp. 183-210. Muscat - Sultanate of Oman: Sultan Qaboos university.

[22] Saleh, A. (2009). Trends trainers and students towards the use of e-learning in social work. *The 22 International Scientific Conference* (pp. 6469-6492). Cairo: Faculty of Social Work, Helwan University.

[23] Abdul Majid, M. B. (2010). Electronic learning in Social Work: Case study in Assiut University. *The 23th International Scientific Conference.* Cairo: Faculty of Social Work, Helwan University.

[24] José Albors-Garrigos, M.-d.-V. S.-O.-C. (2011). The Impact of E-Learning in University Education: An Empirical Analysis in a Classroom Teaching Context,. *17*. Retrieved from http://link.springer.com/book/10.1007/978-3-642-223.

[25] Johnson, E., Hinterlong, J., & Sherraden, M. (2001). *Strategies for Creating MIS Technology to Improve Social Work Practice and Research*. Washington: Center for Social Development George Warren Brown School of Social Work, Washington University.

[26] Ishak, I. S., & Alias, R. A. (2005). DESIGNING A STRATEGIC INFORMATION SYSTEMS PLANNING METHODOLOGY FOR MALAYSIAN INSTITUTES OF HIGHER LEARNING (ISP-IPTA). *Issues in Information System, VI*(1), pp. 1-7. doi:https://d1wqtxts1xzle7.cloudfront.net/52385538

[27] Mandoura, M., & Osama, R. (1989). A comprehensive study on the use of computers in public education with a focus on the experiences and projects of Member States. *Arabian Gulf Message, 9(29)*, 99-183.

[28] World Health Organization (2020). Coronavirus disease (COVID-19) pandemic. https://www.who.int/emergencies/diseases/novel-coronavirus-2019. Accessed 15 June 2020.

[29] Cain, S. (2013). *Key Concepts in Public Relations.* (M. M. Abo Nasr, Trans.) Cairo: The National Center for Translation, Ministry of Culture, pp. 150-151.

[30] Armstrong, . S., 2013. *What Are The Advantages And Disadvantages Of Online Learning?*. [Online] Available at: https://elearningindustry.com/advantages-and-disadvantages-of-online-learning [Accessed 1 August 2020].

[31] Gilbert , J., Morton, S., & Rowley, J. (2007). E-Learning: The student experience. British Journal of Educational Technology. *British Journal of Educational Technology, 38*(4), pp. 560-573. doi:10.1111/j.1467-8535.2007.00723.x

[32] Mahafza, M., & Yehia, A. S. (2010). *The importance of e-learning in institutions of higher education.* Jourdan: Amman for publication and distribution.

[33] Saleh, E. F. (2015). The Moodle Application Constraints among Students in Social Work at Sultan Qaboos University. *2015 Fifth International Conference on e-Learning (econf)* (pp. 514-533). Manama, Bahrain: IEEE. doi:10.1109/ECONF.2015.14

Chapter 3

The Impact of Online Learning Strategies on Students' Academic Performance

Khaled Hamdan and Abid Amorri

Abstract

Higher education institutions have shifted from traditional face to face to online teaching due to Corona virus pandemic which has forced both teachers and students to be put in a compulsory lockdown. However the online teaching/learning constitutes a serious challenge that both university teachers and students have to face, as it necessarily requires the adoption of different new teaching/learning strategies to attain effective academic outcomes, imposing a virtual learning world which involves from the students' part an online access to lectures and information, and on the teacher's side the adoption of a new teaching approach to deliver the curriculum content, new means of evaluation of students' personal skills and learning experience. This chapter explores and assesses the online teaching and learning impact on students' academic achievement, encompassing the passing in review the adoption of students' research strategies, the focus of the students' main source of information viz. library online consultation and the collaboration with their peers. To reach this end, descriptive and parametric analyses are conducted in order to identify the impact of these new factors on students' academic performance. The findings of the study shows that to what extent the students' online learning has or has not led to any remarkable improvements in the students' academic achievements and, whether or not, to any substantial changes in their e-learning competence. This study was carried out on a sample of University College (UAEU) students selected in Spring 2019 and Fall 2020.

Keywords: online learning environment, content-based research, process-based research, success factors assessment

1. Introduction

With the advent of COVID-19 pandemic and the shutdown of universities worldwide for fear of contamination due to the spread of the coronavirus, higher educational institutions have deemed necessary to adopt new teaching strategies, exclusively online, to deliver their curriculum content and keep from the Corona virus widespread at bay [1]. Technology was called upon to play this pivotal teaching/learning online role, as it has influenced people's task accomplishment in various ways. It has become a part of our ever changing lives. It is an important part of e-learning to create relationship-involving technology, course content and pedagogy in learning/teaching environment. Therefore, e-learning is becoming unavoidable in a virtual teaching environment where students can take control of their learning and optimize it in a virtual classroom and elsewhere. So, learning today has shifted from the conventional face to face learning to online learning and to a direct access to information through technologies available as e-learning has proven to be more beneficial to students in terms of knowledge or information acquisition. Online teaching promotes learning by encouraging the students' use of various learning strategies at hand and increases the level of their commitment to studying their majors. Virtual world represents an effective learning environment, providing users with an experience-based information acquisition. Instructors set up the course outcomes by creating tasks involving problem or challenge-based learning situations and offering the learner a full control of exploratory learning experiences. However, there are some challenges for instructors such as the selection of the most appropriate educational strategies and how best to design learning tasks and activities to meet learners' needs and expectations. Various approaches can lead towards strong students' behavioral changes especially when combined with ethical principles. However, with careful selection of the learning environment, pedagogical strategies lining up with the concrete specifics of the educational context, the building of learners' self-confidence and their empowerment during the learning process becomes within reach. Another benefit of using online teaching/learning is that here is a need to explore new teaching strategies and principles that positively influence distance education, as traditional teaching/learning methods are becoming less effective at engaging students in the learning process. Finally, e-learning can solve many of the students' learning issues in a conventional learning environment, as it helps them to attend classes for various reasons, as it has made the communication/interaction between them and their instructors much easier and the access to lectures much more at hand. Students can attend online university courses and at the same time meet other social obligations. Therefore, the circumstances in a learner's life, and whatever problems or distraction he/she may have such as family problems or illnesses, may no longer be an impediment to his education. Learners can practice in virtual situations and face challenges in a safe environment, which leads to a more engaged learning experience that facilitates better knowledge acquisition.

The work presents the educational processes as a modern strategy for teaching/learning. e-learning tends to persuade the users to be virtually available to act naturally. There are a few factors affecting the outcomes such as learning aims and objectives, and different pedagogical choices. Instructors use various factors to measure the learning quality like Competence, Attitude, Content Delivery, Reliability, and Globalization [2–4]. In this work, we are going to pass in review positive and negative impacts of online learning followed by recommendations to increase awareness regarding online learning and the use of this new strategic technology. Modern teaching methods like brainstorming, problem solving, indirect-consultancy, and inquiry-based method have a significant effect in the educational progress [5].

The aim of this research is to examine the effect of using modern teaching methods, such as teacher-student interactive and student-centered methods, on students' academic performance. Factors that may affect students' performance and success- the technology used, students' collaboration/teamwork, time management and communication skills are taken into consideration [6]. It also attempts to identify and to show to what extent online learning environment, when well integrated and adapted in course planning and objectives, can cater for students' needs and wants. Does online teaching make a significant improvement in students' academic performance and their personal skills such as organizations, communications, responsibilities, problem-solving tasks, engagement, learning interest, self-evolution, and abilities to reach their potential? Is students' struggle is not purely academic, but rather related to the lack of personal skills?

2. Online learning experience

There are many motives behind the implementation of the online learning experience. The online learning is mandatory nowadays to all audience due to COVID −19 pandemic, which forced the higher educational authorities to start the online teaching [1]. We believe that we reached a tipping point where making changes to the current learning process is inevitable for many reasons. Today learners have instant access to information through technology and the web, can manage their own acquisition of knowledge through online learning. As a result, traditional teaching and learning methods are becoming less effective at engaging students, who no longer rely exclusively on the teacher as the only source of knowledge. Indeed, 90% of the respondents use internet as their major source of information. So the teacher is new role is to be a learning facilitator, a guide for his students. He should not only help his students locate information, but more importantly question it and reflect upon it and formulate an opinion about it. Another reason for the adoption of the online learning is that higher institution did not hesitate one moment to integrate it as a primary tool of education. So, it transformed the conventional course and current learning process into e-learning concept. The integration of the online teaching into the curriculum resulted in several issues to instructors, curriculum designer and administrators, starting from the infrastructure to online teaching and assessment. Does the current IT infrastructure support this integration? What course content should the instructor teach and how it should be delivered? What effective pedagogy needs to be adopted? How learning should be assessed? What is the direct effect of the online learning on students' performance? [7].

With reference to the survey findings, the majority of students were among the staunch supporters of online learning taking into consideration the imposed COVID-19 lockdown circumstances, as they expressed their full support and confidence in computer skills to share digital content, using online learning and collaboration platforms with their peers, and expressed their satisfaction with the support of the online teaching and learning [8].

However, a small percentage of the survey respondents, expressed their below average satisfaction when higher educational institutions have invested in digital literacy and infrastructure, as they believe they should provide more flexible delivery methods, digital platforms and modernized user-friendly curricula to both students and teachers [9]. On the same lines, the higher education authorities regard the quick and unexpected development of the UAE's higher education landscape, ICT infrastructure, and advanced online learning/teaching methods, imposed by COVID-19, have had a tremendous adverse impact on the students' culture, thus leading to students' social seclusion from their peers, imposing new social norms and behavior regarding plagiarism, affecting students' cultural ethics and learning and collaboration with their peers, when adopting the digital culture [10].

A current study emphasized the need for adoption of technology in education as a way to lessen the effects of Coronavirus pandemic lockdown in education to palliate the loss of face- to- face teaching/learning which has more beneficial aspects of learning for students than online learning as it offers more interactive learning opportunities.

We recommend that all these questions should be taken into consideration when designing a new course i.e. the e-learning strategies, the learners' and instructor's new roles, course content and pedagogy and students' performance/achievement assessment (**Figure 1**). In this experience, we focus only on the implementation of new learning academic objectives- how they are infused into the curriculum and how they are assessed. The ultimate objective of implementing a new learning process is to design a curriculum conveyed by a creative pedagogy and oriented towards the cultivation of a creative person yearning for the exploration of new ideas [11].

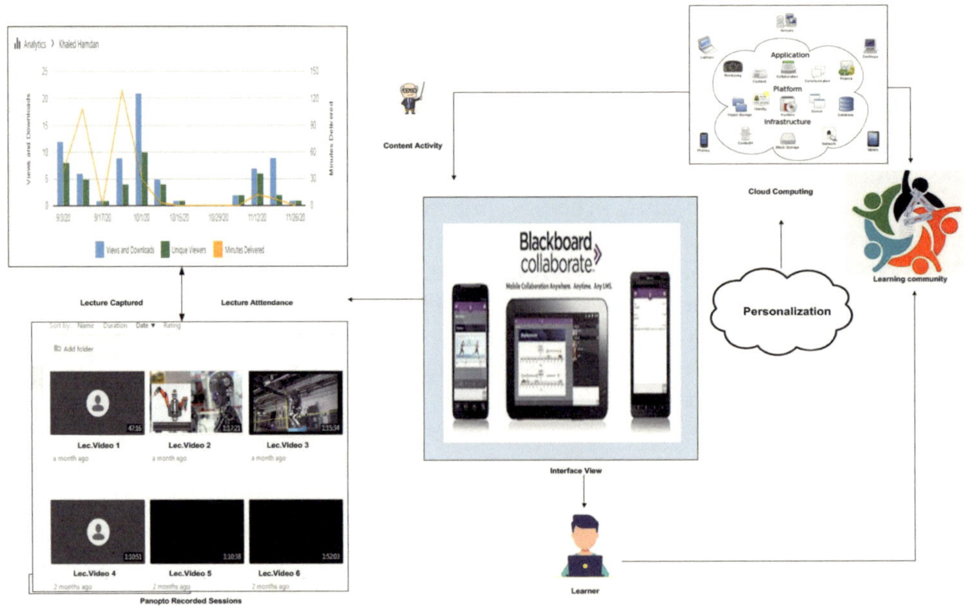

Figure 1.
E-learning approach.

The afore-mentioned objectives lead to design a comprehensive learning experience with new learning outcomes where instructors infuse new practical skills - Critical thinking and Problem-Solving Tasks, Creativity and Innovation, Communication and Collaboration. Other skills are implicitly infused into the curriculum such as, self-independent learning, interdependence, lifelong learning, flexibility, adaptability, and assuming academic learning responsibilities. Online learning is defined as virtual learning using mobile and wireless computing technologies in a way to promote learners' learning abilities [12]. In (**Figure 2**), each component of the e-learning process is defined clearly below [13].

2.1 Active instructor

His role is to facilitate learning process in the virtual classroom, to engage students in the learning process, to allow them to participate in designing their own course content and to contribute to design learning assessment parameters.

2.2 Active learner

He can access course content anytime and from anywhere, engage with his peers in a collaborative environment, formulate his opinions continuously, interact with other learning communities, communicate effectively, share and publish their findings with others in online environment.

2.3 Creative pedagogy

Both instructors and learners decide on what to learn online and how it should be learned. This experience is designed to promote an inquiry and challenge-based learning models where teachers and students work together to learn about compelling issues, propose solutions to real problems and take actions [11]. The approach involves students to reflect on their learning, on the impact of their actions and to publish their solutions to a worldwide audience [14].

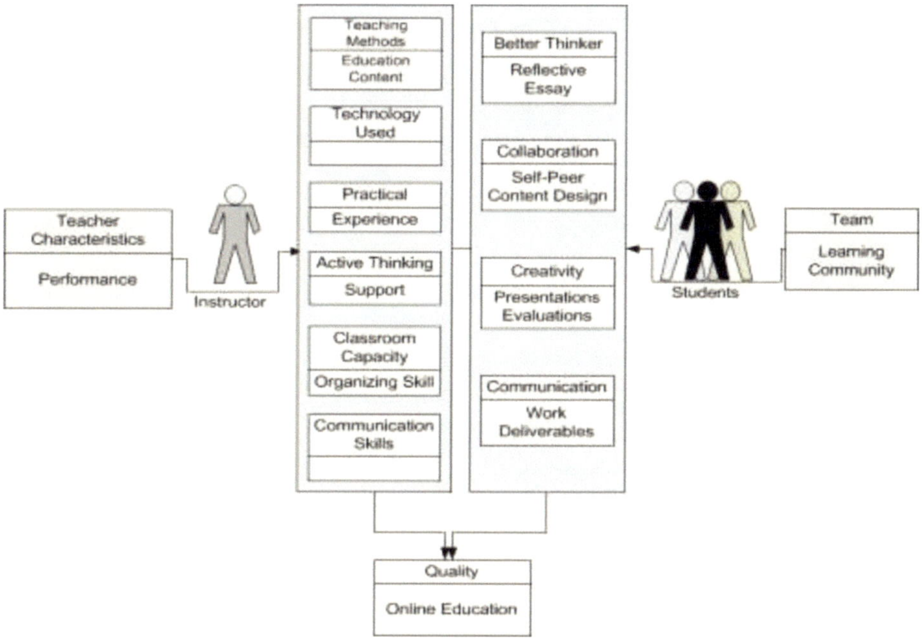

Figure 2.
E-learning process.

2.4 Flexible curriculum

A core curriculum is designed, but the facilitator has the freedom to innovate and customize course content accordingly up to the aspiration of the learners; this means that the learner's knowledge of the material will mainly come from his own online research (formal and informal content), and from his own creativity and collaboration with his peers (teamwork).

2.5 Communities outreach

This allows a group of students to formulate real-world context research question, connect with local learning and global communities to find creative solutions to their problems, create opportunities to connect themselves with international communities. These opportunities will foster students' social and leadership skills [15].

According to students' observation, more than 70% of instructors found that the online learning using Blackboard ultra-collaboration boosts students' learning interest, engagement and motivation. 84% of teachers use required to use interactive tools in order to engage students in presenting and sharing a five minutes presentation to their classmates, write a reflective essay on their experience, be involved in a collaborative project (interest- based learning project). 97% of students contributed to self and peer assessments, and 97% interacted using online management systems. Students were also encouraged to interact with their peers using blackboard group collaborate. Thanks to the online teaching strategy, 70% of students were able to deliver on time their work.

For the study purpose, several assessments components incorporate both individual and group work. For the individual work, each student was required to make an individual presentation on any subject of his own interest, write a reflective essay, self -assessment, class peer assessment, midterm and final exams. For the collaborative work, students were assigned teams and each student should

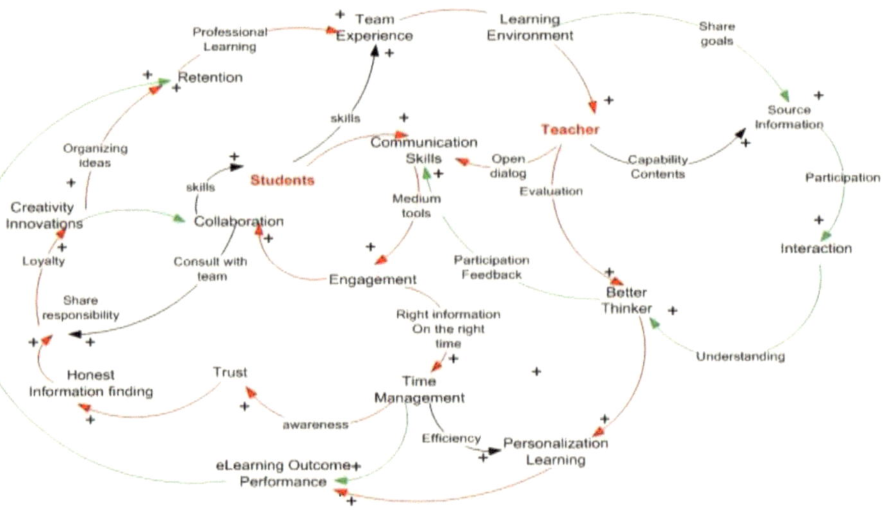

Figure 3.
Conceptual model of students' E-learning environment parameters.

contribute to the project delivered every two weeks in the form of a final presentation and a final project. Rubrics were designed and all students were well instructed to use them. Teachers were trained to monitor and facilitate the experience and the internal learning management systems such as Blackboard.

The subsequent (**Figure 3**) shows the feedback loop of content mapping of factors and their relationships in relation to students' performance and intake. The first feedback loop begins at the node called "Students". The second one begins at the node entitled "Teacher". There are two major positive feedback loops. For instance, a good team improves co-operation and creativity which increase the team's learning experience. Setting clear goals and interactive strategies will enhance online learning and performance results. The E-learning process and the project outcomes are influenced by technology use [13].

3. Research methodology

We studied the impact of online learning using technology in virtual classrooms and the effect of performance factors on students' learning behavior and achievement. The study focused on a sample of 6045 students, collected from the enrolment of University College students in spring 2020, at United Arab Emirates University has used online teaching strategy in comparison to fall 2019 teaching/learning experience, which used conventional teaching strategy involving 7369 students (See **Table 1**). The study shows the learning outcomes are similar for both virtual and conventional learning, although the assessment methods are different. They include students' learning outcomes assessment, testing (assessing

Term	Pass	Not Pass	Total
Fall 2019 (FOF)	6839	530	7369
Spring 2020 (OLA)	5488	557	6045

Table 1.
Students' population.

prior and post knowledge acquisition) and quantitative versus conventional research. The findings of the survey are discussed below. Descriptive statistics were obtained to summarize the sample characteristics and performance variables. Pearson Correlation was used to evaluate the association between the learning outcomes dimensions. Independent Samples t-test was used to compare the mean overall performance of the online learning. Linear Regression was used to determine the impact of the learning characteristics (Critical thinking, Creativity, Communication and Collaboration) on the overall performance score. Factor Analysis was used to study the inter-relationships among the learning characteristics and compare the online methods.

The objectives of the learning process consist of providing a diversified learning environment. The positive impact of this diversity is reflected in the students' performance. Students in various represented colleges have similar passing grades as high (80–98%) for both Online Approach (OLA) and Conventional learning -Face-to-Face (FoF). The University College is the largest college in the University with more than 4000 students. Most of UAEU students start their study in UC; they take English, Arabic, IT and Math (**Figure 4**).

This study was limited to GEIL101 foundation students. Surveys were sent out to all information literacy sections at the end of the first semester 2019/2020, but there were only 87 respondents. The survey had 2 parts, one part is about students' achievement/performance, and the second part use is about online learning in a virtual classroom. All sessions were conducted online by trained instructors in tandem with the University library delivered by professional librarians. In this report, fall 2019 students' data are used as the sample for the study (**Table 2**).

Overall, the results indicate the online learning was beneficial for students as it shown in their academic achievements and in tables below. A significant number of students reported high comfort levels of attending online courses in virtual classroom instead of conventional learning. Results indicated students have a positive

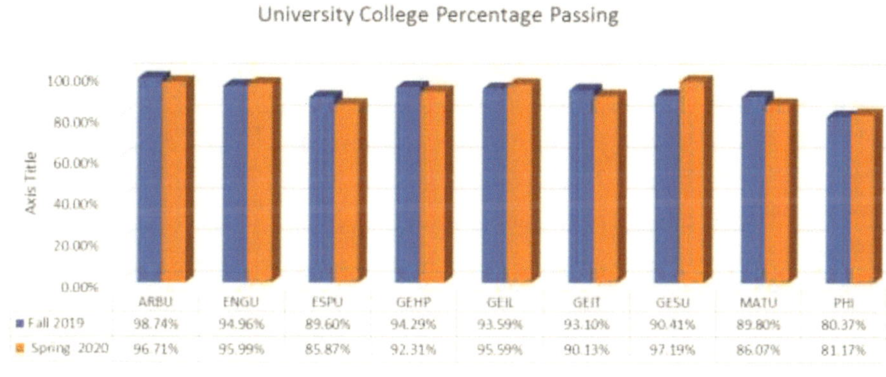

Figure 4.
University college percentage passing rate.

Course title	GEIL101 Information Literacy	Cohort:	Fall 2019
Total number of students	930	Passing	889
Average class size	30	Average grade	95.59%

Table 2.
GEIL students.

reception to online approach rather than traditional classrooms. Additionally, qualitative data identified a clearconsiderations for the integration of new technology into the new teaching and learning experience.

4. E-learning results and analyses

Table 3 shows the IL students' pre and post tests performance. The analysis on the pre and post-tests, using the means comparison and one sample test, shows an increase of students' performance by 84%, the mean of the pre-test is around 7.5 and the post test is 13.85, a significant difference of 6.35. 65% of students score above 60% (passing rate for the course) in the post-test, only 2.4% of students scored above 60% in the pre-test. This means that 97.6% of students did not have basic information literacy knowledge, but after going through intensive 12 week learning under e-learning conditions, 65% achieved the course outcomes with higher scores.

The following tables (**Tables 3** and **4**) shows the students' performance by each learning activity:

The scores in the post-test ranged between 11 and 20, whereas it ranged between 6 to 9 in the pre-test (**Figure 5**).

The above results show that OLA students scored higher than the FoF in the majority of the learning activities. There is an important performance of online students in the midterm and final exams though both approaches where offered the similar assessments criteria under the same test conditions. In the next section, the online learning process validity, the learning activities, and the learning outcome achievements, will be discussed in greater details. Several statistical models, qualitative and quantitative analysis have been applied for this purpose.

Aspect	%Yes
Operational Skills	89%
Use of Technology	90%
Communications Skills	69%
Problem Solving	69%
Formulate Critical opinion	79%
Evaluate information	84%
Collaboration	88%
Sharing findings and ideas	86%
Taking academic responsibilities	88%

Table 3.
Students' academic performance.

5. Impact analysis of the learning activities

It is important for an educator to evaluate which type of learning activity that has an important impact on students' performance. It will help the curriculum designers to adjust and improve the syllabus content accordingly. Two types of analyses are conducted quantitatively and qualitatively; the first analysis relies on the learning activities grades and course final scores. The second one relies on students' feedback through reflective essays and teachers' perception towards their students' learning progress.

DOI: http://dx.doi.org/10.5772/intechopen.94425

Item		Participation Engagement (5%)	Individual Presentation (5%)	Reflective Essay (5%)	Quizzes (10%)	Midterm (20%)	Final (20%)	Project (35%)	Final Grade (100%)
Average		4.61	4.42	4.04	8.85	14.60	12.90	30.55	**80.00**
Students	**Total**								
FoF	796	4.59	4.44	4.02	8.83	14.19	12.44	30.71	**79.25**
OLA	930	4.64	4.33	4.12	8.94	16.43	14.78	30.10	**83.20**

Table 4.
Students' learning activity.

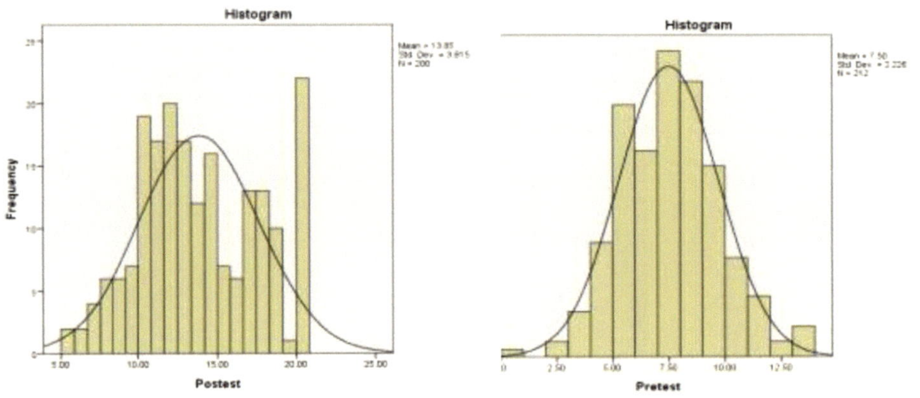

Figure 5.
Pre and post-tests comparison distribution.

5.1 Quantitative analysis

5.1.1 Impact of the learning activities on students' performance

To analyze the significance of each learning activity on students' performance, a regression linear model was used to analyze the impact of each learning skill on students' performance. According to the output report, the model is significant at 95% ($p < 0.000$), and there is a strong correlation between 95.8% of the learning skills and students' performance ($r2 = 0.919$).

Overall, all learning skills strategies have a significant impact on students' performance. Each student's learning skills and their impact will be analyzed. The following graph shows that individual contribution has less impact on the student's performance, but the course component is very important where students demonstrate their interaction with the course content. The quality of the students' online participation, their assiduity and interaction with others and their contribution in the projects are different from class participation. Therefore, statistically speaking, it has a lower impact. So, it is highly recommended to review how this component is graded.

5.1.2 Impact of each learning skill on students' achievement

The following table describes the impact of each individual learning skill on students' performance. To do this analysis, we used Pearson Correlation Coefficient to measure the strength of the linear relationship between the learning skills. The following figure shows the relationship between the learning skills.

From the table below, the test 1 (Midterm Exam) and test 2 (Final Exam) have the strongest impact (754 and 758) respectively on the final grades, even though students scored lower in these activities compared to other assessed learning activities. They are still the most efficient assessment methods to evaluate students' achievement. The projects, individual presentation and reflective essays have also a significant impact on students' performance. The only learning activity with the lowest impact is the individual participation and engagement in the class, which is an important learning activity, and it needs a review on how to assess it in an effective way.

6. Teachers' observations

Students' e-learning performance data is processed and presented. The six characteristic attributes are identified. Each characteristic is divided into further sub-items that are rated from 1 to 5 by the respondents. Then, for each of the six main characteristics, the average of the sub-items rating is calculated. The box plot (see **Figure 6**) shows a detailed distribution of each response. This is made up of the results, comparing the responses given to the different factors affecting learning. The result shows that the teachers rating of the effect of online learning in the following table. Example: 50% of teachers think that 70% of students improved their creativity skills.

Descriptive statistics for the learning variables are shown below in **Table 5**. In general, the mean and median of all the characteristics are quite high-around 3.5 (**Table 6**). Regarding correlations between learning parameters, the results show that almost all characteristics are highly inter-correlated ($p < 0.001$) (See **Table 7**).

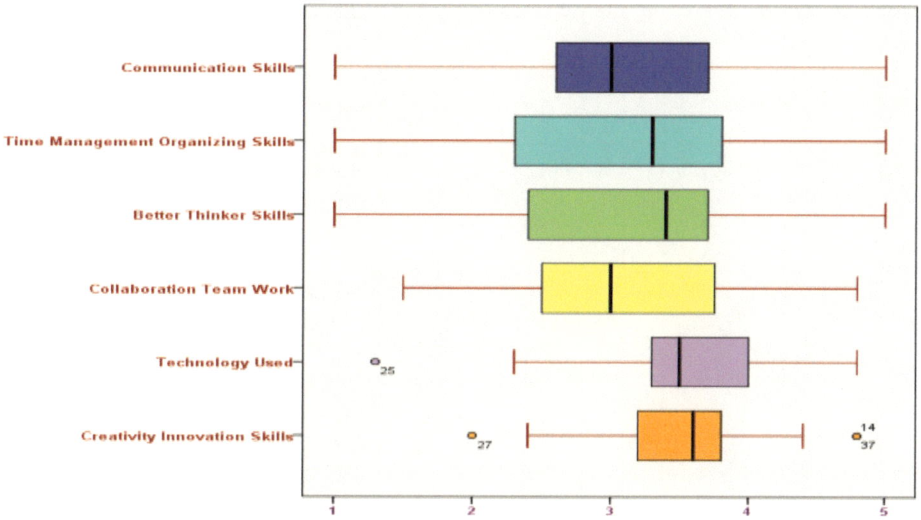

Figure 6.
Using e-learning in the virtual classroom.

Coefficientsa								
Model		Unstandardized Coefficients		Standardized Coefficients	t	Sig.	95.0% Confidence Interval for B	
		B	Std. Error	Beta			Lower Bound	Upper Bound
1	(Constant)	19.445	.992		19.601	.000	17.497	21.393
	IndivContribution	1.122	.147	.090	7.653	.000	.834	1.410
	IndivP resentation	1.878	.151	.161	12.403	.000	1.581	2.175
	ReflectiveEssay	1.719	.099	.237	17.431	.000	1.526	1.913
	Assignments	1.348	.090	.187	14.060	.000	1.159	1.536
	Testi	1.884	.045	.323	22.400	.000	.916	1.092
	Test;	1.858	.035	.407	29.210	.000	.986	1.129

[a]*Dependent Variable: FinalGrades.*

Table 5.
Regression model on learning skill of students' performance.

Correlations

		IndivContribution	IndivPresentation	ReflectiveEssay	Assignments	Testi	Test2	FinalProject	FinalGrades
IndivContribution	Pearson Correlation	1	.130**	.141**	.186**	.159**	.168**	.127**	.299**
	Sig. (2-tailed)		.001	.000	.000	.000	.000	.002	.000
	N	623	623	623	623	623	623	623	623
IndivPresentation	Pearson Correlation	.130**	1	.406**	.328**	.317**	.262**	.420**	.539**
	Sig. (2-tailed)	.001		.000	.000	.000	.000	.000	.000
	N	623	623	623	623	623	623	623	623
ReflectiveEssay	Pearson Correlation	.141**	.406**	1	.429**	.328**	.302**	.473**	.624**
	Sig. (2-tailed)	.000	.000		.000	.000	.000	.000	.000
	N	623	623	623	623	623	623	623	623
Assignments	Pearson Correlation	.186**	.328**	.429**	1	.350**	.240**	.352**	.569**
	Sig. (2-tailed)	.000	.000	.000		.000	.000	.000	.000
	N	623	623	623	623	623	623	623	623
Test1	Pearson Correlation	.159**	.317**	.328**	.350**	1	.549**	.261**	.754**
	Sig. (2-tailed)	.000	.000	.000	.000		.000	.000	.000
	N	623	623	623	623	623	623	623	623
Test2	Pearson Correlation	.168**	.262**	.302**	.240**	.549**	1	.256**	.758**
	Sig. (2-tailed)	.000	.000	.000	.000	.000		.000	.000
	N	623	623	623	623	623	623	623	623

Correlations

		IndivContribution	IndivPresentation	ReflectiveEssay	Assignments	Testi	Test2	FinalProject	FinalGrades
FinalProject	Pearson Correlation	.127**	.420**	.473**	.352**	.261**	.256**	1	.681
	Sig. (2-tailed)	.002	.000	.000	.000	.000	.000		.000
	N	623	623	623	623	623	623	623	623
FinalGrades	Pearson Correlation	.299**	.539**	.624**	.569**	.754**	.758**	.681**	1
	Sig. (2-tailed)	.000	.000	.000	.000	.000	.000	.000	
	N	623	623	623	623	623	623	623	623

***. Correlation is significant at the 0.01 level (2-tailed).*

Table 6.
Correlation between the learning skills on students' academic performance.

Correlations

		Creativity Innovation Skills	Technology Used	Collaboration Team Work	Better Thinker Skills	Time Management Organizing Skills	Communication Skills
Creativity Innovation Skills	Pearson Correlation	1	.393*	.685**	.767**	.659**	.653**
	Sig. (2-tailed)		.019	.000	.000	.000	.000
Technology Used	Pearson Correlation	.393*	1	.632**	.599**	.575**	.543**
	Sig. (2-tailed)	.019		.000	.000	.000	.001
Collaboration Team Work	Pearson Correlation	.685**	.632**	1	.845**	.773**	.836**
	Sig. (2-tailed)	.000	.000		.000	.000	.000
Better Thinker Skills	Pearson Correlation	.767**	.599**	.845**	1	.862**	.897**
	Sig. (2-tailed)	.000	.000	.000		.000	.000
Time Management Organizing Skills	Pearson Correlation	.659**	.575**	.773**	.862**	1	.796**
	Sig. (2-tailed)	.000	.000	.000	.000		.000
Communication Skills	Pearson Correlation	.653**	.543**	.836**	.897**	.796**	1
	Sig. (2-tailed)	.000	.001	.000	.000	.000	

**Correlation is significant at the 0.05 level (2-tailed).*
***. Correlation is significant at the 0.01 level (2-tailed).*

Table 7.
E-learning characteristics.

7. Students' results and analysis

The survey was to collect feedback from students after they started using online learning courses. The effects of this methods on students' learning and understanding A scale of 1–5 range from strongly agree (5) to strongly disagree (1). Different dimensions of online approach are analyzed and Eighty-seven UAE College Students coming from different Universities were asked to give their perception on different aspects of online learning methods.

For the question (1), "Do you like online learning technology?" 84 respondents representing 97.6% of the students said they do. As for the question (2), "Do you feel ready to use online environment?", 61 students representing 71.2% said they do.

While 7 students or 8% said, they do not. Only 19 student or 21.8% were neutral (see **Table 8**).

As for question (3), "whether students have all the required technology tools for online learning", 71 of the respondents representing 83.53% agreed but only 4 students disagreed (See **Table 9**).

Regarding the question (4), as to "whether students have reliable internet connection for online learning, 56 of the respondents representing 64% said that they agreed, while 7 students said that they disagree (See **Table 10**).

For question (5), "Did Online learning help your study when you have flexible schedule?" 53 students representing 63% of the respondents said it helped them because of time restriction. On the other hand, 31 students representing 37% said that time was not visible (See **Table 11**).

For question (6), "Did online learning help you to be more productive?" 38 students representing 45% of the respondents said that online class helped them to be more organized and productive. On the other hand, 19 students representing 23% said that it was not productive for them (See **Table 12**).

	Frequency	Percent
Agree	61	71.2%
Neutral	19	21.8%
Disagree	7	8%

Table 8.
Ready for online transformation.

	Frequency	Percent
Agree	71	83.53%
Neutral	10	11.76%
Disagree	4	4.70%

Table 9.
Do students have the required tools for online learning?

	Frequency	Percent
Agree	56	64%
Neutral	24	27.59%
Disagree	7	8%

Table 10.
Do students have the reliable internet connection for online learning?

For question (7), "How do rate your experience with your team online" 58 students representing 60% of the respondents said that online learning class is like normal class. On the other hand, 9 students representing 10% said that they were not satisfied with online learning (See **Table 13**).

For question (7), "How do rate your internet connectivity and how often problems occurred?" 37 students representing 43% of the respondents said that online class runs into technical issues which lead to reduce their productivity and confidence. On the other hand, 42 students representing 48% said that there were no issues with their internet connections (See **Table 14**).

For question (8), "Did you develop any health issues since the start of online learning? 41 students representing 48% of the respondents said that online class causes health issues which lead to reduce their productivity and confidence. On the other hand, 25 students representing 29% said that there were no health issues using online learning (See **Table 15**).

For question (9), "Rate the distractions you have had online", 31 students representing 37% of the respondents said that online class did not face distractions. On the other hand, 23 students representing 27% said that there were not issues concerning online distraction (See **Table 16**).

	Frequency	Percent
Yes	53	63.10%
No	31	37%

Table 11.
Did you have a flexible schedule when online learning was used?

	Frequency	Percent
Agree	38	45%
Neutral	27	32.14%
Disagree	19	23%

Table 12.
Did online learning help you be more productive?

	Frequency	Percent
Satisfied	52	60%
Neutral	25	29.07%
Unsatisfied	9	10%

Table 13.
How do you rate your online experience with your team?

	Frequency	Percent
Perfect	42	48%
Neutral	28	32.18%
Sometimes / Never	37	43%

Table 14.
How often do you face technical problems?

	Frequency	Percent
Agree	41	48%
Neutral	20	23.26%
Disagree	25	29%

Table 15.
Did you develop any health issues since the start of online learning?

	Frequency	Percent
Unsatisfied	31	37%
Neutral	30	35.71%
Satisfied	23	27%

Table 16.
Rate the distractions you have had at home.

8. Conclusion

The ultimate purpose of this investigation was to explore the impact of online learning on students' academic achievement as the demand has increased in recent times for online courses among institutions and college students who solely rely on flexible and comfortable education. We tried to measure in quantifiable terms the students' final academic performance after their exposure to online learning during this pandemic lockdown. The final results obtained in this study were quite self-eloquent, as they unequivocally show the tremendous impact of e- learning on students' academic performance and achievements, as it can benefit students in many ways, including enhancing and maximizing their learning independence and classroom participation. It is a good experience for students' transitional preparation to pursue college education and seek employment. Students were more engaged in the learning process than in conventional teaching, and online learning experience has revealed that didactic teaching style is no longer effective. They no longer regard teachers as the only source of information, but as learning facilitator and online learning from different internet sources as their main source of information. They have proved that they can assume their responsibilities, contribute to course design assessment and learning process personalization. Online learning also helped overcome time and space constraints imposed by the convention learning process and helped students to effectively communicate their findings and share their ideas with their peers locally and globally. The introduction of a new technology such as the online learning will undoubtedly have more impact on the learning outcomes only if we reconsider the delivery mode, content redesign, new assessment system. A suitable pedagogy and an appropriate content are the most important sources of students' learning motivation. Finally, e-learning has a bright future, tremendous learning potentialities and excellent organizational culture. Universities will incontrovertibly use many of the lessons learned during this pandemic lockdown period of this forced online teaching to adjust curriculum contents, teaching methods/lesson delivery, and assessment tools.

E-learning is here to stay and can make a much stronger contribution to higher education in the years to come. However, there are some negative effects of online class as it does not offer real a face to face contact and interaction with instructors and imposes time commitment and less accountability on students. There are also many online struggles that students face such as the impossibility to stay motivated all the time, as they sometimes feel that they are completely isolated. In addition, instructors feel impotent to control students' cheating, impose classroom discipline. In addition to that, poor students struggle to get the necessary electronic equipment to access this new mode of learning to interact in due time with their instructor, make necessary comments and raise questions to clear ambiguities and any equivocal statements and get appropriate feedback from their instructor.

There are other academic issues that need to be investigated deeply such as the perspectives of higher education quality focusing on the study of cultural, emotional, technological, ethical, health, financial or academic achievements. Furthermore, more academic research should be done about e-learning theories/distance learning to truly improvise a new and adequate teaching/learning approach.

Author details

Khaled Hamdan* and Abid Amorri
UAEU-University College, UAE

*Address all correspondence to: khamdan@uaeu.ac.ae

References

[1] Bao, W. (2020). COVID-19 and online teaching in higher Education: A case of Peking University. Wiley Online Library,2(2),113-115.

[2] Zheleva M., Tramonti M., "Use of the Virtual World for Educational Purposes", in Electronic Journal for Computer Science and Communications, n. Issue 4(2), Burgas Free University, pp. 106-125, 2015.

[3] Usoro, A., & Majewski, G. (2009). Measuring Quality e-Learning in Higher Education international Journal of Global Management Studies (2), 1-32.

[4] Rossing, J. P., Miller, W. M., Cecil, A. K., & Stamper, S. E. (2012). iLearning: The Future of Higher Education? Student Perceptions on Learning with Mobile Tablets. Journal of the Scholarship of Teaching and Learning, 12(2), 1-26.

[5] MacTeer, C. F. (2011). Distance education (Ser. Education in a competitive and globalizing world). Nova Science.

[6] Nathan, S. (2020). AL-FANAR MEDIA covering Education, Research and Culture, Retrieved from https://www.al- fanarmedia.org/2020/05/future-higher-education-go-from-here/

[7] Joshi, H. (2012). Towards Transformed Teaching: Engaging Learners Anytime, Anywhere. UAE Journal of Education Technology and Learning v3, pp. 3:5.

[8] Onyema,E. Eucheria, N Dr. Obafemi, F. , Fyneface, S. Atonye, G. Sharma, A. Alsayed, O. (2020), Impact of Coronavirus Pandemic on Education, Journal of Education and Practice, Vol.11, No.13, 2020

[9] Aristovnik, A.(2020),How Covid-19 pandemic affected higher education students' lives globally and in the United States.

[10] Aman, S. (2020). Flexible learning in UAE: a case for e-lessons post COVID-19 too. *Gulf News*.

[11] Hamdan, K., Al-Qirim, N., Asmar, M. (2012) The Effect of Smart Board on Students Behavior and Motivation, IEEE, 2012, pp. 162-166. International Conference on Innovations in Information Technology (IIT).

[12] Carmozzino, E., Corvello, V., & Grimaldi, M. (2017). Entrepreneurial learning through online social networking in high-tech startups. International Journal of Entrepreneurial Behavior & Research, 23(3), 406-425.

[13] Hamdan,K and Asmar, M (2012), Improving Student Performance Using Interactive Smart Board Technology, Innovations 9TH International Conference in Information Technology, UAEU.

[14] O'Malley, C., Vavoula, G., Glew, J.P., Taylor, J., Sharples, M., & Lefrere, P., (2004). Guidelines for learning/teaching/tutoring in a mobile environment. [Online] Available http://www.mobilearn.org/download/results/guidelines.pdf

[15] Walker, A. A. (2017). Why education practitioners and stakeholders should care about person fit in educational assessments. *Harvard Educational Review*, *87*(3), 426-443.

Chapter 4

A Model of the Continual Adaptive Online Knowledge Assessment System

Miran Zlatović, Igor Balaban and Željko Hutinski

Abstract

This chapter presents a model of a novel adaptive online knowledge assessment system and tests the efficiency of its implementation. System enables continual and cumulative knowledge assessment, comprised of sequence of at least two interconnected assessments, carried-out throughout a reasonably long period of time. Important characteristics of the system are: (a) introduction of new course topics in every subsequent assessment, (b) re-assessment of earlier course topics in every subsequent assessment iteration, (c) in an adaptive manner, based on student's achievements during previous assessments. Personalized post-assessment feedback guides each student in preparations for upcoming assessments. The efficiency has been tested on a sample of 78 students. Results indicate that the proposed adaptive system is efficient on an individual learning goal level.

Keywords: online knowledge assessment, adaptive knowledge assessment, improving classroom teaching, post-secondary education, learning strategies, learning goals

1. Introduction

The courses taught by the authors of this chapter (ICT-oriented, undergraduate university level courses) use a type of accumulative model of tracking students' activities, where multiple traditional written mid-term assessments grant most of the points required to pass the course. A more specific feature of this tracking model is that the units of learning contents are assessed multiple times. In other words, every subsequent mid-term assessment includes the re-assessment of previous content too, but with diminishing contributions – for example, 2nd mid-term assessment might include 40% of the content from the 1st mid-term assessment and 60% of new content, 3rd mid-term might include 10% of the oldest content (1st mid-term), 30% of the older content (2nd mid-term) and 60% of brand new content, etc.

Although we were generally satisfied (in terms of overall course grades) with the results of our traditional non-adaptive pen-and-paper assessment approach, we wanted to explore the possibilities of including Information and Communications Technology (ICT) support and adaptive assessment into the accumulative tracking model, to achieve following improvements:

1. To adapt the re-assessment portion of the mid-term to each individual student, based on the results he/she obtained for that content during previous mid-term:

   - Students that have shown higher levels of mastery of particular content during previous mid-term need not be re-assessed about that content in detail – i.e. they may receive less questions or less complex questions (to demonstrate that they have not forgotten what they had known before).

   - Students that have shown lower levels of mastery of old content should be re-assessed about that content more thoroughly (to demonstrate that currently they have more knowledge than before).

2. To include ICT support into adaptive knowledge assessment process, because manual adaptation of subsequent pen-and-paper mid-terms for each individual student, as suggested above, would be too complex to manage.

Such assessment model should be **continual** (span across multiple connected assessments throughout semester) and **adaptive** (re-assessment part of every subsequent assessment would be adapted to each participant, based on his/her previous results). It would also need to fit our current teaching delivery model, i.e. traditional classroom courses supported by blended e-learning and activity tracking.

With that respect, our primary goal was to explore the possibilities of improving the in-house knowledge assessment process by making it adaptive, but without introducing the complexity of complete adaptive learning systems (which will be mentioned briefly in the opening paragraphs of Chapter 3.

2. Research methodology

To achieve the desired goal (as mentioned in Introduction - inclusion of ICT support and adaptive assessment into our existing accumulative tracking model), we used Design and Development Research (DDR) Method that allows researchers to establish new procedures, techniques and tools based on specific needs analysis [1] and that consists of seven iterative phases [2]. Within the first, "Focus" phase we bounded the scope of the project to ensure that the project pursues an important goal that can be achieved with current resources, which is presented in the introduction section. Within the "Understand" phase we analyzed research literature to investigate the problem (section "The Context of the Study"). Research objectives and hypothesis were then identified within the "Define" phase. The initial solution was designed under the "Conceive" phase (section "Rationale Behind the Proposed Model"). The "Build" phase aimed at developing the model and building a test platform (section "Development of the Model"). We evaluated the efficacy and behavior of the solution in a real context within the "Test" phase (section "Testing the Model"). This chapter, in overall, is part of the last phase in the DDR methodology ("Present"), where we elaborate how the developed solution contributed to solving the problem.

3. The context of the study

The adaptive online education is highly represented in current scientific and professional research, especially the studies focused on adaptive learning and adaptive learning systems (ALS). Here we refer to adaptive learning as a process which creates unique learning experiences for every learner by taking into consideration many learner's traits, such as his/her interests, performance, personality, etc. [3]. Most research efforts in the ALS field are focused on full e-learning systems, which are driven by two main principles: (a) selection and delivery of the appropriate learning contents to each participant, so that (b) each participant can improve the effects of his/her education [4, 5].

Although this chapter follows a similar principle, it does not focus on adaptive education in its broader and general sense. Instead, it puts an emphasis on the process of adaptive online knowledge assessment [6–8], i.e. on the process of selection and application of different types of questions within written online knowledge assessment, in order to improve each student's achievement levels of learning goals. In the context of this chapter, like the approach taken by the Stanford University, we consider learning goals as the statements of "... what we want our students to be able to demonstrate at the end of our class." [9]. Examples of such learning goals can be found in **Table 1**. Achievement of such learning goals can be measured by standard knowledge assessment grading techniques.

3.1 Adaptation and learning strategies vs. learning styles

To be able to consider users' individual differences, ALSs rely on user models [10] that keep track of many elements, including learning styles, learners' personal preferences, prior knowledge, skills and competences. Many studies stress the importance of learning styles during adaptation process. As shown by Soflano, Connoly and Hainey [11], the adaptation based on learning styles in games-based learning (GBL) environment allowed learners to complete the tasks faster, compared to both non-adaptive GBL and to classic textbook learning. Tseng, Chu, Hwang and Tsai [12] report that the approach based upon multiple sources of personalization (learning behavior and personal learning style) is helpful in improving both the learning achievements and learning efficiency of individual students.

Online tests	Learning goal codes	Learning goal descriptions
First test (t1)	LG1	Define decision support systems and expert systems
	LG2	Describe the elements, components, objectives and functions of IS
	LG3	Describe the structure of decision support systems and expert systems
	LG4	Describe the decision-making process and the role of DSS and ES in the decision-making process
	LG5	Describe the types of IS
	LG6	Distinguish the life and development cycle of IS
	LG7	Define types of content search on the Internet
	LG8	Define common Internet services
	LG9	Describe the elements of a computer network
	LG10	Describe the elements, functions and structure of the Internet, intranets and extranets
	LG11	Describe and compare the types of content search on the Internet
	LG12	Describe the ISO/OSI model and TCP/IP model
	LG13	Describe common Internet services
Second test (t2)	LG14	Define concepts of multimedia and virtual reality
	LG15	Describe multimedia systems and virtual reality
Third test (t3)	LG16	Define concepts of the safety and security of IS
	LG17	Describe and explain the safety and security of IS

Table 1.
Learning goals used in Adaptivity application to test the model.

Although adaptations based on learning styles might have a role in improving learning achievements when applied on an entire ALS level, it should be noted that learning styles would not be that useful if they were used as a foundation for adaptations within narrower field of knowledge assessment only. Hartley [13] claims that individual learning styles are mostly static in time and not easily changed, unlike learning strategies which are primarily dynamic, conditioned by current tasks and can be manipulated with during shorter periods. Hartley defines learning strategies as "... the different combinations of activities (i.e. 'strategies') students use while learning.". Similarly, Mayer [14] defines them as "... behaviors of a learner that are intended to influence how the learner processes information". For this chapter, we consider these two basic learning strategies - deep and surface learning, which can be briefly described as follows [15, 16]:

- Surface learning – any combination of the activities used by the students while learning, that lead to the learning aimed at mere reproduction of the contents. Understanding of learning contents is very low or non-existent.

- Deep learning – any combination of the activities used by the students while learning, that lead to the learning aimed at understanding of the contents, i.e. questioning of alternatives, raising additional questions, etc.

We aim to use the feedback part of proposed adaptive system to steer the students towards behaviors and activities which would preferably lead to deep learning while preparing for the re-assessment of earlier learning contents.

Learning strategies, as described above, can be measured by various instruments, such as Study Process Questionnaire [17], although their direct measurement is not in the scope of this chapter. Here we refer to additional study which has shown that learning strategies can be facilitated (stimulated) and have important influence on achievement levels of learning goals [18] – it has been shown that an announcement of any type (form) of online knowledge assessment is not suitable for the facilitation of the more desirable deep learning and that all learning strategies facilitated by such announcements do not equally contribute to the achievement levels of the required learning goals. Zlatović, Balaban and Kermek [18] have demonstrated that a deep learning strategy has a positive effect on results in both essay and multiple-choice types of online assessment, while surface learning strategy has a negative impact on results in online essay, and no impact on results in online multiple-choice question assessment. When it comes to the levels of knowledge, the study has demonstrated that achievements of lower levels of knowledge (rote memorizing, reproduction, understanding) have been primarily stipulated by surface learning strategies which were facilitated by using online assessments containing multiple-choice questions. Achievements of higher levels of knowledge (analysis, synthesis and evaluation) were better when essay-based online assessments were used to facilitate deep learning strategies. Due to all these findings, we decided to incorporate the effects of learning strategies facilitation in proposed model, as an important supportive element in the adaptation of the re-assessment of the old learning contents.

3.2 Feedback

Another major aspect of our model involves feedback which is a major element of quality in teaching and assessment [19, 20]. Students also appreciate the value of feedback and are aware of its importance in achieving learning goals [21]. Maier, Wolf and Randler [22] have examined feedback effects with computer-assisted multiple-tier tests and it was revealed that feedback is more effective when it is designed as elaborated (specific) feedback and that the elaborated feedback is effective when it is perceived as helpful.

By using feedback based on the results of individual's current assessment, the adaptive system we propose will announce to each individual student the following instructions related to the re-assessment part of the next assessment:

1. What type of questions is predominantly going to be used in the following iteration (e.g. essay-oriented questions, matching the terms, fill-in the blanks, multiple choice) and

2. What is the expected difficulty of those questions (i.e. easy, medium or hard)?

Such announcements are supposed to facilitate the appropriate learning strategies (preferably deep learning) during preparations for re-assessment.

3.3 Adaptation throughout a series of assessments

The central aspects of the model we are proposing are the **continuity** of the assessment and the **adaptation** between the series of the connected assessments (i.e. the adaptive re-assessment part of each subsequent assessment).

Review in the field of the adaptive online knowledge assessment reveals that historically most efforts are focused on studying various aspects of adaptability within a single knowledge assessment, usually within a self-assessment and/or formative assessment [23, 24].

However, to continuously monitor students' progress, a continuous knowledge assessment was proposed. McAlpine [25] defines it as "... the more modern form of modular assessment, where judgments are made at the end of each field of study". Continuous knowledge assessment belongs to the group of formative assessment techniques, since it provides plethora of individuals' learning progress indicators while students are still committed to the learning process. Therefore, such indicators can be used to carry-on corrective actions while the teaching process is still ongoing – e.g. to adapt teaching process to the specific needs of participants.

Continuous formative evaluation using ALS system Amrita Learning [26] uses multiple assessments in adaptive manner, but each assessment covers different learning contents and old contents are never re-assessed. Therefore, such adaptation process does not consider the results of earlier assessment(s).

Grundspenkis [8] and Grundspenkis and Anohina [27] have described an adaptive learning and assessment system where concept maps are used as a more machine-friendly replacement for essays. Course contents are introduced gradually in time, through multiple stages. Every subsequent stage can only upgrade existing content from previous stage with new concepts. Adaptive knowledge assessments take place between stages, but although these assessments encompass contents from all available stages (similarity with our approach), the adaptivity is still limited to a single assessment. Adaptivity is reflected via two properties: (i) student can request a task with reduced difficulty, if initial version is too difficult and (ii) system can automatically increase the difficulty of the following task if the student has achieved required score without any reductions. Still, there is no evidence that e.g. an assessment that takes place between stages 2 and 3 takes into consideration the results from the assessment conducted between stages 1 and 2. There are also examples of adaptive and continuous assessment within commercial e-learning platforms – e.g. Khan Academy, whose approaches towards assessing students' mastery of a particular topic is described in [28]. Historically, the Khan Academy used the streak concept, where student had to solve correctly at least 10 problems in a row. Then the system assumes that required proficiency level has been achieved and student can progress further to new topics. More advanced proficiency model replaced the streak approach – next task was selected using logistic regression techniques, considering both previously solved tasks and current proficiency level of a student. While the element of adaptivity over the series of assessments is present, it still lacks the systematic inclusion of older content into upcoming assessments.

Within the area of ALSs we often encounter distinctions mentioning micro- and macro-adaptation. It is suggested by Van Lehn [29] that primary focus of macro-adaptation is application of adaptivity on a global task selection process within entire ITS, while primary focus of micro-adaptations are lower-level in-task interactions. Knowledge assessment is usually considered to belong to the micro-level of an ITS. Results of assessments are then used to update learner models, which are then used in subsequent macro-adaptation activities [24, 30]. Since we propose the adaptive model of continual assessment that is designed primarily to be used standalone, without being part of a larger ALS or ITS, macro-level of adaptation will be represented by adapting the re-assessment part of the next assessment. Results of micro-activities (individual assessments) would update simplified user model (user's achievement levels per topic/learning goal), which is later used to perform macro-adaptation between two assessments.

Review of the available research suggests that sufficient investigation effort has not yet been put into assessment systems which implement adaptivity within series of interconnected assessments, specifically into systems using adaptivity to re-assess previous learning contents. Additional insights about such systems is one of the scientific contributions of this study.

4. Research objectives and hypothesis

In respect to the issues noted from the research literature, the objectives of this study are as follows:

- To develop and test a model of the adaptive online knowledge assessment system that facilitates those learning strategies that lead towards better achievement of the required learning goals.

- To provide feedback to students based on individual results of their online assessments, containing suggestions about the assessment types that are going to be used for the re-assessment of particular learning goals in the next iteration of an adaptive assessment.

In line with the research objectives, the following hypothesis is formulated:

The model is proposed, of the continual adaptive online knowledge assessment system, which leads to better achievements of the required levels of learning goals, by utilizing a personalized feedback to announce what questions types will be selected in the following assessment iteration and by utilizing learning strategies facilitated by such personalized feedback.

5. Rationale behind the proposed model

Based on the findings and the experience from previous research regarding the learning strategies, as well as the other relevant work indicated in previous section, we propose the model of an adaptive online knowledge assessment system, which supports series of assessments connected in a linear way, in a chain-like structure. It is designed to guide the individual towards continuous improvements in achievement levels of required learning goals within traditional higher education class-based courses by focusing on several key aspects:

- Assessment process is carried out continually during longer period (e.g. one semester), throughout a series of assessments following the principles generally common for ALS described in previous section. Necessity for having longer period is also supported by findings from Dembo and Praks-Seli [31], stating that changes in students' learning strategies cannot appear instantaneously, due to them (strategies) being either part of individual's automated behavior patterns or being carried over from other courses.

- Personalized feedback per assessed learning goal (for example, see Maier, Wolf and Randler [22]) will be presented at the end of each assessment, based on individuals' achievement levels per topic/learning goal, suggesting what type of questions will be used next time, to re-assess those learning goals.

- Given the application of above-mentioned feedback and having enough time between two assessments, individuals have enough time to adjust their learning strategies [18, 31] – preferably towards deep learning, so that they are more likely to improve their achievement levels in re-assessed topics.

Inclusion of the following aspects into the proposed assessment model is part of the original contribution of this chapter:

- Every subsequent assessment includes re-assessment of the topics from previous assessments (continual assessment of topics, to stimulate improvements of learning goals' achievement levels – here we build upon findings from the field of cognitive psychology, where it was shown "... that repeated testing of information produces superior retention relative to repeated study, especially when testing is spaced out over time." [32]).

- Adaptive re-assessment of old topics based on individuals' previous achievement levels per old topic/learning goal.

The knowledge assessment model proposed in this chapter represents a type of **continual** (carried-out through multiple iterations during longer period of time, i.e. one semester) and **cumulative** (iterations cannot be considered as mutually independent, because subsequent iterations include **earlier content** alongside **newly introduced content**) knowledge assessment. The first iteration (first assessment) is always non-adaptive. Adaptive assessment phase starts with the second iteration of e-assessment by analyzing individual assessment results from the first iteration, which opens-up a possibility to personalize each students' questions structure just for the re-assessment part of the old topics. In those phases system automatically selects the questions (their number, type and difficulty), based on the built-in adaptivity rules which consider student's previous level of learning goals achievements for a particular learning object (topic). At the end of each assessment, system presents the student with the feedback containing information about the level of achievement per learning goal and the types of questions that will be preferred in upcoming assessment to re-assess earlier learning content (especially for those units of content whose learning goals were not met in a satisfactory manner in current assessment). This information should incite students to change learning strategies they intend to use for the re-assessment of earlier learning content.

Inclusion of adaptivity elements within the above-described type of assessment, as well as modeling and development of a system which selects the types of questions to facilitate learning strategies, which in turn lead to a better achievement of the required learning goals, is an important contribution of this chapter.

6. Development of the model

6.1 Basic structure

Following general practices from the field of adaptive knowledge assessment are integrated within the proposed model (references to the numberings 1 to 3 will be used later in the text as "general practice 1", "general practice 2" and "general practice 3"):

1. Quantitative expression of individuals' success in achieving particular learning goal [34], e.g., using percentage scale that mimics grading system.
2. Multi-level qualitative marking of questions difficulty, in context of the assessment of associated learning goal, e.g. easy/medium/difficult [33, 34].
3. Rule-based approach towards adaptation process [33, 35].

Besides those elements, continual and cumulation properties are paired with adaptivity features are also built into the model. Cumulation property enables the inclusion of desired elements of adaptivity in the assessment system, in a sense that re-assessment of the earlier learning content may become individualized and in accordance with the achievements examinees have demonstrated during previous iterations:

- Individual goal achievements from the previous iterations can be used to formulate the announcement of the type and the difficulty of the assessment that will be used to re-assess these goals in a new iteration.
- The system informs each examinee what type of the assessment will be used in re-assessment of various portions of earlier learning content, so that (i)
    - Such announcements provide **individual** facilitation of learning strategies, and
    - Effects of the facilitated learning strategies lead to the improvements of students' performance.

The basic structure of the proposed assessment model is shown in **Figure 1**. The **cognitive level** is a label assigned to a learning goal, according to Bloom's Taxonomy [36]: 1 – Knowledge ... 6 – Evaluation. It is used to classify learning goals regarding their cognitive levels.

The **learning objects** represent broader units of learning content, to which one or more learning goals are connected.

A **learning goal** is always connected to a particular learning object and a particular cognitive level is assigned to it. Goals also have defined percentage-based thresholds for achievement levels. If the achievement level is below the lowest level, it means that the related learning goal is not achieved; gradual increase in the thresholds reached represents the achievement on a gradually higher level.

The **questions** element represents the assessment questions database and "general practice 2" was followed here. Each question is assigned to one or more **learning goals**. Model supports various types of questions: (i) multiple-choice questions

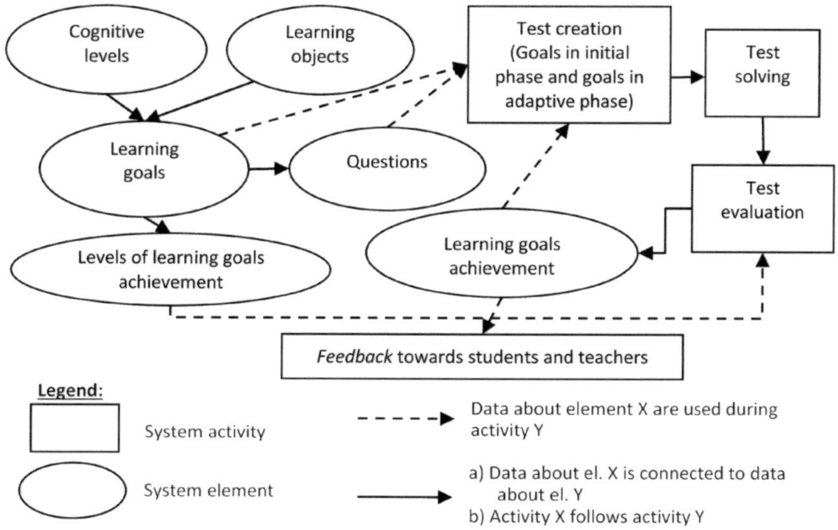

Figure 1.
Basic elements of the proposed model of the continual adaptive online knowledge assessment system.

(both single- and multiple correct answers), (ii) matching questions, (iii) fill-in the blanks and (iv) essay questions. Difficulty of a question within the context of particular learning goal [33] is defined by attaching mandatory qualitative label to each question – three levels of difficulty are supported: easy questions (DL1, "difficulty level 1"), medium-difficulty questions (DL2) and difficult questions (DL3).

All the above-mentioned elements (cognitive levels, learning objects, learning goals, question difficulty levels) are defined manually by the teacher within the proposed system – it is solely their responsibility to set-up the database of interrelated learning goals, objects and questions.

The **assessment creation** activity is a central element of the system and takes into consideration all the other main elements of the system, except for feedback, and also leans on general practice (general practice 3). Learning goals that are being assessed for the first time during an assessment cycle are in the initial phase, which means that adaptivity rules do not apply yet. The goals that are re-assessed in the following iterations are in the adaptive phase and the process of questions selection is fully governed by the adaptive rules and results achieved for that goal in previous iteration.

The **learning goals achievement** element is calculated during the assessment evaluation activity, in-line with the "general practice 1". It is a quantitative indicator of student's level of achievement of a learning goal, expressed as a percentage scale. Although arbitrary number of thresholds can be used to express various achievement levels, proposed model is set to mimic the traditional grading scale:

- Fail (F or 1): 0–49,99%
- Sufficient (D or 2): 50–62,49%
- Good (C or 3): 62,5-74,99%
- Very good (B or 4): 75–87,49%
- Excellent (A or 5): 87,5–100%

The **feedback towards the students** (see **Table 2** for an example) visualizes the individual achievement levels related to the particular learning goals included

(1) Results per Learning Goal (LGs)	(2) Announcement of question types and difficulties to be used for a learning goal re-assessment:
LG: Describing the decision process and the role of DSS and ES within it. **No. of questions:** 3 **Max. points:** 3 **Points achieved:** 3 (100%) **Learning goal achievement level:** Excellent	**If the current achievement level of a learning goal is "Fail":** - > it will be re-tested using difficult questions (predominantly using more demanding essay-type questions) **If the current achievement level of a learning goal is „Sufficient "or „Good":** - > it will be re-tested using medium and difficult questions (predominantly using essays and matching terms/statements questions; less likely by fill-in-the-blanks and multiple-choice questions) **If the current achievement level of a learning goal is "Very good" or "Excellent":** - > it will be re-tested using easy and medium difficulty questions (predominantly using multiple choice, fill-in-the-blanks and matching questions; less likely by short and less demanding essay questions)
LG: Describing the network topologies and elements used to build computer networks **No. of questions:** 4 **Max. points:** 5 **Points achieved:** 3.33 (66.6%) **Learning goal achievement level:** Good	
LG: Describing the ISO/OSI model and TCP/IP model **No. of questions:** 3 **Max. points:** 5 **Points achieved:** 0 (0%) **Learning goal achievement level:** Fail	
etc. results for other learning goals	

Table 2.
Excerpt from an automated feedback presented to student at the end of each assessment.

in assessment and provides personalized suggestions describing what type and difficulty of questions will be used predominantly in following adaptive iteration, during repeated assessment of old learning content.

6.2 Flow of the assessment

The first assessment iteration in the assessment cycle is always non-adaptive, as illustrated in **Figure 2**. In this iteration, since it is the first time that all topics are being assessed, all students will have identical structure of the test. Only teacher (without intervention of the built-in adaptivity mechanics) decides (a) which learning objects and goals to include, (b) what difficulty levels of the questions will be required to assess particular learning goal and (c) how many questions (of required difficulty and type) will be included in the test. Besides already mentioned criteria (objects/goals, difficulty and number of questions), teacher can also define that in the initial phase of the assessment all student will be given either: (i) fully identical set of questions, or (ii) randomly selected questions, or (iii) a mixture of fixed and randomly selected questions.

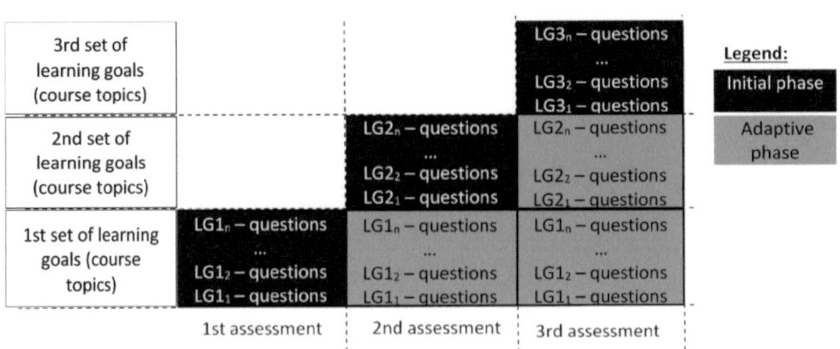

Figure 2.
Flow of the continual and cumulative adaptive knowledge assessment.

Based on individual results from the first iteration, it is possible to adaptively automate and personalize each student's questions structure for the re-assessment of old learning goals in the following iteration. Therefore, the second (and each subsequent) iteration of the assessment implements the cumulation property and it is comprised of the:

- First assessment of **new learning objects** – since these objects enter the assessment for the first time (dark gray rectangles in **Figure 2**), teacher is again responsible for defining all the parameters (as described above), and

- Repeated assessment of **learning objects from the previous iteration** (Property of cumulation) – since these objects need to be assessed repeatedly, they enter the adaptive assessment phase (light gray squares in **Figure 2**) and only the system automatically selects the questions (their number, type and difficulty), based on built-in adaptivity rules (general practice 3) which consider student's previous level of learning goals achievements for that object. Teacher does not have any influence on the question selection process for learning goals that are being assessed repeatedly.

Likewise, the N-th iteration is also cumulative in nature – it includes the first assessment of new learning objects (initial phase with identical assessment structure for all students, teacher defines all parameters for question selection) and the repeated assessment of learning objects which were included in all the previous iterations (without teacher's influence, governed only by built-in adaptivity rules, General practice 3).

Automated process of selecting the questions for learning goals that have entered the adaptive phase relies on five adaptive rules, which will be briefly summarized in following section, for the completeness and clarity of the chapter. More elaborate descriptions and case studies of those rules can be found in [37].

6.3 Adaptive rules

There are three categories of adaptive rules used to select questions for learning goals which have reached the adaptive phase of the assessment. Rules are built around general practices (general practices 1 and 2) and the properties of continuality and cumulation:

1. **Three rules (R1 to R3) to decide the questions difficulty** – the difficulty selection is based on the individual student's achievement level for a learning goal (i.e. score for a group of questions pertaining to that learning goal), in a way that if the achievement level in the previous iteration was:

    - **"Fail"**: select only high-difficulty questions (i.e. highest difficulty available) for that learning goal. This is **rule R1** with the rationale: "improve the non-satisfactory achievement level".

    - **"Sufficient"** or **"Good"**: select medium- and high-difficulty questions available for that learning goal. This is **rule R2** with the rationale: "maintain decent achievement level, with incentive for improvement".

    - **"Very good"** or **"Excellent"**: select easy and medium-difficulty questions available for that learning goal: This is **rule R3** with the rationale: "don't forget about this portion of learning content".

2. **Rule R4 which decreases the number of questions used in the adaptive phase** – both repeated assessment of learning goals from previous iterations

and inclusion of the first-time assessed new learning goals lead to inevitable question inflation (i.e. ever increasing number of questions) and consequently to assessment duration issues (i.e. ever longer duration of the test, to compensate for the ever increasing number of questions). If **N** question were used in **1st iteration**, then at most **N/2** questions will be used in **2nd iteration** for that learning goal, at most **N/3** in **3rd iteration**, etc.

3. **Rule R5 which increases the number of questions only for the individuals with low achievement** – this rule is complementary to the rule R4. If some student has achieved the lowest (i.e. "Fail") level for some learning goal during previous iteration, then due to this rule system will individually increase (only for such student) the total number of questions used to re-assess only that failing learning goal. Rule R5 uses the amount obtained from rule R4 as baseline and adds to it. Nevertheless, it also ensures that the total amount of questions for the re-assessment of failed goal does not exceed the number **N** (no. of questions used for that goal in the first iteration). The rationale behind this rule is the following: because of the student's previous poor achievement for a learning goal, its re-assessment in current adaptive phase should be more thorough for such student.

Regarding rule R1, at first it may seem pedagogically wrong to use only the difficult questions during the re-assessment of failed learning goals. It may very well be perceived as a punishment, but only if those difficult questions **actually were more difficult** than all the questions used in the previous iteration for that learning goal. The responsibility to avoid such unwanted situation lays on the teacher – he/she must include an appropriate mixture of easy, medium and difficult questions for the initial stage of each learning goal. In such circumstances, rule R1 **cannot select even more difficult questions** for failed goals during the adaptive phases – it will merely focus on the pool of questions marked as "difficult" (from the same pool which has already been used in the first iteration), while disregarding less difficult questions. And according to the rules R4 and R5, re-assessment of failed goal also includes less questions, albeit all of them being marked as "difficult".

7. Testing the model

Adaptivity, the web application for continual adaptive online knowledge assessment, was developed based on the proposed model and built upon Microsoft ASP.NET platform (MS Windows Server, MS SQL Server and ASP.NET) in order to test the model. However, detailed description of the web application is not in the scope of this chapter. More elaborate description of Adaptivity's architecture can be found in Zlatović and Balaban [38].

The procedure of testing the effectiveness of the model involved approximately half of the students who regularly attended classes at the "Informatics 2" (convenience sample, N = 78), which is held at authors' university as a part of the undergraduate curriculum for the bachelor's degree in the field of information systems and technology. All students enrolled in "Informatics 2" were divided into two groups (alphabetically, by Faculty administration). We selected randomly one of those groups to participate in experiment. The course is elective and is being taught at the bachelor university level, with first-year students being enrolled predominantly (more than 90% of the population). It is also available for students who attend 2nd and 3rd year of the bachelor program.

Formal curriculum of the course prescribed four written assessments (hereinafter tests) during the semester. The first test was used to verify the functionality of the proposed system in a real environment and under the workload generated by the actual number of users. Therefore, the three remaining tests were included in the research. The type of assessment was cumulative, meaning that each subsequent test included new learning materials along with the old one (as illustrated in **Figure 2**). With respect to the terminology used in previous Section, the individual test in the experimental group matches one iteration within the proposed model of the assessment. All the tests were conducted in strictly controlled environment (in Faculty's computer labs, under teachers' supervision).

7.1 Changes in learning goals achieved

In this section we analyze the results achieved by using Adaptivity to explore whether its usage increased levels of achievement of learning goals that had not been considered satisfactory in previous iterations. **Table 1** shows all the learning goals (LGs) that were examined during the three tests cycle (tests t1, t2 and t3).

Upon completion of all three tests, average achievement scores per learning goals were compared. Prior to any comparisons, all individual achievement scores were converted from absolute points into relative percentages. Absolute points would not make sense here, because each student's assessment in adaptive phase will have different amount of questions used (due to built-in adaptive rules R4 and R5 in particular) and consequentially, absolute points maximum would differ from student to student. Although the distribution of the achievement scores of learning goals in all three iterations did not follow normal distribution (both Kolmogorov–Smirnov and Shapiro–Wilk tests were used), the size of the experimental group ($N = 78$) is large enough to warrant the usage of parametric t-tests [39]. Specifically, two-tailed paired samples t-tests were conducted, because pre- and post-test scores produced by the same students were compared.

Table 3 shows the results of the comparisons made at the end of each iteration and **Table 4** the results of the comparisons made between the first and the final test. Only the learning goals which elicited significant increase or decrease in the average achievements score were kept in those tables. In the first cycle, learning goals LG14 and LG15 were not calculated, because in the second test (t2) those goals were assessed for the first time, so there were no results for them from the previous iteration. Likewise, when displaying the results of the second cycle, LG16 and LG17 are not shown either. Item pairs in tables are encoded using simple LGx_ty scheme, where LGx stands for Learning Goal X (1 < =x < =17) and ty stands for particular test iteration y (1 < =y < =3) – e.g. LG6_t2 represents the score of Learning Goal 6 in test iteration 2.

Paired-samples t-test statistics from **Table 3** show that at the end of the 1st cycle of assessment, only 4 learning goals displayed significant changes in average achievement scores – for three of them (LG8, LG9 and LG13) there is significant increase of the average scores (ranging from 6.51% to 12.18% higher score on the average), while one learning goal (LG10) displayed significant decrease of the average score (17.37% lower score on the average). After the 2nd cycle, statistically significant increases of the average scores were noted for 6 learning goals in total (LG1, LG6, LG7, LG9, LG10 and LG13, ranging from 6.98% to 12.95% higher score on the average) and one learning goal (LG15) has shown statistically significant decrease of the average score (9.14% lower score on the average).

After the 2nd cycle, LGs from 1 to 13 have been adaptively re-tested for the second time, while LGs 14 and 15 have been adaptively re-tested for the first time. Lack of the statistically significant difference in score for LG8 after the 2nd cycle

Differences after the 1st test cycle (test t2 vs. test t1)	Paired Diff. Mean	t	Sig. (2-tailed)
LG1_t2 - LG1_t1	−1.28205	−0.217	0.829
LG6_t2 - LG6_t1	6.19692	1.462	0.148
LG7_t2 - LG7_t1	1.06410	0.183	0.855
LG8_t2 - LG8_t1	6.51282	2.501	**0.014**
LG9_t2 - LG9_t1	9.38013	3.267	**0.002**
LG10_t2 - LG10_t1	−17.37179	−3.479	**0.001**
LG11_t2 - LG11_t1	3.57859	1.035	0.304
LG13_t2 - LG13_t1	12.17949	2.838	**0.006**
Differences after the 2nd test cycle (test t3 vs. test t2)	**Paired Diff. Mean**	**t**	**Sig. (2-tailed)**
LG1_t3 - LG1_t2	10.25641	2.432	**0.017**
LG6_t3 - LG6_t2	9.88244	2.232	**0.029**
LG7_t3 - LG7_t2	10.89744	2.194	**0.031**
LG8_t3 - LG8_t2	1.91026	0.716	0.476
LG9_t3 - LG9_t2	6.97538	2.074	**0.041**
LG10_t3 - LG10_t2	12.94872	2.406	**0.019**
LG11_t3 - LG11_t2	6.10051	1.750	0.084
LG13_t3 - LG13_t2	7.13141	2.236	**0.028**
LG14_t3 - LG14_t2	6.72962	1.808	0.075
LG15_t3 - LG15_t2	−9.13500	−2.462	**0.016**

Table 3.
Comparison of the achievements of learning goals between consecutive tests - comparisons after the 1st cycle (test t2 vs. test t1) and the 2nd cycle (test t3 vs. test t2) of the continual assessment, paired samples t-test ($N = 78$, $df = 77$, $p < 0.05$).

Differences between the first and the final test (test t3 vs test t1)	Paired Diff. Mean	t	Sig. (2-tailed)
LG1_t3 - LG1_t1	8.97436	1.867	0.066
LG6_t3 - LG6_t1	16.07936	4.090	**0.000**
LG7_t3 - LG7_t1	11.96154	2.256	**0.027**
LG8_t3 - LG8_t1	8.42308	2.443	**0.017**
LG9_t3 - LG9_t1	16.35551	5.341	**0.000**
LG10_t3 - LG10_t1	−4.42308	−0.991	0.325
LG11_t3 - LG11_t1	9.67910	2.468	**0.016**
LG13_t3 - LG13_t1	19.31090	4.437	**0.000**

Table 4.
Comparison of the achievements of learning goals between the final and the first test - comparisons between the final test (t3) and the first test (t1) of the continual assessment, paired samples t-test ($N = 78$, $df = 77$, $p < 0.05$).

can be interpreted as the stagnation (compared to the significant increase LG8 has had after the 1st cycle) – slight average increase of 1.91% cannot be taken as statistically significant at $p < 0.05$. Differences in achievement levels for learning goal LG11 show stagnation after both 1st and 2nd cycle of the assessment. Interestingly,

Table 4 suggests that LG11 has significantly higher average score when entire chain of the assessments is taken into consideration.

Results shown in **Table 4** (final test t3 vs. first test t1) include only those learning goals that have been used throughout entire chain of assessments, i.e. only LGs from 1 to 13 (LGs 14 and 15 were introduced in test t2 for the first time, while LGs 16 and 17 were introduced in test t3 for the first time). At the end of the series of assessments, 6 learning goals in total (LG6, LG7, LG8, LG9, LG11 and LG13) have shown statistically significant increase of the average achievement score (ranging from 8.42% to 19.31% on the average).

The results of one learning goal (LG10) have effectively canceled themselves out during the repeated assessments – data from **Table 3** shows that LG10 recorded significant decrease of the score after the 1st cycle and significant increase of the score after 2nd cycle – the results for LG10 after test t3 have become similar to the initial results after test t1. This is shown as statistically insignificant decrease of 4.42% on the average in **Table 4**. Although final results for LG10 indicate stagnation, initial significant decrease of students' score after LG10's first re-assessment has been compensated by significant increase after the second re-assessment of LG10. Similar reasoning can be applied to LG1 too – the decrease of the score after the 1st cycle was not large enough to be considered significant and the increase of the score after the 2nd cycle was significant (**Table 3**). But the final results for LG1 (in **Table 4**) suggest that observed increase for LG1 between the last (3rd test) and the first assessment (1st test) is borderline insignificant at $p < 0.05$, because students had achieved slightly lower score at LG1 during 3rd assessment than during 2nd.

In addition to the already discussed LG10 and LG1, for 5 more learning goals in total (LG2, LG3, LG4, LG5 and LG12) repeated assessment did not cause statistically significant changes in average scores and those LG's were omitted from **Tables 3** and **4**. These results can also be interpreted as the stagnation in the achievement levels.

Based on those indicators, it is shown that the use of the proposed model encourages improvements in the level of achievement for almost 50% of the evaluated learning goals (6 out of 13 goals which have been included in the assessment from the beginning), or at least it enables the retention of the existing levels of the achievement (7 out of 13 goals which have been included in the assessment from the beginning). Constant decrease of the achievement levels has not been noticed at any of the learning goals which have been re-assessed at least twice.

8. Discussion

It has been demonstrated that the application of the Model has positive influence on improving achieved levels of knowledge per individual learning goals being assessed. During the three-test assessment cycle, it was shown that for 6 learning goals there was a global tendency of improving the achievement (i.e constantly increased achievement levels during re-assessments of those learning goals) - predominantly for the more complex goals, which required the ability to describe and understand concepts, not just to recall the facts. For 5 learning goals, there was a global tendency to maintain previous level of achievement. Only one learning goal showed negative initial result, although, as already described, after 2nd iteration that learning goal recorded significant improvement in scores, but not adequate to globally overcome the low score after the 1st iteration. And the improvements for one more learning goal were borderline insignificant.

It has been mentioned in Section 7 that only half of the student population enrolled in course "Informatics 2" were used to test the model (i.e. "experimental group"). One could ask why the results obtained during model testing have not been compared with the results of the other half of the class (i.e. "control group"). Main reason is that there have been too many differences in the overall knowledge assessment process between two groups, for the comparisons to be valid and meaningful. While the "experimental" half of the class used online Adaptivity system, which had provided mixture of various types of questions (multi-choice, fill-in, match, essay), between-assessment adaptation and individualized post-assessment feedback per learning goal, students in so-called "control" half of the class were given only pen-and-paper tests using essay-type questions exclusively, without detailed feedback and without any form of adaptation (i.e. the traditional way of administering the summative assessments within the course).

It must be mentioned that number of re-assessments per LO and LG used in this research (one initial assessment and at most two adaptive re-assessments) may not be enough in terms of proper continual knowledge assessment. Since the assessment results of the experimental group had to be used as a formally valid substitute for the final summative results of the "Informatics 2", the assessment process design for the experimental group could not have diverged too far from the assessment process used for the rest of the class. E.g. fixed and relatively small number of assessments per semester was one of the constraints that had to be adhered to. It would be highly recommended to use more frequent (re)assessments in future research. Nevertheless, despite relatively low number of re-assessments, the proposed model did yield at least the retention of the previously reached levels of achievements (for 7 of 13 LGs), if not slight improvements in levels of achievements during re-assessments (for 6 of 13 LGs).

Another valid question is what type of knowledge has been taught and the type of teaching used. Content of the "Informatics 2" course is related to purely theoretical knowledge, within the area of expertise in ICT belonging to both social and technical sciences. Teaching process had consisted of purely ex-cathedra lectures with supplementary slides and lectures available within learning management system (LMS). Because of the assessed knowledge nature, success percentages in the Adaptivity have been set to mimic traditional grading system, requiring at least 50% success for a positive grade. If necessary, grading scales in Adaptivity can be re-adjusted to fit other areas of expertise, where higher cut-off points may be required for positive grades.

Most of the LGs (see **Table 1**) used in this study are focused on lower levels of knowledge. While not ideal, it is consistent with findings in [8] that even the most sophisticated automated assessment systems do not allow for testing of knowledge which is higher than level 3 or 4 in Bloom's taxonomy. Adaptivity as a system does support usage of essay-type of questions, which must be graded manually by teachers. Therefore, higher levels of knowledge could also be re-assessed in the continual adaptive manner, at the expense of re-introducing increased teachers' workload.

Overall, those findings are in-line with traditional features of continuous assessment, i.e. the ability to apply corrective actions while the education is still ongoing [25, 40] and the superior retention of information due to repeated testing spaced-out over time [32]. These are also in-line with several observations given in [41]: (i) assessment should not encourage surface learning and (ii) adaptive assessment provides benefits to both summative and formative assessment.

Application of the proposed system also helps alleviate one of the biggest practical disadvantages of manual continuous assessment reported in literature – vastly increased teachers' workload, due having to spend more time to prepare and carry out frequent activities to track their learners [30, 42]. Proposed system is fully automating the adaptive portion of the continual re-assessment of old topics, leaving the teacher with task to manually create only the content related to the new topics, which are being assessed for the first-time.

Thus, it is shown that the Model, which employs continual and cumulative approach towards knowledge assessment and which: (a) individually adjusts amount, difficulty and type of questions per learning goal, based on previously demonstrated levels of achievement of learning goals, and (b) announces what types of the assessment will be used to test particular learning goals in the upcoming iteration, has predominantly positive effects on individual's success at the level of particular learning goals, therefore supporting research objectives and hypothesis.

9. Research limitations and future research suggestions

This research was conducted among ICT-oriented higher education students, which have already been using online education before. Therefore the sample used may not represent well the population from other fields of higher education (natural, technical, biomedical, humanistic, etc.) or outside of the higher education (e.g. secondary education, workplace education and/or life-long learning, etc.). Inclusion of respondents from other areas would ensure more varied population of respondents. Also, research was conducted within a course that uses blended education model (mixture of traditional class-based education and elements of online education), therefore it is advised to exercise caution when trying to generalize the results of this study to institutions and environments that practice either self-paced education, full online education, or traditional class-based education. The specifics of the assessment process itself represent another limitation – the assessment was adjusted to fit the continuous monitoring of students' activities in the context of high education that adheres to Bologna Process.

The course was taught by the authors themselves and the authors have also designed the assessments, so a methodological bias needs to be considered when analyzing the results of this study. Further research should include both courses taught by and assessments designed by other teachers too.

We have also included only learner's cognitive abilities. Affective characteristics of students (e.g., motivation, mastery goal orientation), which can also be important when designing adaptive assessment system, were not included. Further research should include broader student modeling. In line with [40], further research could also expand onto teacher responsiveness, which builds upon continuous results provided by the proposed assessment system.

On a different note, the current implementation of the Model could be a worthy contribution to further development of the Adaptive Learning Management systems that consider various users' individual differences. Integration of the proposed Model in such adaptive environment as a complementary to the adaptive lessons could present a significant step forward in the design and implementation of Adaptive Learning Management systems.

10. Conclusion

This study describes original approach related to the modeling and implementation of the continual adaptive online knowledge assessment within class-based courses, where the adaptive aspects of assessment are used to re-assess old topics and are:

1. Applied within the series (or chains) of assessments, and

2. Based on the results that students have achieved in the previous assessments, rather than being based on the results achieved in the current, isolated assessment.

The Model introduces adaptation throughout a series of assessments in order to continuously monitor students and uses immediate feedback (mostly based on recommendations from Rowe and Wood [21] and Maier, Wolf and Randler [22]) as a major element of quality in teaching and assessment, which is given to students at the end of each assessment to facilitate the appropriate learning strategies.

The empirical study of the Model's efficiency has shown that it is possible to design the system for adaptive online knowledge assessment, which can facilitate desirable learning strategies, which in turn lead to the achievement of required learning goals by announcing and using the appropriate types of questions in assessments.

Since it was shown that continual and cumulative adaptive online assessment is an efficient tool for facilitation of the appropriate learning strategies, the results of this chapter can be useful to the educational institutions when designing and implementing online knowledge assessments within class-based courses. The proposed Model also fits particularly well in continual monitoring and evaluation of students' activities which is in line with Bologna Process, and in the same time relieves teachers from heavier workload.

Author details

Miran Zlatović, Igor Balaban* and Željko Hutinski
University of Zagreb, FOI, Varaždin, Croatia

*Address all correspondence to: igor.balaban@foi.hr

References

[1] Richey RC, Klein, JD. Design and development research. New Jersey: Lawrence Erlbaum Associates Inc.; 2007.

[2] Easterday MW, Rees Lewis DG, Gerber EM. The logic of design research. Learning: Research and Practice. 2017;1-30. DOI: 10.1080/23735082.2017.1286367

[3] Yaghmaie M, Bahreininejad A. A context-aware adaptive learning system using agents. Expert Systems with Application. 2011;38(4):3280-3286. DOI: 10.1016/j.eswa.2010.08.113

[4] Hafidi M, Bensebaa T, Trigano P. Developing adaptive intelligent tutoring system based on item response theory and metrics. International Journal of Advanced Science and Technology. 2012;43:1-14

[5] Ahuja NJ, Sille R. A critical review of development of intelligent tutoring systems: Retrospect, present and prospect. International Journal of Computer Science Issues. 2013:10(2):39-48

[6] Avgerinos E, Karageorgiadis A. On an adaptive formative assessment platform for STEM Education. In: IEEE Global Engineering Education Conference (EDUCON); 2017. IEEE; 2017. p. 1216-1224. DOI: 10.1109/EDUCON.2017.7943003

[7] Comas-Lopez M, de la Rubia MA, Sacha GM. Adaptive test system for subjects that simultaneously include theoretical content and numerical problem solving. In: International Symposium on Computers in Education (SIIE); 2018; Jerez, Spain. IEEE; 2018. p. 1-5. DOI: 10.1109/SIIE.2018.8586729

[8] Grundspenkis J. Intelligent Knowledge Assessment Systems: Myth or Reality. In: Lupeikiene A et al., editors. Frontiers in Artificial Intelligence and Applications, vol. 315, Databases and Information Systems X. IOS Press; 2019. p. 31-46. DOI: 10.3233/978-1-61499-941-6-31

[9] Learning Goals. Teaching Commons, Stanford University [Internet]. Available from: https://teachingcommons.stanford.edu/resources/course-preparation/creating-syllabus/learning-goals [Accessed 2020-06-25]

[10] Normadhi NBA, Shuib L, Nasir HNM, Bimba A, Idris N, Balakrishnan V. Identification of personal traits in adaptive learning environment: Systematic literature review. Computers & Education. 2019;130:168-190. DOI: 10.1016/j.compedu.2018.11.005

[11] Soflano M, Connolly TM, Hainey T. An application of adaptive games-based learning based on learning style to teach SQL. Computers & Education. 2015;86:192-211. DOI: 10.1016/j.compedu.2015.03.015

[12] Tseng JCR, Chu H-C, Hwang GJ, Tsai C-C. Development of an adaptive learning system with two sources of personalization information. Computers & Education. 2008;51(2):776-786. DOI: 10.1016/j.compedu.2007.08.002

[13] Hartley J. Learning and studying: a research perspective. USA: Routledge; 1998. DOI: 10.4324/9780203132951

[14] Mayer R. Learning strategies: An overview. In: Weinstein C et al., editors. Learning and Study Strategies: Issues in Assessment, Instruction, and Evaluation. New York: Academic Press; 1988. p. 11.22. DOI: 10.1016/B978-0-12-742460-6.50008-6

[15] Hoeksema LH. Learning Strategy as a Guide to Career Success in Organizations. Leiden University, Netherlands: DSWO Press. 1995.

[16] Marton F, Säljö R. On qualitative differences in learning: I - Outcome and process. British Journal of Educational Psychology. 1976;46:4-11. DOI: 10.1111/j.2044-8279.1976.tb02980.x

[17] Biggs JB, Kember D, Leung DYP. The revised two-factor Study Process Questionnaire: R-SPQ-2F. British Journal of Educational Psychology. 2001;71:133-149. DOI: 10.1348/000709901158433

[18] Zlatović M, Balaban I, Kermek D. Using Online Assessments to Stimulate Learning Strategies and Achievement of Learning Goals. Computers & Education. 2015;91:32-45. DOI: 10.1016/j.compedu.2015.09.012

[19] Peacock S, Murray S, Kelly J, Scott A. The transformative role of ePortfolios: Feedback in healthcare learning. International Journal of ePortfolio. 2011;1(1):33-48

[20] Pacheco-Venegas ND, López G, Andrade-Aréchiga M. Conceptualization, development and implementation of a web-based system for automatic evaluation of mathematical expressions. Computers & Education. 2015;88:15-28. DOI: 10.1016/j.compedu.2015.03.021

[21] Rowe AD, Wood, LN. Student perceptions and preferences for feedback. Asian Social Science. 2008;4(3):78-88. DOI: 10.5539/ass.v4n3p78

[22] Maier U, Wolf N, Randler C. Effects of a computer-assisted formative assessment intervention based on multiple-tier diagnostic items and different feedback types. Computers & Education. 2016;95(1):85-98. DOI: 10.1016/j.compedu.2015.12.002

[23] Conejo R, Guzmán E, Trella M. The SIETTE automatic assessment environment. International Journal of Artificial Intelligence in Education. 2016;26(1):270-292. DOI: 10.1007/s40593-015-0078-4

[24] Chrysafiadi K, Troussas C, Virvou M. A framework for creating automated online adaptive tests using multiple-criteria decision analysis. In: IEEE International Conference on Systems, Man, and Cybernetics (SMC); 2018; Miyazaki. IEEE; 2018. p. 226-231. DOI: 10.1109/SMC.2018.00049

[25] McAlpine M. Principles of assessment. Luton: CAA Centre, University of Luton; 2002.

[26] Raman R, Nedungadi P. Adaptive learning methodologies to support reforms in continuous formative evaluation. In: IEEE International Conference on Educational and Information Technology (ICEIT); 2010. IEEE; 2010. vol. 2, p. V2-429. DOI: 10.1109/ICEIT.2010.5607608

[27] Grundspenkis J, Anohina A. Evolution of the concept map based adaptive knowledge assessment system: Implementation and evaluation results. Scientific Journal of Riga Technical University. Computer Sciences. 2009;38(38):13-24. DOI: 10.2478/v10143-009-0001-2

[28] Hu D. How Khan Academy is using Machine Learning to Assess Student Mastery [Internet]. 2011. Available from: http://david-hu.com/2011/11/02/how-khan-academy-is-using-machine-learning-to-assess-student-mastery.html [Accessed 2020-06-25]

[29] VanLehn K. The behavior of tutoring systems. International journal of artificial intelligence in education. 2006;16(3):227-265.

[30] Rus V, Baggett W, Gire E, Franceschetti D, Conley M, Graesser A. Towards Learner Models based on Learning Progressions (LPs) in DeepTutor. In: Sottilare RA et al., editors. Design Recommendations for

Intelligent Tutoring Systems, Vol 1. U.S. Army Research Laboratory; 2013. p. 183-192.

[31] Dembo MH, Praks Seli H. Students' Resistance to Change in Learning Strategies Courses. Journal of Developmental Education. 2004;27(3): 2-11.

[32] Larsen DP, Butler AC, Roediger III HL. Test-enhanced learning in medical education. Medical Education. 2008;42(10):959-966. DOI: 10.1111/j.1365-2923.2008.03124.x

[33] Hatzilygeroudis I, Koutsojannis C, Papachristou N. Adding adaptive assessment capabilities to an e-learning system. In: Mylonas P et al, editors. SMAP '06, First International Workshop on Semantic Media Adaptation and Personalization; 2006; Athens. IEEE; 2006. p. 68-73. DOI: 10.1109/SMAP.2006.8

[34] Chatzopoulou DI, Economides AA. Adaptive assessment of student's knowledge in programming courses. Journal of Computer Assisted Learning. Wiley. 2010;26(4):258-269. DOI: 10.1111/j.1365-2729.2010.00363.x

[35] Jadhav M, Rizwan S, Nehete A. User profiling based Adaptive Test Generation and Assessment in E-Learning System. In: IEEE 3rd International Advance Computing Conference (IACC); 2013. IEEE; 2013. p. 1425-1430. DOI: 10.1109/IAdCC.2013.6514436

[36] Bloom BS, Engelhart MD, Furst EJ, Hill W, Krathwohl DR. Taxonomy of Educational Objectives, The Classification of Educational Goals, Handbook I: Cognitive Domain. USA: McKay Press; 1956.

[37] Zlatović M, Balaban I. Personalizing Questions Using Adaptive Online Knowledge Assessment. In: eLearning 2015 - 6th International Conference on e-Learning; 2015; Belgrade. Univerzitet Metropolitan: Belgrade; 2015. p. 185-190.

[38] Zlatović M, Balaban I. Adaptivity: A Continual Adaptive Online Knowledge Assessment System. In: Rocha Á et al, editors. Trends and Innovations in Information Systems and Technologies; WorldCIST 2020; Advances in Intelligent Systems and Computing, vol 1161. Cham: Springer. 2020. p. 152-161. DOI: 10.1007/978-3-030-45697-9_15

[39] Lumley T, Diehr P, Emerson S, Chen L. The Importance of the Normality Assumption in Large Public Health Data Sets. Annual Review of Public Health. 2002;23:151-169. DOI: 10.1146/annurev.publhealth.23.100901.140546

[40] Preciado-Babb P, Metz M, Sabbaghan S, Davis B. The Role of Continuous Assessment and Effective Teacher Response in Engaging all students. In: Hunter R, editor. Mathematical Discourse that Breaks Barriers and Creates Space for Marginalized Learners. Leiden, The Netherlands: Brill|Sense;2018. p. 101-119. DOI: 10.1163/9789463512541_006

[41] Challis D. Committing to quality learning through adaptive online assessment. Assessment & Evaluation in Higher Education. 2005;30(5):519-527. DOI: 10.1080/02602930500187030

[42] Timmerman K, Doom T. Infrastructure for Continuous Assessment of Retained Relevant Knowledge. ACM Inroads. 2017;8(2); 73-77. DOI: 10.1145/3095781.3017738

Section 2

Blended Learning

Chapter 5

Blended Learning in Higher Education: Faculty Perspective through the Lens of the Planned Behaviour Theory

Dominique Verpoorten, Johanne Huart, Pascal Detroz and Françoise Jérôme

Abstract

Before the COVID-19 pandemic, the Teaching and Learning Centre of the University of Liège (Belgium) administered a questionnaire to disclose the main predictors of faculty's intention to resort, within a timespan of two years, to blended learning in at least one of their courses. The instrument was constructed according to the Theory of Planned Behaviour, a sound conceptual framework for probing intentions and their antecedents. In the responses of 114 faculty members, multiple regression analyses detected that attitude towards blended learning, subjective norm and perceived control explained 73% of the intention to use blended designs for teaching purposes in a not too distant future. Data treatment also singled out beliefs working indirectly in favour of the intention to use hybrid approaches: the inclination to think of blended learning altogether in a student-centred, conformist and pragmatic way. Moreover, respondents who declared having already used blended learning in the past expressed stronger opinions congruent with the constructs of attitude, norm and perceived control. The results also establish that pre-lockdown e-learning practices remained rather basic. A better knowledge of what can facilitate or impair the diffusion of blended learning is of importance for higher education institutions and their staff training efforts.

Keywords: theory of planned behaviour, blended learning, higher education, predictors of intention, staff development

1. Introduction

1.1 The context of the study

The study reported here has been carried out by IFRES (Institute for Training and Research in Higher Education - http://www.ifres.ulg.ac.be), the Teaching and Learning Centre of the University of Liège, Belgium. In order to adapt and monitor the training sessions and the regular tutoring it offers to faculty members, IFRES periodically conducts surveys on emerging academic topics (use of competency frameworks, mentoring, peer tutoring, classroom of tomorrow, threshold concepts, etc.). In recent years, blended learning (BL) has become an obvious candidate for inquiry among teachers. Investigating the level of use of this instructional practice and eliciting determinants that predict or prevent its implementation is of importance for orienting staff development strategies and reinforcing the overall Scholarship of Teaching and Learning in the university.

2. Blended learning

As a "thoughtful integration of conventional and digital methods of teaching and learning" [1], BL presents as the best breed of two historically separate models of instruction: traditional face-to-face and distributed learning systems [2–4]. In higher education, BL has been lately experiencing an upward trend [5–7], spurred even more by the COVID crisis [8]. Indeed, meta-analyses provide indications that BL has a higher impact on student performance than face-to-face or distance learning alone [9–11]. Benefits have also been reported with regard to engagement in learning [12], student satisfaction [13], drop-out prevention [14], meaningfulness of learning experience [15], seat time reduction [16], and an increased sense of community among learners [17]. Despite its potential, BL is not yet widely embraced on campuses [18–20] or, since the COVID crisis, it has taken impoverished forms of "emergency remote teaching" [21, 22]. Facing this situation, questions should be raised about the reasons that can explain this pattern of moderate adoption. The Theory of Planned Behaviour [23] can shed light on this issue at an individual level of analysis.

3. Theoretical framework: theory of planned behaviour

The Theory of Planned Behaviour (TPB, **Figure 1**) has been used to predict specific behaviours and/or to plan interventions designed to influence behaviour in various domains including education [24–30]. Its predictive reputation regarding behaviour is up to now unchallenged [31]. According to TPB, behaviour can be directly predicted by the intention to adopt it, and intention is itself determined by three essential factors (**Table 1**, column 1):

1. attitude towards the behaviour: it can be defined as the extent to which the target behaviour is regarded as desirable or undesirable. If measured directly, attitude can be expressed in two ways [32]: cognitively (is it good or bad?) and affectively (is it pleasant or not?). Indirect measuring results from multiplying "the beliefs about the consequences of the behaviour" by "the estimation of the value of those consequences".

2. subjective norm: it corresponds to the social judgement that is believed to be associated with the target behaviour. Direct measuring has to consider two types of normative beliefs. The first type is called descriptive norm. It corresponds to the assumed behaviour of one's entourage: are friends, relatives, colleagues, superiors… likely to adopt the behaviour? The second type is called injunctive norm. It consists in estimating the expectations of the entourage in relation to the behaviour to be adopted (or not). Indirect measuring is obtained by multiplying "the beliefs concerning the opinions of relevant persons" by "the motivation for taking those opinions into account".

3. perceived behavioural control: it corresponds to the perception of the control one has over the target behaviour when it comes to adopt it. Does it rely entirely on oneself? Perceived control requires two types of information

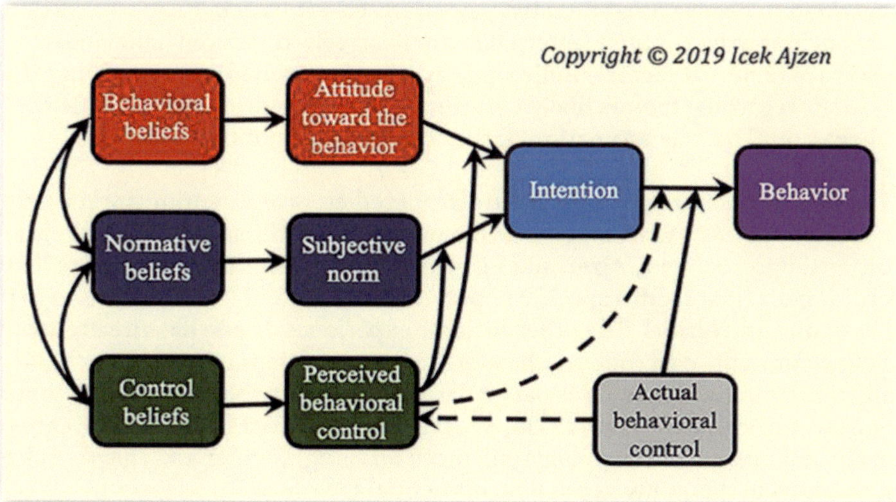

Figure 1.
Synoptic representation of the theory of planned behaviour framework (with permission: https://people.umass.edu/aizen/tpb.diag.html).

Behavioural beliefs in terms of outcomes	Positive outcomes: resorting to BL in my course(s) would make it possible to: • teach the subject at a distance so as to have more in-class time to be devoted to examples, exercises and discussion; • have students work more regularly and be more active throughout the year; • increase student motivation; • enhance student reflection and deep-thinking. Negative outcomes: Resorting to BL would: • cause misunderstanding of the subject without the teacher's noticing and correcting it; • risk losing contact with students.
Normative beliefs	Injunctive: Who would want me to resort to BL in my course(s)? • My students; • Academic authorities; • Colleagues of equal status. Descriptive: Who do I think is likely to resort to BL in their course(s)? • Teachers interested in new technologies; • Teachers for whom research is very important; • Teachers of the young generation.
Control beliefs	Which factors would facilitate or impede my using BL in my course(s)? • The amount of time to be dedicated to modifying my course(s) and to maintaining it (them); • The (lack of) user-friendliness and efficiency of the institutional e-learning platform; • The (lack of) reliable technological infrastructure at the university (computers, WIFI, classroom equipment...); • The focus on research activities rather than on teaching activities for promotion purposes; • Possessing (or not) technical know-how; • The necessity to rethink the pedagogical design of my course(s).

Table 1.
Beliefs related to the use of BL for teaching purposes.

in order to be measured directly: perceived self-efficacy in relation to the behaviour to be adopted (internal factor) and self-attributed behavioural control (external factor). Indirect measuring is obtained by multiplying "the beliefs regarding factors likely to facilitate or to impede the adoption of the behaviour" by "the estimation of the effect intensity of those factors".

The TPB postulates that these three direct predictors of intention are strongly influenced by at least two factors. One factor is context. Because salient beliefs are conditional upon context, Ajzen and Fishbein [33] suggest that researchers identify beliefs for behaviour from a specific population and context (here: restricted to professors of one university). The other factor is experience. If one has already adopted the behaviour in the past, one will be more inclined to adopt it in the future [34]. Taking this factor into account is particularly relevant here because several continuums of technology adoption [35–38] suggest a cumulative effect of experience on intensity and quality of technology-enhanced learning. Gender and age have also been included in this study as possible influential factors of BL adoption.

Ajzen [39] proposes a methodology aiming at constructing the adequate questionnaire in which each construct of the TPB model (attitude, subjective norm, perceived control and intention) should be represented by five or six items. He also recommends to use a seven-point bipolar scale for each item.

4. Theory of planned behaviour and blended learning

Although examples of instructional designs of BL can be found in the relevant literature [40, 41], hardly any systematic and empirical inquiries about the factors working as incentives to use blended approaches to teaching and learning have been carried out up to now. Current literature provides a few adoption and concerns frameworks in relation to BL. Stacey and Gerbic [13] developed a set of recommendations for adopting BL divided them into four categories. Besides recommendations related to students, pedagogy and institutional constraints, one category conveys an explicit concern for teacher-related aspects but without much elaboration. With their "Institutional Blended Learning Adoption Checklist", Graham, Woodfield and Harrison [42] continue in a similar vein, exploring the degree to which institutional strategic, structural, and supporting measures may facilitate or restrain the adoption of BL among higher education teachers, at various levels of familiarity with technology. The contributions of those studies are located at an institutional decision making level.

However, because teachers are at the heart of any educational change process, addressing directly the practitioner level is important. In that regard, a few pieces of work showing interest in the determinants likely to predict the adoption of BL in concrete courses can be found. Through six semi-structured interviews, Mozelius and Rydell [43] spotted four problems and barriers (extra time needed to learn new technology tools, lack of support for acquaintance with critical functions of LMS, and discomfort with understanding and implementing effective online pedagogy) hindering a successful implementation of BL at university, in Sweden. Antwi-Boampong [44] used a grounded theory approach and interviewed 22 teachers to gain an in-depth understanding of the processes influencing the implementation of BL in Ghanaian institutions. In Zimbabwe, Dube [45] interviewed 14 faculty members in order to uncover the challenges they associated with a successful implementation of BL. Apandi and Raman [46] investigated teacher perceptions as an important element in shifting to BL in Malaysian post-secondary institutions. Labelling their work as a "concept paper", the authors primarily intended to complement a technology acceptance model [47] with what they consider as a missing factor of adoption or avoidance: teachers' "techno-pedagogical content knowledge", a notion that has been strongly highlighted by the teacher professional development model TPACK [48]. Ibrahim and Nat [49] tried to identify the factors responsible for motivating instructors to integrate BL into their courses. Based on two categories of motivational factors to be found in the literature on BL, namely extrinsic factors (instructor interactions with technology and with students, academic workload, institutional environment) and intrinsic factors (instructor attitude and beliefs regarding technology and vocational training), the authors designed a synoptic model and tested it on 362 faculty members in Turkey.

Although the above review enumerates valuable contributions, it contains no genuine application of the canonical TPB to BL issues in higher education.

The present study adopts the TPB in order to determine which representations about BL and which intention influencing factors are likely to work as an incentive for higher education teachers to resort to BL in at least one of their courses in a not too distant future.

The following hypotheses guide the study:

1. The TPB constructs "attitude towards the behaviour", "subjective norm" and "perceived behavioural control" significantly predict teachers' behavioural intention regarding BL.

2. Teachers' age and gender influence their behavioural intention regarding BL.

3. Teachers' beliefs indirectly predict their behavioural intention regarding BL.

4. Teachers' past experience influences their beliefs about BL.

5. Methodology

5.1 Instrument

The design of the questionnaire strictly follows Ajzen's methodological guidelines [23, 32, 39] and examples, as described in various papers and on his website (http://people.umass.edu/aizen).

5.1.1 Definition of target behaviour

The first step to create the questionnaire was to delineate the behaviour to be predicted by means of the TPB. According to Ajzen [32], "the behaviour of interest must be clearly defined in terms of its target, action, context, and time elements" (p.2). Consequently, the target behaviour regarding BL was formulated as follows: "to resort to BL in at least one of my courses next year or the year after".

5.1.2 Construction of indirect measures

Indirect measures are displayed in **Table 1**. They are called "indirect" because they are antecedents of the three major predictors of intention, visible in **Table 1**, column 1. In order to get indirect measures, semi-structured interviews took place with members of the target audience [39]. The interviews aimed at determining salient beliefs in relation to each TPB construct.

Salient beliefs are those that interviewees connect most frequently with the target behaviour. Fifteen interviews allowed to reach threshold saturation [50].

An analysis of occurrences identified the most frequently mentioned items in relation to attitude, subjective norm and perceived control. Those items gave rise to the formulation of corresponding items in the questionnaire.

5.1.2.1 Questionnaire items centred on attitude towards the behaviour

Each behavioural belief has to materialise in two items [39]. The first one refers to the strength of the belief (i.e. the degree of agreement with the belief). Considering the topic "more in-class time to be devoted to examples, exercises and discussion", the corresponding item can be formulated as follows: "Resorting to BL in at least one of my courses next year or the year after would make it possible to teach the subject at a distance so as to have more in-class time to be devoted to examples, exercises and discussion" with a seven-point bipolar scale ranging from "not at all probable" to "extremely probable". The second item refers to the desirability of the belief. Drawing on the same example, the corresponding item can be formulated as follows: "More in-class time to be devoted to examples, exercises and discussion is..." with a seven-point bipolar scale ranging from "entirely negative" to "entirely positive". The multiplication of both scores ("strength" multiplied by "desirability") constitutes the behavioural belief.

5.1.2.2 Questionnaire items centred on subjective norm

The same method applies: two items are created for each normative belief. The first item refers to the attitude a reference group is believed to adopt towards the target behaviour whereas the second one reflects the value attributed to such a belief. In other words, the second item deals with respondents' motivation to conform to the postulated attitude of the reference group. For instance, if students constitute the reference group, the first corresponding item can be formulated as follows: "Students think that... resort to BL in at least one of my courses next year or the year after" with a seven-point bipolar scale ranging from "I ought to" to "I ought not to". The second item centred on students as a reference group is: "How do you value your students' opinion about your teaching?" with a seven-point bipolar scale ranging from "not at all" to "enormously". The indicator of the corresponding normative belief is obtained by multiplying "strength" by "motivation to conform".

5.1.2.3 Questionnaire items centred on perceived behavioural control

The method for obtaining control indicators remains unchanged. This time it consists in multiplying the strength of the belief by the perception of control. Considering for instance the time factor, the strength of the belief can be formulated as follows: "Resorting to BL in at least one of my courses next year or the year after will force me to spend ... time modifying my course(s) and maintaining it (them)" with a seven-point bipolar scale ranging from "little" to "a huge amount of". The item related to control perception is: "If I had enough time to modify my course(s) and to maintain it (them) or if I had an assistant to do the job, I would resort to BL in at least one of my courses next year or the year after" with a seven-point bipolar scale ranging from "completely disagree" to "completely agree".

5.1.3 Construction of direct measures

Direct measures are easier to construct. One needs to have at least three items for each construct, and, for each construct, items that cover the two aspects proposed by Ajzen [39]. This construction is summarised in **Table 2**.

Construct	Aspects	Number of items	Examples of items
Attitude towards behaviour	Instrumental aspect	4	"To resort to BL in at least one of my courses next year or the year after would be..." (seven-point bipolar scale ranging from "a bad thing" to "a good thing")
	Experiential aspect	3	"To resort to BL in at least one of my courses next year or the year after would be..." (seven-point bipolar scale ranging from "disagreeable" to "agreeable")
Subjective norm	Descriptive aspect	2	"Most of my colleagues resort to BL in at least one of their courses" (seven-point bipolar agreement scale)
	Injunctive aspect	3	"Most people I approve of would like me to resort to BL in at least one of my courses next year or the year after" (seven-point bipolar agreement scale)
Perceived behavioural control	Capacity aspect	3	"If I wanted to resort to BL in at least one of my courses next year or the year after, I would be able to do it" (seven-point bipolar agreement scale)
	Autonomy aspect	2	"Resorting to BL in at least one of my courses next year or the year after only depends on me" (seven-point bipolar agreement scale)
Intention	No aspect recommended by Ajzen	3	"I intend to resort to BL in at least one of my courses next year or the year after" (seven-point bipolar agreement scale)
Past behaviour	No aspect recommended by Ajzen	1	"Did you happen to use BL in the past?" (yes – no)

Table 2.
Items aiming at direct measurement of the three major TPB constructs.

5.1.4 Supplementary questions

In addition to the focused TPB approach, participants were asked to answer the following questions about their actual e-learning practices:

- Do you publish course contents online? (never-systematically)
- Do you publish supplementary contents (in addition to those dealt with in class) online? (never-systematically)
- Do you communicate with students via the Web (using other technological facilities than email)? (never-systematically)
- Do you propose online-tests to your students? (never-very often)
- Do you propose learning activities (preparations, homework, additional exercises...) online to your students? (never-very often)
- Do you inform yourself during the year about student online activity? (never-very often)
- Do you propose online discussion boards in order to promote debate among students? (never-very often)

- Do you propose to your students group work to be carried out online? (never-very often)
- Do you interact (chat) online with your students? (never-very often)

5.2 Procedure

The regular four-step process was applied:

1. Semi-structured interviews with 15 faculty members in order to identify salient beliefs regarding the use of BL (**Table 1**).
2. Construction of the TPB questionnaire (**Table 2**).
3. Encoding of the questionnaire using the Qualtrics survey tool and submission to the faculty members of the University of Liège by means of a Web-link sent by email.
4. Data collection and analysis.

5.3 Methods of analysis

Responses to the questionnaire on BL were processed by applying the following statistical analyses:

- Descriptive statistics about respondents' gender, age and actual e-learning practices;
- Computation of Cronbach's alphas and of means in order to create the TPB-related constructs based on respondents' evaluation of their constitutive aspects;
- Stepwise multiple regression analyses in order to examine the relationships between: 1) attitude towards the behaviour, subjective norm, perceived behavioural control and intention; 2) attitude towards the behaviour, subjective norm, perceived behavioural control and indirect predictors;
- Multivariate analyses of variance (Student's t-test) in order to find out 1) if previous use of BL is influenced by age, and 2) if respondents' beliefs are impacted by previous use of BL.

5.4 Participants

Faculty in charge of teaching activities constituted the population of interest for our study. Therefore, the questionnaire was addressed by email to the faculty members of the University of Liège (Belgium).

6. Results

6.1 Response rate

Out of 600 faculty members, 114 returned a fully workable questionnaire. Genders are distributed in 57% male and 43% female. Ages range from 23 to 69 years, with a mean age of 43.84 years (SD = 10,52).

6.2 Intention variable and its direct predictors: Reliability and consistence

Considering a total of 114 respondents, Cronbach's alphas for the items directly related to attitude (7 items), to subjective norm (5 items), to perceived control (5 items), and to intention (3 items) amount respectively to .97, .96, .75, and .79. The constructs can be regarded as reliable provided that their corresponding alphas are superior to .70.

6.3 Regression analyses on the direct predictors of intention

Stepwise multiple regression checked the significance of direct predictors (**Table 1**) in relation to the dependent variable 'intention' (**Table 3**). The portion of intention variance that can be explained by all three direct predictors amounts to 73% (*R2* adjusted = .72, p = .02). (Two additional variables – age and gender of respondents – were added to the best-fitted model but turned out to be non-significantly influential. Therefore, the corresponding models are not displayed).

The break-down for the three direct predictors reveals that each of them separately predicts intention at the significance level of .05: 49,9% of intention variance can be attributed to attitude (ß = .65, $p < .001$), 15,5% to perceived control (ß = .19, p = .002) and 10,9% to subjective norm (ß = 0.12, p = .029).

6.4 Regression analyses on the indirect measures of intention predictors

Stepwise multiple regressions were conducted in order to find out about the impact of respondents' beliefs on the direct predictors of intention. The first stepwise regression aims at explaining attitude by means of behavioural beliefs (**Table 1**, line 1). The portion of attitude variance that can be explained by the model amounts to 56% (*R2* adjusted = .55, p = .007). Two variables out of 6 explain this portion of variance (**Table 4**). The other four variables have been excluded because they brought no incremental change to the model. The two influent behavioural beliefs predicting attitude at the significance level of 0,05 are "Teach the subject at a distance so as to have more in-class time to be devoted to examples, exercises and discussion" (ß = .22, p = .007) and "Increase student motivation" (ß = .59, $p < .001$).

The second stepwise regression aims at explaining subjective norm by means of normative beliefs (**Table 1**, line 2). The portion of norm variance that can be explained by the model amounts to 36% (R2 adjusted = .35, p = .008). Two variables have been retained by the model (**Table 5**). The other four variables have been excluded because they brought no incremental change to the model. The retained behavioural beliefs predicting subjective norm at the significance level of .05 are the injunctive norm "Colleagues of equal status" (ß = .48, $p < .001$) and the belief corresponding to the descriptive norm "Teachers of the young generation" (ß = .22, p = .008).

The third stepwise regression aims at explaining perceived control by means of control beliefs (**Table 1**, line 3). The portion of control variance that can be explained by the model amounts to 7% (*R2* adjusted = .06, p = .004). One variable has been retained by the model (**Table 6**). The other five variables have been excluded because they brought no incremental change to the model. The single behavioural belief which predicts perceived control at the significance level of .05 is "The user-friendliness and efficiency of the institutional e-learning platform" (ß = .27, p = .004).

Model	R	R-Squared	Adjusted R-Squared	Standard Error of Estimate	Modification of statistics				
					Variation of R-Squared	Variation of Function	DOF1	DOF2	Significant Variation of Function
1	.832[a]	.692	.689	113,953	.692	251,853	1	112	.000
2	.849[b]	.722	.717	108,858	.029	11,728	1	111	.001
3	.856[c]	**.733**	.726	107,009	.012	4870	1	110	**.029**

Dependent variable: intention.
[a]*Predictors: (Constant), attitude.*
[b]*Predictors: (Constant), attitude, perceived control.*
[c]*Predictors: (Constant), attitude, perceived control, norm.*

Table 3.
The three traditional predictors of intention are active in BL intention – Summary of models.

DOI: http://dx.doi.org/10.5772/intechopen.95375

Model	R	R-Squared	Adjusted R-Squared	Standard Error of Estimate	Modification of statistics				
					Variation of R-Squared	Variation of Function	DOF1	DOF2	Significant Variation of Function
1	.729[a]	.531	.527	.89090	.531	121,160	1	107	.000
2	.750[b]	**.562**	.554	.86517	.031	7458	1	106	**.007**

[a]*Predictors: (Constant), item belief-attitude3 (motivation).*
[b]*Predictors: (Constant), item belief-attitude3 (motivation), item belief-attitude1 (exercises).*

Table 4.
Two behavioural beliefs influence the predictor "attitude towards BL" – Summary of models.

Model	R	R-Squared	Adjusted R-Squared	Standard Error of Estimate	Modification of statistics				
					Variation of R-Squared	Variation of Function	DOF1	DOF2	Significant Variation of Function
1	.568[a]	.323	.316	103,930	,323	50,533	1	106	.000
2	.606[b]	**.367**	.355	100,943	.044	7365	1	105	**.008**

[a] *Predictors: (Constant), item belief-norm3 (colleagues).*
[b] *Predictors: (Constant), item belief-norm3 (colleagues), item belief-norm6 (young-teacher).*

Table 5.
Two normative beliefs influence the predictor "subjective norm" – Summary of models.

Model	R	R-Squared	Adjusted R-Squared	Standard Error of Estimate	Modification of statistics				
					Variation of R-Squared	Variation of Function	DOF1	DOF2	Significant Variation of Function
1	.278[a]	**.077**	.069	139,247	.077	8893	1	106	**.004**

[a]*Predictors: (Constant), item belief-control (platform).*

Table 6.
One control belief influences the predictor "perceived behavioural control" – Summary of models.

6.5 Statistics related to previous use of blended learning

When asked if they had already used BL in the past, 61% of participants answered positively, while the remaining 39% answered 'no'. Interestingly, age was not a predictor of participants' previous use of BL (ß = .003, p = .954). A T-test comparison of the groups "previous use of BL" versus "no experience of BL" delivers significant differences for all indirect predictors of intention identified above (**Table 7**).

BL-related beliefs to be rated on a seven-point bipolar scale	Previous use of BL (no/yes)	N	Mean	Standard deviation	t	p	d
Outcome evaluation "Teach the subject at a distance so as to have more in-class time to be devoted to examples, exercises and discussion"	No	43	4,21	1612	−3.46	<.001	.67
	Yes	70	**5,31**	1673			
Outcome evaluation "Increase student motivation"	No	43	3,86	1612	−3.88	<.001	.75
	Yes	70	**4,87**	1154			
Injunctive norm "Colleagues of equal status"	No	42	3,83	,853	−2.43	.017	.47
	Yes	67	**4,33**	,991			
Descriptive norm "Teachers of the young generation"	No	42	4,10	1185	−2.67	.009	.52
	Yes	69	**4,75**	1253			
Facilitating factor "The user-friendliness and efficiency of the institutional eLearning platform"	No	43	3,58	1577	−2.74	.007	.53
	Yes	70	**4,29**	1446			

Table 7.
BL-related beliefs are reinforced by previous use of BL.

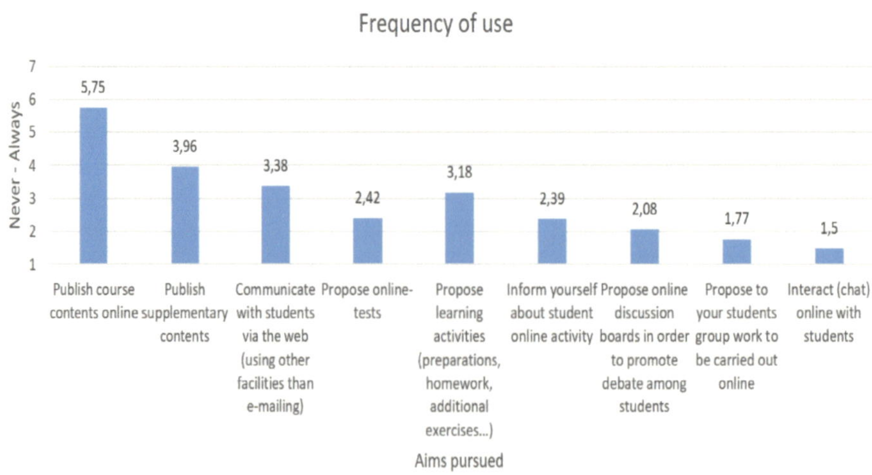

Figure 2.
Self-expressed technology-enhanced practice is basic in the sample.

6.6 Statistics related to current e-learning practices

The supplementary questions about actual technology-enhanced learning practice disclose teachers' current practice, mostly associated with transmission of contents and communication with students, and less with student-centred activities (**Figure 2**).

7. Discussion

The study confirms that the intention to resort to BL for teaching and learning purposes in a not too distant future is massively predicted by the three canonical perceptions highlighted by the TCP: attitude towards the behaviour, subjective norm and perceived behavioural control. On the other hand, respondents' age and gender do not influence their intention to use BL in their courses. Therefore, if faculty were to be persuaded to adopt BL, no special attention would have to be paid to those attributes.

The study also uncovers several specific beliefs acting as indirect predictors of intention: BL motivates students, BL makes room for exercises to take place during the course, using BL is an expectation of colleagues, using BL is a feature of young colleagues, the LMS can be a barrier to BL. However, the direct predictors are not fully predicted by those second-line beliefs. This means that other beliefs play an active role in predictability of the three constructs related to intention. Nevertheless, the coefficient of partial determination computed for each significant belief makes it possible to list and to hierarchize those beliefs and thus, with a view to pragmatism, to set priorities among the arguments most likely to work in favour of the intention to use BL.

As for behavioural beliefs, the most salient one is related to the idea that BL enhances student motivation. The second student-centred attitudinal belief significantly promoted by respondents touches upon the gain of in-class time to be dedicated to more examples, exercises and discussion. In this regard, respondents' opinions coincide very much with one of the most frequently reported pedagogical strengths of BL [51] and the germane notion of flipped classroom [52]. Should a Teaching and Learning Centre promote the use of BL among the faculty members of its university, it could especially emphasise this pedagogical aspect. Interestingly, the respondents who declared having used BL in the past believe still more strongly in the motivation enhancing power of BL and in the opportunity to devote more in-time class to active learning than traditional teaching methods usually allow for. Experience sharing of concrete instantiations of those beliefs could be considered with a view to stimulating reflection around BL.

As for normative beliefs, respondents value uppermost the opinion of colleagues of equal status. Pressure exerted by colleagues to adopt BL seems to be perceived more strongly than any kind of demand formulated either by institutional authorities or by students. Such sensitiveness in relation to colleagues can be interpreted as a wish to conform to peers' expectations regarding teaching and learning practices based on hybrid environments. In that regard, inviting teachers versed in BL to communicate about their experience with BL to colleagues with no experience of it would probably have some convincing power. The belief according to which young teachers are more attracted to BL than teachers with other profiles does not converge with the lack of correlation between the age of respondents and their experience of BL or their intention to use BL. However, the respondents with BL experience have manifested a slightly stronger opinion in favour of that belief. Such a lack of consistence is hard to explain and no satisfying explanation could be put forward.

As for control beliefs, the user-friendliness of the institutional e-learning platform is the only aspect influencing significantly the perception of behavioural control towards BL. Consequently, the e-learning platform can be seen as a major technical facilitator of BL. Such a pragmatic approach to BL could be entertained by offering faculty effective training and service in relation to the platform. However, encouraging teachers to make a more sophisticated use of it than it seems to be currently the case would also be advisable. Presently, e-learning practices mainly consist in giving students access to course contents online and in the communication around those contents.

The obtained results should not be generalised as they chiefly concern one Belgian institution. However, literature on BL indicates to some extent that the beliefs put forward by this study could be shared by a larger community. Moreover, as already mentioned, if the salient beliefs identified by the study can be regarded as levers in favour of BL, acting on such levers is worth a trial. On the whole, rooting faculty development actions in evidence-based approaches like the TPB and its emphasis on obstacles and incentives to adopt a specific behaviour can help policy makers, academic authorities or teaching and learning centres to guide, structure, and promote more effectively innovative approaches to teaching and learning.

The study presented here also points towards an obvious further piece of research: relaunching a TPB-based inquiry on BL after the pandemic and check whether the predictors of intention and their underlying beliefs have been affected by this constrained "emergency remote teaching" [21–22]. In this perspective, the current study, taking place just before the lockdown, could somehow serve as a useful yardstick to calibrate possible evolutions of faculty readiness to practise BL. For Teaching & Learning Centres, it would be very interesting – and conceivably somewhat depressing – to establish whether a nasty virus has done more in several months for the promotion of BL in teachers' minds than years of patient argumentative work in favour of thoughtful hybrid instructional design. Of course, recent circumstances have given rise to a series of articles regarding technological adaptation and BL efforts due to the COVID-19 pandemic across the globe [8, 53–56]. However, contrasting empirical pre- and post-lockdown data obtained through a comparable and well-documented research methodology would have a value of its own.

Author details

Dominique Verpoorten*, Johanne Huart, Pascal Detroz and Françoise Jérôme
IFRES (Institute for Training and Research in Higher Education), Traverse des Architectes, B63b, University of Liège, 4000 Liège, Belgium

*Address all correspondence to: dverpoorten@uliege.be

References

[1] Laurillard D. Thinking about Blended Learning. December: A paper for the Thinkers in Residence programme. Royal Flemish Academy of Belgium for Science and the Arts; 2014

[2] Garrison D, Vaughan N. Blended Learning in Higher Education: Framework, Principles, and Guidelines. Jossey-Bass; 2012. 272 p.

[3] Graham C. Blended learning systems: Definition, current trends, and future directions. In: Bonk CJ, Graham CR, editors. The Handbook of Blended Learning: Global Perspectives, Local Designs. San Francisco: Pfeiffer Publishing; 2006. pp. 3-21

[4] Stein J, Graham C. Essentials for blended learning: A standards-based guide. New York: Springer. 2014. DOI: 10.4324/9781351043991

[5] Garrison D, Kanuka H. Blended learning: Uncovering its transformative potential in higher education. The Internet and Higher Education. 2004;**7**(2):95-105

[6] Educause. Horizon Report 2020. Teaching and Learning Edition. Louisville CO: EDUCAUSE; 2020.

[7] Porter W, Graham C, Spring K, Welch K. Blended learning in higher education: Institutional adoption and implementation. Computers and Education. 2014;**75**(3):185-195

[8] Crawford J, Butler-Henderson K, Rudolph J, Malkawi B, Glowatz M, Burton R, et al. COVID-19: 20 countries' higher education intra-period digital pedagogy responses. Journal of Applied Learning & Teaching. 2020;**3**(1):9-28

[9] Bernard R, Borokhovski E, Schmid R, Tamim R, Abrami P. A meta-analysis of blended learning and technology use in higher education: From the general to the applied. Journal of Computing in Higher Education. 2014;**26**(1):87-122

[10] Chien Y, Chang, Chang C. Do we click in the right way? A meta-analytic review of clicker-integrated instruction. Educational Research Review. 2016; 17: 1-18.

[11] Means B, Toyama Y, Murphy R, Baki M. The effectiveness of online and blended learning: A meta-analysis of the empirical literature. Teachers College Record. 2013;**115**(3):1-47

[12] Dziuban C, Graham C, Picciano A. Research Perspectives in Blended Learning. New York: Routledge; 2013. 376 p.

[13] Stacey E, Gerbic P. Teaching for blended learning - research perspectives from on-campus and distance students. Educational and Information Technologies. 2007;**12**(3):165-174

[14] López-Pérez M, Pérez-López M, Rodríguez-Ariza L. Blended learning in higher education: Students' perceptions and their relation to outcomes. Computers & Education. 2011;**56**:818-826

[15] McCarthy J. Blending virtual and physical classrooms to enhance the first year experience. In same places, different spaces. In: Proceedings of the ASCILITE conference; 2009; Auckland. New Zealand.

[16] Baepler P, Walker J, Driessen M. It's not about seat time: Blending, flipping, and efficiency in active learning classrooms. Computers & Education. 2014;**78**:227-236

[17] Rovai A, Jordan H. Blended Learning and Sense of Community: A Comparative Analysis with Traditional and Fully Online Graduate Courses.

The International Review of Research in Open and Distributed Learning. 2004; 5(2). DOI: 10.19173/irrodl.v5i2.192

[18] Dahlstrom E, Bichsel J. ECAR Study of Undergraduate Students and Information Technology. Research Report. EDUCAUSE: Louisville, CO; 2014

[19] Goffe W, Kauper D. A survey of principles instructors: Why lecture prevails. The Journal of Economic Education. 2014;**45**(4):360-375

[20] Watts M, Becker W. A little more than chalk and talk: Results from a third national survey of teaching methods in undergraduate economics courses. Journal of Economic Education. 2008;**39**(3):273-286

[21] Hodges C, Moore S, Lockee B, Trust T. Bond a. EDUCAUSE Review: The difference between emergency remote teaching and online learning; 2020, March 27

[22] Butler-Henderson K, Crawford J, Rudolph J, Lalani K, Sabu K. COVID-19 in higher education literature database (CHELD V1): An open access systematic literature review database with coding rules. Journal of Applied Learning & Teaching. 2020;**3**(2):1-6

[23] Ajzen I. The theory of planned behavior. Organisational behavior and human decision process. 1991;**50**:179-211

[24] Barnard-Brak L, Burley H, Crooks S. Explaining youth mentoring behavior using a theory of planned behavior perspective. International Journal of Adolescence and Youth. 2010;**15**(4):365-379

[25] Cheon J, Lee S, Crooks S, Song J. An investigation of mobile learning readiness in higher education based on the theory of planned behavior. Computers & Education. 2012;**59**(3):1054-1064

[26] Detroz P, Huart J, Loye N, Piazza A, Giet D, Burette S, et al. L'intention d'utiliser les référentiels de compétences. Le cas des maitres de stage en faculté de médecine. Revue des Sciences de l'Education. 2019;**45**(1):108-132

[27] Goh E, Ritchie B. Using the theory of planned behavior to understand student attitudes and constraints toward attending field trips. Journal of Teaching in Travel & Tourism. 2011;**11**(2):179-194

[28] Kam C, Hue M, Cheung H. Academic dishonesty among Hong Kong secondary school students: Application of theory of planned behaviour. Educational Psychology. 2018;**38**(7):945-963

[29] MacFarlane K, Woolfson L. Teacher attitudes and behavior toward the inclusion of children with social, emotional and behavioral difficulties in mainstream schools: An application of the theory of planned behaviour. Teaching and Teacher Education. 2013;**29**:46-52

[30] Moss N, O'Connor E, White K. Psychosocial predictors of the use of enhanced podcasting in student learning. Computers in Human Behavior. 2010;**26**:302-309

[31] Armitage C, Conner M. Efficacy of the theory of planned behaviour: A metaanalytic review. British journal of social psychology. 2001;**40**(4):471-499

[32] Ajzen I. From intentions to actions: A theory of planned behavior. In: Kuhl J, Beckmann, J, editors. Action control: From cognition to behavior. Berlin/Heidelberg. Germany: Springer-Verlag. 1985;**1985**:11-39

[33] Ajzen I, Fishbein M. The influence of attitudes on behavior.

In: Albarracin D, Johnson B, Zanna M, editors. The Handbook of Attitudes. Mahwah, New Jersey: Lawrence Erlbaum Associates; 2005. pp. 173-221

[34] Conner M. Armitage, C. J. extending the theory of planned behavior: A review and avenues for further research. Journal of applied social psychology. 1998;**28**(15):1429-1464

[35] Davies R. Understanding technology literacy: A framework for evaluating educational technology integration. Tech Trends. 2011;**55**(5):45-52

[36] Dwyer D, Ringstaff C, Sandholtz J. Changes in Teachers' beliefs and practices in technology-rich classrooms. Educational Leadership. 1991;**48**(8):45-54

[37] Hall G, Dirksen D, George, A. Measuring Implementation in Schools: Levels of Use. Austin: SEDL; 2006. 81 p.

[38] Moersch C. Levels of technology implementation (LoTi): A framework for measuring classroom technology use. Learning and Leading with Technology. 1995;**23**(3):40-42

[39] Ajzen I. Constructing a TpB Questionnaire: Conceptual and Methodological Considerations. 2006.

[40] Ferdig R, Baumgartner E, Hartshorne R, Kaplan-Rakowski R, Mouza C. Teaching, Technology, and Teacher Education during the COVID-19 Pandemic: Stories from the Field. Association for the Advancement of Computing in Education (AACE); 2020.

[41] Defaweux V, Delbrassine D, Dozo B-O, Etienne A-M, Centi V, D'Anna V, Multon S, Pesesse L, Stassart C, Van de Poël J-F, Wagener A, Weatherspoon A, Verpoorten D. To combine a MOOC to a regular face-to-face course – A study of three blended pedagogical patterns. In: Proceedings of Work in Progress Papers of the Research, Experience and Business Tracks at EMOOCs 2019 - European MOOCs Stakeholders Summit. Aachen. Germany: CEUR Workshop Proceedings; May 2019. pp. 210-217

[42] Graham CR, Woodfield W, Harrison JB. A framework for institutional adoption and implementation of blended learning in higher education. The internet and higher education. 2013;**18**:4-14

[43] Mozelius P, Rydell C. Problems affecting successful implementation of blended learning in higher education: The teacher perspective. International Journal of Information and Communication Technologies in Education. 2017;**6**(1):4-13

[44] Antwi-Boampong A. Towards a faculty blended learning adoption model for higher education. Education and Information Technologies. 2020;**25**:1639-1662

[45] Dube S. Educators' Pedagogical Concerns on Blending ICTs in Teaching. In: Proceedings of the European Conference on e-learning. Kidmore End. UK: Academic Conferences International Limited; 2017. pp. 150-155

[46] Apandi A, Raman A. Factors affecting successful implementation of blended learning at higher education. International Journal of Instruction, Technology, and Social Sciences. 2020;**1**(1):13-23

[47] Vankatesh V, Davis F. A theoretical extension of the technology acceptance model: Four longitudinal field studies. Management Science. 2000;**46**(2):186-204

[48] Koelher M, Mishra P. Technological pedagogical content knowledge: A framework for teacher knowledge. Teacher College Record. 2006;**108**(6):1017-1054

[49] Ibrahim M, Nat M. Blended learning motivation model for instructors in higher education institutions International. Journal of Educational Technology in HigherEducation. 2019; 16(12).

[50] Laforest J, Rainville M. Trousse diagnostique de sécurité à l'intention des collectivités locales. Guide d'organisation d'entretiens semi-dirigés avec des informateurs clés. Québec, Canada : Institut national de santé publique du Québec; 2019.

[51] Boelens R, De Wever B, Voet M. Four key challenges to the design of blended learning: A systematic literature review. Educational Review Research. 2017;**22**:1-18

[52] Kim M, Kim S, Khera O, Getman J. The experience of three flipped classrooms in an urban university: An exploration of design principles. Internet and Higher Education. 2014;**22**:37-50

[53] Adedoyin O, Soykan S. COVID-19 pandemic and online learning: The challenges and opportunities. Interactive Learning Environments. 2020. DOI: 10.1080/10494820.2020.1813180

[54] Flores M, Swennen S. The COVID-19 pandemic and its effects on teacher education. European Journal of Teacher Education. 2020;**43**(4):453-456

[55] Reich J. Remote Learning Guidance from State Education Agencies during the COVID-19 Pandemic: A First Look. 2020. Available from: https://osf.io/k6zxy

[56] Vlachopoulos D. COVID-19: Threat or Opportunity for Online Education? Higher Learning Research Communications. 2020; 10(1). DOI:10.18870/hlrc.v10i1.1179

Chapter 6

Mainstreaming Blended Learning in a Low-Income University

Mildred Atieno Ayere

Abstract

Due to the COVID-19 pandemic, Maseno University (MU) began to consider institutional shift from traditional face-to-face (F2F) instructions to online and blended modes of teaching and learning. The university was able to draw from its experience with adapted flexible and blended learning (FBL) approaches for high enrollment common courses already offered to students on the Learning Management System (LMS). Several questions have been raised: How to preserve what most lecturers consider as most essential — the regular student interaction, the freewheeling give-and-take discussion sessions — if the class cannot be together in the same physical space at the same time? How to make a synchronous activity dependent course and make it work in a completely asynchronous environment? How to handle the practical based subjects on the online platform? And even if the university is able to find acceptable answers to these questions, where would it begin? However, MU did not try to reinvent the wheel. There were already examples of good practice in a number of common courses had been running on the LMS. The available courses already had a blend of both theory and practical base. The university sought assistance from schools and departments that already had parts of their programmes running on the LMS. They were able to tap into their expertise and get introduced to a valuable collection of resources about online distance teaching and learning (ODTL). That, in turn, assisted the university to develop online or blended versions of its regular F2F courses that far surpassed expectations, judging from how well their courses performed, and get ready for any other unexpected circumstance equal or similar to which the world has had to live through the COVID-19 pandemic.

Keywords: blended learning, common courses, face to face learning, high enrollment courses, low-income university, online learning, online distance teaching and learning

1. Introduction

Lecturers especially in Africa's Higher Education Institutions (HEIs) are facing unprecedented change, with often larger classes, more diverse students, demands from government and employers who want more accountability and the development of graduates who are workforce ready, and above all, needing to cope with an ever-changing technological landscape [1, 2]. To handle changes of this nature, lecturers and instructors need a theoretical base and knowledge that provide a solid foundation for their teaching, no matter what changes or pressures they face. There is need, therefore, to study and understand the underlying principles that guide effective teaching in an age when everyone, and in particular the students, are using and understanding technology better than their teachers especially in the developing world. A framework and a set of guidelines need to be developed by a university with vast knowledge and practice in online learning to build an appropriate model, theoretically sound, which allows making decisions coherently about pedagogical foundations of teaching, low cost but versatile technologies that can be deployed for classroom use and hybrid ad online delivery based on their vast experience in handling classes in technology rich ecologies. This can be done while keeping in mind that every subject discipline is different, and every lecturer has something unique and special to bring to their teaching which needs exploiting and nurturing to its full potential.

The need for this kind of mentorship from Universities already practicing blended learning is dire with the developments witnessed in the recent past where the COVID-19 pandemic has rendered all institutions non-operational from basic to higher education institutions (HEIs) in a country like Kenya [3, 4]. The basic education institutions would have been seeking mentorship from the HEIs but as it is, the HEIs were all shut down and looking to institutions in the west for support and mentorship. This kind of scenario spelled the urgency for this book project so that in future, HEIs in developing countries, more specifically Kenya, could have Maseno University (MU) as a mentor within its borders that the government can turn to for guidance and leadership in a major shift from face to face (F2F) to online classroom delivery mode. Recently, the COVID-19 pandemic forced a major global experimentation with remote teaching. But most of the experts agree that remote teaching as applied was an emergency measure from which lessons learned must not be lost but documented for future. There are many indicators that this crisis has transformed the education sector and good practice when document, will provide useful lessons in the post-COVID-19 period. As this crisis-driven experiment was launched at MU, it is expected that the process must not be lost as it proves useful guidelines for other universities hoping to be part of this shift.

As MU eCampus team began to consider institutional shift from F2F to online and blended modes on behalf of the University Management, despair almost overwhelms the team. Several questions were raised: How to preserve what most lecturers consider as most essential — the regular student interaction, the freewheeling give-and-take as discussion on a particular source or topic take place — if the class cannot be together in the same physical space at the same time? How to take a course that seemed to depend on synchronous activity and make it work in a completely asynchronous environment? And even if acceptable answers to these questions are found, where would the university begin? Fortunately, the university did not try to reinvent the wheel. The university received assistance from colleagues from Open University of Catalonia (OUC), Association of Commonwealth Universities among others who were more familiar with the online world than the colleagues from MU. Faculties from MU were able to tap into their expertise and get introduced to a valuable collection of resources about online teaching and learning. That, in turn, helped MU to develop online or blended versions of its regular F2F courses that far surpass expectations, judging from how well their courses have performed, and get ready for any other unexpected circumstance equal or similar to which we have lived facing the pandemic.

Today, the outburst in developments in educational technology and the fact that the ed-tech arena is a crowded field may overwhelm. At any given time, there is at least one app or platform screaming about how it is the newest, best, easiest tool for online courses [5]. And that app or platform is just as likely to be gone within a year as it is to become and remain a valuable teaching tool. How does one make a decision on good digital tools that (a) afford students the means of interacting substantively with lecturer and with one another, (b) enable a deep engagement with course materials or applications, and (c) affordable in low-income institution like MU? Yet still, in the shift in learning modes, several variables need to be considered: The planning process, learner characteristics, design and delivery methods, learning contexts, workplace environment and the already existing barriers to this shift. A successful shift, however, needs to move beyond asking which method is most effective to the important role of pedagogy that actually takes into account a social element in online delivery which is important to student engagement and knowledge acquisition [6]. One important pedagogical theory that addresses this is constructivism. It offers a model that addresses the social needs of students as well as providing an opportunity for critical inquiry and subsequent knowledge acquisition. However, for attitudes to change and trust to be built there is need to co-develop online systems where university management teams are involved in decision making based on existing university delivery systems. However, knowing about pedagogy and practicing the pedagogy are two different things. In this project, it is hoped that mentorship by Open University of Catalonia (OUC) or any other informed user would inculcate correct attitudes and a shift in institutional culture at MU that would allow for development of the expected institutional culture that blends with constructivism as a classroom would take root. This would open the door for setting the correct environmental climate needed to introduce online and blended learning as modes of practice at MU.

Maseno University already had a robust and very interactive learning management system running on Moodle (Modular Object-Oriented Dynamic Learning Environment). However, the institution has not been able to adopt online and blended learning because of shortcomings that need to be addressed in this project. The chief of these being lack of policy to guide the uptake of fully online and blended learning for faculty and students; insufficient knowledge of pedagogical orientations needed to implement these new modes of instructional delivery; and a model for carrying out mass capacity building for lecturers to allow them to develop and teach online and blended courses.

The goal of this chapter is to document the processes the university had to go through in making the shift from a traditional face to face institution to a modern university having F2F, blended and online learning. The processes it had to consider were: carry out capacity building for lecturers in online pedagogy, content development and facilitation in a bid to build a new university community culture that is positive towards affordances of online and blended learning; and expand its technology infrastructure to support the twenty thousand plus students at the university.

The specific objectives of this chapter are to document how to:

a. Mainstream quality conceptual pedagogy for online and blended learning that would create a change process with a genuine paradigm shift in instructional strategies within the institutional;

b. Create a model for online and blended content development that allows seamless shift in learning modes within a traditional face to face university, especially set up for MU;

c. Prepare a set of mechanisms, and resources for training of staff to learn to teach online;

d. Design a policy to guide online and blended learning activities with the university; and

e. Choose low cost but effective technologies for classroom instruction in the light of existing economic constraints within the University.

2. Maseno University eCampus

The eCampus was established in the year 2007 to spearhead the development of institutional policies and strategies for promoting the innovative use of information and communications technologies (ICTs) to benefit learning, teaching and research activities in Maseno University. Located in Kisumu City, the eCampus boasts of an open office work environment that models good office practice to the university community. As currently constituted, the eCampus operates on a different time, different place (home study, computer conferencing, tutorial support by e-mail and fax communication), recognized as Scenario 4 in the Commission of University Education (CUE) Open Distance and eLearning (ODeL) standards and guidelines as stated in the Universities Standards, 2014.

The eCampus of Maseno University is a pioneer workstation using modern technologies to offer quality higher education for learners within the region and globally. This involves use of the internet to support teaching and learning activities. Developed around a web-based learning management system (LMS), this approach has attracted a large number of undergraduate and postgraduate students who registered for differentcertificate, diploma and degree programmes spanning seven schools within the university. In addition, eCampus provides an ambient platform that mounts university common courses offered to all students registered for various undergraduate programmes in all the campuses of MU, irrespective of their mode of study i.e. full-time, part-time, weekend, sandwich or eLearning. These courses are mandatory and are currently offered online at the eCampus of Maseno University through the LMS, also known as the Maseno University eLearning Portal. To achieve quality eLearning standards on programmes offered at the eCampus, there is a robust quality and effective monitoring and evaluation mechanism in place.

The eCampus operations are domiciled in 4 key support areas: Content Development; Learner Support Services; Capacity Building; and Research, monitoring and Evaluation. The functions of each of these key areas are discussed in the sections that follow.

2.1 Content development

The content development follows internationally acceptable norms [7–9] and all content offered at the eCampus is developed by the content expert nominated by the department offering a specific programme at the eCampus. The programmes offered at eCampus are provided on a modular basis to give maximum flexibility to the participants as well as on a blended basis as part of regular full time face-to-face programmes. The programmes specify core materials to be covered and guidelines detailing total content required for completion. The eCampus technical team (Instructional designers, systems support specialists and graphic designers) and the host Departments are jointly responsible for capacity building for module development, evaluation and related quality assurance procedures.

Module development, delivery and assessment are undertaken by a course development team (course developer, editor and reviewer) in the host departments as appointed by the Dean, in line with the University Statutes. This team is assisted by a support team (instructional designer, graphic designer, multi-media specialist, eLearning System support specialist, eLibrary assistant and copyright officer) from eCampus so as to ensure that guidelines for content development, review, uploading, packaging and branding are adhered to. Each module provides clear learning outcomes, course content, instructional mode and assessment methods. The content development flow is represented in **Figure 1** [10].

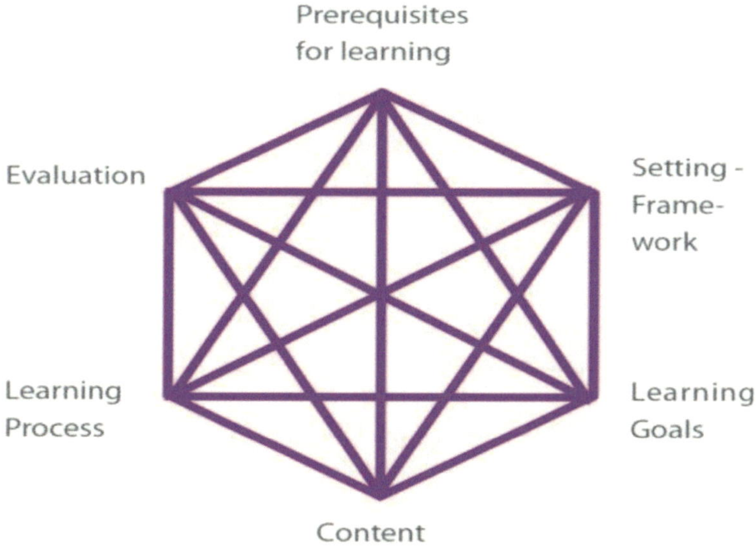

Figure 1.
Didactical relationship model by Charlotte Lærke Weitze [10].

The eCampus uses an improved model of the didactic relationship in its content development by considering the target group for which content is intended; The content itself in terms level in the curriculum; The targeted learning outcomes; The pedagogical approach the content is hinged on; Organization of the content which in most cases is from simple to complex; The learning activities that enable the learner to achieve the outcomes in the shortest time possible; The assessment of student learning. To help further clarify issues in content development, the eCampus furnishes its content development experts with a content review rubric adapted from the Commonwealth of Learning. The rubric is used to focus the content development by considering the following key aspects: Navigation/Orientation (e.g., the course site is well organized and easy to navigate from the course home page to the course units, links, forums, etc.); Content (learners can engage with content together with peers as expectations are clear); Instructional Design (the content is pedagogically sound); Good flow in course structure; Student support structures are considered in the development; Technology or Media used is clear and available to learners; Assessment is ingrained in the developed material; and lastly quality assurance measures are considered in every part of the content development. It follows therefore that the eCampus endeavors to provide high quality online programmes that are supported by renown researchers [2] who believe that quality online programmes should beOpen: learning resources are accessible and available, including after the course; Navigable: well-planned interfaces allow students to find what they need; Learning: sites are designed to develop knowledge, skills, attributes and identity; Interactive: dialog is supported among and between teachers and learners; Networked: curriculum and activities foster broad-reaching connections; and Engaging: teachers invite, model and sustain enthusiastic presence for learning. These sentiments are summarized in the **Table 1** below.

2.2 Learner support services

The eCampus has invested significantly in an online based learning management system (LMS). The learning content is uploaded to the learning management system. The LMS supports upload of multimedia and well as text-based resources.

Open	Navigable	Learning	Interactive	Networked	Engaging
Create links from and to key industry research & websites.	Develop, share & follow a consistent Program glossary of educational terms.	Identify the key digital tools that graduates are likely to use and include them in the course.	Create a marked Discussion Forum and post a clear marking guide. Model strong interaction.	Dedicate marks to students posting completed assessment on a digital portfolio	Create & post an auto-biographical video about you and what attracted you to the taught discipline.

Table 1.
Description of quality online programmes [11].

Student and course lecturers communicate using both synchronous and asynchronous instructional tools. Learner support assistants headed by a coordinator ensure the learning processes are efficient and effective. This is achieved by promoting effective Learner-Learner and Learner-Lecturer interactions employed through online learner support services.

As confirmed by research [12, 13] some of the most important online teacher competencies drawn from the experience at the eCampus include: communication skills; technological competence; provision of informative feedback; administrative skills; responsiveness; monitoring learning; and providing student support. The problems of the distance learners are unique and require to be handled differently. The efficiency of the delivery system will greatly depend not only on efficient modes of providing services but also on the staff of the university. The Online Support Service System should be developed for the learner community, along with other electronic media services [14]. In fact, a well-designed learner support system for the distance learning is a system for fostering creative, critical and independent thinking skills which inculcates deep learning [15]. The practice at eCampus was designed to avoid obvious pitfalls in online learning such as high attrition and repetition rates normally associated with unfacilitated online instructional practices [16]. The eCampus further believes as affirmed by research that good learner support services provide online learners with coaching and mentorship programmes to help them discover their interests; develop self-motivation, innovativeness and excellence in performance. This prepares them with essential skills for life and the workplace such as leadership, communication, self-awareness into their own strengths and weaknesses, initiative, problem-solving, innovation and critical thinking [17]. The learner support practice at eCampus can best be summarized in **Figure 2** that follows as described specialists [18, 19].

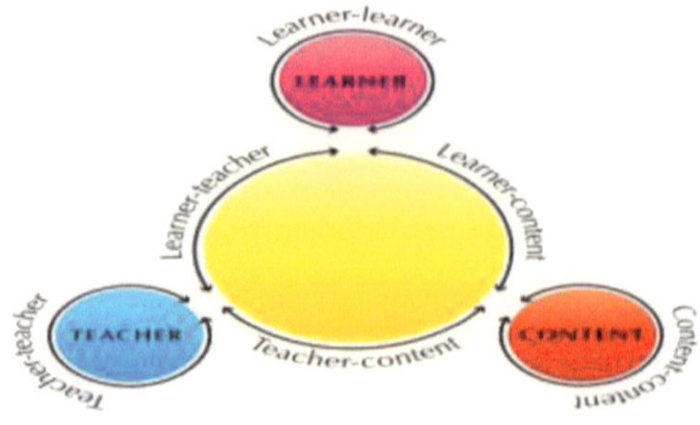

Figure 2.
Interaction and learner support [19].

2.3 Capacity building

The eCampus continues to organize online training for course lecturers, editors, reviewers, supervisors and facilitators to enable them to develop modules, edit content, review online modules, teach and supervise learners and offer online support to eLearning students. A mandatory foundation course is offered to course lecturers, editors, reviewers, supervisors and facilitators before embarking on specialized blended training. These training sessions are developed to ensure adherence to MU good practice guidelines for online interaction which is in line with international best practice especially during the pandemic [20–22].

HEIs in Africa like Maseno eCampus face the challenge of responding to the expanding demand for tertiary education while maintaining or enhancing the quality of their course offerings. This demand has led to some HEIs introducing the use of interactive web technologies to support their distance teaching and learning practices [23]. However, academic staff at these institutions may struggle to provide sufficient support to online learners in part due to inadequate staff capacity in terms of familiarity with and use of online communication tools and virtual learning environments. It is therefore necessary to develop capacity building strategies that are self-sustaining in such an institution.

Two key considerations from research [24] drive capacity building initiatives at the Maseno University eCampus. These are that in designing effective distance education programmes, engagement with and feedback from the learner is critical, and open-source solutions may be effective in meeting teaching objectives. Second is that in training initiatives for staff capacity building in HEIs that are just starting out in online learning initiatives: it is imperative for trainees to understand the relevance of the technology for the existing ecosystem and build for sustainability through the development of demand-driven country-specific and institution affordable applications. Capacity building at the eCampus relies mainly on the blended mode because the staff come from geographically dispersed locations; have limited flexibility because of work schedules and would face challenges attending fully in-person training; have limited daily time to devote to capacity building and would benefit from courses being split into short modules; have reliable access to the necessary technology and basic computer and internet skills; and appreciates learning at their own pace.

The paper hypothesizes a four-part framework to define the e-learning capacity gaps that these circumstances appear to represent: the “instructional design capacity gap”, the “production capacity gap”, the “tutorial capacity gap” and the “community building gap” [25]. Capacity building must be at the heart of moving from theory to practice. Increasingly, individuals need to understand different perspectives in their endeavor to manage the complexities of real-world problems [26]. This is particularly true in the case of the Nexus Approach which has been extensively borrowed and applied by the eCampus, which examines the challenges related to interconnected resources and in this case, the needs of staff at the university. It is clear that for capacity building measures to be successful, innovative approaches are required. The Nexus approach advocates for an inclusive approach to capacity building by anchoring all capacity building approaches on institutional policy; allowing dialog among participants while using the free flow of information to share best practice from participants. The outcome can only be scientific if informed by research during the capacity building session, and this builds into institutional practice (**Figure 3**) [26].

The other model used in all capacity sessions at the eCampus is mentorship. Mentoring can help staff overcome difficulties in mastering several subjects in higher education while reducing failure rates and lowering dropout rates. Mentees

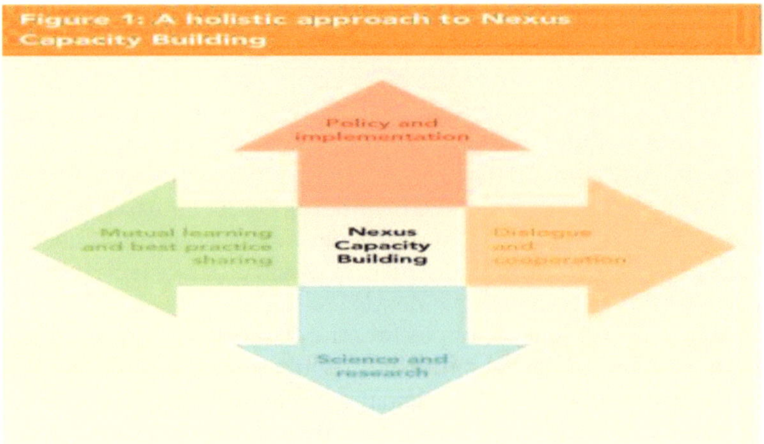

Figure 3.
The nexus approach to capacity building [26].

receive personalized direction to improve attitudes, values, and skills needed to master the new issues in the curriculum and develop self-confidence in teaching with technology [26]. Mentoring programmes as used at the eCampus provide the necessary guidance and support in content and/or pedagogy, to aid technology novice lecturers in their ongoing professional development. Mentors in this case are colleagues in more advanced specific technology knowledge within the university or other educational consultants providing outside, research-based perspectives on the subject [27]. The eCampus uses mentorship at two levels in its capacity building session: The school champions are academic staff that have grasped the concepts and as a result provides mentorship at school level; they also use learner support assistants who are mainly administrative staff but with good technology skills and are then mentored by the eCampus technical staff to provide the needed technical support at school level. The two groups of staff are core to all capacity building activities at the eCampus. In developing countries like Kenya, access to and quality of education are being addressed by e-learning strategies and especially mentorship of academic staff serving as a useful tool of capacity building [28] in eLearning methodologies and practices.

2.4 Research monitoring and evaluation

Monitoring and Evaluation (M&E) are two distinct but complementary processes that mutually reinforce each other. In general, M&E is designed to monitor the impact of a policy, or progress of programme activities, against the overall goals, objectives and targets. M&E also assesses the outcome relevance of an activity, and the impact of a programme, or effectiveness of a policy, as well as its efficiency and sustainability [29]. OECD-DAC [30] defines monitoring as "the ongoing, systematic collection of information to assess progress towards the achievement of objectives, outcomes and impacts," and it defines evaluation as "the systematic and objective assessment of an ongoing or completed project, programme or policy, its design, implementation and results, with the aim to determine the relevance and fulfillment of objectives, development efficiency, effectiveness, impact and sustainability. This unit at the eCampus of Maseno university does both monitoring and evaluation of the systems, programmes, learning outcomes and learning processes. It is this unit at the eCampus that ensures that quality procedures and processes are followed and adhered it. It also carries out periodic evaluations that inform policy and practice.

The Research, Monitoring and Evaluation (RM&E) Unit at the eCampus aims at improving the quality of its programmes operations and services. It further aims at maintaining high-quality outcomes in the physical and virtual spaces of the eCampus as per the approved quality assurance practices. This is achieved through on-going monitoring and evaluation of content development, learner support, capacity building and administrative processes at the eCampus. As such, the RM&E unit does not only conduct a review against the Commission for university Education ODEL Standards and Guidelines, but it also picks on the good practices and standards from international institutions with which the eCampus benchmarks, as well as quality improvement schemes like the Commonwealth of Learning (CoL) Quality Assurance rubric, ECBCheck and ACDE quality toolkit. Since student learning is the focal point of the eCampus, the RM&E unit examines all activities at the eCampus which contribute to quality learning outcomes.

The eLearning Postgraduate Research Support platform has been designed for the postgraduate student, and the aim is to support students at all levels of the postgraduate studies. As such, this area will link the student to fellow graduate students in all Schools and Departments within Maseno University eCampus. This allows students to share and discuss coursework and research experiences with other participants (peer researchers) and supervisors.

One key area of concern had been the postgraduate students' research process. Due to the concerns raised on the process, the eCampus created a post-graduate students research support area to assist in continuous monitoring and evaluation of the research processes. Specifically, given the challenges students face at various levels of research phase of their studies, such as formulating research/study/project concepts, study/questionnaire designs, study methodologies, data collection strategies, data analyses and interpretations as well as write-ups, it was realized that mentorship through sharing of experiences and expertise is the only sure way to unlock students' research potential, improve their research skills and accelerate the pace of post-graduate studies. The discussions are accessible to all online participants, facilitators, supervisors and lecturers as they are free to comment and assist.

The role of the Coordinator in charge of Research, Monitoring and Evaluation (RM&E) at eCampus is to coordinate all monitoring and evaluation activities including the graduate students on the eLearning platform. It is hoped that students shall be able to access supervisors, research information and resources needed for post-graduate studies. Through this platform, the eCampus endeavor to offer real time monitoring and support to individualized challenges in the research phase of learning. This is an example of an open but innovative way of offering online monitoring and mentorship not only to students but also to the supervisors both in knowledge and use of online technological tools in research.

3. Change process that cause genuine paradigm shift in university instructional strategies

In order to make the institutional transition from possible, organizations and institutions interested in adopting blended learning models must have a clear vision and a strong support from the various stakeholders involved in the change process [31–33]. The eCampus identified three such change agents. The first is that adoption of the blended learning model must be part of the educational institution's strategy. The second factor is related to the organizational support, understood as facilitating conditions. Facilitating conditions in this case was the degree to which individuals believed that sufficient resources existed to support learning in a blended setting. Facilitating conditions have been conceptualized in terms of training and provision of organizational support. The third factor was the organizational capabilities to effectively execute and deliver a blended learning program. Here organizational capabilities are understood as the organization's ability to manage all the people involved in a learning process to gain advantage [34–36]. This means that low-budget institutions should focus first on helping instructors shift to student-centered styles of pedagogies before making large investments in IT infrastructure.

When we consider the culture of the HEI as a set of instructional values, traditions, and beliefs ingrained in the fabric of the educational community, the idea of cultural change offers both promise and pause for HEIs looking to implement a blended learning program. Cultural change does not happen overnight, and can create significant growing pains for those with longstanding ideas about educational practices. Proper implementation of this shift depends on a leadership team that sets clear goals and acts in support of those goals [1] and, in turn, ensures that teachers are prepared to successfully adopt new technologies and pedagogies [37, 38].

eCampus identifies with researchers who maintain that Innovation in education can be particularly challenging because change has the potential to affect student achievement [39]. Creating a culture of innovation also requires structure and process, capacity, resources, policy environments, and learning agendas [40].

i. Structure and process includes the formal systems in the institution, some of which may need to be altered during the transition to blended learning. It also includes the habits of stakeholders and how those habits are reinforced. Building a blended learning culture may require educators and students to build new habits.

ii. Capacity, in terms of culture, is less about physical capacity and more about mindset and the ability to carry forward the blended plan. An institution that has capacity will exhibit a growth mindset and show diligence and patience in pursuit of blended learning.

iii. Resources include the obvious financial considerations, but also include time and team resources. Successful institutions pay particular attention to balancing time and human considerations to keep the culture on track.

iv. Policy environments include both the written and unwritten institutional policies that enable or prevent the changes needed to support blended learning. Maseno University as an institution had to look for ways to make blended learning easy and attractive to implement.

v. Learning agendas should include an emphasis on measuring progress and managing the change process. Progress should be measured against the SMART goals created by the institutional leadership team and by student achievement data.

3.1 Blended learning model as an institutional strategy

Blended learning is a formal education program in which a student learns at least in part through online delivery of content and instruction with some element of student control over time, place, path, and/or pace. The methodology behind blended learning is to combine classroom learning with mobile learning and online learning. Maseno University already has a robust and very interactive learning management system running on Moodle (Modular Object-Oriented Dynamic Learning Environment). However, the institution had not been able to adopt online for its regular face to face students because of tradition. In the advent of the COVID-19 pandemic, the institution had to find a strategy that fitted closely with its already existing resources, facilities and a ready workforce. It was out of this analysis that the institution settled on a model that had originally suggested by Bhaskar [41] It compares well with other models [42–45]. This model fits the practice at the university as it already has a digitally literate workforce; an operational and robust learning management system; already trained pool of lecturers able to develop and facilitate online courses and able to act as mentors to the rest; organizational objectives supportive of blended learning; a student pool that already has common IT skills because all their courses is taught with IT; and it has an existing library of printed instructional materials already in use in the traditional classroom. Tech teams have identified seven main modes of practicing blended learning: Lab rotation, station rotation, individual rotation, flipped classroom, a la carte, and enriched virtual. However, the model [41] below converges around 6 main modes which are all practiced at the Maseno University eCampus. These modes are: Face-to-face Driver – the teacher guides learning with technology as a supplementary resource; Rotation – the learner has a fixed schedule rotating between face to face and online schedules; Flex - the model where most of the learning is done online and the face-to-face model exists to provide on-site support; Online Lab - a model of blended learning that characterizes programs that rely on an online platform to deliver the entire course while teachers interact with students through pre-recorded videos, audio and video conferences or discussion forums and email; Self-Blend - a fully individualized approach that allows students to choose to take one or more courses online to supplement their traditional school curriculum; and Online Driver- involves online platform as well as teachers to deliver the curricula and students work from remote locations most of the time but come to school for required face-to-face classes (**Figure 4**) [41].

The practice in MU was a blend of these six models from one extreme end to the other. For example, some lecturers had face to face classes but occasional sent work or instructions to students through short messaging services (SMS) or WhatsApp. Others had all the content on LMS and students only consulted where there was a need. Yet still a big majority gave all instructions fully in F2F classes only. It is these

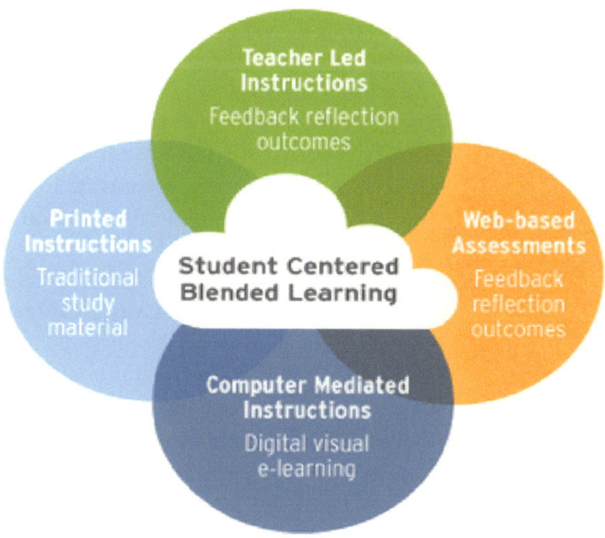

Figure 4.
Model of blended learning [41].

extremes that forced the university to come up with the blended approach as the university strategy for instructions.

3.2 Resources to support the blended learning strategy

MU already had a robust and very interactive learning management system running on Moodle platform. Moodle is free and open-source LMS which easily integrates to other systems like the University Management Information System (MIS) for seamless flow of information from the classroom to management. The current MU learning management system also allows for notes and assignment uploads by both lecturers and students. Besides content, the LMS has a web-conferencing facility that allows lecturers to capture what they are teaching to be uploaded online for students. This web-conferencing facility has also assisted with defense for post-graduate student, especially those that cannot attend the F2F defenses either because of geographical location or a tight work schedule or any other genuine reason.

MU had trained some of its lecturers in online content development and delivery. Specifically, the lecturers from the following schools had already been trained on several occasions and were able to develop online content and facilitate online teaching.

a. School of Art and Social Sciences – Mainly lecturers from the Department of Socially and Anthropology

b. School of Business and Economics – Almost all lecturers

c. School of Computing and Informatics – Almost all lecturers

d. School of Education – Only one quarter of the lecturers from the School have received some meaningful training

e. School of Mathematics Statistics and Actuarial Science – Three quarters of the lecturer

f. Planning and Architecture – Almost all lecturers

g. School of Public Health and Development – Only lecturers from Department of Public Health lecturers

The other 4 schools within the university had not been trained and had no capacity as at now to develop or teach on the online platform. It was therefore important to have capacity building of lecturers to be able to turn their face-to-face content into e-content. Currently, the University had a total of 102 courses each having at least 5 modules, making e-content development a capital investment that would require proper planning to finance.

3.3 Organizational capabilities to effectively execute and deliver a blended learning programme

For students and staff to have meaningful engagement in the online platform, a number of materials and equipment needed to be made available. These include:

a. Computers or other hand held devices

b. Internet bundles

c. Online library resources

3.3.1 Basic computers for students and staff

It can be estimated that almost 80 percent of Maseno University students do not own basic computers. A big percentage of staff on the other hand had their personal Computers that they use in and out of the campus. It is important to note however that that there were still staff who did not own any personal computers. Therefore the university management made a big investment in computer resources within the computer labs for students where they get practical experience for the Information Technology courses it offers to all undergraduate students. But with the rise in undergraduate student numbers, the resources are still not enough. This means that in the current situation brought about by COVID-19 pandemic, it would be very difficult to engage student in online learning as most of them have been relying on University computer labs to get access. Staff offices are also fitted with computers that have internet access and this allows them to share the computers for work purposes. However, the University came up with a policy on "Bring your own device (BYOD)", so that students would be in a position to own at least some basic computer for classroom use. Such a policy was easier to implement for new students by including it in their calling letters. For continuing students, it required a lot of sensitization to get them to acquire computers and also implementation of the online examinations mandated every student to have a laptop with internet and a webcam. The examinations therefore became catalysts for the BYOD policy and accelerated its implementation.

3.3.2 Internet bundles

Maseno University students have always relied on the university Wi-Fi for their online engagement in academic work. Online learning requires dependable and constant internet for learning to succeed. The University through Kenya Education Network (KENET) engaged the local telecommunication companies through a government to private sector partnership programme on affordable internet provision to students. They offered the students an education bundle of 10GB at approximately 5 USD with unlimited access for one month. This allowed students to study from wherever they were and in future likely to ease the bandwidth demands within the University.

The offer from the telecommunication companies was very helpful for students who were at a place that had network connection. Even though most parts of Kenya are covered by these companies, it must be noted however that there are several regions in Kenya that still lack connectivity (National internet penetration stands at 43%, [46]). This makes it difficult to engage students equitably without bias on the online platform while they are at home because of diversity in locations and internet environment. The arrangement with private telecommunication providers has proved useful for students in the light of blended learning implementation as an institutional policy in future.

3.3.3 Library resources

Within the university Learning Management System, Maseno University has an e-library with an e-librarian deployed to assist students with access to virtual library resources. Access to e-resources is through the Maseno University website and online public access catalog (OPAC). The only missing link was for the e-library to install an EZ-proxy to allow students to access all electronic resources the University subscribes to from the comfort of their homes. Due to improved practice in blended learning at the university, the librarian developed innovative ways to make immense contribution in the knowledge era by supporting knowledge gathering, creation and dissemination using new technology-based tools. With these new developments, it is still instructive to note that most of the traditional professional knowledge that defines librarianship will remain essential; the profession will also need a new set of skills to adapt to the evolving environment of higher education [47]. He goes on to assert that responsive and scalable organization needed today and even more in the future will rely on a culture that embraces user awareness and engagement. It is also important to note that user populations will continue to evolve and libraries need robust user assessment programs that can scale what they learn about changing populations to revise and extend services with limited growth in resources. They also need to develop learning cultures that harvest trends, skills and local institutional dynamics delivering service and value to users and institutional decision makers. Scaling what they learn and what they do will better position the libraries for tomorrow's educational environment.

3.3.4 Student assessment

Blended learning at Maseno University drew a lot of its lessons on online assessment from its common courses that were already available on the online platform. These courses already attracted large student populations of up to six thousand students in one single offer. They included HIV/AIDS Course, Communication Skills, Common IT courses for School of Medicine and Nursing, and Common mathematics courses. For these courses to run successfully, all Continuous assessment Tests (CATs) were done on the online platform that allows for computer-based assessment. The Moodle platform used in the LMS was customized for computer-based assessment and an in-built grade book allows the students to view their results immediately. In the current situation where the University closed before summative assessment was undertaken, it became an urgent need to explore and identify software that could be used to offer the examinations online for students. This also meant that the policy examinations had to be reviewed to embed the

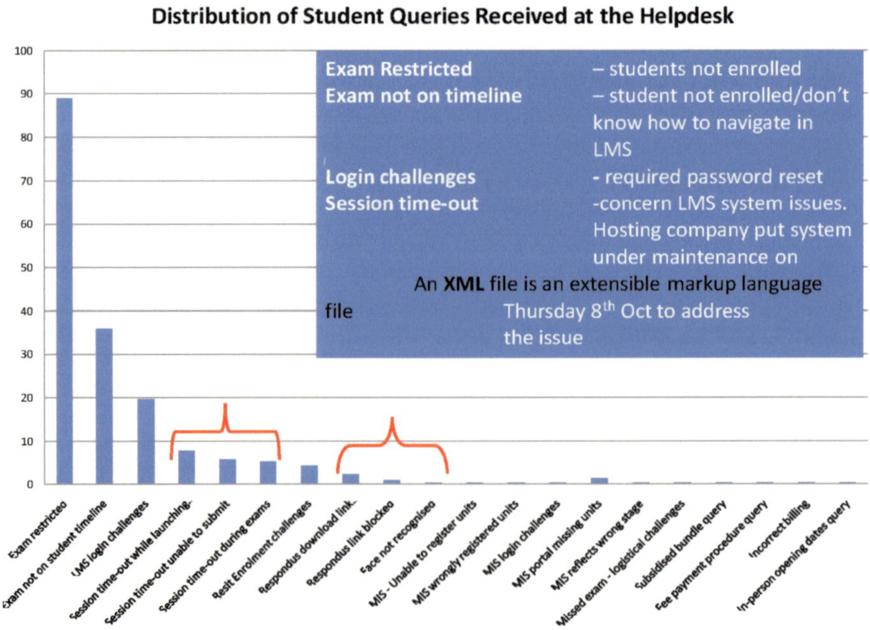

Figure 5.
Distribution of student queries from the helpdesk [48].

online examination component in the existing policy. This is because the examination policy had no provision for online examinations. With the reviewed policy, the University embarked on extensive planning for its first ever summative examinations covering all undergraduate students. This required the upgrade of the existing LMS from a concurrency of 1000 to 3000 and in a mode that was compatible with the safe exams browser; purchase of other software for examination like the script conversion software from word to Moodle compatible XML file. The team then embarked on a search for an online proctoring examination system existing currently in the market and yet affordable for use with the large number of students at the university. The experience and challenges experienced in these first online exams is presented in **Figure 5** [48].

3.3.5 Quality assurance measures in place

All Maseno University courses presented to Commission for University Education (Kenya) for approval to ensure they meet the requisite internal and external quality assurance mechanisms and standards. All the courses are approved for three different modes of offer: Face to Face offer, Blended Learning offer, and Online learning offer. This allows the university to be ready for any of these modes of offer by using the same content, but variation brought about by the classroom activity used.

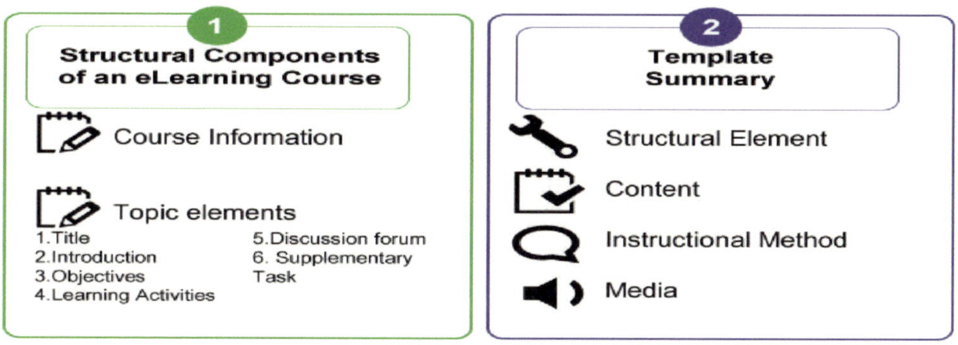

Figure 6.
Internal Maseno university eCampus QA tools for content development [49].

Figure 7.
eCampus Online Content Review Tools [49].

Furthermore, the eCampus has developed a series of tools that are used internally to measure and monitor quality both at the point of development and offer. Samples of these tools are appended below (**Figures 6** and 7) [49].

4. Choosing low cost but effective technologies for classroom instructions in the light of existing economic constraints within a university

In considering effectiveness, researchers contend that BL coalesces around access, success, and students' perception of their learning environments. Success and withdrawal rates for F2F and online courses are compared to those for BL as they interact [50] and outcomes show that BL students are more successful than either face to face or fully online learners. Blended learning is an innovative concept that embraces the advantages of both traditional teaching in the classroom and ICT supported learning including both offline learning and online learning. It has scope for collaborative learning; constructive learning and computer assisted learning (CAI). Blended learning needs rigorous efforts, right attitude, handsome budget and highly motivated teachers and students for its successful implementation because it incorporates diverse modes so it is complex and organizing it is a difficult task. The cost-effectiveness therefore of a BL technology is based on learner perception of the specific technology. According to the UNESCO Handbook [51] on flexible learning, affordable technologies largely available for institutions in Africa are categorized as in **Figure 8** [52] that follows.

The type of technologies for BL are based on six dimensions resources serve in a BL environment, namely infrastructure, learning tools, learning resources, teaching and learning methods, services for teachers and students, and cooperation between enterprise, government, and schools/institutions. These technologies were costed and presented to the university in terms of priority and summarized in the **Table 2** [53] that follows.

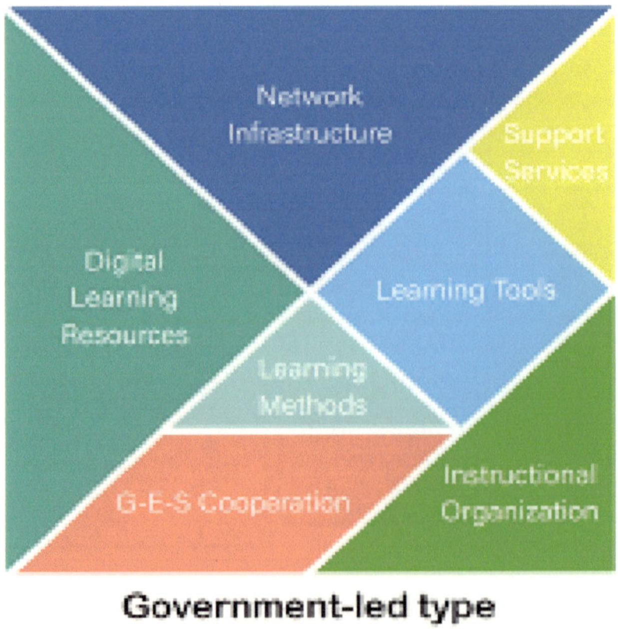

Figure 8.
Affordable technologies [52].

One Time Cost	Periodic Cost	Recurring Costs
• Bandwidth & Wireless/Wired Connectivity • Furniture • Power Access (laptop carts and/or wired outlets) • Design, Implementation & Consulting Services • Initial Professional Development	• Technology devices • Headphones and Other Accessories	• Learning management System • Licenses for Digital Content & Tools • Licenses for HLMS or Other Integrated Platforms • Blended Learning technical leads • Increased IT Support or IT staff

Table 2.
Priority on Technology for Blended Learning adapted from blended learning toolkit [53].

4.1 The MOODLE learning management system infrastructure

The main infrastructure at the eCampus for BL is the learning management system which runs on Moodle and supported by the Moodle community through continuous development and improvement. There are about 20 different types of activities available to Moodle users (forums, glossaries, wikis, assignments, quizzes, polls, scorm players, databases etc) and each can be customized to suit the user organization. This activity-based model permits combining of activities into sequences and groups, which can help a teacher guide participant through learning paths [54]. This LMS has been customized in such a way that it supports all the operations of the university listed above including student communities, administrative centres and teacher support areas. This becomes clear when we examine a representation of the eCampus at a glance presented as a **Figure 9** [55] below.

The use of technologies to enhance teaching and learning and help instructors and departments to process administrative work in Maseno University is flexible. A variety of simple web 4.0 tools are used to help learners generate content and interact with peers, such as blogs, wikis, and social networks [56]. Additionally, several technology-based communication mediums, such as emails, WhatsApp and instant messaging

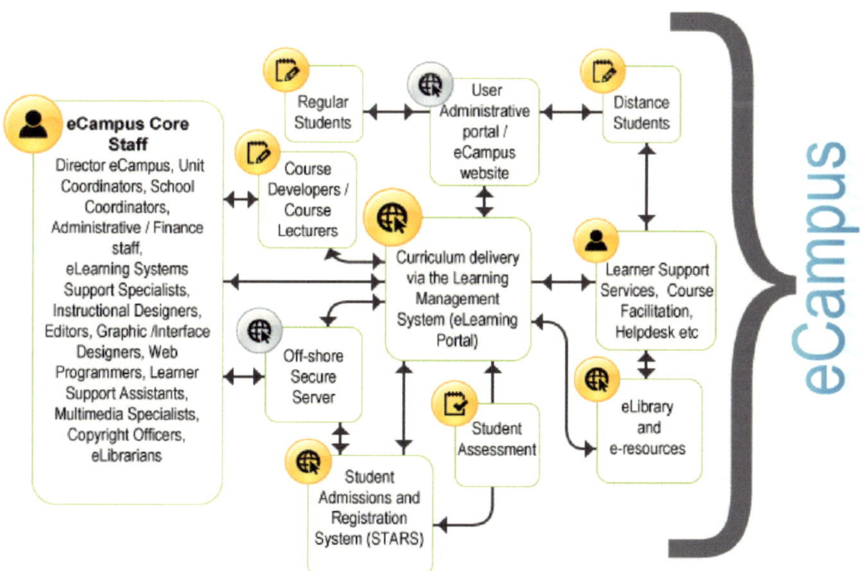

Figure 9.
Maseno university eCampus at a glance [55].

applications are used. This makes the instructors and administrative staffs' work much more convenient.Originally online learning in Maseno was limited to a few digital tools such as multimedia courseware, learning objects and on-line forum discussions, it has since expanded to include video conferencing in addition to audio and video streaming.

4.2 Gaps identified in the universities resource provision

The university set up a committee to assess the prevailing gaps in its provision of resources for blended learning and the following were duly identified.

eLearning Multimedia Spaces – these are physical spaces designated for content development and fully equipped with software and digital resources to enable formatting course content, audio and video recording, editing and upload of these resources onto the LMS.

Smart Classrooms – These are large lecture halls customized mounted with large screens and speakers to support BL. This allows it to accommodate the large numbers of students who may attend Common Units or courses with large student population. These halls are customized to hold the necessary multimedia equipment and fitted with smart screens where students can follow the scheduled live session as required and others from external locations following on their computers or phones.

Internet Access Points – these are necessary to allow for students' access to Learning Management System.The limited number of Wi-Fi access points across the university needed to be increased to allow for social distancing in an effort to meet the Ministry of Health (MoH) and Ministry of Education (MoE) requirements for social distancing and prevent crowding at the available access points.

Dedicated Computer Laboratory Space - To cater for the students who may desire to access the eLearning Platform (LMS) content while they are within the university grounds, but do not have web-enabled personal devices, a dedicated laboratory space equipped with access terminals and internet connectivity are required.

Capacity Building Gaps - There have been capacity building trainings for the teaching staff across Schools. Most of the trainings have however focused on online content development and the spread has not been uniform. Out of the thirteen Schools in the university four have received adequate exposure; three have received moderate exposure while five have received minimal exposure. The committee therefore identified the following as eLearning capacity gaps among the teaching staff to adequately handle the requisite components of eLearning: online content development; e-facilitation and e-moderation; technical skills for LMS; familiarity with proctoring systems for online assessment and skills to ensure quality assurance. The committee further identified the need for collaborations and mentorship that will lead to the development of these capacities with institutions and organizations such as University of Edinburgh, Association of Commonwealth Universities, The United Nations Educational, Scientific and Cultural Organization (UNESCO), Proctorio (an online examination proctoring company) and Cisco Systems. Further, the committee recommended pursuit of partnerships with institutions and organizations such as Volkswagen, Safaricom and Airtel that can facilitate acquisition of laptops for both teaching staff and students at low cost in order to improve access to eLearning.

Human Resource Gaps - In order to achieve quality in teaching and learning the committee noted that the university needs a strong and qualified staff in online pedagogy. For this to be actualized human, the committee noted that there was need to improve technical staff at the School of Education that trains in pedagogy of teaching and learning and the eCampus that trains in online pedagogy. Additional teaching and technical Staff in the School of Educationincluded Technician specialized in operations, Management & Maintenance; Technician specialized in multimedia Production, Multimedia production, Graphic Art and Photography, and Audio Visual projectionist.

Additional technical staff for required at the eCampus included a Coordinator for Research Monitoring and Evaluation to be responsible for quality assurance and standards, Copywrite Editor, Multi-Media resource Specialist, Web programmer, Graphic Designer, Data base administrator, and a Systems Specialist.

5. Lessons learned from MU's transition from face to face to online and blended learning

The transition in MU from F2F to ODTL became a learning laboratory for the university in various aspects of online and blended learning. The lessons learned can broadly be categorized into the following six areas: Attitude of Lecturers and Students; Online Assessment; Technologies; The Digital Divide; Change management; Capacity Building Best practice.

5.1 Attitude of lecturers and students

The forced shift from F2F to online and blended learning exposed the fact that a majority of lecturers and students had a strong negative attitude towards online learning activities. This came out mainly through the various social media platforms used by lecturers and students. The best lesson however was that with continued use, the attitude continued to improve. Secondly, the prevalent attitude made the university go back to the drawing board of having to deal with the negative attitude to improve future engagement as supported by other researchers [57–59].

5.2 Online assessment

The online assessment undertaken at MU during this period realized that the proportion of students who were eligible to do exams was 70.4%, meaning that 29.6% of the entire student population had not paid fees and/or registered in MIS hence were ineligible to take the examinations. It was further realized that only 32.4% of the total student population potentially qualified to progress to the next academic level. Nationally, this was the best performing university in online examinations both numerically and qualitatively, which was a good report for the university. But considering the low output from students, pertinent issues were raised on online assessment and by extension online learning. The barriers to assessment were more technological in nature as opposed to pedagogical. Most students had laptops that could not support the proctoring software; a large population had no laptops, network connectivity, and network coverage in their localities. A few students however cited lack of lecturer support during the online examinations as well as challenges with the proctoring software. These challenges became learning points in preparing students for the subsequent examinations. The best outcome from this experience though was the fact that the university integrated online examinations in its examination policy which opened the door for online examinations as a practice in the university. It further exposed the technical staff at the eCampus to a variety of proctoring soft-wares which allowed the team to identify a cost-effective proctoring system.

5.3 Technologies

One of the key benefits from the shift to online and blended learning in MU is the new technological investments the university management had to make in new learning technologies which will make immense contribution to improvement of the quality and equity towards course content and facilitation of online learning [60]. Continued use of these technologies (Zoom, BigBlueButton, LMS, examination proctoring system, video creation software etc.) is naturally killing technophobia and ushering the university into a new dawn.

5.4 The digital divide

The shift exposed the deep digital divide among government sponsored students in public universities. This was possibly the greatest hindrance to students realizing the full potential of e-learning, yet lecturers still expected students to submit assessment tasks and engage with course activities on the LMS. This confirms the sentiment that due to high level of digital divide between Africa countries and other nations of the world the global information society benefits are but mirage to the larger Africa society vis-à-vis higher educational institutions (HEIs) in Africa [61]. This digital divide among government sponsored students at MU is caused by social exclusion, digital exclusion and access factors [62–64] which has further led to digital exclusion. The digital exclusion was even direr among learners with special needs in MU as was the case for this learners in other institutions [65]. But hope is not lost as this exposure has led to Higher Education Loans Board in Kenya creating a fund for provision of laptops for government sponsored students in public universities in Kenya.

5.5 Change management

Implementing online education, the MU team discovered that it requires a comprehensive strategic approach to change management [66, 67]. The MU experience further exposed the fact that student attitudinal issues were as a result of challenges with access to technological tools needed. On the other hand, the lecturer attitudinal issues were mainly as a means of resisting change [68]. It is from this experience that the MU team learned that the most suitable way for change management in eLearning environment is capacity building and the negotiatory process of persuading the lecturers with a view to enhancing their digital literacy and thus gradually changing their attitude in a positive direction.

5.6 Capacity building best practice

Through the concluded experiences the following principles were realized through capacity building sessions: High relevance between online instructional design and student learning; Effective delivery of online instructional information impacts online learning; Adequate support provided by faculty and learner support assistants to students improves learning; High-quality and participatory and activity oriented content improves the breadth and depth of student's learning [69].

6. Conclusion

This chapter gives a detailed account on the need for Maseno University to adapt a flexible and blended learning approach which was as a result of the disruption caused by COVID-19. It gives details of the planning, the training and resource mobilization that was undertaken to make the move to blended learning possible. Throughout, the chapter refers to mentorship, training and studies of best practice that assisted in the transition from F2F to ODTL. It is hoped that other low budget universities can learn from this experience and have the courage to use low-cost technologies available in the market to give its students quality learning and collaborative experiences HEI students benefit from in blended learning.

Author details

Mildred Atieno Ayere
Maseno University, Kisumu, Kenya

*Address all correspondence to: mayere@maseno.ac.ke

References

[1] Osman, R. & Walton, E. (2020, August). The long-term goal for universities – Quality blended learning. University World News, The African Edition. https://www.universityworldnews.com/post.php?story=202008240939215

[2] Association of Commonwealth Universities (2020). Partnership for Enhanced and Blended Learning (PEBL). https://www.spheir.org.uk/partnership-profiles/partnership-enhanced-and-blended-learning

[3] Van der Merwe, C. (2020). Blended learning 'future of African higher education' https://www.researchprofessionalnews.com/rr-news-africa-pan-african-2020-5-blended-learning-seen-as-the-future-of-african-higher-education/

[4] Myroslava, P., Salla, A. & for the ARCADE consortium (2016) The experiences of lecturers in African, Asian and European universities in preparing and delivering blended health research methods courses: a qualitative study, Global Health Action, 9:1, DOI: 10.3402/gha.v9.28149

[5] Teräs, M., Suoranta, J., Teräs, H. & Curcher, M. (2020). Post-Covid-19 Education and Education Technology 'Solutionism': a Seller's Market. Postdigit Sci Educ 2, 863-878 (2020). https://doi.org/10.1007/s42438-020-00164-x

[6] Raja, R. &Nagasubramani (2018). Impact of Modern Technology in Education. Journal of Applied and Advanced Research 3(S1):33. https://www.researchgate.net/publication/325086709_Impact_of_modern_technology_in_education

[7] JISC (2020). Developing blended learning approaches. https://www.jisc.ac.uk/guides/creating-blended-learning-content

[8] Sinha, B. & Sahay, S. S. (2017). eContent: An Effective Tool For Blended Learning. National conference on "Emerging Trends in Education, January 2017. https://www.researchgate.net/publication/330650968_e-Content_An_Effective_Tool_For_Blended_Learning

[9] Huntley, J. & Neuberger, L. (2020). Digital and Blended Learning as a way to Improve Employment and Entrepreneur Outcomes. https://www.accenture.com/_acnmedia/pdf-5/accenture-digital-learning-report_short-version.pdf

[10] Weitze, C. L. (2016). Designing for Learning and Play - The Smiley Model as Framework. file:///C:/Users/USER/AppData/Local/Temp/CLWeitze_Designing_for_Learning_and_Play_The_Smiley_Model_as_a_Framework.pdf

[11] Kinash, S. (2019). How to Design & Deliver Quality Online Education. Education Technology Solutions. https://educationtechnologysolutions.com/2019/06/how-to-design-deliver-quality-online-education/

[12] Jordan, C. (Ed). (2017). Applying Best Practice Online Learning, Teaching, and Support to Intensive Online Environments: An Integrative Review. Frontiers in Education https://www.frontiersin.org/articles/10.3389/feduc.2017.00059/full

[13] Yuen, A. H. K. (2010). Blended Learning in Higher Education: An Exploration of Teaching Approaches. https://www.researchgate.net/publication/228718427_Blended_Learning_in_Higher_Education_An_Exploration_of_Teaching_Approaches

[14] Chattopadhyay, S. (2014). LearnerSupport Servicesin Open Distance Learning System:Case Study on IGNOU. http://eprints.rclis.org/29071/1/Learner_Support_Service_ODL_NSOU.pdf

[15] Gao, S. (2012). Learner Supportfor Distance LearnersA Study of Six Cases of ICT-basedDistance Education Institutions in China. Studies in International and Comparative Education. https://www.diva-portal.org/smash/get/diva2:570145/FULLTEXT01.pdf

[16] Shikulo, S. & Lekhetho, M. (2020). Exploring student support services of a distance learning centre at a Namibian university, Cogent Social Sciences, 6:1, DOI: 10.1080/23311886.2020.1737401

[17] Njui, H. M. (2018). Significance of Learner Support Services in Delivering Holistic Quality Education in Learning Institutions in Kenya

[18] Roddy, C., Amiet, D. L., Chung, J., Holt, C., Shaw, L., McKenzie, S., Garivaldis, F., Lodge, J. M., & Mundy, M. E. (2017). Applying Best Practice Online Learning, Teaching, and Support to Intensive Online Environments: An Integrative Review. https://www.frontiersin.org/articles/10.3389/feduc.2017.00059/full

[19] Anderson, T. (2016). The Enigma of Interaction. https://virtualcanuck.ca/2016/03/03/the-enigma-of-interaction/

[20] UNESCO. (2020). Beyond Disruption: digital learning during the COVID-19 pandemic. https://en.unesco.org/news/beyond-disruption-digital-learning-during-covid-19-pandemic

[21] Council of Europe (2020). A Roadmap for Action on the Council of Europe education response to COVID-19. https://rm.coe.int/making-the-right-to-education-a-reality-in-times-of-covid-19-a-roadmap/16809fee7b

[22] VVOB. (2020). Capacity development from a distance: 3 good practices. https://www.vvob.org/en/news/apacity-development-from-a-distance-3-good-practices

[23] Malinson, B. & Krull, G. (2013). Building Academic Staff Capacityto Support Online Learningin Developing Countries. https://files.eric.ed.gov/fulltext/EJ1018279.pdf

[24] Hansen, S. (Ed). (2018). Capacity Building in aChanging ICT Environment. International Telecommunication Union https://www.itu.int/dms_pub/itu-d/opb/phcb/D-PHCB-CAP_BLD.01-2018-PDF-E.pdf

[25] Aczel, J.C., Peake, S., & Hardy, P. (2008). Designing capacity-building in e-learning expertise: Challenges and strategies. Computers & Education 50(2):499-510

[26] Meyer, K. (2017). Capacity Building and Governance https://flores.unu.edu/en/news/news/technical-report.html

[27] Tinoco-Giraldo, H., Sanchez, E. M. T., & García-Peñalvo, F. J. (2020). E-Mentoring in Higher Education: A Structured Literature Review and Implications for Future Research. file:///C:/Users/USER/AppData/Local/Temp/sustainability-12-04344-v2.pdf

[28] Graves, S. M., Abbitt, J., Klett, M. D., & Wang, C. (2009). A Mentoring Model for Interactive Online Learning in Support of a Technology Innovation Challenge Grant. Innovation Challenge Grant. https://files.eric.ed.gov/fulltext/EJ856112.pdf

[29] Zaheer, M., Jabeen, S., & Majeed, M. (2015). Role of e-learning in capacity building: An Alumni View. Open Praxis 7(1):71-81, DOI: 10.5944/openpraxis.7.1.143

[30] UNESCO (2016). Designing effective monitoring and evaluation of education systems for 2030: A global synthesiss of policies and practices. http://www.unesco.org/new/fileadmin/MULTIMEDIA/HQ/ED/pdf/me-report.pdf

[31] OECD-DAC (2008). DAC Principles for Evaluation of Development

Assistance. https://www.oecd.org/development/evaluation/2755284.pdf

[32] Wang, L. (2020, November). Achieving access to quality blended learning for all. University World News, The Global Window on Higher Education https://www.universityworldnews.com/post.php?story=20201120123658883

[33] Govindarajan, V. & Srivastava, A. (2020). What the Shift to Virtual Learning Could Mean for the Future of Higher Ed. https://hbr.org/2020/03/what-the-shift-to-virtual-learning-could-mean-for-the-future-of-higher-ed

[34] Mpungose, C. B. (2020). Emergent transition from face-to-face to online learning in a South African University in the context of the Coronavirus pandemic. *Humanities and Social Sciences Communications*,7(113), 2020. https://www.nature.com/articles/s41599-020-00603-x

[35] Julien, G. & Dookwah, R. (2020). Students' transition from face to face learning to online learning at higher education: A case study in Trinidad and Tobago. *Educational Research and Reviews,*15(8), pp. 487-494, August, 2020. https://www.researchgate.net/publication/343996620_Students_transition_from_face_to_face_learning_to_online_learning_at_higher_education_A_case_study_in_Trinidad_and_Tobago

[36] Otten, L. (2020). Transitioning to Online Learning. https://diverseeducation.com/article/186510/

[37] Lederman, D. (2020). How Teaching Changed in the (Forced) Shift to Remote. https://www.insidehighered.com/digital-learning/article/2020/04/22/how-professors-changed-their-teaching-springs-shift-remote

[38] Horn, M. B. & Staker, H. (2015). Blended- Using Disruptive Innovation to Improve Schools. file:///C:/Users/USER/AppData/Local/Temp/Horn_Staker2015pp169-187.pdf

[39] Gonzales, S. (2013). Examining the relationship among high-school teachers' technology self-efficacy, attitudes towards technology integration, and quality of technology integration. https://search.proquest.com/openview/5fa924366fe2168c177a3cb827ee044f/1?pq-origsite=gscholar&cbl=18750&diss=y

[40] Shaunessy, E. (2007). Attitudes toward information technology of teachers of the gifted - Implications for gifted education. 50th Annual Conference of the National-Association-for-Gifted-Children, Volume: 51

[41] Duty, L., & Kern, T. (2014). So you think you want to innovate? Emerging lessons and a new tool for state and district leaders working to build a culture of innovation. Retrieved from http://learningaccelerator.org/media/29004d8f/Assessing%20Culture%20of%20Innovation_2Rev-TLA__10.9_final.pdf

[42] Bhaskar, S. K. (2013). Different forms of Blended Learning in Classroom. https://edtechreview.in/trends-insights/trends/562-different-forms-of-blended-learning-in-classroom

[43] Porter, W. W., Graham, C. R., Spring, K. A., & Welch, K. R. (2014). Blended learning in higher education: Institutional adoption and implementation. Computers & Education, 75, pp185-195, June 2014. https://www.sciencedirect.com/science/article/abs/pii/S0360131514000451

[44] Poon, J. (2013). Blended Learning: An Institutional Approach for Enhancing Students' Learning Experiences. *MERLOT Journal of Online Learning and Teaching*, 9(2), 271-288, June 2013. https://jolt.merlot.org/vol9no2/poon_0613.pdf

[45] Anthony, B., Kamaludin, A., Romli, A., Raffei, A. F. M., Phon, D. N., Abdullah, A. & Ming, G. L. (2020). Blended Learning Adoption and Implementation in Higher Education: A Theoretical and Systematic Review. Tech Know Learn. https://doi.org/10.1007/s10758-020-09477-z

[46] Graham, C. R., Woodfield, W., & Harisson, J. B. (2012). A framework for institutional adoption and implementation of blended learning inhigher education. Internet and Higher Education, 18 (2013) 4-14. https://blendedtoolkit.wisc.edu/wp-content/uploads/2015/03/Framework-for-Institutional-Adoption-and-Implementation-of-Blended-Learning-in-Higher-Education.pdf

[47] Internet World Stats 2020 https://www.internetworldstats.com/africa.htm

[48] The Andango Committee. (2020). Maseno Univesity Report of the Performance of Online Examinations. Unpublished Maseno University Report.

[49] eCampus. (2020). Revised Course Development Framework. Unpublished Maseno University eCampus publication

[50] Keisling, B. (2018). Blended learning: Scaling library services and instruction to support changing educational landscapes. https://www.emerald.com/insight/content/doi/10.1108/LM-08-2017-0080/full/html

[51] Dziuban, C., Graham, C.R., Moskal, P.D. et al. Blended learning: the new normal and emerging technologies. Int J Educ Technol High Educ 15, 3 (2018). https://doi.org/10.1186/s41239-017-0087-5

[52] Huang, R.H., Liu, D.J., Tlili, A., Yang, J.F., Wang, H.H., et al. (2020). Handbook on Facilitating Flexible Learning During Educational Disruption: The Chinese Experience in Maintaining Undisrupted Learning in COVID-19 Outbreak. Beijing: Smart Learning Institute of Beijing Normal University.

[53] Hannon, K. & Macken, C. (2014). Blended and Online Learning Curriculum Design Toolkit. https://www.latrobe.edu.au/__data/assets/pdf_file/0006/602178/Blended-learning-Toolkit-v4.pdf

[54] Underhill, D. (2013). Moodle and Constructivism. http://etec.ctlt.ubc.ca/510wiki/Moodle_and_Constructivism

[55] eCampus . (2012). The eCampus of Maseno: 1 year on. Unpublished Maseno University eCampus publication

[56] Gordon, H. (2014). Flexible Pedagogies: technology-enhanced learning. https://www.heacademy.ac.uk/sites/default/files/resources/TEL_report_0.pdf

[57] Omar, N. D., Hassan, H., & Atan, H. (2012). Student Engagement in Online Learning: Learners Attitude Toward E-Mentoring. The 3rd International Conference on e-Learning ICEL2011, 23-24 November 2011, Bandung, Indonesia. https://link.springer.com/article/10.1007/s42438-020-00155-y

[58] Zhu, Y., Au, W., & YATES, G. C. R. (2013). University Students' Attitudes toward Online Learning in a Blended Course. A Paper Presented in AARE Conference in Adelaide. https://files.eric.ed.gov/fulltext/ED603297.pdf

[59] Valantinaite, I. & Sedereviciute-Pa-ciauskiene, Z. (2020). The Change in Students' Attitude towards Favourable and Unfavourable Factors of Online Learning Environments. file:///C:/Users/USER/Downloads/sustainability-12-07960.pdf

[60] UNESCO. (2020). COVID-19 and higher education: Today and tomorrow. Impact analysis, policy responses and recommendations http://www.iesalc.unesco.org/en/wp-content/uploads/2020/04/COVID-19-EN-090420-2.pdf

[61] Ilevbare, G. E. (2019). Bridging the Digital Divide: The Role of Higher Education Institutions in Getting Africa Closer to the Global Information Society. https://events.aau.org/corevip/wp-content/uploads/sites/3/2019/11/BRIDGING-THE-DIGITAL-DIVIDE.-THE-ROLE-OF-HIGHER-EDUCATION-INSTITUTIONS-IN-GETTING-AFRICA-CLOSER-TO-THE-GLOBAL-INFORMATION-SOCIETY.pdf

[62] Khalid, S. & Pedersen, M. J. L. (2016). Digital exclusion in higher education contexts: A systematic literature review. 2nd International Conference on Higher Education Advances, HEAd´16, 21-23 June 2016, València, Spain. Procedia - Social and Behavioral Sciences 228 (2016) 614-621. https://pdf.sciencedirectassets.com/277811/1-s2.0-S1877042816X00146/1-s2.0-S1877042816310205/main.pdf?

[63] O'Malley, B. (2020). Digital divide 'catastrophic' for many students – World Bank. https://www.universityworldnews.com/post.php?story=20201121084401266

[64] Matlali, L. (2020). How can Africa prepare its education system for the post-COVID world? https://www.weforum.org/agenda/2020/10/how-can-africa-pivot-its-education-system-using-enthusiasm-of-covid-reset/

[65] Oguna, D. W. & Cherotich, W. (2020). Expanding Inclusion of Learning Opportunities for Children with Special Education Needs. https://palnetwork.org/expanding-inclusion-of-learning-opportunities-for-children-with-special-education-needs/

[66] Navarro, P. How economics faculty can survive (and perhaps thrive) in a brave new online world. The Journal of Economic Perspectives, 29, 4 (2015), 155-176.

[67] Lisewski, B. (2016). Implementing a learning technology strategy: top–down strategy meets bottom–up culture. https://www.tandfonline.com/doi/full/10.1080/0968776042000216228

[68] Parlakkılıç, A. (2014). Change Management in Transition to E-learning System. http://qqml.net/papers/September_2014_Issue/338QQML_Journal_2014_Parlakkilic_Sept_637-651.pdf

[69] Bao, W. (2020). COVID-19 and online teaching in higher education: A case study of Peking University. Human Behavior and Emerging Technologies 2(11)

Chapter 7

Using Synchronous vs. Asynchronous Methods during the COVID-19 Pandemic in Malaysia: Preservice and In-Service Teachers' Perspectives

Charanjit Kaur Swaran Singh, Noor Alhusna Madzlan, Eng Tek Ong, Revathi Gopal, Mazura Mastura Muhammad, Siti Shuhaida Shukor, Nor Azmi Mostafa, Tarsame Singh Masa Singh and Mahendran Maniam

Abstract

The world witnessed the outbreak of the Coronavirus (2019-nCoV) with lockdowns that forced most schools and other educational institutions to close down. Alternative approaches in the form of synchronous and asynchronous methods were adopted to ensure continuity in teaching and learning in this new norm of providing emergency remote education. This chapter aims at presenting preservice and in-service teachers' views on using synchronous versus asynchronous teaching and learning methods during the COVID-19 pandemic in Malaysia. Data were elicited from three groups of preservice teachers and one group of in-service teachers from three different courses in one teacher education university in Malaysia. Implementation of the e learning approaches including synchronous and asynchronous sessions was planned carefully based on the course learning outcomes. Important elements such as identification of the learning platform, delivering and conveying information to preservice teachers about the e-learning activities, assessment strategies, attendance, and students' reflection were taken into consideration.

Keywords: synchronous method, asynchronous method, preservice teachers, in-service teachers, COVID-19, Malaysia

1. Introduction

The world witnessed the outbreak of the Coronavirus (2019-nCoV) with lockdowns that forced most schools and other learning institutions to close down. Alternative approaches in the form of synchronous and asynchronous methods were adopted to ensure continuity in teaching and learning in this new norm of emergency remote education. The COVID-19 outbreak has led most educators to using the blended synchronous approach to cover teaching and learning in the higher education context [1]. The blended synchronous approach promotes learning that allows students to engage online at their own pace at different locations in learning as they are unable to join traditional face-to-face classes at the universities. However, this barrier does not limit and constrain learning as sharing of knowledge and collaboration still take place [1]. Only a handful of studies have been carried out to show the positive results of the blended synchronous approach [2, 3]. More studies are needed to be carried out to explore how educators and students benefit from different kinds of blended synchronous approaches.

Access to ICT-supported teaching and learning was made possible for students in higher education institutions (HEIs) to study online despite the COVID-19 pandemic outbreak. This is supported by previous studies [4, 5]. Past studies focused on students' achievement and satisfaction in learning [6, 7], but the benefits of online real-time presentation learning and comparison studies focused on the effectiveness of online learning [6, 7]. Nevertheless, studies on asynchronous and synchronous learning in the context of higher learning institutions are scarce.

Students in HEIs embrace both face-to-face and offline teaching and learning modes. Due to the pandemic outbreak, face-to-face classes were replaced with asynchronous and synchronous online teaching and learning methods to ensure continuation in instruction. Synchronous learning is online learning that employs video conferencing and other multimedia techniques to allow lecturers and students to interact with each other at the same time even if they are not at the same place. It is, therefore, also referred to as "live" or real-time instruction. Asynchronous learning is offline teaching and learning that allow students to learn independently, as there is no real-time interaction with anyone. According to previous research [8, 9], students can benefit more when these face-to-face and online teaching and learning modes are blended together. Chen et al. [2] noted that blending face-to-face and offline teaching modes enable lecturers in the HEIs to come up with ground-breaking innovation in pedagogy to enhance educational learning experiences linking to ICT. However, many controversial issues arise from implementing both asynchronous learning and synchronous learning as compared with face-to-face lectures.

This study is guided by the Community of Inquiry (CoI) framework proposed by Garrison et al. [10]. The CoI framework represents students' experiences in asynchronous and synchronous online teaching and learning. Students are viewed as an educational CoI who continuously collaborate and engage in meaningful and purposeful critical discussion to reflect and construct mastery of learning. Meaningful educational experiences develop at the juncture of teaching, social, and cognitive occurrences. The CoI framework shows a process of developing constructive and meaningful learning experiences from the three main components namely social, cognitive, and teaching presence.

According to Garrison et al. [11], social presence refers to participants' ability to recognize and stay connected with the community (e.g., during the course of study), relay and communicate in a meaningful way in their surroundings, and develop positive relationships by exhibiting unique individual personalities. Teaching presence refers to the strategy, design, and simplification to promote cognitive and social processes for the need to ensure the realization of personal and meaningful processes engaging in the education context in order to achieve the learning outcomes [12]. Cognitive presence refers to learners' motivation to be able to create and confirm meaning through sustained reflection and communication [12].

1.1 Context of the study

This chapter aims at presenting preservice and in-service teachers' views on using synchronous vs. asynchronous methods during the COVID-19 pandemic in

Malaysia. How did the students perceive the blended synchronous approach on attaining the planned learning outcomes? In this context, the term "educators" is used for both "preservice" and "in-service" teachers who were students at the university. The findings of this study highlight information regarding educators' teaching and learning practices involving ICT. With regard to this aim, this study addressed the following two research questions:

- What are the experiences of the educators in synchronous learning situations?
- What are the experiences of the educators in asynchronous learning situations?

2. Methodology

This study employed a qualitative research design that reports the findings about the experiences of preservice and in-service teachers in asynchronous and synchronous learning mode during their teacher education program at the university. All the participants of the study are studying and have enrolled in the same teacher education university. This qualitative study explored and made sense of human views, perspectives, experiences, and communication that would permit searching further into the phenomenon being investigated from the participant perspectives [13].

2.1 Research participants and sampling

The research participants were selected based on purposeful sampling [13]. This sampling method allows the researchers to select information-rich cases related to the phenomenon of interest. In this case, the phenomenon of interest refers to participants who were exposed to the use of the asynchronous method.

There are three groups of research participants who participated in this study. The first group consists of 26 preservice teachers enrolled in the English Grammar course and the second group consists of 67 preservice teachers from the Final Year project who were taught and exposed to the asynchronous method. Among the preservice teachers, only seven were agreed to share their reflections on the use of the asynchronous method. The third group consists of six postgraduate students who were exposed to the synchronous learning method. Out of the six postgraduate students from the third group who have registered for the current trends in English language teaching (ELT) course, only four submitted their reflections on the use of the synchronous method. Only one lecturer participated in the study and this lecturer taught all the three groups using both the synchronous and asynchronous methods.

2.2 Data collection

2.2.1 Synchronous learning

Synchronous learning is possible when the students have good access and connection to the Internet. All the teaching and learning materials were prepared based on the course Proforma, an official document that contains all the important details of the course synopsis, course learning outcomes, detailed assessment activities, assignments to be completed within the stipulated time of the study in a semester. Each semester consists of 14 weeks of lectures.

The lecturer is allowed to be flexible in terms of teaching and learning whereby after the teaching session ends, the lecturer can incorporate games in the form of Kahoot quizzes to assess student understanding and mastery of the topics taught.

Lecturer-student engagement and student–student engagement are allowed for idea exchange after the lecture. For synchronous learning, both the lecturer and students have to be online at the same time. This means the lectures, students' presentations, assessments, and discussions would take place at a specified time given by the lecturer. When students are online, they are allowed to participate and interact with other students at the time set by the lecturer. For this study, the students are aware of their lecture schedule that have been fixed on every Saturday. For this purpose, the students would spend some time to do revision based on the topic assigned for discussion before they attend the lecture.

As for the postgraduate class, the lecturer taught the students synchronized online teaching and learning for 2 h. During the session with the postgraduate students, they were allowed to interrupt the lecture to pose questions related to the topics taught. Students were allowed to interact with one another after the lecture session ended. Students were asked to share their views on topics discussed.

2.2.2 Asynchronous learning

Asynchronous learning was designed to fulfill the learning needs of students who could not access or have poor Internet connection due to their location or remoteness. The lecturer recorded the lesson on a weekly basis via the Zoom platform. Then, the video-recorded lesson of the week would be saved and transferred into an MP4 file to be shared with the students through WhatsApp. In other words, students in the asynchronous learning group would listen to the video-recorded lesson at their own pace and time. The lecturer gives the student a time frame for mastering and understanding the video lesson. As for asynchronous learning, the lecturer followed the course Proforma. Students were allowed to text their lecturer to seek assistance if they encountered problems in understanding the video content.

3. Data analysis

Data obtained from the students' personal reflective notes were analyzed thematically [13]. The themes were derived from the students' reflective notes. The selected excerpts from the students' personal reflective notes were coded and analyzed thematically and then categorized into themes and sub-themes as shown in **Table 1**. The end of every excerpt is attached with a [Tn], where n indicates the participant. Hence, as shown in **Table 1**, two major themes were identified in relation to using synchronous vs. asynchronous methods through qualitative thematic analysis of the open-ended question.

The themes are divided based on the two research questions. The themes that emerged under the "What are the experiences of the educators in synchronous learning situation?" are divided into perceived advantages and perceived challenges in synchronous learning situations. Under the main theme of perceived advantages, the sub-themes include opportunities for digital collaboration ideas, opportunities to engage students for learning, and opportunities for collaboration. As for the perceived challenges, only one sub-theme emerged lack of information to align technology with teaching objectives.

As for the second research question, "What are the experiences of the educators in asynchronous learning situation?" two main themes namely perceived advantages and perceived challenges emerged for the asynchronous learning situation. Under the main theme of perceived advantages, five sub-themes emerged namely opportunities to access learning materials, opportunities for Community of inquiry, opportunities to collaborate with peers, opportunities for self-directed learning,

Themes	Sub-themes	Selected excerpts
Question: What are the experiences of the educators in synchronous learning situations?		
Perceived advantages	Opportunities for digital collaboration ideas	Her lecturer decided to start by sharing simpler digital collaboration ideas, recorded YouTube channels, and game-based learning platforms such as Kahoot [A1] Educators need to start learning and using technology in the classroom, and parents need to be onboard by supporting schools in utilizing digital education tools [D1]
	Opportunities to engage students for learning	Engaging students as much as possible in discussions and providing guidance (with the aid of technologies [B1] Synchronous learning allows the lecturer to still control the class and give instant feedback to the students on [C1] Students get excited to learn through online and are very engaged [D1]
	Opportunities for collaboration	According to Student D1, he and his classmates love to collaborate and be involved in class discussions [D1]
Perceived challenges	Lack of information to align technology with teaching objectives	The main concern should be how to better combine information technologies with teaching objectives [B1]
Question: What are the experiences of the educators in asynchronous learning situations?		
Perceived advantages	Opportunities for learning	The asynchronous learning allowed him to access the learning materials anytime [SA] Asynchronous learning can provide students with opportunities and advantages for learning [SA] Asynchronous learning gives students the freedom to access it whenever they want, there is a possibility that students might not view the recorded lessons or the uploaded materials [SE] She expressed that she could choose whenever she wanted to study the subject or topic [SF] I find asynchronous learning has provided students with the privilege of learning independently without having to worry about Internet accessibility [SG]
	Opportunities for Community of inquiry	He further shared that he was able to discuss and create a community of inquiry and learning by collaborating with his peers [SA]
	Opportunities to access learning materials	I can collaborate with peers [SC]
	Opportunities for self-directed learning.	Asynchronous learning allows her to learn at her own pace [SB]
	Opportunities to self-monitor learning	I have to undergo online learning and self-monitoring because of the pandemic, she admitted that she is now a lot more aware of tasks given [SC] She shared that she was still able to study at her own pace with asynchronous learning [SD]
Perceived challenges	Poor access to the Internet	He encountered problems accessing learning materials online due to poor Internet access [SA]
	Lack of interaction with peers	The risk with asynchronous learning is that it can be a lonely experience not having classmates and the lecturer around to share ideas and knowledge [SB] Asynchronous learning lacks classroom engagement as students learn in different periods [SF]

Table 1.
Selected excerpts from the students' personal reflective notes.

and opportunities to self-monitor learning. As for the perceived challenges, only two sub-themes emerged namely poor access to the Internet and lack of interaction with peers.

3.1 Findings from the asynchronous learning group

As seen in **Table 1**, the main and sub-themes that emerged based on the students' personal reflective notes were analyzed thematically to show how the participants benefited from using synchronous vs. asynchronous methods based on their perceived advantages and perceived challenges.

3.2 Findings from the asynchronous learning group

3.2.1 Perceived advantages in asynchronous learning situation

3.2.1.1 Opportunities for learning

According to student A, he finds that asynchronous learning can provide students with opportunities and advantages for learning. He had to return to his hometown after the lockdown. However, the asynchronous learning method assisted him in accessing materials in a more convenient way as he did not have to worry about poor Internet connection anymore. The asynchronous learning allowed him to access the learning materials anytime.

Next, with asynchronous learning also, Student A could refer to the learning materials from time to time. The asynchronous learning method allowed him to permanently store and save learning materials in his personal computer. He expressed that whenever he faced any confusion or if he was unable to understand certain topics, he would just need to refer to the learning material that his lecturer has provided to them through any approachable platform such as the MyGuru platform (Learning Management System set up by the university). However, he shared that his lecturer permitted him to personally text or mail her if he wanted to enquire about topics taught through the recorded lessons.

As for Student G, he finds asynchronous learning has provided students with the privilege of learning independently without having to worry about Internet accessibility. As he acknowledged, synchronous learning requires the two-way interaction with students and lecturers, of which classes are conducted online, and many of them have difficulties and issues pertaining to that matter. Students in rural or underdeveloped areas may experience inaccessibility as some regions lack a proper or stable Internet connection. Thus, asynchronous learning offers a more flexible, relaxing, and organized time management for students to learn subjects on their own time and in a preferred space without having to worry about "always on" Internet connection.

Besides that, asynchronous learning equips students with more opportunities to learn in a compact and wholesome experience. In this case, Student G believes that students are more organized in grasping knowledge and obtaining resources faster than having to rely on lecturers solely. Students may ask lecturers for further justification and may contact them efficiently without having to worry about missing out in classes. Student G believes that the learning process should be focusing at his own pace and how he can understand particular subjects without rushing and fear of missing out. Therefore, his choice in online learning leans strongly toward asynchronous, as it offers him the choice to learn better and improve his learning experience in his own way, to provide himself with the time he needs to learn certain topics in a more comprehensive manner.

Lastly, Student G rarely frets about getting a poor connection, because he has a strong, stable connection in his house due to WIFI. However, those students, who are poor, underprivileged and may not afford to pay expensive bills weekly or monthly, may find this issue extremely worrying because they might not catch up with online classes. Hence, lecturers may share their materials online, and students are free to check and complete their tasks within the time frame given. All in all, asynchronous learning provides flexibility, a better learning experience, and affordability for all students. Student G advocates asynchronous learning as the main online education experience.

According to Student E, asynchronous learning gives equal learning opportunities to both students with a stable and unstable Internet connection as the materials or lessons uploaded by the educator can be downloaded and reviewed over a longer period. Compared to synchronous online learning where students are expected to attend class within a set time, asynchronous learning offers students the flexibility to do so. This is especially advantageous to the students who have part-time jobs or a large family, which makes it harder for them to attend online classes at fixed times.

While living at home, students may have to prioritize other matters than their studies such as helping their family's business or taking care of their younger siblings; so, asynchronous learning is a solution that benefits these students. Next, since asynchronous learning helps students to store the materials and lessons in their own storage space, there is little concern of some students being left behind in a lesson compared to their friends. With synchronous learning, some students might miss classes and the ongoing lesson might not be recorded by the lecturer. This is different from asynchronous learning where one can access the stored data wherever and whenever needed. However, as asynchronous learning gives students the freedom to access it whenever they want, there is a possibility that students might not view the recorded lessons or the uploaded materials. As a suggestion, the educator can ask students to summarize their findings from the lessons or the materials within a period and upload them on a platform set by the lecturer. Questions and instructions such as "What are the important points that you get from this particular lesson?" or "Summarise your findings from this week's video" will encourage students to review the materials.

3.2.1.2 Opportunities for community of inquiry

Asynchronous learning provides the opportunities for students to be able to discuss and create a community of inquiry and learning by collaborating with peers. One advantage of asynchronous learning is that it is hassle-free for students who had to balance their time with house chores and studies especially when they had to learn and join online learning in their homes because of the movement control order.

3.2.1.3 Opportunities to access learning materials

The asynchronous method adopted by the lecturer was quite helpful for so many reasons. It is convenient and adaptable despite the condition. Student C expressed that asynchronous learning works well only if there is enough guidance and useful materials provided. She believes that being in university means one has to learn to be independent and cannot expect the lecturers to spoon-feed students all the time. At the same time, she also feels that lecturers should equip students with proper notes and tasks for a particular course; then, asynchronous learning will be more effective.

According to student C, if a new subtopic in a subject of the syllabus is introduced, sufficient materials should be provided so that the students can comprehend the content delivered confidently. "Hence why I think asynchronous learning could still work provided materials are given beforehand." The material in this context also means additional notes that students can make full use of to do reading to gain more understanding of the assignment. For example, "an assignment is given based on Week 7 material posted on Myguru. The material stated should then be easily accessed by students and lecturers to monitor as well. With this clear instruction, I think more students will benefit from it. Explanations are also needed with the materials provided. Some may not have the coverage to access classes online; therefore, some of my lecturers opted to prerecord their lessons to be accessed whenever the rest are able to. One of the disadvantages of using asynchronous learning is when some subjects lacked guidance in explaining the subject or requirement of each task. Some students have been experiencing this over the online distance learning (ODL) and it affects their work pace."

According to Student C, asynchronous learning builds up individual discipline. She admitted that she used to depend a lot on attending physical classes to stay updated on her learning; however, ever since they had to undergo online learning and self-monitoring because of the pandemic, she admitted that she is now a lot more aware of tasks given. Asynchronous learning requires one to be diligent in accessing the materials or search on each subject's requirement and this is why she thinks in a way that it builds more positive character in students if it is taken seriously. It helps an individual in being independent to go out of the comfort zone to reach out to lecturers themselves for inquiries and work through their assignments with all the information they have gathered.

3.2.1.4 Opportunities for self-directed learning

Student B believes that learning took place better *via* asynchronous learning. She further shared that asynchronous learning may seem a little difficult for some students because they do not have the lecturer present physically in front of them to explain certain topics. She also believes that this learning method depends on the individual. Asynchronous learning allows her to learn at her own pace and time and she feels that many would not take advantage of it by learning what is given later and maybe skip parts if they are lazy to listen to the lectures.

Student B shared that she personally prefers the asynchronous learning method. It allowed her to access the recorded lectures within a flexible time frame. Furthermore, she relates her learning to her introverted attitude as a student as she prefers to learn individually at a very quiet place. She shared that the asynchronous learning method was similar to researching about something she could not master and by doing this, she could learn better. She shared that when a lecture is going on, it cannot be repeated and that one needed to catch up really fast when the lecturer is speaking. But through asynchronous learning and materials given to her, she could replay the material whenever she needs to and learns better in a sense. Learning in an asynchronous learning environment is reasonable due to the pace.

Student B prefers to study at her own pace. She does not feel pressured while learning this way; she said that while "someone does a face-to-face meeting; you feel pressured where you have to be attentive and keep jotting things down as they speak. This also helps us in terms of replay the lecture, take notes and practice it without the concern of you being worried of the speed of lecturers when they conduct a class."

Besides that, Student B feels that online learning saves a lot of money where she just has to submit her work online and does not have to print anything before submitting it to the lecturer. In this manner, Student B shared that she could save cost and paper. Learning individually is totally fine but when it comes to group work, it is a little hard to contact especially those who do not have a stable or good Internet connection in their areas. It is best to segregate tasks than sending in and compiling it when it is done. Student feedback should be collected for the upcoming semester, to lessen group work if needed.

The risk with asynchronous learning is that it can be a lonely experience not having classmates and the lecturer around to share ideas and knowledge in a better way. The intellectual energy is not delivered in the same way. It is even difficult to have everyone sharing ideas and discussing online simply because they do not wish to but when one is in class one has to discuss. There would be a lack of discussion and feedback when asynchronous learning takes place. Basically, asynchronous learning is where students get all the vital materials to learn and it is up to them to complete learning at their own convenience.

3.2.1.5 Opportunities to self-monitor learning

Based on Student D's reflection, she found asynchronous learning brought convenience in her studies. This is because she realized that the entire learning now would depend on a good Internet service for her to complete her studies in current semester due to the COVID-19 pandemic. She shared that she was still able to study at her own pace with asynchronous learning. Some students with poor Internet access were unable to join the online learning classes and this disrupted the learning process merely for students in rural areas. Student D was grateful as some of her classes initiated asynchronous learning style, and this enables her to keep track of her studies in her free time by watching the videos and notes uploaded by the lecturers. Other than that, regarding attendance, there should be other ways such as giving homework to ensure student attendance is acknowledged so that students will not be accused of being absent. All in all, it is not wrong to have online classes but educators really need to consider other students who are having Internet difficulties as well. This could be simply solved by having a survey on what option the students prefer. Student D concluded by stating asynchronous learning was always the better option.

3.2.2 Perceived challenges

3.2.2.1 Poor access to internet

Student A views asynchronous learning can be difficult for those having problems with Internet connection. He encountered problems accessing learning materials online due to poor Internet access. He had to find ways to solve this problem so that he could view the recorded lecture videos posted by his lecturer.

3.2.2.2 Lack of interaction with peers

Student F shared that asynchronous learning was being implemented during the whole semester due to the pandemic happening in the country. Thus, some lecturers opt to use asynchronous learning for the whole semester. Student F felt that asynchronous learning helped her in learning the subject or the topic better since it offered flexible time. Student F expressed that she could choose whenever she wanted to study the subject or topic. The learning session can be accessed at her own time because it was done as a podcast or prerecorded lecture.

She felt that asynchronous learning lacks classroom engagement as students learn in different periods. If she had confusion regarding a topic, she was unable to get immediate feedback from friends as they might have not learned it yet; but using asynchronous learning, she could read and learn the topic at her own pace.

There is no pressure for Student F to complete the topic before the next class. This gives Student F the chance to review the information, take notes, and complete the tasks provided at her own pace.

Student F feels comfortable as she does not have to rush to complete the tasks. This is because she feels that she gets more opportunities to learn or explore more about the topic. But sometimes she feels asynchronous learning as a lonelier learning experience since it cannot deliver the same vibe or energy as a real-time interaction. This can interface with the debate or discussion between the classmates, and the students might have a lack of social interaction and classroom engagement. Lastly, if given a choice, she would choose a mixed type of learning as both types of learning to have their advantages and disadvantages.

3.3 Findings from the synchronous learning group

3.3.1 Perceived advantages in synchronous learning situation

3.3.1.1 Opportunities for digital collaboration ideas

Student A1 is a postgraduate student and is also working as a teacher at the same time. She experienced the synchronous learning due to the COVID-19 pandemic and lockdown that forced the entire higher learning institutions to close down. She expressed that the world she knew was about to undergo one of the most dramatic changes ever experienced. As for her postgraduate lesson made possible *via* synchronous learning, she shared that her lecturer set up a message group for her group to communicate important details about the classes and also to share other concerns related to teaching and learning activities.

She also feels that the lecturer's approach to set up a message group has been very comforting as it allowed them to share their concerns and has brought them even closer together as a team. For teaching and learning to take place in this pandemic situation, her lecturer applied synchronous learning approach to teach the current trends in English language teaching course. Her lecturer used one platform namely Zoom for students to join the class. Her lecturer decided to start by sharing simpler digital collaboration ideas, recorded YouTube channels, and game-based learning platforms such as Kahoot! Student A1 shared that her lecturer was aware of the lack of resources faced by some students, but she also knew how popular and powerful the mobile phone is and how it can be used to overcome the huge digital divide.

Synchronous learning employs video conferencing and other multimedia techniques to allow lecturers and students to interact with each other at the same time even if they are not at the same place. It is therefore also referred to as "live" or real-time instruction. In addition, synchronous learning also provides discussion rooms that allow students to ask questions and share ideas online. During the discussion period in her class, her lecturer observed the interaction among students and the discussion content of the whole class, and gave students appropriate support whenever needed.

In order to prevent the problems of distraction during the course program, the lecturer asked students to answer some questions by text or audio. All such conversations along with contents can be recorded using tools such as Zoom and made available to the students for review either after completion of the class or in the form of course material for asynchronous learning. This possibility does not exist in traditional face-to-face teaching.

First day of the live online learning experience was a mixture of excitement, worry, and apprehension. The experience of synchronous teaching and learning has been both challenging and rewarding. Student A1 expressed that the purpose of communication is not limited to imparting knowledge but it helps her to learn and retain the information shared during the teaching and learning session. Lecturer's amiable nature can inspire students to participate more during the instruction and also express their anxiety coping with challenges and stress during the COVID-19 pandemic. It shows them other possibilities and encourages them on their journey to learn a foreign language, which is likely to play an important role in their future.

3.3.1.2 Opportunities to engage students for learning

Synchronous sessions should be dedicated to three major tasks rather than just knowledge delivery on the teachers' part so as to help students as much as possible: making comments on students' learning progress (praise, encourage, remind, urge, punish, etc.) and giving more specific feedback (and sometimes quiz may be used to assess students' self-learning outcomes), engaging students as much as possible in discussions and providing guidance (with the aid of technologies, this process can be made more interesting than traditional classroom discussion, e.g., ask students to do online voting for the best work and explain why), and finally question and answer. The first task helps to urge sluggish students to work harder while further motivating those hard-working learners. The other two attend to students' needs of instant communication with teachers and fellow students, and clarifications of confusions in learning. For older learners, for example, students in tertiary institutions, and interactions with teachers and students are especially important. After all, good command of knowledge cannot be achieved through cramming; it should be constructed and absorbed [B1].

The interactive process of discussions, debates, brainstorming, sharing, questioning, and answering, under teachers' guidance, is the very process of knowledge construction and absorption. Student B1 said "in the current course we are taking, students are always encouraged to offer opinions, which is greatly beneficial. For example, on the topic of assessment, our teacher asks us to share our understandings of "assessment", "test", "measurement" and "evaluation", and talk about ways of assessments we adopted in our teaching (most of us are both graduate students and schoolteachers at the same time) before giving her own opinions and other academic explanations. This is a much better way for us students to gain a deeper understanding of assessment than simply giving definitions of the above four concepts." All in all, synchronous sessions are essential in ICT. The main concern should be how to better combine information technologies with teaching objectives. Learning and practice are always best for teachers in ICT education.

Synchronous learning can be defined as all types of learning in which students and teachers are in the same place, at the same time, in order for learning to take place. This includes in-person classes and live online meetings when the whole class or smaller groups get together. Student C1 said "during this Covid-19 pandemic breakdown, most of the learning institutions have opted to proceed with the teaching and learning process by using online platform to deliver the lessons. My lecturer conducted her online lessons via the Zoom platform. As stated in the schedule, we have to attend our online sessions for four hours and we do have breaks in between. My lecturer usually teaches during the first hour followed by discussion based on the topic presented."

According to Student C1, her lecturer makes the lesson interesting and to ensure the students pay full attention, she prepares some questions for discussion that are usually related to their teaching experiences. Her lecturer checks on their discussion and they are also instructed to do a presentation on the matter discussed. To ensure no students will be left out due to some technical glitches or connection breakdown, her lecturer records all the sessions and delivers them *via* WhatsApp. The benefits that student C1 can point from having this synchronous learning is that the lecturer has the ability to still control the class and give instant feedback to the students on the subject taught in the session. Although it is conducted virtually, the students can still give their cooperation in participating in each in-class activity prepared. Through the implementation of synchronous learning virtually, student C1 thinks that it is the right time for every educator to self-check their self-efficacy in handling IT and conducting virtual classes. This is in-line with the demand of our current students who obviously are so attached to gadgets. Student C1 expressed that is really exciting having the class online as it suits the students' technology competency.

3.3.1.3 Opportunities for collaboration

Student D1 reflected on the synchronous learning approach which was used by his lecturer during the COVID-19 pandemic. Synchronous learning is learning that takes place simultaneously in real time. Learners attend class at a scheduled time either in a traditional classroom or *via* the web using various technologies. As we know, all the schools and higher learning institutions have been shut down for almost 3 months during this pandemic. So, his lecturer opted to teach the post-graduate class by using the Zoom platform. Usually, the link is given 15 minutes before the class. All the lecture notes, task sheets, and YouTube videos will be given through the MyGuru platform. His lecturer records the Zoom sessions and then shares the recorded lessons to the group *via* WhatsApp. Students then can view the lesson anytime that they want to recall what they have learned on that day. After the lecture session, his lecturer has discussion, question, and answer sessions with the group before the class ends.

According to Student D1, relying only on synchronous lectures using the Zoom platform is ideal. In these times, online platforms are the only way to ensure teaching and learning are not affected. If teachers and lecturers cannot teach, students are the ones who are most impacted. E-learning is the future of education. Educators need to start learning and using technology in the classroom, and parents need to be onboard by supporting schools in using digital education tools. Students get excited to learn online and are very engaged. He shared that his lecturer has ensured that she supplements extra reading materials with other engaging activities such as discussions. This can further inform the lecturer whether the students had understood the subject, or the topic area taught.

Student D1 also believes that time always moves forward, so as a student he needs to keep updated and follow the trends in online learning. Synchronous learning implementation made the students more excited in using the technology to learn. This helps to enhance the lecturer-student relationship. He looks forward to the classes as technology makes learning more fun and meaningful. According to Student D1, he and his classmates love to collaborate and be involved in class discussions.

3.4 Perceived challenges

3.4.1 Lack of information to align technology with teaching objectives

Student B1 expressed her main concern on how lecturers can plan and implement teaching and learning to make it more meaningful for students to learn. The main problem would be to find solutions to combine information technologies with teaching objectives. Learning and practice are always best for teachers in ICT education.

4. Discussion

The use of asynchronous and synchronous learning methods both pose advantages and disadvantages based on the data obtained from the preservice and in-service teachers' reflective notes. One obvious problem faced by the preservice teachers in the asynchronous learning approach was to stay connected with peers to exchange ideas and discuss topics related to the recorded lessons. Preservice teachers who experienced the asynchronous learning approach expressed the lack of opportunity and engagement to interact with peers and also the lecturer to get immediate feedback. Preservice teachers said that the synchronous learning approach could not deliver the same vibe or real-time interaction as compared to the face-to-face or the traditional teaching approach.

A combination of both asynchronous and synchronous learning approaches can promote the development of social interaction and community of inquiry in the education landscape. This is supported by Zawacki-Richter [14] who investigated the impacts of the COVID-19 on teaching and learning at universities in Germany. Findings showed that both e-learning and face-to-face learning have advantages and disadvantages of using digital media for instruction. Educators can be creative to offer students "a different kind of learning" [15]. This is supported by a diversified resources and materials that can be problem-based, cooperative, collaborative, interactive, flexible, and self-directed. Nevertheless, more focus should be given to the types of pedagogical added value e-learning can offer, relying on the needs of the students, and the course content that will be taught.

The findings of this study are supported by many authors (e.g., [16–19]) on the need for educators to devise a balanced ODL strategy whereby preservice teachers can experience and attend both asynchronous and synchronous learning approaches in order to provide equivalent learning opportunities. On the other hand, preservice teachers admitted that they could not stay focused and follow the face-to-face lectures accordingly given their limited attention span. Some of them even expressed that they lacked the confidence to pose questions to their lecturers when they attend the face-to-face online lectures. The reasons given were mainly due to their fear of the lecturer, besides feeling timid and inhibited [20]. It is noted that educators must embrace some flexibility in their teaching approach and offer choices for students to adopt both asynchronous and synchronous learning approaches.

Studies on both asynchronous and synchronous learning approaches are in their infancy. Findings from this study suggest that both asynchronous and synchronous learning approaches offer a variety of educational, practical, and economic advantages. Universities worldwide can still increase their student intake with greater enrolment although knowing the fact that classroom space would be an issue but given the nature of the synchronous learning approach, they can still accept a huge population of students [21, 22]. Synchronous learning approach can offer students equal and comprehensive learning experiences beyond geographical borders [23, 24]. Education now is open to everyone including those working full time, and parents looking after children as they can join off or on campus to pursue their studies [25]. Students who join online distance learning or remote learning can now ask questions *via* online, add comments, and literally get engaged in discussion in a similar vein as compared to the on campus students [22]. As a result, it creates an opportunity to create a community of inquiry to interact socially and intellectually to share knowledge through the asynchronous learning approach [21, 26].

Khalil et al. [27] investigated undergraduate medical students' views regarding the effectiveness of synchronized online learning at Unaizah College of Medicine and Medical Sciences, Qassim University, Saudi Arabia, due to the ongoing

COVID-19 pandemic. A qualitative research design was employed by using focus group discussions synchronously comprising of seven open-ended questions. Findings revealed that online sessions were time saving and their performance improved as a result of the time used wisely. However, participants expressed other challenges such as their behavioral challenges during the synchronous learning session, technical, and also online exams. Participants showed their interest toward online learning for the future academic years. Both the asynchronous and synchronous learning approaches are essential parts of the information and communications technology.

5. Conclusion

In this information age, ICT in education has become widely accepted, generally actualized and greatly developed around the world, not to mention the incredibly vital role, ICT has been playing in this COVID-19 pandemic when face-to-face classroom instruction is rendered risky. ICT benefits learners by offering them vast digital resources at their fingertips and giving them the freedom to tailor their own learning timetable, among many other advantages. While some learners' motivations and interests are boosted with the highly raised autonomy, instant feedback and discussions are in great need for them as always, and some students, especially those young students, may slack off in asynchronous sessions, for want of self-discipline and self-learning strategies. That is why synchronous sessions are indispensable in ICT, and synchronous sessions are the ones making ICT real education instead of merely a collection of advanced and powerful tools.

Conflict of interest

The authors declare no conflict of interest.

Author details

Charanjit Kaur Swaran Singh[1*], Noor Alhusna Madzlan[1], Eng Tek Ong[2], Revathi Gopal[3], Mazura Mastura Muhammad[1], Siti Shuhaida Shukor[3], Nor Azmi Mostafa[1], Tarsame Singh Masa Singh[4] and Mahendran Maniam[3]

1 Faculty of Languages and Communication, English Language and Literature Department, Universiti Pendidikan Sultan Idris, Tanjong Malim, Perak Darul Ridzuan, Malaysia

2 Faculty of Human Development, Sultan Idris Education University, Malaysia

3 Faculty of Languages and Communication, Universiti Pendidikan Sultan Idris, Tanjong Malim, Perak Darul Ridzuan, Malaysia

4 English Language Unit, Language Department, Institute of Teacher Education, Bukit Mertajam, Penang, Malaysia

*Address all correspondence to: charanjit@fbk.upsi.edu.my

References

[1] Szeto E. A comparison of online/face-to-face students' and instructor's experiences: Examining blended synchronous learning effects. Procedia—Social and Behavioral Sciences. 2014;**116**:4250-4254

[2] Chen N-S, Ko H-C, Kinshuk, Lin T. A model for synchronous learning using the Internet. Innovations in Education and Teaching International. 2005;**42**(2):181-194

[3] Hastie M, Hung I-C, Chen N-S, Kinshuk. A blended synchronous learning model for educational international collaboration. Innovations in Education and Teaching International. 2010;**47**(1):9-24

[4] Stacey E, Wiesenberg F. A study of face-to-face and online teaching philosophies in Canada and Australia. Journal of Distance Education. 2007;**22**(1):19-40

[5] Szeto E. Transforming learning and teaching in higher education: The impact of ICT on pedagogy, peer interaction and support in a networked virtual learning environment. International Journal of Learning. 2011;**17**(11):205-214

[6] Brown BW, Liedholm CE. Can web courses replace the classroom in principles of microeconomics? The American Economic Review. 2002;**92**(2):444-448

[7] Smith GG, Ferguson D, Caris M. Teaching college courses online vs face-to-face. T.H.E. Journal. 2001;**28**(9):18-16

[8] Nicol DJ, Minty I, Sinclair C. The social dimensions of online learning. Innovations in Education and Teaching International. 2003;**40**(3):270-280

[9] Tu C-H, McIsaac M. The relationship of social presence and interaction in online classes. The American Journal of Distance Education. 2002;**16**(3):131-150

[10] Garrison DR, Anderson T, Archer W. Critical inquiry in a text-based environment: Computer conferencing in higher education model. The Internet and Higher Education. 2000;**2**(2-3):87-105

[11] Garrison DR, Anderson T, Archer W. Critical inquiry in a text-based environment: Computer conferencing in higher educationmodel. The Internet and Higher Education. 2000;**2**(2-3):87-105

[12] Anderson T, Rourke L, Garrison DR, Archer W. Assessing teaching presence in a computer conferencing context. Journal of Asynchronous Learning Networks. 2001;**2**(3):152-158. Retrived from: http://www.aln.org/alnweb/journal/jalnvol5issue2v2.Htm

[13] Patton MQ. Qualitative Research and Evaluation Methods. 3rd ed. Thousand Oaks, CA: Sage Publications; 2002

[14] Varutharaju E, Ratnavadivel N. Enhancing higher order thinking skills through clinical simulation. Malaysian Journal of Learning and Instruction. 2014;**11**:75-100

[15] Zawacki-Richter O. The current state and impact of Covid-19 on digital higher education in Germany. Human Behavior and Emerging Technologies. 2021;**3**:218-226. DOI: 10.1002/hbe2.

[16] Kerres, M. Bildung in der digitalen Welt: Wir haben die Wahl. In: denk-doch-mal.de, Online-Magazin für Arbeit-Bildung-Gesellschaft, Ausgabe. 2018;**2**(8):1-7. (Berufliches) Lernen in digitalen Zeiten

[17] Popov O. Teachers' and students' experiences of simultaneous teaching in an international distance and

on-campus master's programme in engineering. The International Review of Research in Open and Distance Learning. 2009;**10**(3):1-17. Retrieved from http://www.irrodl.org

[18] Turoff M. An end to student segregation: No more separation between distance learning and regular courses. In: Paper Presented at the TeleLearning '99 Conference, Montreal, Canada. 16 M. Bower et al. Computers & Education. 2015;**86**:1e17

[19] Waddoups GL, Howell SL. Bringing online learning to campus: The hybridization of teaching and learning at Brigham Young University. The International Review of Research in Open and Distance Learning. 2002;**2**(2):1-21. Retrieved from: https://scholarsarchive.byu.edu/facpub/549

[20] Hill P. Online delivery educational models: A descriptive view. EDUCAUSE Review. 2012;**47**(6):84-97

[21] Rogers PC, Graham CR, Rasmussen R, Campbell JO, Ure DM. Case 2dBlending face-to-face and distance learners in a synchronous class: Instructor and learner experiences. Quarterly Review of Distance Education. 2003;**4**:245-251

[22] White CP, Ramirez R, Smith JG, Plonowski L. Simultaneous delivery of a F2F course to on-campus and remote off- campus students. TechTrends. 2010;**54**(4):34-40. DOI: 10.1007/s11528-010-0418-z

[23] Cunningham U. Teaching the disembodied: Othering and activity systems in a blended synchronous learning situation. The International Review of Research in Open and Distance Learning. 2014;**15**(6):33-51. Retrieved from: https://files.eric.ed.gov/fulltext/EJ1048222.pdf

[24] Norberg A. Blended learning and new education logistics in Northern Sweden. In: Oblinger DG, editor. Game Changers: Education and Information Technologies. Boulder, CO: Educause; 2012. pp. 327-330

[25] Pope C. Breaking down barriers: Providing flexible participation options for on-campus courses. In: Paper Presented at the Fifth Education Research Group of Adelaide Conference; Adelaide, Australia. 2010

[26] Park YJ, Bonk CJ. Is online life a breeze? A case study for promoting synchronous learning in a blended graduate course. MERLOT Journal of Online Learning and Teaching. 2007;**3**(3):307-323. Retrieved from http://jolt.merlot.org

[27] Khalil R, Mansour AE, Fadda WA, Almisnid K, Aldamegh M, Al-Nafeesah A, et al. The sudden transition to synchronized online learning during the COVID-19 pandemic in Saudi Arabia: A qualitative study exploring medical students' perspectives. BMC Medical Education. 2020;**20**:285. DOI: 10.1186/s12909-020-02208-z

Chapter 8

STEAME Model in Action: Challenges and Solutions in Mastering the Digital Culture

Eugenia Kovatcheva and Milena Koleva

Abstract

Due to the digital transformation of everyday practice the process of education has become more complicated than ever before. The role of teachers is more complex as they are not the only source of information and knowledge for their students anymore. Formally or informally, they need to help students develop new competencies and prepare them for the unknown future in the fast-growing and changing labor market. Essential part of these new competencies lies in the interconnected fields of Science, Technology, Engineering and Mathematics. In order for students to obtain them a variety of learning approaches have to be applied in an interdisciplinary educational environment and digital culture. The new generations of digital natives grow up with a set of skills about engaging in the digital world as a basic knowledge. Furthermore, to provide students with more holistic understanding the concepts of Arts are integrated with STEM to become STEAM education. This chapter presents extended education model taking STEM and STEAM to the next level and bringing the Entrepreneurship discipline to create an integrated STEAME curriculum. This chapter presents an integrated STEAME curriculum model, methodology for its implementation and STEAME classroom and environment design as a new education approach to tackle the challenges of the development of skills for the 21st century.

Keywords: Digital Culture, Education, Challenges and STEAM, Education for sustainable development (ESD), digital natives

1. Introduction

Nowadays the world is changing faster than ever affecting all aspects of our lives including the way students learn and teachers have to respond quickly to their learning needs. Global economy and job market have also imposed challenges with a higher demand of new qualifications and skills. In order to be competitive, the workforce has to adapt with the same speed and according to the expectations and needs of the contemporary employers. This adaptation is not possible without the crucial role of education as its main objective is to transfer the knowledge to the next generations as Montessori said that the education is natural process for humans achieved by meeting the complex challenges in the real world [1].

And from Seymour Papert's constructionism point of view "*students construct mental models to understand the world around them*" [2]. The information technologies support additional possibilities - created public entity can be shared. This leads to change towards a digital culture for students as digital natives and digital immigrants - most of the teachers [3]. The synergy of disciplines in the classroom will give students a broader vision of the world as it is in its integrity. In the past 20 years such pedagogical approach has been developed to create STEM (Science, Technology, Engineering, Mathematics) education. It is further upgraded to include arts and become STEAM and now entrepreneurship is integrated as well to become STEAME.

The interdisciplinary STEAME (Science, Technology, Engineering, Arts, Mathematics, and Entrepreneurship) education focuses on developing such essential skills as creativity, problem-solving, engineering literacy and entrepreneurial spirit. STEAME as a newly developed approach for integration of these disciplines conveys very good results and positive feedback so far. This is directly related to the fact that in the past few years pursuing STEM careers has decreased and the education system needs to make extra efforts to encourage students to work in these fields. This would be possible and much easier by applying innovative methods, approaches, tools and technologies to the education process. Furthermore, teachers who are digital immigrants need to be supported in this endeavor by development of new skills and methodologies like innovative thinking, design thinking, lean and agile methodologies, new role of a coach and mentor. Teachers have to prepare students for real life full with technologies and necessity of faster adaptation and flexibility.

What kind of new knowledge and skills students should develop at school level? Are these sufficient and well accepted by employers? How are students motivated to learn and develop their abilities?

These and many other questions are asked by teachers. The complexity of our dynamic world puts the focus on the development of interdisciplinary knowledge, abilities and skills. STEM (Science, Technology, Engineering and Mathematics) upgraded to STEAM (Science, Technology, Engineering, Arts and Mathematics) and the newest STEAME (Science, Technology, Engineering, Arts, Mathematics and Entrepreneurship) are empower schools to improve science and technology development.

This chapter presents a model for implementation of STEAME (Science, Technology, Engineering, Arts, Mathematics and Entrepreneurship) education and provides an overview of how to be designed and integrated at school level.

2. Bulgarian roots

The interdisciplinary approach has deep roots in Bulgarian education. Scientific research on the effective utilization of computers and information technologies in the middle school has been done in Bulgaria as early as the end of 70-ies [4]. The Research Group in Education (RGE) at the Bulgarian Academy of Science and Ministry of Education developed a curriculum in which the cross-disciplinary study of language and mathematics (actually one of their text titles: Language and Mathematics) and Logo-based computer are in a synergy. The learning activities played prominent roles for students' motivation and their understanding of the complexity and dynamics of the world around them.

The research group had the task to develop and experiment with new curriculum based on the following principles:

- integration of academic disciplines;

- learning through action and discovery.

The developed curriculum was implemented in 29 schools from different parts of Bulgaria in the period from 1979 to 1991. It was an experiment conducted by scientists across all fields. Prominent poets, writers, artists, cartoonists, musicians took part in the development of the textbooks (**Figure 1**). The leader of the authors' team was Blagovest Sendov. It is renowned for its intriguing texts (Valeri Petrov and Marko Ganchev), artistic design of Donyo Donev, the ideas for language integration with mathematics (Rosalina Novachkova, Blagovest Sendov and Boyan Penkov).

During the first four years, computer science was an element of encyclopedic training. Some basic computer concepts (algorithm, coding, decoding, table, graph, procedure, data) were applied in various learning activities.

The textbooks and classes developed on the basis of Logo stimulated and supported the research style of learning in all classes. The specifics of the traditional school with fixed classes and relatively large groups of students were taken into account. This required a certain modification of the flexible style of work experimented in the USA and England by teams of experts in psychology, computer science, artificial intelligence, with groups of children in the framework of ambitious projects for schools of the future.

The experiment finished thirty years ago. However, the society was not ready for that. This was the start of applying new approaches and use of technology to develop the necessary digital culture.

During periods of dynamic changes and advances of technology teachers and students have access to them. The new information technologies (IT) look attractive for the younger (digital natives) generations and intimidating for older generations (digital immigrants). The teachers are afraid that IT prevents them from being professional in their fields when they are not fluent in technologies [5]. Under this pressure somehow teachers forget to transfer the most important message to the students – love for studying. Nevertheless, the educational big challenges are *where, which*, *how* and *why* to use IT. The most important in the new pedagogical approach supported by technologies is that it has to be active and student-centered. The theoretical knowledge of active learning is not enough to be applied easily and to present adequately the teacher's expertise.

This experiment was a base for further scientific research on the effective utilization of computers and information technologies in the middle school has been done in RGE [6, 7]. This research is intensified in the context of several European projects [8] and it is still an inspiration for ongoing research tailored to the new

Figure 1.
Textbooks: Logo - 1st grade, 3th iand 4th.

generations. One of the main directions of the educational design is inquiry-based learning for interdisciplinary education [9–18].

The improvement of learning methodologies is a long process. The results are visible at least 10 years after the application. Most of the current teachers are focused on their topic(s) and the interdisciplinary approach integrated with new technologies for teaching and learning is a challenge for them.

3. STEAME curriculum

The technology-driven economy and skilled workforce in STEM (Science, Technology, Engineering and Mathematics) fields are considered the driving forces for innovation and growth. However, a number of European studies register a declining interest in students' interest and enthusiasm in STEM education. Thus, motivating secondary school students towards STEM careers is becoming a critical task. However, in a traditional school curriculum all or most of subjects constituting STEAM are taught separately. There needs to be curriculum adaptation to adjust the current one to the changing and emerging needs of all learners. Curricula are changed according to the new requirements and expectations, policies, priorities, circumstances. It has to reflect the different abilities of students and their strengths in different areas [19, 20].

School curricula must favor applied knowledge, inquiry-based teaching and invention: students' individual strengths emerge as they are confronted with challenges. Students acquire independent thought, learn to make decisions and act on them. At higher levels the overall educational programs giving content, mindsets, competencies, and skills works together with other special programs like internships and intensives. Educational goals must be centred around experience-based knowledge to develop critical reflection and commitment to action. In advanced courses students work independently and are encouraged to offer thoughtful responses to given questions and to think more abstractly. Through work-based experiences in STEAM subjects and Career Development programs focused on entrepreneurship, students develop an aptitude for real-world leadership and problem solving focusing on teamwork, communication and interpersonal skills.

4. Methodology

4.1 STE(A)M(E) – why?

Twenty years ago, the term STEM was introduced by scientific administrators at the U.S. National Science Foundation (NSF) as curriculum that is centred on education in the disciplines of science, technology, engineering, and mathematics [21]. STEAM variations are STEAM (A for Arts) and STEAME (E for Entrepreneurship).

STEM is a curriculum-based approach integrating four disciplines: science, technology, engineering and mathematics. This model of teaching and learning allows better understanding of these subjects in their mutual correlation and application in the real world. Science includes physics, biology, chemistry. The paradigm of synergy among them is based on the real-world examples and challenges [21, 22].

The integration of arts into this approach leads to the existence of STEAM model. This complimentary subject provides students with such skills as creativity, artistic abilities and knowledge about the world of arts. It allows teachers to better prepare them and to nurture artistic development. STEAM education leads to better preparation of 21st century innovators, leaders, educators and learners because to follow STEAM approach means to create, to take risks, to meet the problems and to find solutions [23].

The newest educational approach is STEAME [24] where entrepreneurship presents the last "E". These approach guides and builds one new layer of understanding of the real world - entrepreneurial mindset together with research, creativity, logical and critical thinking.

STEAME is introduced as results of the Erasmus+ KA2 project STEAME: Guidelines for Developing and Implementing STEAME Schools, project No. 2019-1-CY01-KA201-058240. This research presents the STEAME methodology as an upgrade of RGE's approach.

STEAME is challenging for teachers as any new cross-disciplinary educational approach and methodology. From one side they have to improve their ability to work in synergy and to cover a broad range of disciplines and teaching styles. On the other hand, they have to motivate students in these areas which are not that attractive and complex to learn. According to John Dewey education is *not a preparation for life; it is life itself*. Teachers should prepare students to realize the integrity and interconnectivity of the world and give them the opportunity to dive deeper into technical/scientific and artistic/humanistic fields to develop their real potential.

How to motivate and teach/train digital natives for the diversity today and the unclear future with disappearing and emerging professions? The answer could be STE(A)M(E)!

STEM - > STEAM - > STEAME education are not in opposition, each one enriches and expands (**Figure 2**) the scope of the previous one [25]. They:

- enrich school philosophy for curriculum which engages teachers and students;
- bring education to meet the needs of the dynamic 21st century in an integrated and holistic way
- develop a creative collaborative space for students and teachers in an integrated curriculum;
- can be inspired by real projects implemented in the learning programs;
- engage students in considering synergy of five sides of knowledge: culture, relations, criticism, vision and ethics, and its action which is transformative learning.

Seymour Papert says: *You Can't Think About Thinking Without Thinking About Thinking About Something*. In STEAME education creativity and problem-solving

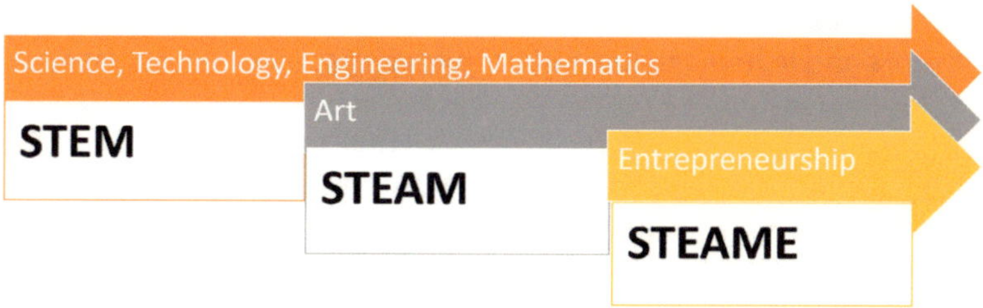

Figure 2.
STEM - > STEAM - > STEAME.

skills are on focus. Design and design thinking develop creativity and innovation, and have become increasingly important in the development and implementation of the integrated STEAME education. Design thinking is a problem-solving iterative approach traditionally applied by designers. It is now applied in business, education, and other fields to tackle problems and challenges following human-centered approach of six-step iterative process: Empathise, Define, Ideate, Prototype, and Test can be applied for science, technology, engineering, mathematics, arts and entrepreneurship [26]. Design of STEAME curriculum starts with empathy of digital natives. The learners are in the center of the training. Their understanding is crucial for effective learning. The digital immigrants have to be aware for their specifics. When creating such curriculum the following objectives are set:

- to connect concepts, ideas and different perspectives to provide new and innovative valuable propositions,
- to test them and re-elaborate with experience.
- to incorporate elements from other creative and design disciplines.

To facilitate and enhance the successful implementation of the model, learning units are designed and developed according to a number of learning cycles that, following a sequence of stages, promote the development of this independent, meaningful learning. Inspired by the model of Kolb [27] and St Ignatius' teachings [28] five stages are proposed for the development of a learning cycle:

4.1.1 Experiential context

"From known to unknown". It is first stage which gives students an introduction to the topic. The aim is to motivate students through their own experience and context so that they can have an initial general overview on the subject and the context in which it is especially relevant, or where the contents to work on can be applied.

4.1.2 Reflective observation

The aim of this stage is to encourage students to ask questions, to question themselves, as there cannot be significant learning if one does not ask oneself or questions about it. It can be a question, a number of questions, a conflict, or a gap between what I know and what I need to know or do; all that drives students into action and hence, to the construction and reconstruction of knowledge.

4.1.3 Conceptualization

The aim of this stage is to bring students closer to the theoretical approaches that have been developed in a specific scientific or technical area: the answers given by authors and schools to key issues in each discipline. Conceptual learning is based on the acquisition of knowledge, scientific terminology, facts and data, methods and strategies, principles and theories that make up the scientific and technical knowledge of each discipline. As the aim of the course is to move knowledge into action, it should be noted that Design Thinking is a new discipline in the academic world. It is a scientific approach that is closer to practice and used by designers as a problem-solving method. So, there are many real examples that can illustrate this phase.

4.1.4 Active experimentation

In this fourth learning stage, we consider how students can apply the contents they have just worked on. It refers to the theoretical/practical relationship and includes any activity (exercises, internships, projects, research work, designs or any other active proposal to be carried out by students on a specific subject, year or degree) that promotes the development of students' competences concerning the application of concepts, theories or models in order to strengthen them, use them for problem solving or to design or implement a model or strategy.

4.1.5 Assessment

We cannot complete a learning cycle without asking ourselves what we have done and what we have achieved. This is a final point to a learning cycle and it can be the beginning of a new one to refine all the concepts and skills that have not been sufficiently achieved in the previous one. Therefore, it helps go deeper into the subject in an iterative way.

This learning approach allows the training to be: Interactive: among participants, and among them and the users/customers, the teachers, tutors and business people that can take part in the training (in the Entrepreneurship discipline in STEAME); Participatory: making the team central for the learning process; Practical: learning by applying the skills and concepts gained in class in real life; Elicitive: learning from the experience of the participants.

4.2 Core challenges

Change and adaptation of methodologies, models and approaches require time and preparation including setting expectations, overcoming negative perceptions and attitudes, resistance to change. Myths are born, too. For example, in the early years of IT implementation [5] some teachers thought IT prevents their professionalism; the good teacher should know everything, etc. Nowadays students know more than their teachers. In the information age student behavior and knowledge are accumulated from diverse sources and means of communication. New myths are born such as finding the recipe for the successful and intriguing teaching.

Similar myths can appear in the implementation process of STE(A)M(E) education. There are curriculum development difficulties, lack of teaching resources and leaving the comfort zone when implementing the new process.

The core challenges in STEAME implementation are (**Figure 3**):

- Environment (physical and learning materials)
- Research and development capabilities
- Team capability and integration
- Digital transformation mechanism [29].

Development of a **user-friendly environment** supports effective teaching and learning and assures sustainability of educational project. The learning environment for STEAM(E) education can be as important to student success as quality instruction and course curricula. And in today's world, that means outfitting students and teachers with the right set of resources.

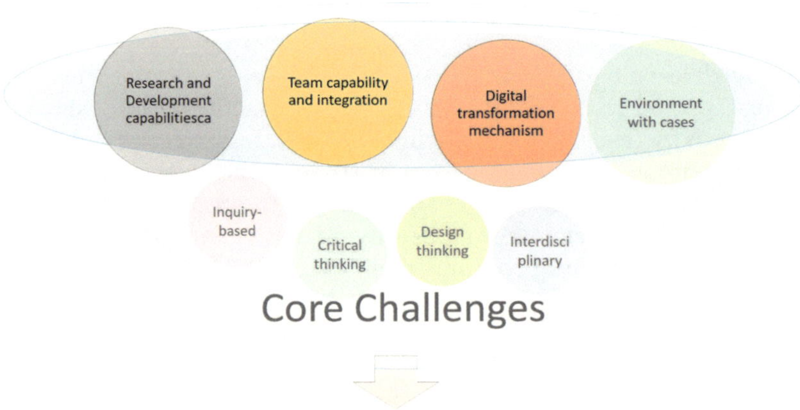

Figure 3.
Core challenges.

The STEAME program should facilitate design, not the other way around. The physical space can align with the principles of student agency, and teacher's flexibility, and choice that are at the core of the new model. Once is determined how students and teachers will interact with STEAME Curricula and blended learning, then the space could be planed accordingly.

The classroom layout should be aligned with the outcomes, that schools' Principles and teachers aim to achieve, when going STEAME and blended oriented.

Improvement of research and development capabilities: the use of case studies and real examples as sources are important to motivate students and help them choose their future career development.

In parallel the team efficiency, dynamics and competences are **developed**: it is essential in order to improve teaching and research capabilities. The team composition and **rapport** are critical for the success and development of effective training. The essential part in the digital transformation involved in this process is the use of **new, fast and frequently changing** digital technology to solve problems. Focusing on the transformation of scientific research topics, the transformation of advanced technology that is "unreachable" into a cognitive curriculum will help participants understand the development trend in advance and clarify future goals.

Attention should be paid when **the independent curricula are developed in combination** with the traditional approaches and systems, the national legislation, the contextual circumstances, digital transformation and innovation level, and the advantages of the research and development. There are already various good practices developed by individual schools across Europe and within the framework of EU and other projects.

The present case study is based on experimentation run in Bulgarian private school – Private English Language school Prof. Ivan Apostolov, partner in the project Guidelines for Developing and Implementing STEAME Schools.

The school has undertaken a pilot STEAME project for the students in 10th grade. For the purposes of the experiment a sample inquiry-based learning and creativity plan (IBLCP) was created. It is based on the integrated teaching process conducted by teachers in profiling disciplines (Entrepreneurship and Economics) and subjects from scientific and technological fields. The main thesis of the experiment is to create a model for applying the paradigm of STEAME training in an innovative way, looking for application of the synergistic effect of the studied subject areas in natural and applied sciences to an entrepreneurial outcome.

The main goal of the STEAME project (2019–1-CY01-KA201–058240) and the experiment in the Bulgarian school is to create an innovative model for applying the STE(A)M(E) paradigm, i.e., synergy of the classical disciplines with entrepreneurial outcomes and support of digital technologies.

The **learning objectives** are the acquisition of set of cross-disciplinary knowledge, abilities and skills.

One of the key success factors in this process is the flexibility and application of such approaches as: inquiry-based learning, cross-disciplinary teaching, problem-based learning, project-based learning, case-based learning.

Teachers develop and apply the so called learning and creativity plans instead of the traditional plans. They are used as guidelines with main steps, organizational matters, y-based learning for generating a creative plan for STEAME training, is based on the study of cases for interdisciplinary scientific, social, project and business realizations, as in addition to gather and analyze the necessary information, in order for teachers and students to identify disciplinary and interdisciplinary links with studied, in previous periods or at present, subject areas. This approach allows to demonstrate exploration skills by teachers and students, both in the period of research and analysis of the cases studied, and in the process of implementation of STEAM project development and its orientation to entrepreneurial results.

The model requires **students to develop and improve**:

Analysis of case studies and solutions. Inquiry-based approach is well known and applied by the teachers. Students also have experience in case-based learning and.

The model requires **teachers to master** the adaptation of the Interdisciplinary training and curricula; application of Inquiry-; Problem- and Project-based training approaches as well as the Case study description, decomposition and analysis.

Cross-disciplinary STEAME methodology. Together with mathematics and physics, the students are introduced to engineering inventions; technological innovations; robotics; information and communication technologies. Fine, monumental and graphical arts are part of the process, too. The STEAME model integrates the following social and behavioral disciplines taught at school: Sociology (Social Anthropology), Economics, Entrepreneurship, Ethnography.

Soft skill such as personal skills (creativity, critical thinking, emotional intelligence, etc.); interpersonal skills (leadership, social awareness, teamwork, communication, presentation, etc.); time management and stress resistance.

The model was tested with five teachers of the respective disciplines and five teams of students in 10th grade [30]: Team 1 – Mathematics and Arts; Team 2 – Arts and Chemistry; Team 3 – Anatomy and Arts; Team 4 – Engineering/Technology and Physics; Team 5 – Entrepreneurship.

All student teams worked on topics defined as projects within the described fields of their teams. They developed final presentations of the main findings and conclusions form their research and experiments.

5. Design the STEAME school and classroom

5.1 Main principles and tools

If the School is going STEAME and blended oriented to promote student and teacher agency, then the classroom should be redesigned to give many options and locations to teach and learn. The classroom layout must facilitate the outcomes that are expected.

Few innovative approaches for new organizational structure and design are applied:

Blended training system, based on real good industry and business practices and principles as:

- the optimal and efficient Lean Toyota Production System, Japan [31],
- the flexible and optimized programming methodologies in IT- Agile [32]
- the innovative models of production, business and life behavior - Design thinking of IDEO [33]

Flipped classroom [34]- a type of blended learning where students are introduced to content at home and practice working through it at school. It is a common practice for new content introduction.

IT tools for education support – there are many tools for online learning and for organization of the learning process.

Case study sets as:

- Epic [34] case study & analysis for STEAME Inquiry based learning within the frames of the School's Curricula.
- Backlog [35] is created on the base of conducted inquires in IBLCP in the framework of STEAME thematic plan.

5.2 Design and development

What should the STEAME classroom look like – students in rows, teachers writing on chalkboards, textbooks and so on? Technology and modernity of our times will transform the school and the classroom. In STEAME classroom, students and teachers are empowered to apply blended personalized learning and teaching. Through STEAME didactic technologies, time, classroom space, and teachers themselves become more flexible and adaptable. Students set their own goals and monitor their own progress under the umbrella of data-driven, targeted instruction and coaching. It means that students and teachers must have access to a structure for achieving relative curricula independence.

The mission of STEAME schools is to oppose the challenges of next endeavors in students 'life. The fundamental characteristic of this approach is to help students to understand who they are, what their interest and values are, what are their abilities, skills and talents. Teachers in the classroom can guide and motivate students as needed. The STEAME learning and training space is a joint classroom and there are three designated spaces for students and teachers to work – STEAME space, Science space and Creative space.

Personalized technology-driven approach is new and STEAME schools' premises must be designed from the ground up with this paradigm in mind. What about the existing school campuses? They should be adapted in order to meet the STEAME model.

What does the STEAME classroom look like?

The answer of this question is developed under the Erasmus+ project STEAME (2019-1-CY01-KA201-058240) where the team of Private English language school Ivan Apostolov created a pilot design of STEAME classroom.

The STEAME learning and training space is a joint classroom infrastructure with three designated spaces for students and teachers to work – STEAME space,

Science space and Creative space (**Figure 4**). The classrooms are separated for each grade level, and for STEAME activities and the Humanity sciences, as well, but they should be supplemented by two auxiliary classrooms.

First, it should be a large room, open space interior design, and flexible infrastructure, because each place has its own identity within the STEAME classroom for blended learning;

Second, the classroom should be very purposefully designed in order the layout to allow teachers and students to organize in-class activities exactly what it needs to be;

Third, the nomenclature of different spaces in the school, is important to be clearly specified, because the role of Project-based, Inquiry-based, and Discovery-based learning that are the three basic learning methodologies applied in STEAME schools is critically important to be allocated appropriately;

Forth, the classrooms are separated for each grade level, and for STEAME activities and the Humanity sciences, as well, but they should be supplemented by two auxiliary classrooms (for STEAME by a seminar room and for Humanity's by a Lab;

Fifth, the organization of the space in the STEAME school is determined by different learning environments, and each environment is defined by the furniture, the architecture or space, and the finishes, for example:

- Introspective space for personalized learning, individual research activities, assisted by online or offline content (texts, graphs, pictures, audio and video content) digitally delivered via Chromebooks;

- Exchange space for collaborative learning with peer delivered content;

- Direct instruction space for limited number of students (10 to 12) focused around a whiteboard, smartboard, flipchart, and/or projector for direct delivery of educational content by the instructor;

- Studying space which is soft seating informal environment where independent individual or group (in small groups) learning can take place;

- Feedback space for the teachers in the STEAME learning process.

Sixth, in the STEAME classroom must support critical thinking collaboration with technology-enabled, teacher's led instruction for each grade, as well as, to be

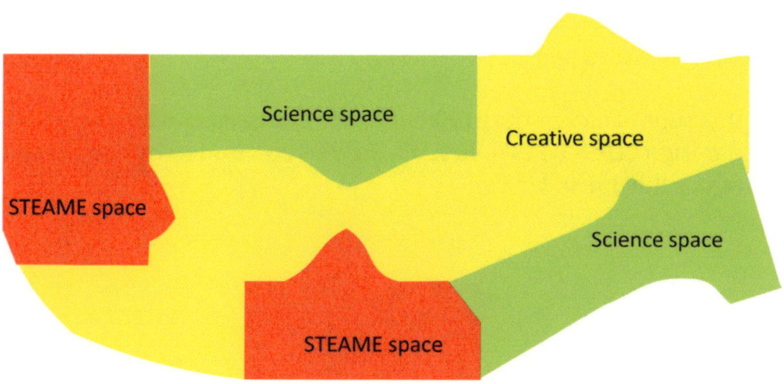

Figure 4.
STEAME classroom according the vision of Deyan Doykov, teacher at School Ivan Apostolov [30].

designed for structured group work within the project-based learning, in the same time a specific classroom space must be available for big ideas, discussions and connections;

Seventh, the classroom should be designed in such a way, to support independence end personal space for individual work;

Eight, the classroom space should support students' assessment and possibility for measurement of their personal and collective progress;

Ninth, the design of the classroom must support the STEAME teaching mode for providing life-changing opportunities and post-secondary success;

Tenth, STEAME classroom must support the roadmap for all other interdisciplinary educators.

The STEAME school model should ensure the interdisciplinary approach of its topics, incorporating a multifaceted exploration and study of a subject that ensures transferable knowledge and its applications. The synergy of disciplines with cross-thematic approach builds a more holistic understanding of the real world with real applications of abstract concepts. This motivates students to find solutions to real challenges.

6. Conclusion

The world is facing challenges in terms of meeting the changing social, economic and technological advances. The labor market is developing faster than ever with many new jobs emerging and some traditional ones – disappearing. These circumstances require new sets of skills and knowledge. Some of them are creativity, problem-solving, teamwork, leadership, digital literacy, social awareness, emotional intelligence, and entrepreneurial mindset. Educational systems have to be more flexible, creative and effective in order to meet the demand of the labour market of these new skills. The integration of Science, Technology, Engineering, Arts, Mathematics and Entrepreneurship into a new STEAME model and curriculum at school level provides a new paradigm and approach for preparation of students to empower them with skills and knowledge for the future.

It leverages on the STEM (Science, Technology, Engineering and Mathematics) and STEAM (Science, Technology, Engineering, Arts and Mathematics) education and incorporates Entrepreneurship as a subject area.

The integrated STEAME curriculum model is developed for the needs of the education of 21st century and based on the conducted experimentation and research proves to be successful.

Acknowledgements

This paper is supported by the project High5: Transdisciplinary methodology for Integrated design 2019-1-PL01-KA203-065784 co-funded by the Erasmus+ Programme of the European Union.

Author details

Eugenia Kovatcheva* and Milena Koleva
University of Library Studies and Information Technologies, Sofia, Bulgaria

*Address all correspondence to: e.kovatcheva@unibit.bg

References

[1] Montessori M, The Absorbent Mind, Henry Holt and Company, 1995, ISBN 0805041567, 9780805041569 p.8

[2] Alesandrini, K. & Larson, L. (2002). Teachers bridge to constructivism. The Clearing House, v75 n3 p118-21 Jan-Feb 2002, ISSN: ISSN-0009-8655

[3] Prensky M, Digital Natives, Digital Immigrants, From On the Horizon MCB University Press, Vol. 9 No. 5, October 2001

[4] Sendova E, Constructionism as Educational Philosophy and Culture in Bulgarian Context - In Memory of Seymour Papert, Papert, S. (2005). You can't think about thinking without thinking about thinking about something. Contemporary Issues in Technology and Teacher Education, 5(3/4), 366-367. (appear in Bulgarian Language)

[5] Stefanova E., Nikolova N., Kovatcheva E., Boytchev P., Sendova E., Myths and Realities about Technology Enhanced Learning, In Proceedings of First International conference Software, Services and Semantic Technologies (S3T), Sofia, Bulgaria, October 28-29, 2009, Ed. D.Dicheva, R. Nokolov, E.Stefanova, pp.116-123, ISBN 978-954-9526-62-2

[6] Sendova, E. & Nikolov, R., Problem Solving Scenarios in Secondary School Textbooks in Informatics and Mathematics. In G. Schuyten & M. Valcke (Eds.) Proceedings of the Second European Logo Conference, Gent, Belgium, 1989, pp685-693.

[7] Nikolov R, A Learning Environment in Informatic, PhD Thesis, Sofia University, 2. 1987

[8] Nikolov, R., Nikolova, I., Stefanov K, Research and Educational projects at CIST 3. (Center for Information Society Technologies), FMI Conference "Pioneers of the Bulgarian Mathematics", 8-10 July, 2006

[9] Chehlarova T, Sendova E., Stefanova, Dynamic tessellations in support of the inquiry-based learning of mathematics and arts, In proceeding of Int. Conf. Constructionism 2012, Athens, Greece, pp 570-574

[10] Kenderov, P. & Sendova, E., Enhancing the inquiry based mathematics education, UNESCO, International Workshop: Re-designing Institutional Policies and Practices to Enhance the Quality of, Teaching through Innovative Use of Digital Technologies, 14 – 16 June 2011, Sofia, 56-70

[11] Sendova, E. & Grkovska, S., Visual Modelling as a Motivation for Studying Mathematics and Art, EUROLOGO'2005). In Gregorczyk, G et al (Eds.) Proceedings, EUROLOGO'2005, 12-23

[12] Stefanova E., Boytchev P., Kovatcheva E., Nikolova N., Sendova E. A handbook 1. for the ICT teachers for 7th grade, Anubis, 2008 (in Bulgarian)

[13] Stefanova E., Boytchev P., Kovatcheva E. Nikolova N., Sendova E. Textbook You and IT handbook for 7th grade, Anubis, Sofia, 2008 (in Bulgarian)

[14] Sendova E., Stefanova E., Kovatcheva E., Nikolova N., Boytchev P., ICT Teachers' handbook, Anubis, Sofia, 2007 (in Bulgarian)

[15] Dobreva M., Kovatcheva E., Nikolova N., Sendova E., Stefanova E., Learn and Create with a Computer: an ICT handbook for 6th grade, Anubis, Sofia, 2007 (in Bulgarian)

[16] Dobreva M., Kovatcheva E., Nikolova N., Sendova E., Stefanova E., The computer in my World: Handbook in Information Technologies for 5th degree, Anubis, Sofia, 2006, ISBN-10:954-426-726-3 (in Bulgarian)

[17] Dobreva M., Kovatcheva E., Nikolova N., Sendova E., Stefanova E. ICT Teachers' handbook, Anubis, Sofia, 2006 (in Bulgarian)

[18] United Nations. (2015). Transforming our world: The 2030 agenda for sustainable development. https://sustainabledevelopment.un.org/post2015/transformingourworld/publication [Accessed: 2020-08-20]

[19] Deloitte, IT worker of the future: a new breed, https://www2.deloitte.com/content/dam/Deloitte/uk/Documents/technology/deloitte-uk-it-worker-of-the-future.pdf [Accessed: 2020-08-20]

[20] Deloitte, Moving Toward New Heights Deloitte Education Industry Report 2017, https://www2.deloitte.com/cn/en/pages/technology-media-and-telecommunications/articles/deloitte-education-industry-report-2017.html

[21] Hallinen J, STEM education curriculum, Encyclopedia Britannica, https://www.britannica.com/topic/STEM-education

[22] Hom E, What is STEM Education?, https://www.livescience.com/43296-what-is-stem-education.html#:~:text=STEM%20is%20a%20curriculum%20based,an%20interdisciplinary%20and%20applied%20approach [Accessed: 2020-08-20]

[23] Institute for Arts Integration and STEAM, What is STEAM Education? Comprehensive Guide, https://educationcloset.com/what-is-steam-education-in-k-12-schools/#whysteam [Accessed: 2020-08-20]

[24] STEAME 2019-1-CY01-KA201-058240, Guidelines for Developing and Implementing STEAME Schools, https://steame.eu/wp-content/uploads/2019/11/Press-release-STEAME-EN.pdf [Accessed: 2020-08-20]

[25] Taylor, P, Why is a STEAM curriculum perspective crucial to the 21st century?, https://research.acer.edu.au/cgi/viewcontent.cgi?article=1299&context=research_conference [Accessed: 2020-08-20]

[26] Kovatcheva E, Campos J.A., Del Val Roman, J.L., Dimitrov G.P., Petrova P., Design Thinking In Higher Education, In EDULEARN19 Proceedings, ISBN: 978-84-09-12031-4 / ISSN: 2340-1117, doi: 10.21125/edulearn.2019

[27] Kolb, D. A., Learning style inventory technical manual. Boston, MA: McBer. 1976

[28] Gil Coria, E., La pedagogía de los jesuitas ayer y hoy. Madrid: Universidad Pontificia Comillas, 1999

[29] Wang X, Hu W, Guo LThe Status Quo andWays of STEAM Education Promoting China's Future Social Sustainable Development, Sustainability 2018, 10, 4417; doi:10.3390/su10124417

[30] Doykov D, Developing and Implementing STEAME Schools - Inquiry Based Learning and Creativity plan, Published Prof. Ivan Apostolov, 2020

[31] Harris, L, Lean Manufacturing Made Toyota the Success Story it is Today, Investing in our Economy, Spring 2007, http://www.rcbi.org/index.php/viewarticle/130-capacity-magazine/spring-2007/features/336-lean-manufacturing-made-toyota-the-success-story-it-is-todayinvesting-in-our-economy [Accessed: 2021-01-08]

[32] AltexSoft, Agile Project Management: Best Practices and Methodologies, Whitepaper, https://www.altexsoft.com/media/2016/04/Agile-Project-Management-Best-Practices-and-Methodologies-Whitepaper.pdf [Accessed: 2021-01-08]

[33] IDEO, What is Design Thinking?, https://www.ideou.com/blogs/inspiration/what-is-design-thinking [Accessed: 2021-01-08]

[34] Pratt K., Kovatcheva E.P., Designing Blended, Flexible, and Personalized Learning. In: Voogt J., Knezek G., Christensen R., Lai KW. (eds) Second Handbook of Information Technology in Primary and Secondary Education. Springer International Handbooks of Education. Springe, Cham, 2018, DOI https://doi.org/10.1007/978-3-319-53803-7_49-1, Online ISBN 978-3-319-53803-7

[35] Roberts S, Gebhardt G, Bergen M Making the Case for Cases, Part 1: EPIC Case Studies 101, 2016, https://www.epicpeople.org/case-for-cases-part-1/

Section 3

Education in Emergencies

Chapter 9

Education in Emergencies, Mental Wellbeing and E-Learning

M. Mahruf C. Shohel, Arif Mahmud, Munira Azhar Urmee, Muhammad Naveed Anwar, Mohammad Mojibur Rahman, Dev Raj Acharya and Md. Ashrafuzzaman

Abstract

The world has been going through an unprecedented situation due to the world-wide health crisis created by the COVID-19 pandemic. It affected all sectors across the globe, including education. This chapter highlights the importance of education in emergencies and how a situation like the COVID-19 pandemic creates challenges alongside opportunities to learn for personal and professional development as well as to ensure mental wellbeing of individuals through e-learning. The chapter explores literature to draw on different perspectives regarding the issues related to effectiveness in handling education and learning in an emergency in addition to preparedness for post and future emergencies. However, it focuses mainly on the role of the education sector in supporting individuals, especially learners and educators during and after emergencies. It also reflects on educational professionals' work with students during this pandemic i.e. how educational professionals report on their adaptation journey and how the pandemic impacted the ability to serve and engage learners. From the professionals' best practices to assist students in being successful through online education or hybrid teaching and learning formats, many opportunities arose to shape and reform education for a better future and transform the process of lifelong learning. This chapter outlines strategies, in general, for the education sector, and in particular, institutions and individuals to be better prepared for future emergencies through the opportunities e-learning offers.

Keywords: Anxiety, Blended Learning, COVID-19, Digital Transformation, Education in Emergencies, E-Learning, Emergency Remote Education, Emerging Technologies, Fear, Home Learning, Mental Wellbeing, Online Education, Online Distance Teaching and Learning, Personal Development, Professional Development, Social Communication, Strategies and Psycho-social Interventional Steps, Technological Adaptation and Integration

1. Introduction

The COVID-19 pandemic has impacted on every aspect of human life [1–4]. The pandemic showed that human society has been unprepared for this unprecedented circumstance. In reality, there are many things to learn from this situation for preparing to address similar emergencies in the future. The education sector was not spared as education systems all over the world were abruptly shut down, forcing students and teachers to switch into emergency remote education (ERE) using online and other distance teaching and learning approaches [5]. Closures of educational institutions and interruption of education affected more than 1.6 billion enrolled students of all ages which equaled nearly 94% of the global student population [6, 7]. As a response to the COVID-19 crisis, emergency remote education was put into practice to ensure the continuity of education for students via home learning supported by the educational institutions. However, teachers and students alike witnessed that emergency remote education is not just a case of 'learning from home' but that a reinterpretation of pedagogical approaches to adjust to the 'new normal' situation [8]. Educators and practitioners, with short notice and little preparation time, were confronted with redesigning their curricula, changing their pedagogical and assessment practices from face-to-face to online virtual classrooms and embracing additional pastoral care of their students in order to maintain their wellbeing and the quality of the educational experience and performance.

The rapid shift of formal face-to-face teaching and learning to being online distance teaching and learning left teachers, parents and other stakeholders lacking in confidence that students were receive an appropriate education through the virtual or digital learning environments or workplaces as well as concerns about safety and security [8]. Sudden switching from face-to-face to online teaching and learning, and the speed of the change and transition have given limited space and time for many teachers and learners to develop the necessary knowledge, understanding and skills needed to teach and learn online. It has been challenging for many educators to learn and use various tools and techniques and create engaging learning opportunities in the unfamiliar virtual learning environments or digital workspaces [9]. The crisis further revealed the flaws in the global education systems and taught a lesson that in this twenty-first century with all technological advancement, most nations are not prepared for educational crises, which require new approaches to education and emerging innovative pedagogies.

The effect of the COVID-19 pandemic on the education sector has halted the traditional education system but has also fostered innovation due to the challenges of the crisis. This not only included switching from face-to-face to online distance teaching and learning, but also unparalleled parental involvement in children's education, and the development of families' coping mechanisms when forced to 'self-quarantine' or work from home. In the vein of challenges and learning opportunities, this chapter outlines strategies, methods, and tools to address the prevention of gaps in continuing education during these unprecedented times. This chapter focuses on three questions in order to better understand and suggest recommendations for policy and practice in the context of education in emergencies:

1. What is education in emergencies?

2. Why is mental wellbeing important during a crisis time?

3. How can e-learning help individuals, including teachers and students cope with the situation and at the same time support their personal and professional growth?

2. Education in emergencies (EiE): challenges and opportunities of teaching and learning online

Education, in general, is 'life-saving, life-sustaining and life-transforming lifelong process' ([10], p. 2) and in emergencies, it creates the learning opportunities for individuals and can equip them to face on-going crises as well as crises to come [11].

Education in emergencies (EiE) has been defined in such a way that educational needs are met along with humanitarian assistance provided, to protect individuals in a crisis [10]. Education in emergencies is based on the concept of "education as a humanitarian response" [12–14]. That is why, the UNHCR ([15], online), explains that "[e]ducation in emergencies provides immediate physical and psychosocial protection, as well as life-saving knowledge and skills (for example, with respect to disease prevention, self-protection, and awareness of rights). If children and youth receive a good quality education in a safe manner during and after an emergency, they will be exposed less frequently to activities that put them at risk. They will also acquire knowledge and mental resources that increase their resilience to help them to protect themselves".

Education in emergencies covers "education that protects the wellbeing, fosters learning opportunities and nurtures the overall development (social, emotional, cognitive, and physical) of children affected by conflicts and disasters" ([16], p. 23; [17], p. 4). Therefore, education in emergencies could be defined as "education that is provided during times of crisis created by conflicts or disasters" ([10], p. 2). However, any conflict or disaster destabilises, disorganises or destroys the existing education system, and requires an integrated process of crisis and post-crisis assistance to continue education [18]. During any natural or man-made crisis, education in emergencies "increasingly serves as shorthand for schooling and other organised studies, together with 'normalising' structured activities, arranged for and with children, young people and adults whose lives have been disrupted by conflict and major natural disasters" ([19], p. 4).

According to UNESCO ([18], p. 11), "the rationales of the educational responses in emergencies are to provide humanitarian assistance as follows:

- Education helps meet the psychological needs of children affected by conflicts or disasters which disrupts their lives and social networks.

- Education is a tool for protecting and safeguarding children in emergencies as they are extremely vulnerable in situations.

- Education provides a channel for conveying health and survival messages as well as tools and techniques for teaching new skills and values, such as peace, tolerance, conflict resolutions, democracy, human rights, environmental conservation.

- Education for All (EFA) is a tool for social cohesion, whereas educational discrepancies lead to poverty for the uneducated and fuel civil conflict.

- Education is vital to the reconstruction of the socio-economic and cultural basis of family, local and national life and for sustainable development and peacebuilding".

In order to minimise the effect and maximise the impact of education in emergencies, emerging technologies have been used increasingly for teaching and learning for more than two decades. Technological advancement also enriches the teaching materials, makes the best use of time and allows having live, visual and authentic learning conditions which ignite learners to absorb knowledge [20, 21]. It is important for educators to understand and command the new technologies and be able to use them in the process of learning. However, this does not mean that technology takes over the instructor's tasks and human presence in the learning process. Technology is there only as learning support to strengthen material explanations from an instructor and for students to understand concepts better and develop skills. Thus, the presence of an instructor is necessary for the detailed explanation of the contents and learning process, and they must respond to the new technology and its role in the learning [22].

Online distance learning (ODL) is the use of the internet and some other important technologies to develop materials for educational purposes, instructional delivery and management of the educational programmes [23, 24]. There are two types of online distance learning - asynchronous and synchronous online learning which are often compared, but for online learning to be effective and efficient, instructors, organisations and institutions must be aware of the benefits and limitations of both [25]. The consistent growth in technology and internet accessibility has increased the thrust for online teaching and learning [26], but Joshi et al. [27] concluded that the instructional achievement of online learning is debatable because of the absence of face-to-face relationship among learners and learning facilitators (i.e. teachers, instructors or trainers). However, there are clear distinctions between adequately planned online learning experiences and courses presented online as a response to the crisis [5, 28]. Online learning during this pandemic is referred to as 'emergency remote education', 'emergency remote learning' or 'emergency remote teaching and learning' because it is in contrast with the quality or effectiveness of providing education online [5, 29].

Due to the COVID-19 pandemic, online distance teaching and learning have become a necessity to maintain continuity of education. This pandemic has made the educational institutions and other organisations go online and become agents of change and digital transformation. Some educators and learners were reluctant to accept the emerging technologies for online teaching and learning or training for professional development at the beginning of the pandemic. They thought that their disciplinary teaching and learning approaches might not be suitable through online teaching and learning. For example, some modules in science and engineering programmes require physical demonstration or lab work so that student can have face-to-face interactions with their teacher to understand practical aspects and learn. As a result of lockdown, they had to change or alter their approaches to adjust with emergency remote teaching and learning so that they can continue their education programmes and complete their courses in time.

For online distance teaching and learning, virtual connections to the university's servers to access the software and tools had been helpful in supporting the learning for both students and faculty members. In most universities, there have been live lectures, seminars or labs which may have also been pre-recorded or recorded live sessions uploaded and e-resources to make them accessible at any time from anywhere. It is a great opportunity from the students' point of view that they can access the materials at anytime from anywhere and revisit or revise the available resources [30, 31]. One of the main advantages of the use of technology is that a large number of students can join online session at one time. For example, most of the UK universities have capacity to have 250+ students to join in their online session(s) at the same time.

Although there have been many challenges and difficulties to operate emergency remote teaching and learning (ERTL), for example, as already mentioned above that there are many courses or modules which require practical sessions or lab demonstrations [29]. So, the importance of face-to-face pedagogical approaches cannot be denied, but considering the current emergency situation imposed by the COVID-19 pandemic, online delivery of education seems to be the best alternative for the continuity of education [5]. Some universities across the globe have adopted a blended or hybrid learning approach following government guidelines, where the situation permitted. Alongside online session, whenever health regulations supported, there were arrangements for face-to-face sessions which improve the learning process and student engagement and satisfaction.

There have been many other issues in terms of online distance learning for students and teaching for staff, such as the availability internet (with a reasonable speed), a modest device (i.e. mobile phone set, tablet, laptop or computer with headphone and microphone), and a space where they could sit comfortably, quietly, without distractions to participate in teaching and learning. Many universities of the developed nations (e.g. UK, USA, Japan) have done their best to support their students and staff. For instance, these universities allow their students and staff to borrow laptop or desktop computers, headphones with microphones, and ergonomic keyboards and chairs (especially for staff). However, there are only limited resources and obviously not all universities can provide such resources to all staff and students which is another challenge of emergency remote online learning.

Considering the above benefits and challenges of online distance teaching and learning, it is crucial to go on with emergency remote (online distance) teaching and learning especially at this point of time (during the lockdown in the pandemic). Despite many barriers and challenges, online teaching and learning have undoubtedly improved further with the passage of time. The current trend shows that the tendency for online distance teaching and learning has gone up as compared to previous years [32] as this pandemic has left no other satisfactory choice than learning mostly online. Providing education online gives the option for people to learn, increase their knowledge and skills, and make the best use of their time especially during lockdown, isolation and quarantine. Being stuck at home, people may find more time to keep them engaged in learning activities [5, 29].

3. Mental wellbeing and its importance while providing education in emergencies

An individual's mental wellbeing is significantly important during a time of crisis to reduce the risk to mental health, especially psychological stability and morale [33–35]. As defined, mental health is a condition of a person that includes emotional, psychological, and social wellbeing [36]. It affects how people think, feel, and act so that they can manage their stress and anxiety. Around the world, people have been managing mental health and mental illness in different ways [37]. In the current situation imposed by the COVID-19 pandemic, many individuals including students and educators may have experienced mental stress and distress [38, 39] due to the changes in personal, social and economic circumstances such as being stuck at home, domestic violence, unemployment, loss of a job, loss of loved one or family breakdown [40–43]. Such mental stress can create various kinds of feelings or behaviours which directly or indirectly impact on their health and wellbeing, learning and educational attainments [44]. These could include sleeping too much or too little, getting away from usual activities, feeling low energy, feeling hopeless and down, developing habits of smoking or drinking, getting confused or upset, being worried about the current situation and the unseen and unpredictable future [40–43].

Mental wellbeing is ubiquitous in learning, and mental health affects cognition differently [45]. Likewise, O'Regan [46] described mental wellbeing as being vital during online learning and his research has put mental health at the centre of the teaching and learning process. Mental health has been seen to be significant in learning as it relates to and acts as a driving force for academic achievement, motivation, efficiency, identity formation, individual development, and overall wellbeing; yet it may negatively influence the achievement of learning outcomes, progress, and experience [47–51].

During the pandemic, the burning question in the context of education is: how can educators keep their learners engaged and motivated when many of them suffer from economic deprivations, losses of loved ones, health issues or lack of resources?

COVID-19 and the consequences of social distancing have brought anxiety and self-doubt for many individuals [41]. In this situation, many other questions arise: How can educators go through such challenging times, while improving their educational practices and the quality of learning of their learners? How can they keep their students motivated and encourage them about learning and education where the future seems blurred?

Due to the multifaceted impact of the situation, it is suggested that students should be connected with other people, be physically active, learn new skills, create positive feelings and be mindful [52]. However, what are the practicalities of such suggestions when a student seeks help for a mental health problem during his or her educational journey? Some students may need clinical treatment of their mental illness and it could be difficult for them to get the right guidance and treatments. Therefore, an integrated strategic support should be in place to help these kinds of learners including psychological, social and financial supports.

Considering the various impacts of the COVID-19 pandemic on learning, students require help and support in different areas. The support initiatives should include, but not limited to curriculum, class duration, teaching methods and techniques, teacher-students relationship, exam preparation, online extra-curricular activities, managing finances, mindset about online class. They should also be supported in coping with isolation and homesickness while they are stuck at their accommodations, and maintaining relationships with families and friends from a distance [38, 39, 53–55] (**Figure 1**).

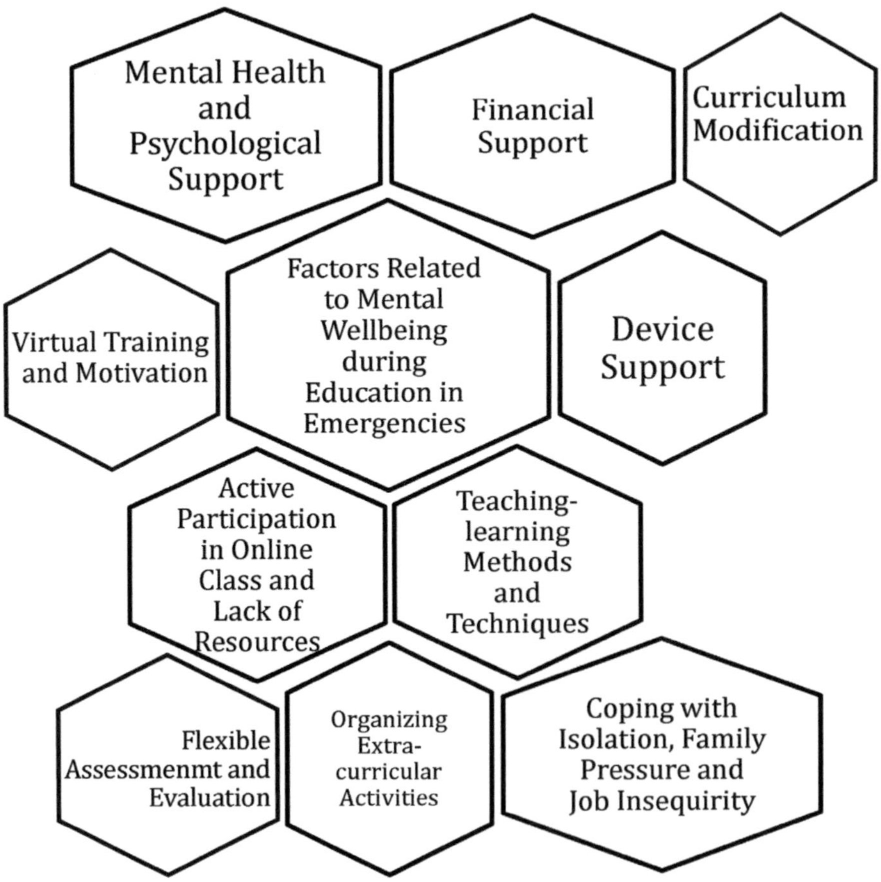

Figure 1.
Factors need to be supported for individuals' mental wellbeing during education in emergencies.

Ensuring an emotionally healthy e-learning environment and recognising mental wellbeing in learning are important for both learners and teachers. These are fundamental components of quality dynamic in learning and cognitive success [56]. The whole body, including affective, emotional, physiological, motivational, and expressive elements, is implicated in mental wellbeing [51, 57]. The correlation between cognition and mental health is bidirectional, which means that cognition and mental health operate in two ways, so both must be better understood [58].

Baker et al. [59] highlighted that the elements that trigger learning challenges and disruptive behaviours may be caused by boredom and misunderstanding, whilst also asserting that concentration is a factor for better learning. These variables are determined by various interface qualities, pedagogical values and resources. O'Neil and Spielberger [60] contended that extreme stress and pressure degrade understanding and thus inadequate learning (all of which may have been exacerbated by the COVID-19 pandemic) may be elicited by limited memory, attention span or decision-making, regardless of having the engaged motivation. In addition, LePine et al. [61] found that *challenge*-related stress had a positive relationship to learning performance, and that *barrier*-related stress had a negative relationship to learning performance and mental health in an e-learning context. They also indicated that these stress-learning performance relationships had been partly mediated by fatigue and the desire to learn. As a consequence, changes in motivation, loss of focus and control, and significant tension that the student experiences are the problems that both the student and the teacher must resolve.

In an online teaching and learning setting, even with a synchronous teacher present, it is difficult for teachers to notice or discuss any mental health-related issues with individual students. Subsequently, it is even more difficult to recognise such unproductive emotional states such as boredom, and irritation. It is certainly not enough for the teacher to evaluate students' success by monitoring quantitative facts, like the frequency of tasks, the number of posts and the grades earned [62]. If a teacher neglects or is unaware of the mental health issues of any student and the reasons that cause the student to act as he or she does, then the teacher will not be able to promote the concentration of the student or to enhance his or her potential achievement.

Culture, age and gender are also elements that impact mental health problems in e-learning. This is evident in how some learners prepare for online tests or feels online test anxiety, how they communicate feelings virtually, how they respond to student-teacher relationships and communications, and how they react to online verbal and non-verbal stimuli [63]. Male students appear to show higher levels of negative emotions and greater emotional arousal [64] while female students appear to be more open to obtaining teacher support [65]. It is worth noting that mental wellbeing and emotions are experienced by all those participating in the e-learning process (i.e., learners, teachers, support staff) and are crucial to the relationship with and between these individuals [66]. Fiedler and Beier [58] indicated that an educational environment such as an e-learning context is "full of experience, anxiety, and fun, anger, and satisfaction, dissatisfaction, and pride" (p. 36). Negative experiences of mental health problems such as frustration can be compounded in an online distance teaching and learning setting as there is no physical connection with peers and teachers and, for many, there are only a few mental health support systems that are accessible or suitable.

These mental health problems can be alleviated by developing awareness and getting prompt, personalised support. Developing digital self-efficacy and technological proficiency can also minimise some fears and anxieties while individuals engage in a self-regulated learning process [67, 68]. Teachers, who aim to teach more online and welcome change, will relieve some of their students' worries and anxieties about teaching online [69, 70]. For students, mental wellbeing may be improved by taking part in evidence-based online teaching and learning orientation [71], by getting access to course materials as early as possible, by warm welcoming addresses from the teacher, or by continuous teaching presence in an e-learning setting [72]. Further support strategies for test, technology and second-language anxieties can also be introduced [73, 74].

Teachers' roles in ensuring students' mental health and wellbeing in learning and online teaching are similarly complex, as positions vary widely across higher education and within e-learning. There are, nonetheless, several recommendations for higher education lecturers who are teaching online that can be obtained from research. To maintain a safe and creative virtual space for learning, the online distance higher education teachers can take a significant responsibility [75]. Concerning mental health and wellbeing throughout the learning process, teachers should "pay close attention to learners' epistemic wellbeing to foster their self-regulated knowledge generation" ([45], p. 15) through students' voices. Thus, "[t]eaching and learning practices which foster both cooperation and competition, independence and self-evaluation, can build the strength of students' voices in ways that do not deny learners' self-identity and values" ([76], pp. 333–334). Higher education lecturers, who develop their own modules, in their module design, they should take into consideration, recognise and acknowledge the importance of good mental health in learning and incorporate tailored interventions, feedback and advice, and support accordingly [48].

Chen et al. [77] make the clear yet important argument that student satisfaction is a key element in the successful implementation of the e-learning programme. Students' high satisfaction of learning, as they claim, is associated with lower dropout rates, increase engagement, learning success and dedication to the programmes they enrolled. There is evidence, however, that students with high levels of mental health problems prefer to keep their difficulties concealed rather than disclosing them [77]. Moreover, students with these forms of concealed wellbeing problems generally drop out of learning and tend to avoid continuing e-learning. As these students do not, in fact, highlight the problems to others, the issues are perpetuated and do not get discovered. Course designers and researchers should thus be mindful when determining the quality of the e-learning course on the basis of basic end-of-course surveys. Researchers should consider how to capture the hidden mental wellbeing of students in addition to collecting students' impressions before they get disaffected and drop out of the course. Satisfaction and good mental wellbeing are therefore significant in e-learning and online education.

After a long period of emergency remote learning and lockdown due to the COVID-19 pandemic, learners are struggling with academic engagement and as their institutional face-to-face teaching and learning has been disrupted. They are also deprived of their friends' and associates' physical presence in their everyday life. In such circumstances, learners are unable to share their emotions with their peers. Moreover, learners are being pressured by teachers and parents to complete the syllabus or course content in order to maintain academic performance. Here it must be mentioned that even in a pandemic situation, there is no change in parental expectation of getting higher marks in exams from their children. However, only a few changes could be considered by parents such as shortening a more extended curriculum and changing traditional paper-pencil assessment procedures to be able to produce a digital copy of the exam script [78, 79].

Due to sudden switching to emergency remote teaching and learning, learners are not prepared, and they are less confident to follow the virtual instructions of their teachers. Some primary and secondary level students become dependent on their parents or other family members to participate in their virtual class due to lack of technological skills for using online learning tools [80–82]. As a result, students become less self-esteemed and motivated to learn as well as possessing little enjoyment in a virtual classroom [83, 84]. These are the common scenarios of the poor mental state of students in underdeveloped and developing countries. Therefore, students should be provided with various kinds of help and support to cope with mental health issues. These supports could include helping in exam preparation, managing finances, personal tutoring, supporting for coping with homesickness, maintaining relationships with families or worrying about future employment or career prospects.

4. The future: technological adaptation and integration for blended or hybrid learning

The effect of the sudden change and immediacy of emergency remote teaching and learning was challenging for many educators, including lecturers and support staff [85, 86]. The COVID-19 pandemic has required a long-term adjustment with clear consequences for teaching and learning settings, and conventional face-to-face lessons are being transformed to incorporate a combination of synchronous and asynchronous pedagogical approaches and delivery methods. Although many teachers and academics have expertise and experience with designing, developing, delivering and assessing blended and e-learning, there remain many academics and educators that do not hold the expertise or knowledge to cope with such a shift. As a result, education work settings have become more collegial and collaborative with colleagues supporting one another. Educators are helping each other to make this continuous professional development process moving forward by offering not only course design and development support but also instructional tips. This process of collegiality support the transformation of traditional education, to enable it to be successful, through blended and online experiences, in developing better learning outcomes for their students [87]. While collegiality is good to see, it is placing an additional burden on all staff members with an already strained workload.

Nevertheless, the focus should be on the lived experiences of the teachers who support other colleagues and can offer lessons, experiences, and tips towards supporting their colleagues that will be lost if not documented in a timely fashion. Therefore, documentation of one's own experience and sharing such knowledge with others is essential. This would also provide an opportunity to develop an instructional guideline as well as policy and procedural recommendation tools to assist others. This strategy helps to recreate instructional reflective learning in a collegial environment in which the organisation moves from self-sustaining strategy towards recognising its own success. The willingness of academics to support each other shows the importance of collegiate unions, while showcasing strategies, innovative pedagogy, engagement styles and assessment alternatives, which are all new ideas for most organisations under current education in emergencies. This could offer a unique chance to document the knowledge and lessons learnt, as well as to take a long-term perspective of the systemic effect and e-learning opportunities.

For educational institutions to go ahead with e-learning, it is vital to ensure inclusiveness of provisions that all students be considered, as well as what policies and practices must be introduced to accommodate and address the needs of all stakeholders, now and in the future. One of the best approaches is to keep record of the experiences through the lens of educators and academics who are at the forefront of teaching and learning.

To maintain learners' effective virtual learning which will enhance their mental wellbeing and will fulfil the goal of education in emergencies (EiE) the following specific strategies and psycho-social interventional steps may be appropriate:

1. In the light of the theories of Socrates and Plato the virtual class as well as distant teaching and learning tasks should be of essence or form (means an existence which is separated from its individual manifestations) based [88]. In this way, e-learning should be focused on basic ideas about all relevant aspects of life, especially dealing with ongoing emergency including what is important, what to do, where to go and how to cope with different situations.

2. From May's existential psychological perspective on 'Normal or Healthy Anxiety' [88] which is conducive to personal growth - a virtual class climate can be created in which all learners feel a 'normal' or 'healthy' anxiety to engage. In this way, the learners' anxiety about virtual class could be positive, which will enhance their learning.

3. According to Rogers [88], learners, teachers and parents in pandemic circumstances need to accept virtual or emergency remote education. Therefore, new coping strategies or new ways of coping should be introduced among education stakeholders and beneficiaries. Basic technology skill-based virtual training programmes need to be implemented for students, teachers, administrators and parents so that they will be able to use different e-learning tools including conferencing tools such as Zoom, Google Classroom, Microsoft Team, Skype, Blackboard Collaborate etc. independently.

4. Becoming enlightened through Rogers' [88] point of view on personality, virtual learning should be self-explorative. The virtual class climate should be positive for students' expression of opinion, feelings, belief and decision making. Thus, individual presentation, dual presentation and discussion, group presentation and discussion and webinars can all be incorporated into online classes. In this way, students will be able to realise their inner potentials and teacher-centric lecture time will be reduced. Research shows that the discussion method is better than the lecture method in terms of students' academic achievement [89]. This practice will also reduce students' anxiety and increase participation and engagement in e-learning.

5. Many educational and cultural practices could be interchangeably used in online and traditional educational approaches [90]. Students are equally valued in all respects by teachers whether they are on campus face-to-face class or in a virtual class. Such unconditional acceptance and empathy should be expressed by teachers towards all students. If a teacher calls the students by name, monitors all students and provides positive and constructive feedback to each of the students virtually, students will own such a class and be motivated to engage academically.

6. According to Piaget [91], primary education learners are in the concrete operational stage of cognitive development and therefore they might not be able to think in the abstract ways that come in the formal operational stage of adolescence. This means a teacher's virtual instruction for primary level learners in virtual class should be as specific, clear and experiential as possible. For example, in a distant learning virtual classroom clear-cut verbal instruction should be provided in order not to confuse the students. On the one hand, students of this age could be asked to make different materials relevant to their textbook topics. In this way, such learners will experience their text-book topic empirically. On the other hand, secondary, higher secondary and tertiary level students may be better able to deal with abstract instructions which can develop their creative and critical thinking.

7. The curriculum may be shortened, specific, explorative, need-based, life skills and culture oriented. The need to develop 21st-century competencies has received global recognition [92–94], but instructional methods have not been reformed yet to include the teaching of these skills. Multiple frameworks include creativity, critical thinking, communication, and collaboration as the foundational competencies which it is advocated should be incorporated in curricula across all levels of education. The challenges in building foundational competencies through designing new curriculums and implementing pedagogy necessitate specialised training. Regardless of such training, pedagogy can be affected by educators' individual perceptions of it, financial pressures, access to resources, societal problems, and the sheer speed of international transitions, in addition to other factors. With the introduction of digitalisation into the sphere of education, it is unknown if educational barriers have been eliminated or removed through e-learning or, whether it became a further barrier in maintaining inequalities in education.

8. Considerations should be given to education sessions, as the number of lessons may be increased or decreased for an 'optimum period' considering the nature of emergencies, i.e. the COVID-19 pandemic. The student's levels, needs, requirements and contexts should be considered when making such decisions. At the end of the day, the focus of e-learning should be all about the students' academic attainments – their learning, their academic results, and so much more. Educators and learning organisations will be able to better develop their online, satisfy students' needs, and place themselves in a dynamic global market if they have a better understanding of the online process and how to better support educators in their teaching and students in their learning journey [95].

9. Any events that take place outside of the regular (compulsory) curriculum are referred to as "extracurricular activities" [96]. Cultural and extracurricular programmes can be carried out through webinars which will decrease students' academic and other stress. These kinds of webinars or e-learning activities will enhance students attachment and engagement with their teachers, classmates and institutions. In turn, these will decrease their engagement with destructing activities online. Through these extracurricular online activities students should have the opportunity to sing, dance, play a role or debate as well as virtually connect with one another from their home setting [97]. Virtual quizzes or art competitions can be held to engage the students and keep them busy in a constructive way [97, 98].

10. Physical education should be compulsory and incorporated into the curriculum by which an instructor will conduct a class on physical exercises virtually. Students will follow the instructor's instructions virtually and will do physical exercises from their home. This type of physical activity session should be monitored by the teacher or a professional instructor. The following four themes have been identified as important for the future of physical education and are prevalent in the online physical education course: 1) appropriate curriculum for students, 2) individualised option for students, 3) family-friendly content, and 4) lessons that involve students in developing long-term, healthy lifestyle behaviours [99]. While completing assignments and working out in their own environment, students in an online physical education (PE) class practice self-directed learning habits, and they often become health advocates in their own homes [100].

11. The term "morality" refers to the theoretical, systemic, and logical analysis of human actions and interactions. It concerns human behaviour, where moral activity is practical [101]. Values are associated with human beliefs and attitudes. Society, spirituality and culture have strong connections with morals, values and ethics [102–104]. Religious education (RE) has a greater impact on preparing young people to live and work in a diverse community than any other subjects [105]. Online religion-focused education should be available in order to enhance and connect with learners' moral development during the emergency.

12. Everyone, including children, young people, young adults, students, and scholars, is influenced by online learning. Virtual classes can exacerbate underlying mental health issues for many students. Others may experience new mental health and mood changes due to the pandemic and online learning [106]. Basic safety awareness based virtual classes also should be taken by learners of all ages to be aware of how to ensure safety against viruses, abuse, mental health issues and online safety.

13. Assessment methods have an impact on how students learn, and online assessments must be structured to encourage students to engage in positive learning behaviours [4]. Online assessment procedures should be flexible as now education is being provided in emergency situations. On the basis of virtual class attendance, virtual class participation and rate of academic engagement in virtual class-assessment should have monitored. The proportion of paper-based traditional tests should be reduced as much as possible and continuous, holistic assessment must be focused [86]. Particularly, physical, religion and safety awareness-based educational topics should be measured visually and verbally that is through viva voce among the students.

14. Free internet connections [107] such as open WiFi facilities [54] must be available for the sake of students' academic advancement in underprivileged areas of under developing and developing countries. Financial support must be given to poor students to buy handheld devices (i.e. smart mobile, tablet or laptop) and internet data [38, 39]. Ergonomically designed and comfortable tables and chairs should be provided to poor and physically disabled students at home. Educational mobile apps must be developed for children, adolescents, adults, and also for physically disabled students, for those who have hearing problems and for learners who are partially or fully blind. By providing these financial supports and other essential resources, students should be able to do their works including attending virtual classes at home with safety and security. This would be the reflection of Maslow's theory of self-actualization where the first two steps of basic needs are fulfilled [88]. Furthermore, Lewin's 'life space' concept [88] also considers the learners' physical and psychological aspects of life.

15. According to existentialist Binswanger [88], the learners' surrounding world of things and events must be considered. Therefore, he emphasises, how the learner communicates with surroundings and his or her subjective experience of self must be considered. To fulfil this issue, educational and school psychologists and family therapists should be virtually paired with teachers, students and parents. With the help of virtual psychotherapy and mental health clinicians, students will be able to improve their mental health and wellbeing and acknowledge the meaning of life in emergencies.

16. Decentralisation of education is not an end in itself, but it may be an important means of improving education [108]. Decentralisation is described as "possibly the single most advocated reform for improving the provision of such basic services as education and health in developing countries" in the literature on education ([109], p. 131). Decentralised power such as power given to local authorities should be implemented in the education sector for developing and under-developing countries. In this way, individual and cultural area-based students' needs should be explored.

17. There is a need for more empirical research in the field of education in emergencies (EiE) to support advanced understandings of learner engagement, mental health and wellbeing issues, interactive activities in remote teaching and learning, and building effective collegiate communities [10]. Moreover, real and perceived social learning activities towards supporting the individuals' cognitive engagement and learning outcomes, career development and personal performance behaviours are equally important to improve the quality of e-learning for individuals in emergencies.

18. There is currently a significant void, and future studies could concentrate more on in-depth study of online instruction practices, step-by-step implementation, and the most successful online course design and instruction practices [95]. However, during emergencies, educational researchers (including teachers, administrators, leaders) should engage to conduct participatory and critical action research in different learning environments or modalities (i.e. face-to-face, online and blended) to better understand different delivery modes and improve their practices.

5. Conclusion

The current COVID-19 pandemic has forced public and private organisations, companies and institutions as well as individuals to change their behaviours during lockdown to maintain social distancing. As a result, 'working from home' and 'home learning' using digital technologies have become the new norm. However, technological advancement has already led to the digital transformation of everyday life, and technology-enhanced learning has already been widely adopted by many education institutions across the globe. In the sudden emergency remote teaching and learning, especially designing and delivering education at short notice, has made digital technologies a ubiquitous requirement for teachers and students to continue their teaching and learning, and especially for higher education institutions to provide education. Such new paradigms have led the education sector worldwide to change the ways of teaching and learning in a significantly short period of time, which creates both challenges and opportunities.

Teaching and learning are essential parts of the rounded development of individuals to unfold their potential. However, the perspectives of individuals involved in teaching and learning through the unprecedented time during the COVID-19 pandemic are crucial to understand the barriers and challenges of the situation. Teachers as practitioners have important insights to offer into how they overcome the difficulties through changes in practice and innovations in pedagogical methods and approaches using different digital or non-digital teaching and learning platforms and different tools and techniques. Therefore, research needs to be carried out to identify the good practices of teaching and learning and proper use of emerging technologies in order to understand the role of digital education in the context of the twenty-first century.

Even though numerous programmes have been delivered through e-learning in different educational institutions including schools, colleges and universities, this is the first time for most teachers and students to use virtual teaching and learning tools and technologies in their full-time education programmes. In this vein, the chapter has explored how experienced and new users of emerging technologies are dealing with the new circumstances. Interest in artificial intelligence and online technologies [110–112] has amplified significantly in universities, showing that there are useful platforms in aiding teaching and learning as well as increasing students' motivation and engagement. Thus e-learning has created new avenues for the education sector worldwide and shown its potential to support mental wellbeing.

Author details

M. Mahruf C. Shohel[1]*, Arif Mahmud[2], Munira Azhar Urmee[3], Muhammad Naveed Anwar[4], Mohammad Mojibur Rahman[5], Dev Raj Acharya[6] and Md. Ashrafuzzaman[7]

1 Institute of Development Studies, University of Sussex, Brighton, United Kingdom

2 Department of Education, University of Roehampton, London, United Kingdom

3 Department of Psychology, Jagannath University, Dhaka, Bangladesh

4 Department of Computer and Information Sciences, Northumbria University, Newcastle, United Kingdom

5 Institute of Education and Research, University of Dhaka, Dhaka, Bangladesh

6 Institute of Health, University of Wolverhampton, Wolverhampton, United Kingdom

7 Department of Education, Bangabandhu Sheikh Mujibur Rahman Digital University, Bangladesh, Gazipur, Bangladesh

*Address all correspondence to: mahruf.shohel@yahoo.co.uk; m.m.c.shohel@alumni.manchester.ac.uk

References

[1] Bacher-Hicks, Andrew, Goodman, J. and Mulhern, C. (2020). *Inequality in household adaptation to schooling shocks: Covid-induced online learning engagement in real time*. No. w27555. National Bureau of Economic Research.

[2] OECD. (2020). OECD Policy Responses to Coronavirus (COVID-19): Youth and COVID-19: Response, recovery and resilience, Retrieved from https://www.oecd.org/coronavirus/policy-responses/youth-and-covid-19-response-recovery-and-resilience-c40e61c6/

[3] Raaper, R, and Brown, C. (2020). The Covid-19 pandemic and the dissolution of the university campus: Implications for student support practice." *Journal of Professional Capital and Community*.

[4] Rahim, A. F. A. (2020). Guidelines for online assessment in emergency remote teaching during the COVID-19 pandemic. Education in Medical Journal, 12(2):59-68. https://doi.org/10.21315/eimj2020.12.2.6

[5] Shohel, M. M. C., Ashrafuzzaman, M., Mahmud, A., Ahsan, M. S., and Alam, A. T. M. (2021). Education in Emergencies, Inequalities, and the Digital Divide: Strategies for Supporting Teachers and Students in Higher Education in Bangladesh. In, L. Kyei-Blankson, J. Blankson and E. Ntuli (eds). *Handbook of Research on Inequities in Online Education During Global Crises*. Hershey, USA: IGI Global.

[6] United Nations (UN). (2020). *Policy Brief: Education During Covid-19 And Beyond*. New York, USA: United Nations. Retrieved from https://www.un.org/development/desa/dspd/wp-content/uploads/sites/22/2020/08/sg_policy_brief_covid-19_and_education_august_2020.pdf

[7] UNESCO. (2020). UN Secretary-General warns of education catastrophe, pointing to UNESCO estimate of 24 million learners at risk of dropping out, Retrieved from https://en.unesco.org/news/secretary-general-warns-education-catastrophe-pointing-unesco-estimate-24-million-learners-0

[8] Rapanta, C., Botturi, L., Goodyear, P. Guàrdia, L. and Koole, M. (2020). Online University Teaching During and After the Covid-19 Crisis: Refocusing Teacher Presence and Learning Activity. Postdigit Sci Educ **2,** 923-945 (2020). https://doi.org/10.1007/s42438-020-00155-y

[9] Bradbury, B. L., Suarez-Sousa, X. P., Coquyt, M., Bockelmann, T. L., and Pahl, A. L. (2020). Teaching Under Crisis: Impact and Implications of the COVID-19 Pandemic on Education in Minnesota. The Interactive Journal of Global Leadership and Learning, *1*(2), 2.

[10] Shohel, M. M. C. (2020). Education in emergencies: challenges of providing education for Rohingya children living in refugee camps in Bangladesh, Education Inquiry, DOI:10.1080/20004508.2020.1823121

[11] Sinclair, M. (2001a). Education in Emergencies. In Crisp, J., Talbot, C. and Cipollone, D. B. (eds.), Learning for a Future: Refugee Education in Developing Countries. Lausanne: United Nations Publications, pp.1-84.

[12] Kagawa, F. (2005). Emergency education: A critical review of the field. Comparative Education, 41(4), 487-503.

[13] Retamal, G., and Aedo-Richmond, R. (Eds.). (1998). Education as a humanitarian response.

[14] Sinclair, M. (2006). Education in Emergencies. In Commonwealth

Secretariat (Eds.), Commonwealth education partnership 2007 (pp. 52-56). Cambridge, UK: Nexus Strategic Partnerships.

[15] UNHCR. (2015). Emergency handbook: Education in emergencies. Geneva: UNHCR. Retrieved from https://emergency.unhcr.org/entry/101908/education-in-emergencies

[16] Sinclair, M. (2002). Planning education in and after emergencies. Paris: UNESCO.

[17] Kamel, H. (2006). Early childhood care and education in emergency situations. Paris: UNESCO.

[18] UNESCO. (2002). Guidelines for education in situations of emergency and crisis: EFA strategic planning. Paris: UNESCO.

[19] Sinclair, M. (2001b). Education in Emergencies. In J. Crisp, C. Talbot, and D. B. Cipollone (Eds.), Learning for a future: Refugee education in developing countries (pp. 1-83). Geneva: Switzerland. UNHCR (United Nations High Commissioner for Refugees 20).

[20] Kaharuddin, A. (2018). The communicative grammar translation method: a practical method to teach communication skills of English. ETERNAL (English, Teaching, Learning, and Research Journal), Vol. 4, N. 2, pp. 232-254.

[21] Susikaran, R. S. A., and Phil, M. (2013). The use of multimedia in English language teaching. Journal of Technology for ELT, Vol. 3, No. 2, pp. [PAGE No.]

[22] Gilakjani, A. P. (2017). A Review of the Literature on the Integration of Technology into the Learning and Teaching of English Language Skills. International Journal of English Linguistics, Vol. 7, No. 5, pp. 95-106.

[23] Fry, K. (2001). E-learning markets and providers: Some issues and prospects. Education+ Training, 43(4/5), 233-239. https://doi.org/10.1108/EUM0000000005484.

[24] Means, B., Toyama, Y., Murphy, R., Bakia, M., and Jones, K. (2009). Evaluation of evidence-based practices in online learning: A meta-analysis and review of online learning studies.

[25] Hrastinski, S. (2008). Asynchronous and synchronous e-learning. Educause Quarterly, 31(4), 51-55.

[26] Tallent-Runnels, M. K., Thomas, J. A., Lan, W. Y., Cooper, S., Ahern, T. C., Shaw, S. M., and Liu, X. (2006). Teaching courses online: A review of the research. Review of Educational Research, 76(1), 93-135. https://doi.org/10.3102/00346543076001093

[27] Joshi, O., Chapagain, B., Kharel, G., Poudyal, N. C., Murray, B. D., and Mehmood, S. R. (2020). Benefits and challenges of online instruction in agriculture and natural resource education. *Interactive Learning Environments*, 1-12. http://doi.org/10.1080/10494820.2020.1725896

[28] Hodges, C., Moore, S., Lockee, B., Trust, T., and Bond, A. (2020). The difference between emergency remote teaching and online learning. *Educause Review*, (March 27, 2020). https://er.educause.edu/articles/2020/3/the-differencebetween-emergency-remote-teaching-and-online-learning.

[29] Shohel, M. M. C., Sham, S., Ashrafuzzaman, M., Alam, A. T. M., Mamun, A. A. and Kabir, M. M. (Under Review, 2021). Emergency Remote Teaching and Learning: Digital Competencies and Pedagogical Transformation in Resource-Constrained Contexts. In, M. Islam, S. Behera and L. Naibaho (eds). *Handbook of Research on Asian Perspectives of the Educational Impact of COVID-19*. Hershey, USA: IGI Global.

[30] King, E., and Boyatt, R. (2015). Exploring factors that influence adoption of e-learning within higher education. British Journal of Educational Technology, *46*(6), 1272-1280.

[31] Violante, M. G., and Vezzetti, E. (2015). Virtual interactive e-learning application: An evaluation of the student satisfaction. Computer Applications in Engineering Education, *23*(1), 72-91.

[32] Duffin, E. (2020) E-learning and digital education - Statistics and Facts. Available at: https://www.statista.com/topics/3115/e-learning-and-digital-education/ [Last accessed: 11th October 2020]

[33] Gruber, J., Prinstein, M. J., Clark, L. A., Rottenberg, J., Abramowitz, J. S., Albano, A. M., ... and Weinstock, L. M. (2020). Mental health and clinical psychological science in the time of COVID-19: Challenges, opportunities, and a call to action. American Psychologist.

[34] Holmes, E. A., O'Connor, R. C., Perry, V. H., Tracey, I., Wessely, S., Arseneault, L., ... and Bullmore, E. (2020). Multidisciplinary research priorities for the COVID-19 pandemic: a call for action for mental health science. *The Lancet Psychiatry*.

[35] Kontoangelos, K., Economou, M., and Papageorgiou, C. (2020). Mental health effects of COVID-19 pandemia: a review of clinical and psychological traits. Psychiatry investigation, *17*(6), 491.

[36] Galderisi, S., Heinz, A., Kastrup, M., Beezhold, J., and Sartorius, N. (2015). Toward a new definition of mental health. World Psychiatry, *14*(2), 231.

[37] U.S. Department of Health and Human Services. (2020). What is mental health? Available at: https://www.mentalhealth.gov/basics/what-is-mental-health and retrieved on 14.10.2020.

[38] Daily Sun. (2020). An analysis of Bangabandhu Digital University on online education amid corona crisis, Daily Sun, May 20, 2020. Retrieved from https://www.daily-sun.com/post/480389/An-analysis-of-Bangabandhu-Digital-University-on-online-education-amid-corona-crisis

[39] Dutta, S. and Smita, M. (2020) The Impact of COVID-19 Pandemic on Tertiary Education in Bangladesh: Students' Perspectives. Open Journal of Social Sciences, **8**, 53-68. doi: 10.4236/jss.2020.89004.

[40] Elmer, T., Mepham, K., and Stadtfeld, C. (2020). Students under lockdown: Comparisons of students' social networks and mental health before and during the COVID-19 crisis in Switzerland. Plos one, *15*(7), e0236337.

[41] Sahu, P. (2020). Closure of universities due to coronavirus disease 2019 (COVID-19): impact on education and mental health of students and academic staff. Cureus, *12*(4).

[42] Wang, X., Hegde, S., Son, C., Keller, B., Smith, A., and Sasangohar, F. (2020). Investigating mental health of US college students during the COVID-19 pandemic: cross-sectional survey study. Journal of medical Internet research, *22*(9), e22817.

[43] Zhai, Y., and Du, X. (2020). Addressing collegiate mental health amid COVID-19 pandemic. Psychiatry research, *288*, 113003.

[44] Son, C., Hegde, S., Smith, A., Wang, X., Sasangohar, and F. (2020). Effects of COVID-19 on College Students' Mental Health in the United States: Interview

Survey Study J Med Internet Res, 22(9):e21279 URL: https://www.jmir.org/2020/9/e21279 doi: 10.2196/21279

[45] Vogl, E., Pekrun, R., Murayama, K., and Loderer, K. (2019). Surprised–curious– confused: Epistemic emotions and knowledge exploration. Emotion. 1- 17. Advance online publication. doi:10.1037/emo0000578

[46] O'regan, K. (2003). Emotion and e-learning. Journal of Asynchronous learning networks, 7(3), 78-92.

[47] Ainley, M. (2008). Interest: A significant thread binding cognition and affect in the regulation of learning. International Journal of Psychology, 43(3-4), 17-18.

[48] Arguel, A., Lockyer, L., Kennedy, G., Lodge, J. M., and Pachman, M. (2019). Seeking optimal confusion: a review on epistemic emotion management in interactive digital learning environments. Interactive Learning Environments, 27(2), 200-210.

[49] Artino, A. R. (2012). Emotions in online learning environments: Introduction to the special issue. The Internet and Higher Education, 15(3), 137-140. doi:10.1016/j.iheduc.2012.04.001

[50] Jackson, C. (2010). Fear in education. Educational Review, 62(1), 39-52. doi:10.1080/00131910903469544

[51] Pekrun, R., and Linnenbrink-Garcia, L. (2014). Introduction to emotions in education. In R. Pekrun and L. Linnenbrink-Garcia (Eds.), International Handbook of emotions in education (pp. 698). New York, NY: Routledge.

[52] National Health Service UK. (2019). 5 steps to mental wellbeing. Available at: https://www.nhs.uk/conditions/stress-anxiety-depression/improve-mental-wellbeing/ and retrieved on 14.10.2020.

[53] Adnan, M., and Anwar, K. (2020). Online Learning amid the COVID-19 Pandemic: Students' Perspectives. Journal of Pedagogical Research, 1, 45-51, https://doi.org/10.33902/JPSP.2020261309

[54] Ahmed, M. (2020). Tertiary Education during Covid-19 and Beyond. The Daily Star. https://www.thedailystar.net/opinion/news/tertiary-education-during-covid-19-and-beyond-1897321

[55] Aslan, I., Ochnik, D. and Çınar, O. (2020). Exploring Perceived Stress among Students in Turkey during the COVID-19 Pandemic, Int. J. Environ. Res. Public Health, 17, 8961; doi:10.3390/ijerph17238961

[56] Pekrun, R., Vogl, E., Muis, K. R., and Sinatra, G. M. (2017). Measuring emotions during epistemic activities: The epistemically-related emotion scales. Cognition and Emotion, 31(6), 1268-1276. doi:10.1080/02699931.2016.1204989

[57] Immordino-Yang, M. H., and Damasio, A. (2007). We feel, therefore we learn: The relevance of affective and social neuroscience to education. Mind, brain, and education, 1(1), 3-10.

[58] Fiedler, K., and Beier, S. (2014). Affect and cognitive processes in educational contexts. In R. Pekrun and L. Linnenbrink-Garcia (Eds.), Educational handbook series: International handbook of emotions in education. New York, NY: Routledge/Taylor and Francis. 36-55.

[59] Baker, R. S., D'Mello, S. K., Rodrigo, M. M. T., and Graesser, A. C. (2010). Better to be frustrated than bored: The incidence, persistence, and impact of learners' cognitive–affective states during interactions with three different computer-based learning environments. International Journal of Human-Computer Studies, 68(4), 223-241.

[60] O'Neil, H. F., and Spielberger, C. D. (Eds.). (1979). Cognitive and affective learning strategies. Academic Pr. 1979.

[61] LePine, J. A., LePine, M. A., and Jackson, C. L. (2004). Challenge and hindrance stress: relationships with exhaustion, motivation to learn, and learning performance. Journal of applied psychology, 89(5), 883.

[62] Jivet, I., Scheffel, M., Specht, M., and Drachsler, H. (2018). License to evaluate: Preparing learning analytics dashboards for educational practice. In *Proceedings of the 8th international conference on learning analytics and knowledge*(pp. 31-40).

[63] DeCuir-Gunby, J. T., and Williams-Johnson, M. (2014). Culture and emotions: Implications for education. In R. Pekrun and L. Linnenbrink-Garcia (Eds.), International handbook of emotions in education (pp. 539-558). New York, NY: Routledge and Taylor and Francis.

[64] Schweder, S., and Raufelder, D. (2019). Positive emotions, learning behavior, and teacher support in self-directed learning during adolescence: Do age and gender matter? Journal of Adolescence, 73, 73-84. doi:10.1016/j.adolescence.2019.04.004

[65] Arroyo, I., Burleson, W., Tai, M., Muldner, K., and Woolf, B. P. (2013). Gender differences in the use and benefit of advanced learning technologies for mathematics. Journal of Educational Psychology, 105(4), 957-969. doi:10.1037/a0032748

[66] Quinlan, K. M. (2016). How emotion matters in four key relationships in teaching and learning in higher education. College Teaching, 64(3), 1- 11. doi:10.1080/87567555.20 15.1088818

[67] Cantabrana, J. L. L., Rodríguez, M. U., and Cervera, M. G. (2019). Assessing teacher digital competence: The construction of an instrument for measuring the knowledge of pre-service teachers. Journal of New Approaches in Educational Research, 8(1), 73-78. doi:10.7821/naer.2019.1.370

[68] Wingo, N. P., Ivankova, N. V., and Moss, J. A. (2017). Faculty perceptions about teaching online: Exploring the literature using the technology acceptance model as an organizing framework. Online Learning, 21(1), 15-35.

[69] Floyd, A., and Preston, D. (2018). The role of the associate dean in UK universities: Distributed leadership in action? Higher Education: The International Journal of Higher Education Research, 75(5), 925-943. doi:10.1007/s10734-017-0178-1

[70] Schmidt, S. W., Hodge, E. M., and Tschida, C. M. (2013). How university faculty members developed their online teaching skills. Quarterly Review of Distance Education, 14(3), 131-140.

[71] Abdous, M. H. (2019). Influence of satisfaction and preparedness on online students' feelings of anxiety. The Internet and Higher Education, 41, 34-44. doi:10.1016/j.iheduc.2019.01.001

[72] Conrad, D. L. (2002). Engagement, excitement, anxiety, and fear: learners' experiences of starting an online course. American Journal of Distance Education, 16(4), 205-226. doi:10.1207/S15389286AJDE1604_2

[73] Huang, P. & Hwang, Y. (2013). An Exploration of EFL Learners' Anxiety E-learning Environments. Journal of Language Teaching and Research, 4 (1): 27-35.

[74] Shahi, M. A. J. (2016). The impact of E-learning on improving Iranian EFL learners' language skills: decreasing learning anxiety. Journal of Fundamental and Applied Sciences 8(3):261. DOI:10.4314/jfas.v8i3s.180.

[75] Tezcan-Unal, B., Winston, K., and Qualter, A. (2018). Learning-oriented quality assurance in higher education institutions. Quality in Higher Education, 24(3), 221-237. doi:10.1080/13538322.2018.1558504

[76] Ingleton, C. (1995). Gender and learning: Does emotion make a difference? The International Journal of Higher Education and Educational Planning, 30(3), 323-335. doi:10.1007/BF01383756

[77] Chen, N. S., Lin, K. M., and Kinshuk. (2008). Analysing users' satisfaction with e-learning using a negative critical incidents approach. Innovations in Education and Teaching International, 45(2), 115-126.

[78] Aucejo, E. M., French, J., Araya, M. P. U., and Zafar, B. (2020). The impact of COVID-19 on student experiences and expectations: Evidence from a survey. Journal of public economics, *191*, 104271.

[79] Dong, C., Cao, S., and Li, H. (2020). Young children's online learning during COVID-19 pandemic: Chinese parents' beliefs and attitudes. Children and Youth Services Review, *118*, 105440.

[80] Dhawan, S. (2020). Online learning: A panacea in the time of COVID-19 crisis. Journal of Educational Technology Systems, *49*(1), 5-22.

[81] Nambiar, D. (2020). The impact of online learning during COVID-19: students' and teachers' perspective. The International Journal of Indian Psychology, *8*(2), 783-793.

[82] Novianti, R., and Garzia, M. (2020). Parental Engagement in Children's Online Learning During COVID-19 Pandemic. Journal of Teaching and Learning in Elementary Education (Jtlee), *3*(2), 117-131.

[83] Aboagye, E., Yawson, J. A., and Appiah, K. N. (2021). COVID-19 and E-learning: The challenges of students in tertiary institutions. *Social Education Research*, 1-8.

[84] Rannastu-Avalos, M., and Siiman, L. A. (2020, September). Challenges for Distance Learning and Online Collaboration in the Time of COVID-19: Interviews with Science Teachers. In *International Conference on Collaboration Technologies and Social Computing* (pp. 128-142). Springer, Cham.

[85] Ferri, F., Grifoni, P., and Guzzo, T. (2020). Online Learning and Emergency Remote Teaching: Opportunities and Challenges in Emergency Situations. *Societies*, *10*(4), 86. MDPI AG. Retrieved from http://dx.doi.org/10.3390/soc10040086

[86] Wal, M. (2020). COVID-19: Introducing a strange transition in our education system, The Daily Star, Retrieved from https://www.thedailystar.net/lifestyle/news/covid-19-introducing-strange-transition-our-education-system-1914933

[87] Shohel, M. M. C., Ashrafuzzaman, M., Islam, M. T., Shams, S. & Mahmud, A.(2021d). Blended Teaching and Learning in Higher Education: Challenges and Opportunities, In, Loureiro, S. M. C. (eds.). Handbook of Research on Developing a Post-Pandemic Paradigm for Virtual Technologies in Higher Education, pp.27-50, Hershey, USA: IGI Global.

[88] Hergenhahn, B. R. (4th Ed.). (2001). An introduction to the history of psychology. Wadsworth, a division of Thomson Learning, United States of America.

[89] Urmee, M. A. and Ahmed, M. F. (2019). Impact of teaching method on academic achievement. Jagannath University Journal of Psychology, 9 (1), 43-50.

[90] Paul, J. and Jefferson, F. (2019). A Comparative Analysis of Student Performance in an Online vs. Face-to-Face Environmental Science Course From 2009 to 2016, https://doi.org/10.3389/fcomp.2019.00007, Retrieved from https://www.frontiersin.org/articles/10.3389/fcomp.2019.00007/full

[91] Slavin, R. E. (3rd Ed.). (1991). Educational psychology theory and practice. Prentice- Hall, Inc.

[92] Care, E., Kim, H., Vista, A., and Anderson, K. (2018). Education System Alignment for 21st Century Skills: Focus on Assessment. *Center for Universal Education at The Brookings Institution*.

[93] Jacobson-Lundeberg, V. (2016). Pedagogical Implementation of 21st Century Skills. Educational Leadership and Administration: Teaching and Program Development, *27*, 82-100.

[94] Van Laar, E., Van Deursen, A. J., Van Dijk, J. A., and De Haan, J. (2017). The relation between 21st-century skills and digital skills: A systematic literature review. Computers in human behavior, *72*, 577-588.

[95] Sun, A., and Chen, X. (2016). Online education and its effective practice: A research review. Journal of Information Technology Education: Research, 15, 157-190. Retrieved from http://www.informingscience.org/Publications/3502

[96] Ahmad, M., Rahman M. F., Ali, M., Rahman F. N. and Al-Azad M. A. S. (2015). Effect of Extra Curricular Activity on Student's Academic Performance, JAFMC Bangladesh, 11(2)

[97] Cook, B. R. and Babon, A. (2016). Active learning through online quizzes: better learning and less (busy) work, Journal of Geography in Higher Education, http://dx.doi.org/10.1080/03098265.2016.1185772, Retrieved from https://www.researchgate.net/publication/303119454_Active_learning_through_online_quizzes_better_learning_and_less_busy_work

[98] Marcell, M. (2008). Effectiveness of Regular Online Quizzing in Increasing Class Participation and Preparation, International Journal for the Scholarship of Teaching and Learning, 2(1), Georgia Southern University, retrieved from https://www.researchgate.net/publication/253991170_Effectiveness_of_Regular_Online_Quizzing_in_Increasing_Class_Participation_and_Preparation

[99] Williams, L. M. (2013). A Case Study of Virtual Physical Education Teachers' Experiences in and Perspectives of Online Teaching. Graduate Theses and Dissertations. http://scholarcommons.usf.edu/etd/4962

[100] Kane, J., and Wagner, J. (2007). Teaching and learning physical education online. In C. Cavanaugh and R. Blomeyer (Eds.), What works in K-12 online learning (pp. 105-123). Eugene, OR: International Society for Technology in Education.

[101] Churchill, L. R. (1982). The teaching of ethics and moral values in teaching: Some contemporary confusions. The Journal of Higher Education, 53(3), 296-306. doi: 10.2307/1981749

[102] Chowdhury, M. (2016). Emphasizing Morals, Values, Ethics, And Character Education In Science Education And Science Teaching, The Malaysian Online Journal of Educational Science, 4(2), Retrieved from https://files.eric.ed.gov/fulltext/EJ1095995.pdf

[103] Rennie, L. (2007). Values of science portrayed in out-of-school contexts. In D.

[104] UNESCO. (1991). Values and ethics and the science and technology

curriculum. Bangkok, Thailand: Asia and the Pacific Programme of Educational Innovation for Development.

[105] Conroy, J. C., Wenell, K. J., and Lundie, D. E. (2013). Does religious education work? A multi-dimensional investigation. London-New Delhi-New York-Sydney: Bloomsbury.

[106] High Focus Centers. (2020). The Effects of Online Learning on a Teen's Mental Health, Retrieved from https://highfocuscenters.pyramidhealthcarepa.com/the-effects-of-online-learning-on-a-teens-mental-health/

[107] UNESCO IESALC. (2020). COVID-19 and higher education: Today and tomorrow, Impact analysis, policy responses and recommendations, Retrieved from https://www.iesalc.unesco.org/en/wp-content/uploads/2020/05/COVID-19-EN-130520.pdf

[108] Behrman, Jere R.; Deolalikar, Anil B.; Soon, Lee-Ying (2002): Conceptual Issues in the Role of Education Decentralization, ERD Working Paper Series, No. 22, Asian Development Bank (ADB), Manila, http://hdl.handle.net/11540/2062

[109] Chann, A. (2016). Popularity of the decentralization reform and its effects on the quality of education. *Prospects Comparative Journal of Curriculum, Learning, and Assessment,46*(1), 131-147.

[110] Bhattacharjee, D., Paul, A., Kim, J. H., and Karthigaikumar, P. (2018). An immersive learning model using evolutionary learning. Computers and Electrical Engineering, 65, 236-249.

[111] Loureiro, S.M.C., Guerreiro, J., Eloy, S., Langaro, D., and Panchapakesan, P. (2019). Understanding the use of Virtual Reality in Marketing: A text mining-based review, Journal of Business Research, 100, 514-her education: A systematic review of the literature. Computers in Human Behavior, 87, 192-206.

[112] O'Connor, E. A., and Domingo, J. (2017). A Practical Guide, With Theoretical Underpinnings, for Creating Effective Virtual Reality Learning Environments. Journal of Educational Technology Systems, 45, 343-364.

Chapter 10

Emergency Remote Teaching during COVID-19 Pandemic: Roles of Educators in Malaysia

Jowati Juhary

Abstract

This chapter responds to the needs of educators in preparing to teach online fully due to the pandemic, COVID-19. This scenario becomes the new normal in the teaching and learning process during the COVID-19 pandemic. The main objective of this chapter is to investigate the roles of educators in one public higher learning institution in Malaysia during emergency remote teaching due to the COVID-19 outbreak. Emergency remote teaching is argued to be the answer to the sudden change from face-to-face teaching to a fully online teaching environment. Data for this chapter were collected through an online survey distributed to potential respondents. Adopting a case study and quantitative approach to research, descriptive and inferential statistical analysis were conducted and presented. Preliminary findings suggest two key challenges. Firstly, educators were ready to embark on transformative emergency remote teaching. Nonetheless, they were not sure of the differences between emergency remote teaching and online teaching; these two have different pedagogical approaches. Secondly, and perhaps most importantly, educators were able to use appropriate platforms and applications during the pandemic; however, they did not have ample time to study other platforms and applications. By this, the author argues that some educators have various options to choose from but may lack the knowledge and understanding on how these options work best. In accepting the new normal in teaching and learning, educators must be open to new and creative strategies to engage students during 100 percent online learning.

Keywords: COVID-19, emergency remote teaching, new normal, online presence, online teaching

1. Introduction

First discovered in December 2019, the COVID-19 pandemic has arguably affected sectors such as businesses, tourism and education of countries all over the world (see [1, 2]). Particularly relevant and significant for this chapter is how educators are coping with teaching fully online; for some educators, teaching fully online happens for the first time in their live. In Malaysia, the education landscape is about to be changed forever. With new normal of teaching and learning, primary and secondary schools, together with higher learning institutions are now faced with enormous tasks to ensure that students acquire the knowledge that have been arranged for their levels accordingly. Trained to teach physically or in face-to-face sessions, educators in Malaysia need to step up and provide a different level of commitment to teaching [3].

IntechOpen

2. The context of the study

Data for this chapter were collected at the National Defence University of Malaysia (NDUM). The NDUM is the only tertiary military institution in Malaysia, awarding undergraduate and postgraduate degrees. For the undergraduate student population, there are about 65 percent military cadets and 35 percent civilian students (about 24 percent of these students are also enlisted in Reserve Officers Training Unit or ROTU). It is a residential campus since 98 percent students live on campus. Currently, there are 17 academic undergraduate programmes offered to students, including Engineering programmes, Maritime programmes and Strategic Studies and Management programmes. Military cadets and ROTU students have to attend military training on campus during the weekends and holidays. Especially for the military cadets, they have to also participate in physical exercises, rollcalls and other military administrative duties on daily basis.

The second semester of the Academic Session 2019/2020 has started when the government of Malaysia introduced and enforced the Movement Control Order (MCO) to stop the spread of COVID-19. The MCO started during the fifth week of the semester; this was when the face-to-face sessions had started, and after that the teaching and learning processes resumed online, fully. During this MCO, which started on the 18th of March 2020, all students, including the military cadets were transported home to be with their families. The semester resumed online a week after the students had settled comfortably at home. The remaining online sessions included lectures, tutorials, assignments, tests as well as final examinations. It needs to be emphasised that some planned teaching and learning activities were not able to be conducted due to the MCO such as fieldtrips, laboratory works and industrial training.

There are two research questions for this research; first, on the educators' readiness to teach online fully from the aspect of their pedagogical readiness. By pedagogical readiness, it is argued that there are differences in the practical applications of emergency remote teaching and online teaching (see [4, 5]). Second, on the platforms, tools and applications used for online teaching. Given that the MCO came as a surprise, educators had no choice but to comply with the existing platforms, tools and applications in completing their teaching responsibilities. These two research questions answer the main objective of this chapter, which is to understand the roles of educators during emergency remote teaching.

There are four key terms used throughout this chapter that must be explained. Firstly, emergency remote teaching, which refers to a temporary and unplanned teaching solution due to a sudden change of the teaching environment. Secondly, the term new normal, which suggests that new practices and routines that must be followed in the current situation. Thirdly, online presence refers to the presence of educators online to assist students, and the amount of presence depends on the students' competency level. The last term is online teaching, that is the process of teaching conducted fully online, with planned and established curricula, including teaching and learning materials, learning activities and assessments.

2.1 Online teaching and emergency remote teaching

Previous research on online teaching and emergency remote teaching are included in order to provide critical background on what should be the roles of educators during this COVID-19 outbreak. It is argued that emergency remote teaching must not be equate to online teaching (fully), considering the differences in their educational approaches [6]. Further, the critical key to differentiate the two is the insufficient time to properly plan for curriculum transformation; emergency remote teaching does not have the luxury of planning [7].

2.1.1 Online teaching

The effectiveness and drawbacks of online teaching and learning, or simply online education, have been debated for decades. Scholars from all over the world have looked at various research studies, theories, models, standards and evaluation criteria, which focus on quality online learning, online teaching and online course design (see [5]). Before further discussions are held, it is appropriate to provide a conceptual definition of online education for this chapter. According to Bakia et al. [8], online education, which includes online teaching and learning can be used to refer to "a wide range of programmes that use the Internet to provide instructional materials and facilitate interactions between teachers and students, and in some cases amongst students as well." Accordingly, online education can be fully online, with all instructions taking place through the Internet, or online elements can be combined with face-to-face sessions known as blended learning (see also on blended learning [9]).

Online teaching cannot be explained properly without the discussions on online learning. This is because the two depend on each other; therefore, critical aspects of online learning will also be highlighted. For example, Hoi et al. [10] found in their study that based on the types of learning tasks and the forms of feedback information, online learning can be divided into three major categories: (a) online supervised learning where full feedback information is always available, (b) online learning with limited feedback, and (c) online unsupervised learning where no feedback is available. What Hoi et al. suggest is that the presence of educators online can be based on the amount of assistance needed by the students. In addition, Means et al. [11] explored the online learning design options by listing various moderating variables, including roles of students and educators, as well as ratio of students during the online lessons. These design options are summarised in **Table 1**.

What could be discerned from **Table 1** are twofold. First, online education for both teaching and learning would require careful planning in order to ensure that the curricula are delivered effectively, and that students and educators are able to work synchronously or asynchronously online. Manfuso [12] in her research also found that designing an effective online course could take weeks and months. Second, roles of students and educators are not definite; accordingly, and when appropriate, both students and educators can negotiate what they need to be doing.

In addition, according to Boon [13], educators' presence in an online learning and teaching environment is important in engaging students. Despite the options offered that educators may choose to have a smaller or zero presence online (refer to **Table 1**), Boon proposed several facilitation strategies that can make students more motivated and interested in their learning; these require active and *big* presence of the educators online. **Table 2** illustrates these strategies.

It is evident that, regardless of whether educators have small or big presence online, students need to know that they are not alone in the virtual classrooms. The author argues that in choosing to be present small or big online, several factors must be taken into consideration, including students' level of competency in the course and students' availability to be online (access and data consumption). Some students may be left to assume more independent learning online, and some may require the utmost assistance imaginable. As Hoi et al. [10] have put forth that online feedback to students depend on the students' capability to learn independently or dependently. The next section explores emergency remote teaching in detail, and highlights differences between online teaching and emergency remote teaching.

Moderating Variables	Important Aspects
Modality	• Fully online • Blended (over 50% online) • Blended (25–50% online) • Web-enabled face-to-face
Pacing	• Self-paced (open entry, open exit) • Class-paced • Class-paced with some self-paced
Student Ratio	• < 35 to 1 • 36–99 to 1 • 100–999 to 1 • > 1000 to 1
Pedagogy	• Expository • Practice • Exploratory • Collaborative
Roles of Online Assessment	• Determine if students are ready for new contents • Tell system how to support the students (adaptive instruction) • Provide students or teachers with information about the learning state • Input to grade • Identify students at risk of failure
Instructor Role Online	• Active instruction online • Small presence online • None
Student Role Online	• Listen or read • Complete problems or answer questions • Explore simulations and resources • Collaborate with peers
Online Communication Synchrony	• Asynchronous only • Synchronous only • Some blend of both
Source of Feedback	• Automated • Teachers • Peers

Table 1.
Online design options [11].

2.1.2 Emergency remote teaching

Emergency remote teaching is arguably a new concept derived due to the pandemic [5]. It is also suggested to be one of the educational responses to the COVID-19 outbreak [6]. When the need for schooling arises, emergency remote teaching becomes a temporary solution in order to allow students to continue with

What to do?	How to do?	Online tools to use
Offer synchronous online office hours to support student learning and knowledge development	• Face-to-face meetings • Telephone consultations • Online audio/video	• Collaborate (Blackboard Learn) • Skype • Google Hangouts
Engage in personal communication with students, individually or as a group	• Email greetings • Posted or recorded welcome messages (audio or audio + video) • Post announcements on the course page	• Email • Blackboard Video Tool • Other lecture capture software (such as Camtasia, Mediasite)
Provide recorded lectures and assignment explanations	• Audio + video (highly recommended) • Audio only (at minimum)	• Mediasite • Audacity (audio only) • Screencast-o-matic • PowerPoint (with audio)
Provide direct (synchronous instruction)	• Develop seminar or lecture courses • Facilitate meetings with students • Set up student group work space	• Google Hangouts
Interact regularly with students, individually or in groups	• Email • Participate in online group discussions • Conduct chat sessions with individuals or groups	• Collaborate (Blackboard Learn) • Google Hangouts
Create a positive learning environment to stimulate learning	• Show respect for students by appropriate conversational tone and word choice	• Email

Table 2.
Selected facilitation strategies [13].

their lessons [14]. Despite being unsure of emergency remote teaching, educators have to continue to teach. According to Talidong [15] in her study of teachers involved in emergency remote teaching, the main findings of this study emphasise several aspects such as the positive outlook, concern for students, and instructional strategies of the Philippine teachers in implementing emergency remote teaching. Despite the difficulties to arrange lessons virtually from distance, the respondents were aware of the instructional strategies that could be employed.

In an attempt to ensure that teaching and learning online is effectively and successfully achieved, Whittle et al. [16] proposed a framework for emergency remote teaching. These scholars combined two frameworks – Sawyer's [17] framework for creating a learning environment and Garrison and Arbaugh's [18] community of inquiry framework for online learning – to develop the emergency remote teaching environment framework. Findings from this study suggest that educators need to reaffirm their online presence by guaranteeing that they are visible accordingly either within or outside of the online teaching sessions.

Some educators may find it difficult to conduct online assessments during the emergency remote teaching phase. Rahim [19] suggested nine aspects that must be

Characteristics	Emergency Remote Teaching	Remote Teaching	Enhanced Remote Teaching	Online Teaching
Planning	• None	• Developed incrementally and added regularly based on the progress of students • May be adjusted weekly • Existing courses moved to online environment • Lack of analysis, design, planning and evaluation	• Existing courses moved to online environment • Feedback from learners helping to inform course elements • Developed Incrementally • When face-to-face instruction resumes, likely to return to face-to-face delivery	• The use of a framework (such as ADDIE or other models) to support development • Developed specifically and intentionally to be delivered online, irrespective of the status of pandemic
Preparation	• Less than 1 week	• 2 weeks to 3 weeks	• Variables	• Variable, but usually anywhere from 4 months (1 term) up to 1 year
Design	• Designed as face-to- face cr hybrid	• Designed as face-to-face or hybrid • Designed by faculty members with varying levels of experience with learning technologies	• Designed as face-to-face or hybrid • Designed by faculty members with varying levels of experience with learning technologies • Informed by training and workshops to support the development of 2–3 student self-directed learning experiences	• Designed for online • Designed with instructional designer and media support • Various technologies have been chosen and tested for specific learning activities to facilitate a self-directed learning experience

Characteristics	Emergency Remote Teaching	Remote Teaching	Enhanced Remote Teaching	Online Teaching
Development Frameworks	• Often developed and adjusted on a weekly basis, with consideration of an overall course blueprint	• Adjusted on a weekly basis, with consideration of an overall course blueprint	• Adjusted on a weekly basis, with consideration of an overall course blueprint	• Fully developed at the start of the course • May go through multiple iterations before development is considered complete
Content	• Minimal to no change • Transferred from in-class to learning management system • Mostly text-based • Required resource already in place and used by students	• Use of existing content already developed • Possible supplemental content added, ideally in multimedia format	• Enhancement of existing content already developed • Increase of supplemental and supportive materials • Increasing balance of dynamic and static resources	• Selected, developed and implemented as part of the design and development process • Greater preference for multimedia resources • Use of dynamic learning activities • Greater reliance on advanced features of learning management system, such as intelligent agents
Educators' Presence	• Active instructor presence • Synchronous, in alignment with scheduled class times, with additional availability, as required to support student adjustment to online environment	• Active instructor presence • Primarily synchronous, in alignment with scheduled class times • Recordings of synchronous 'classes' may be available following the class	• Active instructor presence • Mix of synchronous and asynchronous classes, with many classes following a weekly scheduled class time • Recordings of synchronous 'classes' may be available following the class • Additional recordings may be made in advance and made available in lieu of synchronous class	• Typically designed for students to complete as self-directed, with regular monitoring and check-ins with instructor • Typically asynchronous, but may have synchronous elements

Characteristics	Emergency Remote Teaching	Remote Teaching	Enhanced Remote Teaching	Online Teaching
Assessments and Evaluations	• Use existing assessments, with alternative assessments necessary in certain cases • In some cases, substantial completion ("80%") was sufficient for completion	• In the majority of cases, using existing approved course outlines, with Course Section Information (CSI) addendum • Use existing assessments, with alternative assessments necessary in certain cases	• Updates to curriculum • CSI documents to detail delivery expectations • Use existing assessments, with alternative assessments necessary in certain cases	• Utilising same course outline, with modifications to the CSI document to denote delivery expectations • Assessments designed for online learning environment

Table 3.
Selected characteristics of emergency remote teaching compared with online teaching [4].

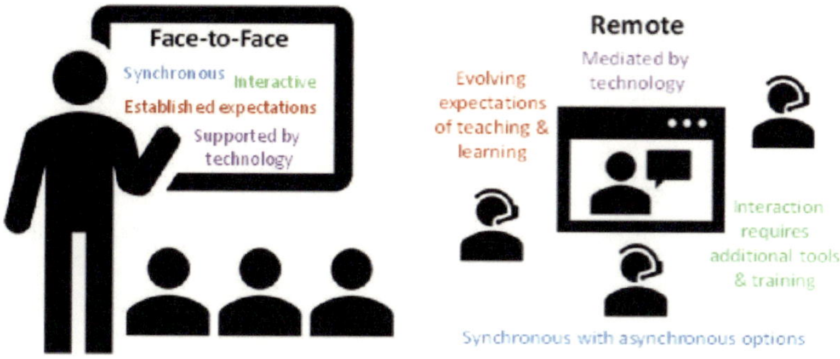

Figure 1.
The scenario between face-to-face sessions and emergency remote teaching [4].

considered when conducting online assessments during this phase. These include evaluating prerequisites for implementing online assessment; ensuring alignment of assessment activities with stated learning objectives; addressing the diversity of students' situations; maintaining a good balance of formative and summative assessments; stimulating student learning with online assessment; considering format; scheduling and timing of tests; establishing clear communication to students regarding assessment matters; ensuring high-quality feedback; and addressing assessment validity threats. Although all these aspects can be familiar to some educators, others may find them new, yet helpful during this time of crisis.

A group of educators at Algonquin College [4] described the differences and evolutions from emergency remote teaching to eventually, online teaching (see **Table 3**). What is reiterated is the fact that emergency remote teaching is a non-planned teaching strategy, and it is just a temporary measure. To demonstrate further the meaning of emergency remote teaching, **Figure 1** confirms some characteristics of emergency remote teaching, including the evolving expectations of the educators as well as students, and synchronous with asynchronous options for teaching and learning.

Based on **Table 3**, it can be concluded that when an academic programme is planned properly to be offered virtually, it can be categorised as online education; teaching and learning will be conducted online. Emergency remote teaching can ultimately become online teaching once it has stabilised and matured; by this, the author argues that there must be proper and adequate time allocated to design and develop the curricula, including the learning materials, activities and assessments.

To sum up this section, both online teaching and emergency remote teaching should be used in different educational situations. What the teaching world is facing now may best be solved by emergency remote teaching because educators are put into the positions of teaching online fully without having the time to plan, design and select the best teaching tools for the students.

3. Methodology

This research employed a case study approach in order to understand the challenges faced by educators teaching during the pandemic. Stake [20] noted that there are three kinds of case studies, namely intrinsic, instrumental and collective. An intrinsic case study focuses on understanding a specific case rather than focussing on a common understanding. Conversely, a collective case study is about understanding more than one case either at one site or multiple locations. Using Stake, this research is an instrumental case study, where it focuses on gaining a general understanding of an issue by studying a particular case, educators at the NDUM.

Case studies have many advantages, such as allowing for comparative study and the support for generalisations [21, 22]. They are also empirically strong because they are grounded in observable realities. However, there are also weaknesses, the main one being that they lack statistical reliability because they can be narrow in their focus. Gummesson [23] counter-argued on the weaknesses of the case study method by insisting that statistical or scientific methods are less insightful in instances where understanding human behaviour is more important. In addition, the case study approach does not rule out statistical analysis. The current research uses quantitative data for descriptive and inferential analysis. This quantitative approach is chosen because the author wants to gauge the general perspectives of educators at the Defence University on teaching during the COVID-19 pandemic.

3.1 Population and sampling

There are 340 active academics at the NDUM during the period of data collection. The author chose convenience sampling because the potential respondents can be reached easily through WhatsApp and emails. There were 63 respondents out of 340 academics (18.5 percent), who answered the online survey, and these were the basis for analysis and discussion in this chapter. The author did not force academics to complete the survey since it was on voluntary basis. Despite this small number of respondents, the author opines that the data were sufficient for preliminary discussions on emergency remote teaching.

3.2 Research instrument and data collection

An online survey was used to collect data. Using Google Forms, items were arranged according to sections explained later. The survey can be found at https://bit.ly/2Zaozjc (see **Figure 2** for the screenshot of the survey), and it was available from the 5th of September until the 18th of September 2020 (about two weeks). Two methods were used to invite potential respondents; first, WhatsApp messages were sent to groups of faculties and academic centres at the NDUM, and second, emails were sent to all academics at the NDUM.

Items in the survey were divided into a demographic section, perceptions about online teaching and emergency remote teaching section, and commentary section. Two types of scales were used in the survey, a 4-point likert and 5-point likert scale, together

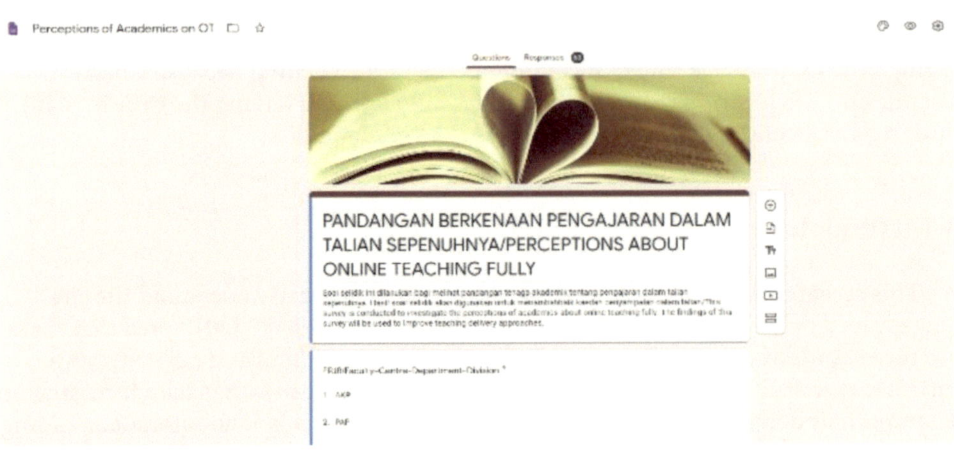

Figure 2.
The screenshot of the online survey.

with 'Yes,' 'No' and 'Not Sure' scale. As emergency remote teaching is barely known to most educators, the author has specifically prepared four items on emergency remote teaching. Further, the items in the survey mostly originated from the existing literature on online teaching and emergency remote teaching. The survey was bilingual in order to cater for local and international academics at the Defence University.

3.3 Data analysis

The final data collected from 63 respondents were analysed using Statistical Package for Social Sciences (SPSS) Version 25, and they were presented in mostly descriptive statistics. Whilst descriptive data were used to answer the research questions posed earlier, inferential data provided different perspectives on the current teaching situations. Data analysis involved the use of frequency tables and graphs for percentages and figures. Since the objective of the paper is to investigate the roles of educators during the pandemic, descriptive data obtained were able to shed lights into the situations faced by the respondents. Meanwhile, inferential statistics were able to illustrate the relations or significance of variables in this study.

4. Findings

4.1 Demographic information

There are seven faculties and academic centres at the Defence University; given this, the online survey was only open to academics under these faculties and centres. Although there are also academics appointed as fellow researchers in centres of excellence at the Defence University, they are also part of these seven faculties and academic centres. **Figures 3–6** illustrate the demographic information of the research respondents. To explain further the labels for the faculties and academic centres, below is the explanation for the acronyms used,

a. AKP – Defence Fitness Academy

b. PAP – Centre for Foundation Studies

c. PB – Language Centre

d. FKJ – Faculty of Engineering

e. FPPP – Faculty of Defence and Management Studies

f. FPKP – Faculty of Medicine and Defence Health

g. FSTP – Faculty of Science and Defence Technology

Based on **Figure 3**, it is evident that the respondents of this study mostly came from the Language Centre, 24 respondents, and the least number of respondents came from two faculties, the Defence Fitness Academy and Faculty of Medicine and Defence Health, with three respondents each. In terms of age range, most respondents were between 36 to 40 years old (24 respondents) and the least number of respondents was at the range of 25 to 30 years old (two respondents).

In addition, most respondents have more than 10 years of teaching experience (31 respondents); nonetheless, it should be emphasised that the older the academics were does not equate to more years in teaching. This could be explained by the fact

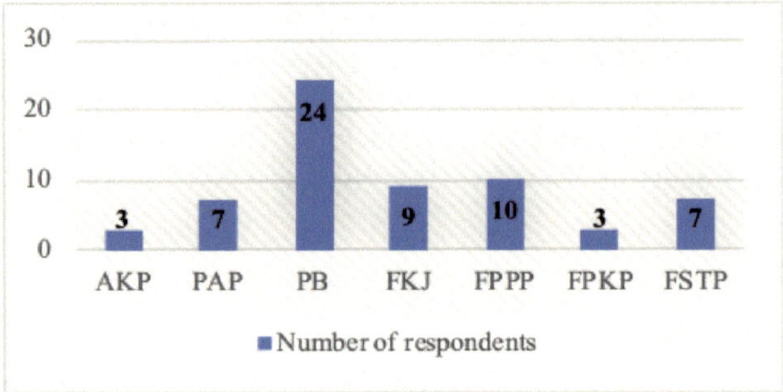

Figure 3.
The respondents and their respective faculties/academic centres (in number).

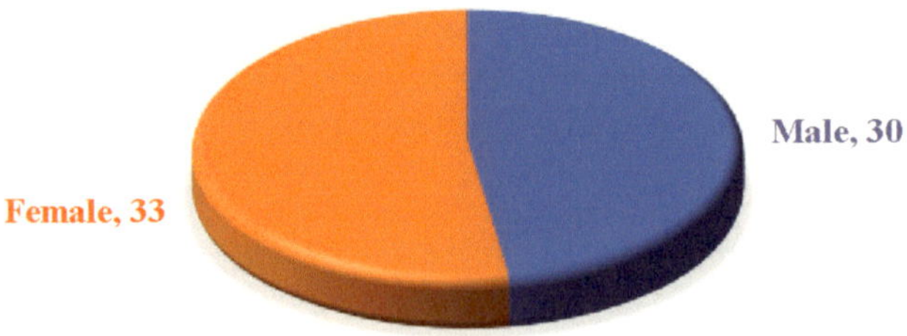

Figure 4.
The gender of the respondents (in number).

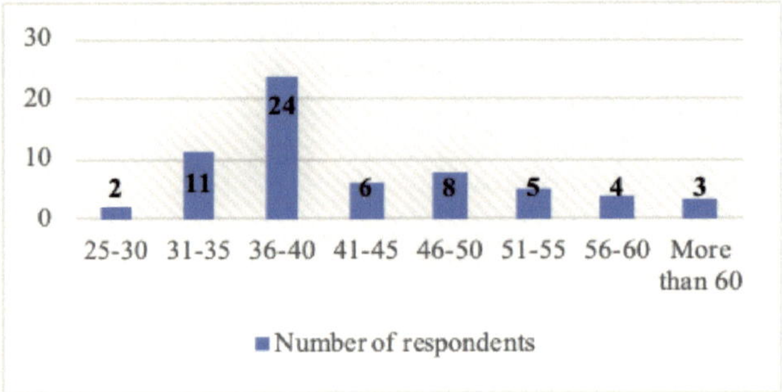

Figure 5.
The age of the respondents (in number).

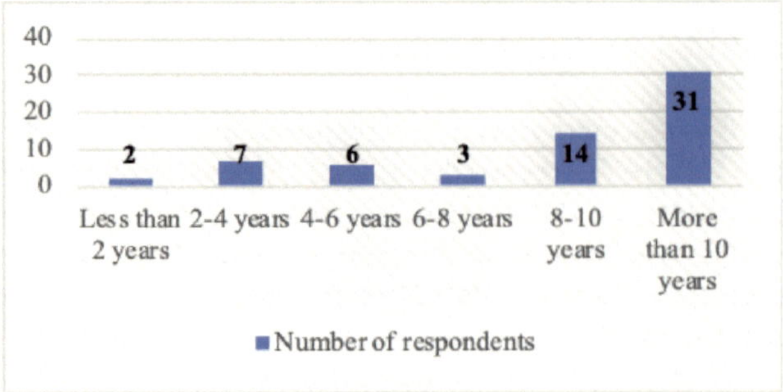

Figure 6.
Years of teaching experience of the respondents (in number).

that some join teaching profession at a later age after gaining industrial experience. Further, the number of female respondents was slightly higher than the male counterparts; in actual fact, this is the real resemblance of the total academic population at the NDUM, with about 50.3 percent female academics.

4.2 Descriptive findings

Data are explained in two main categories, including respondents' perceptions about online teaching and their knowledge about emergency remote teaching, and respondents' choice of platforms, strategies and applications during the pandemic. The first item asked was whether the respondents had experienced teaching fully online. 44 respondents (69.8 percent) confirmed that they have had the experience, and 19 respondents responded 'No' to this item. This item is key in understanding the responses for the subsequent items asked. The author opines that some respondents have not been involved completely in teaching online fully because they teach the Foundation and Diploma students, who were not in sessions from March until July 2020.

The next three items sought respondents' knowledge and awareness on the differences between emergency remote teaching and online teaching. The findings are summarised in **Figures 7–9** below. It can be discerned from these figures that respondents at the NDUM were not sure of what emergency remote teaching is and its differences to online teaching. The majority of the respondents chose 'Not Sure' for these three items. This is not surprising since emergency remote teaching is a new and temporary solution to teaching in times of crisis.

The respondents were also asked on the perceptions about teaching online fully. **Figure 10** illustrates the views of all respondents. A 4-point likert scale was used for this item, ranging from 'Strongly Not Effective' (1) to 'Strongly Effective' (4). As can be observed, 44.4 percent of the respondents (28 people) opted for 'Not

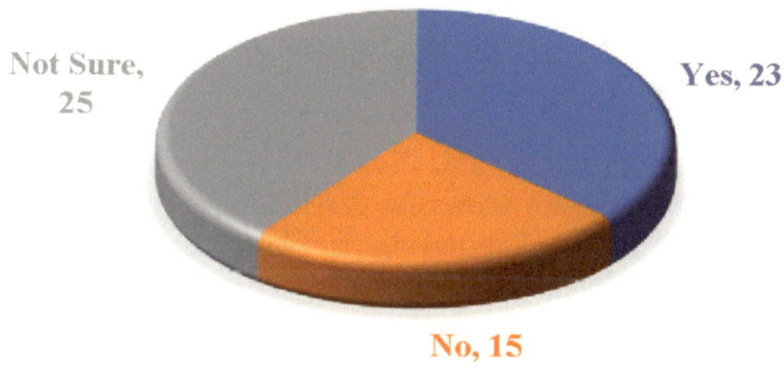

Figure 7.
Responses to the item "Understand the concept of Emergency Remote Teaching" (in number).

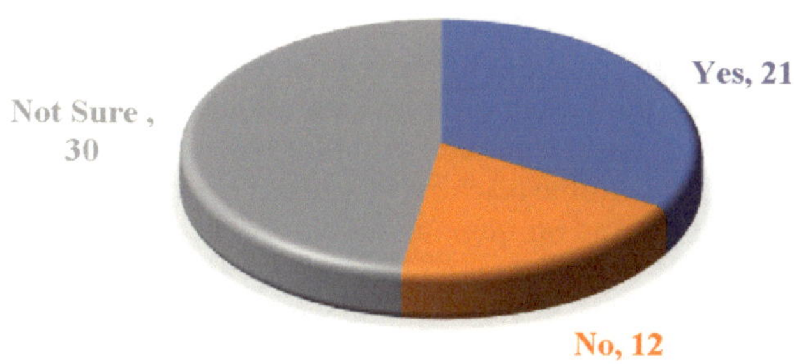

Figure 8.
Responses to the item "Able to distinguish between emergency remote teaching and online teaching" (in number).

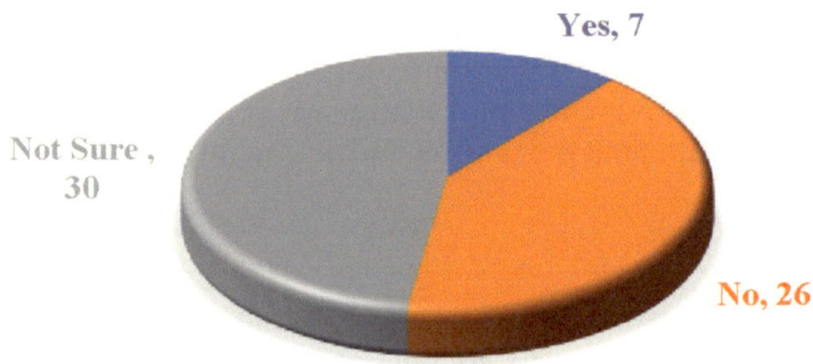

Figure 9.
Responses to the item "Emergency Remote Teaching and Online Teaching are similar" (in number).

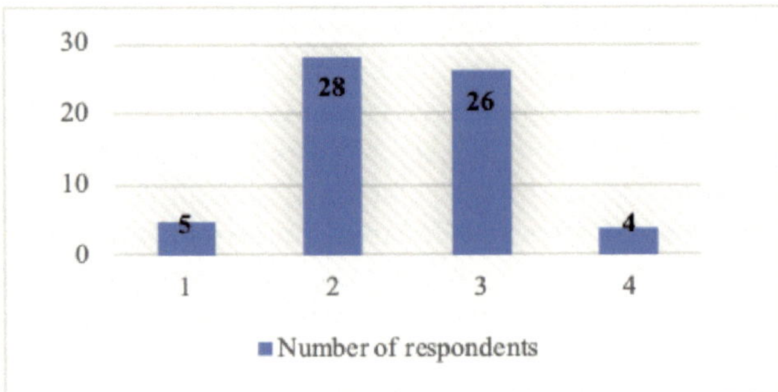

Figure 10.
Responses to the item "Perceptions about teaching online fully" (in number).

Effective,' and 7.9 percent (5 people) opted for 'Strongly Not Effective.' Combining these two scales makes up for the slight majority of the respondents, who opined that teaching online fully lacks effectiveness (33 respondents or 52.3 percent).

In addition, **Tables 4** and **5** tabulate the views of the respondents on what platforms and strategies that they used the most during the pandemic and the most effective platforms and strategies in their opinions. From **Table 4**, it can be deduced that WhatsApp is often (19 respondents) and always (18 respondents) used by the respondents, together with MS Teams for Video Conferencing (51 respondents) and Quizzes (34 respondents). Further, **Table 5** shows similar platforms and applications that the respondents believed to be the most effective (combining 'Effective' and 'Strongly Effective'), WhatsApp and MS Teams for Video Conferencing and Quizzes with 44, 58 and 53 respondents, respectively. In additions, respondents also opined that Al-Fateh e-Learning Portal, Google Forms, Google Meet and Zoom to be effective platforms too.

4.3 Inferential findings

This section explains the relations between selected items in the survey. Four sets of items will be tested on the strength of relations, and they are firstly correlation between years of teaching experience and the ability to distinguish between emergency remote teaching and online teaching (**Figure 11**); secondly, between opinions about teaching online fully and opinions about blended teaching (**Figure 12**); thirdly, between years of teaching experience and perceptions about blended teaching (**Figure 13**); and lastly between years of teaching experience and opinions about teaching online fully (**Figure 14**).

There are numerous ranges and interpretations on the correlation indicators (see **Table 6**); the author opts for the indicators by Sarwono [24] simply because the indicators are more representative of the author's data. The indicators are divided

Online Teaching Platforms/Scales	Never	Rarely	Sometimes	Often	Always
WhatsApp	9	6	11	19	18
Al-Fateh e-Learning Portal	9	8	12	20	14
MS Teams (Video Conferencing)	1	4	7	25	26
Kahoot!	33	4	15	8	3
Google Forms	13	7	19	12	12
MS Teams (Quizzes)	13	5	11	16	18
Exam.Net	50	3	3	5	2
Google Meet	24	9	10	16	4
Twitter	56	3	1	3	0
Facebook	52	6	0	5	0
Telegram	38	5	9	7	4
Skype	35	11	7	9	1
Zoom	16	9	13	19	6

Table 4.
Responses to the item "Online teaching platforms and strategies that respondents use the most" (in number).

Online Teaching Platforms/Scales	Strongly Not Effective	Not Effective	Effective	Strongly Effective
WhatsApp	4	15	27	17
Al-Fateh e-Learning Portal	5	11	33	14
MS Teams (Video Conferencing)	0	5	29	29
Kahoot!	11	17	29	6
Google Forms	1	8	43	11
MS Teams (Quizzes)	4	6	37	16
Exam.Net	17	17	26	3
Google Meet	10	11	31	11
Twitter	38	22	11	0
Facebook	29	23	10	1
Telegram	19	20	22	2
Mentimeter	20	23	19	1
Skype	13	20	26	4
Zoom	10	11	36	6

Table 5.
Responses to the item "Online teaching platforms and strategies that are most effective" (in number).

into six ranges; they begin with '0' to indicate no correlation of the variables, and end with '1' to depict a perfect correlation between two variables. Correlation data can also be positive and negative, indicating the directions of the relations.

Based on **Figures 11–14**, it can be concluded that there are negative and positive correlations between the items; positive correlation suggests that when one variable increases, the other also increases, and negative correlation indicates otherwise. For example, there is a very weak correlation (negative, −.071) between years of teaching experience and the ability of respondents to distinguish between emergency

Correlations

		Years of Teaching Experience	Differentiate Emergency Remote Teaching and Online Teaching
Years of Teaching Experience	Pearson Correlation	1	-.071
	Sig. (2-tailed)		.580
	N	63	63
Differentiate Emergency Remote Teaching and Online Teaching	Pearson Correlation	-.071	1
	Sig. (2-tailed)	.580	
	N	63	63

Figure 11.
Correlations between teaching experience and ability to differentiate emergency remote teaching and online teaching.

Correlations

		Opinions about Teaching Online Fully	Blended Teaching more suitable for the Respondents
Opinions about Teaching Online Fully	Pearson Correlation	1	.407**
	Sig. (2-tailed)		.001
	N	63	63
Blended Teaching more suitable for the Respondents	Pearson Correlation	.407**	1
	Sig. (2-tailed)	.001	
	N	63	63

**. Correlation is significant at the 0.01 level (2-tailed)

Figure 12.
Correlations between opinions about teaching online fully and opinions about blended teaching.

Correlations

		Years of Teaching Experience	Blended Teaching more suitable for the Respondents
Years of Teaching Experience	Pearson Correlation	1	-.175
	Sig. (2-tailed)		.170
	N	63	63
Blended Teaching more suitable for the Respondents	Pearson Correlation	-.175	1
	Sig. (2-tailed)	.170	
	N	63	63

Figure 13.
Correlations between teaching experience and opinions about blended teaching.

remote teaching and online teaching (see **Figure 11**). What this suggests is that as the years of teaching experience increase, the respondents were perhaps not able to distinguish between emergency remote teaching and online teaching.

Meanwhile **Figure 12** illustrates a sufficient correlation (positive, .407) between opinions of respondents about teaching online fully and blended teaching. Thus, as more respondents chose to agree with teaching online fully is

Correlations

		Years of Teaching Experience	Opinions about Teaching Online Fully
Years of Teaching Experience	Pearson Correlation	1	.126
	Sig. (2-tailed)		.324
	N	63	63
Opinions about Teaching Online Fully	Pearson Correlation	.126	1
	Sig. (2-tailed)	.324	
	N	63	63

Figure 14.
Correlations between teaching experience and opinions about teaching online fully.

Range	Interpretations
0	No correlation
0.00–0.25	Very weak correlation
0.25–0.50	Sufficient correlation
0.50–0.75	Strong correlation
0.75–0.99	Very strong correlation
1	Perfect correlation

Table 6.
Correlation indicators (positive and negative) [24].

less effective, the more they opined that blended teaching is suitable for them. Further, **Figure 13** demonstrates that there is a very weak correlation (negative, −.175) between years of teaching experience and opinions about whether blended teaching is suitable for the respondents; as the years of teaching increase, the respondents' view on whether blended teaching is suitable for them decreases. In addition, **Figure 14** illustrates that there is a very weak correlation (positive, .126) between years of teaching experience and opinions about teaching online fully. This illustrates that as years of teaching experience increase, the views that teaching online fully is not effective also increase, although the correlation is relatively small and weak.

5. Discussions

From the data presented in the previous section, the author argues that, especially for the inferential statistics, too many respondents opted for 'Not Sure' when asked about emergency remote teaching and online teaching. In their defence, the author opines that since emergency remote teaching appears out of a sudden, these respondents may not be able to clearly define between emergency remote teaching and online teaching. Nonetheless, the data become a benchmark for the next step that must be taken by all educators in preparing for the unknown challenges.

Two research questions were posed earlier. The first is whether the educators at the NDUM were ready to embark on teaching during times of crisis, and the second is the platforms, tools and applications that were used by the educators during the pandemic. For the first research question, the author argues that the majority of the respondents were ready to teach during the pandemic; nonetheless, they were not able to clearly distinguish between their teaching situation and environment at the time, which is emergency remote teaching and online teaching. This is based on **Table 4**, where the respondents were able to name the platforms and applications used for teaching, and **Table 5**, where they gave their perspectives on the effectiveness of the platforms and applications used.

Regardless of this, most respondents responded 'Not Sure' for survey items on differences between emergency remote teaching and online teaching, understanding of what emergency remote teaching is, and on whether both concepts are similar (refer to **Figures 7–9**). In addition, some respondents claimed in the commentary section of the survey that face-to-face teaching is never to be replaced by emergency remote teaching or online teaching. They believed that teaching conducted fully online is not effective. The inferential statistics also support this (see **Figure 12**); most respondents opined that teaching online fully is not effective, and that blended teaching suits them better (as the number of respondents choosing teaching online fully is ineffective increases, so does that number of respondents who agreed that blending teaching is suitable for them).

For the second research question, it is found that most respondents utilised WhatsApp and MS Teams (for video conferencing and quizzes). Although the other options were also selected by some of the respondents (see **Tables 4** and **5**), the author argues that these two platforms and applications are easily accessible to both educators and students. Almost all have WhatsApp application installed in their mobile phones, and MS Teams is subscribed by the NDUM.

The author also argues that where some of the platforms and applications have never been used by the respondents, the sudden change of teaching scenario and environment does not warrant time for the respondents to explore these other platforms and applications, such as Twitter, Facebook and Exam. Net (56, 52 and 50 respondents, respectively had never used these during the pandemic). Further, based on the commentary section of the survey, a few respondents opined that in order to utilise some of the platforms and applications, *educators and students* require a stable connection to the Internet and a huge data consumption; the question remains whether both educators and students have these Internet stability and ample Internet data.

Given all these discussions, the author opines that the most important finding of this study is the roles of educators in an emergency remote teaching environment. There are two main roles. Firstly, educators must be prepared to have an online presence; either a small or big online presence depends on the students' level of competency of the lessons. This online presence is crucial in motivating and encouraging the students to stay focus and active online. Secondly, choosing the best and most suitable platforms is also important. There are no fixed rules on choosing what is best for both the students and educators. Notwithstanding this, knowing what the students require and their capability to be online may dictate the choice of suitable strategies and platforms in an emergency remote teaching environment.

6. Recommendations

Two recommendations can be offered based on the findings of this study. First, the academics must be made aware of the differences between emergency remote teaching and online teaching. Knowing and understanding of what emergency remote teaching is allow the academics to choose the most appropriate teaching platforms, strategies and applications post COVID-19. Where students are still required to learn online, so does the teaching practice continue online. **Table 3** may be of assistance to all educators, who want to ensure that their teaching benefits the students.

Second, the administrators of the higher learning institutions (and secondary as well as primary schools) may need to invest on redesigning and revamping the existing curricula in order to match post COVID-19 teaching and learning environment. The educational institutions must be ready to offer systematic and effective online education, including online activities, learning and teaching interactions, materials and assessments. Redesigning and revamping the curricula become necessary as some learning and teaching activities cannot be executed online; thus, other platforms and strategies must be chosen and applied to give students the knowledge, exposure and experience that they need.

7. Conclusion

The objective of this chapter is to identify the roles of educators, especially at the NDUM during the COVID-19 outbreak. Two research questions have been answered using the case study and quantitative approaches to research. This chapter has presented data that lead to three major findings. First, despite being ready to teach online fully, some respondents at the NDUM were not able to distinguish between emergency remote teaching and online teaching. Based on the data, the respondents are unsure of the differences between the two; both adopt different strategies of teaching.

Second, based on the data too, the respondents opined that WhatsApp and MS Teams are two platforms and applications that they used the most and were the most effective employed during this time of crisis. Although there are no specific guidelines on what strategies and platforms that must be adopted, the respondents chose what were the most convenient to them. These options *may* and *may not* be effective for all students, and these may be investigated in the near future.

Third, there are two major roles of educators teaching during the COVID-19 pandemic, including educators' willingness to have an online presence and the ability to choose the best teaching and learning platforms and applications. Educators' online presence, either big or small, encourages and motivates students to actively participate during online learning sessions. Students know that they are not alone; there are peers as well on educators to support them. When educators have established this online presence, they become indirectly aware of the platforms and applications that could be beneficial and effective for the teaching and learning activities, online.

Future research may want to also focus on collecting opinions from a bigger population, across the nation, and may want to investigate the journey of educators at primary and secondary schools. Comparing what happened during the teaching processes at various institutions may help academics to improve their teaching strategies and allow academics to learn from one another. As the new normal in teaching and learning is here to stay, educators must brave the challenges that come in various forms and aspects; they must be prepared to adapt and adopt new concepts of teaching, whatever these might be!

Conflict of interest

The author declares no conflict of interest.

Notes/thanks/other declarations

The author thanks all survey respondents for their time and cooperation in completing the online survey, which is available at https://bit.ly/2Zaozjc.

Author details

Jowati Juhary
National Defence University of Malaysia, Kuala Lumpur, Malaysia

*Address all correspondence to: jowati@upnm.edu.my

References

[1] Buheji M, da Costa Cunha K, Beka G, Mavrić B, de Souza YLdC, da Costa Silva SC, Hanafi M, Yein TC. The Extent of COVID-19 Pandemic Socio-Economic Impact on Global Poverty: A Global Integrative Multidisciplinary Review. American Journal of Economics. 2020; 10,4: 213-224. DOI: 10.5923/j.economics.20201004.02

[2] Demirbas D, Bozkurt V, Yorgun S, editors. The COVID-19 Pandemic and Its Economic, Social, and Political Impacts. Istanbul: Istanbul University Press, 2020

[3] Hibrahim MA. Pensyarah Belum Sedia Mengajar Secara 'Online' (Lecturers are not ready to teach online). Sinar Harian. 2020, 17 November. Available from: https://www.sinarharian.com.my/article/110517/BERITA/Nasional/Pensyarah-belum-sedia-mengajar-secara-online [Accessed: 2020-11-18]

[4] Characteristics of Remote and Online Teaching – Learning and Teaching Services, Algonquin College [Internet]. 2020. Available from: https://www.algonquincollege.com/lts/files/2020/05/Characteristics-of-Remote-and-Online-Teaching.pdf [Accessed: 2020-09-11]

[5] Hodges C, Moore S, Lockee B, Trust T, Bond A. The Difference Between Emergency Remote Teaching and Online Learning [Internet]. 2020. Available from: https://er.educause.edu/articles/2020/3/the-difference-between-emergency-remote-teaching-and-online-learning [Accessed: 2020-09-02]

[6] Bozkurt A, Sharma, RC. Emergency remote teaching in a time of global crisis due to Corona Virus pandemic. Asian Journal of Distance Education. 2020;15,1: i-vi. DOI: 10.5281/zenodo.3778083

[7] Abdalellah OM, Basim AK, Abdul N, Vigil JV. Emergency remote teaching during Coronavirus pandemic: the current trend and future directive at Middle East College Oman. Innovative Infrastructure Solutions. 2020;5,72:1-11. DOI: 10.1007/s41062-020-00326-7

[8] Bakia M, Shear L, Toyama Y, Lasseter A. Understanding the Implications of Online Learning for Educational Productivity [Internet]. 2012. Available from: https://tech.ed.gov/files/2013/10/implications-online-learning.pdf [Accessed: 2020-08-14]

[9] Horn M, Staker H. Blended: Using Disruptive Innovation to Improve Schools. San Francisco: Jossey-Bass, 2014

[10] Hoi SCH, Sahoo D, Lu J, Zhao P. Online Learning: A Comprehensive Survey [Internet]. 2018. Available from: https://arxiv.org/pdf/1802.02871.pdf [Accessed: 2020-09-18]

[11] Means B, Bakia M, Murphy R. Learning Online What Research Tells Us About Whether, When and How. London: Routledge, 2014

[12] Manfuso LG. From Emergency Remote Teaching to Rigorous Online Learning [Internet]. 2020. Available from: https://edtechmagazine.com/higher/article/2020/05/emergency-remote-teaching-rigorous-online-learning-perfcon [Accessed: 2020-09-01]

[13] Boon B. Active Online Teaching Strategies – Sharing Best Practices [Internet]. 2015. Available from: https://www.researchgate.net/publication/272680707_Active_Online_Teaching_Strategies-Sharing_Best_Practices. [Accessed: 2020-08-15]

[14] Golden C. Remote Teaching: The Glass Half Full [Internet]. 2020.

Available from: https://er.educause.edu/blogs/2020/3/remote-teaching-the-glass-half-full [Accessed: 2020-09-02]

[15] Talidong KJB. Implementation of emergency remote teaching (ERT) among Philippine teachers in Xi'an, China. Asian Journal of Distance Education. 2020;15,1: 196-201. DOI: 10.5281/zenodo.3881825

[16] Whittle C, Tiwari S, Yan S, Williams J. Emergency remote teaching environment: a conceptual framework for responsive online teaching in crises. Information and Learning Sciences. 2020; 121, 5/6: 311-319. DOI: 10.1108/ILS-04-2020-0099

[17] Sawyer RK, editor. The Cambridge Handbook of the Learning Sciences 2nd ed. New York: Cambridge University Press, 2005

[18] Garrison DR, Arbaugh JB. Researching the community of inquiry framework: review, issues, and future directions. The Internet and Higher Education. 2007;10, 3: 57-172

[19] Rahim AFA. Guidelines for online assessment in emergency remote teaching during the COVID-19 pandemic. Education in Medical Journal. 2020;12, 2:59-68. DOI: 10.21315/eimj2020.12.2.6

[20] Stake RE. The Art of Case Study Research. Thousand Oaks: Sage Publications, 1995

[21] Eisenhardt KM. Building Theories from Case Study Research. Academy of Management Review. 1989; 14, 4: 532-550. DOI: 10.2307/258557

[22] Cohen L, Manion L, Morrison K. Research Methods in Education 6th ed. London: Routledge, 2007

[23] Gummesson E. Qualitative Methods in Management Research. London: Sage Publications, 2000

[24] Sarwono J. Path Analysis Dengan SPSS. Jakarta: PT Alex Media Computindo; 2012

Chapter 11

Developing Professionals: Experience from a Distance Learning Short Course during the COVID-19 Pandemic

Beatriz De Castro Magalhães, Adriana Vieira Nobre, Rachel Cardoso De Almeida, Laís Barreto De Brito Gonçalves, Liz Marjorie Batista De Freitas Leite, Maria Do Socorro Vieira Lopes, Jucier Gonçalves Júnior, Evanira Rodrigues Maia and Grayce Alencar Albuquerque

Abstract

The developing and delivering of distance education (DE) courses in the *stricto sensu* reality in nursing arises in order to strengthen training processes in this area to sensitize critical and reflective professional performance. Thus, this book chapter seeks to report the experience of master's students of the Academic Master's Course in Nursing at the Regional University of Cariri, Ceará, Brazil, in the construction and tutoring of a course in the DE modality. Descriptive study, of the experience-report type, resulting from the elaboration and development of a short course on COVID-19, offered in the modality of distance learning, by *stricto sensu* postgraduate students, destined to graduate nursing students. The experience of developing the short course was positive in the sense of teaching practices, and occurred collectively, through discussions and exchange of knowledge between professors and students, in a planned and organized way. Even before operational limitations, the total process of planning, designing, developing and delivering the short course was considered a successful experience. The recognition of the potentialities and difficulties of the process helped formulating and applying the short course, always based on objectives centered on the perspectives of the students and tutors.

Keywords: COVID – 19, Education, Distance, Andragogy, Critical reasoning, Learning, Nursing, Brazil

1. Introduction

Education is considered an indispensable tool for the possibility of social ascension and better living and working conditions [1]. With the advent of the industrial revolution in England, during the 18th century, new professional profiles began to be required, no longer contemplated only with basic education, under the limits of the banking model of education [2].

In the Brazilian context, the teaching-work linking began to be thought of with the institutionalization of the public school in the 20th century, whose goal was training workers, still configured as an exclusion, not solving, for example, the problem of illiteracy, which is still one of the challenges in the 21st century added to so many others, such as the teaching-technology relationship [3].

In addition, teaching in the 21st century was, and continues to be, marked by challenges related to the insertion of communication and information technologies in teaching and learning environments, as well as by the reinforcement of the professor's role in promoting inclusive learning that regards diversity and the linking of new technologies to the educational process [4].

The new profiles required led to the stimulation of the teaching career aimed at strengthening the student capacity anchored in the tripod intellectual capacity; reading of the reality and its transformation by experience; factors highlighted in Higher Education [2] and with important impacts on professional qualification. In addition to the qualification of profiles and training of professionals, the need for scientific instrumentalization is urgently required, important for developing an evidence-based professional practice, especially when considering some professions, such as Nursing, recognized as a science through research based on high scientific rigor; mostly performed by *stricto sensu*[1] post-graduate courses [5].

Graduate courses in the *stricto sensu* modality should anchor their educational processes in the autonomy and critical reflection of students, aiming not only at the training of future professors, but also of professionals capable of replicating the ethical and scientific precepts that contribute to valuing research and science [5]. However, the current epidemiological context of the COVID-19 pandemic imposed a surprising and challenging reality on the educational scenario due to the need for social distancing [6].

However, those courses were affected by the current epidemiological context of the COVID-19 pandemic, which imposed a surprising and challenging reality on the educational scenario, due to the need for social distancing [7].

Thus, the follow-up of face-to-face courses in the online format began to be boosted, which, despite being considered an alternative, implies challenges, not only for those with limitations of access to technical and digital resources, but also for the teaching community, which identified the need to rewind and adapt to new methodologies of remote teaching (synchronous and asynchronous) and/or Distance Learning (DL) [6].

In this scenario, there came the need for online courses, which, despite considered an alternative, entails challenges not only to those who do not have access to technical and digital resources satisfactorily, but also to the teaching community, who faced the need to re-develop and adapt new methodologies to remote Education or Distance Learning (DL) [8], and among those institutions, the Academic Master's Program in Nursing (AMPN) of the Regional University of Cariri (URCA) stands out, inserted in the countryside of Ceará, in northeastern Brazil.

It is noteworthy that, in this region, where the course is located, only 51% of households have access to the Internet [9], which entails more challenges to the continuity of teaching activities [10]. In this sense, specifically in the AMPN, the challenges imposed motivated professors and students to rethink their subjects,

[1] Courses offered by universities, usually state and federal, from which students are dedicated to conducting research and teaching training.

such as the discipline of Higher Education Methodology (HEM), aiming to resolve barriers in the teaching and learning process amid the need to refine classes to the remote modality, as well as contribute, in some way, to coping with the current pandemic.

Thus, based on the principles of andragogy and meaningful learning, focusing on the student figure in the scenario of his/her learning [11], the professors of the discipline of Higher Education Methodology of the aforementioned course, aiming to stimulate innovation, inciting teaching practice and immersing the master's students in the reality faced by teaching in pandemic times, established as one of the activities of the discipline the development of distance courses for the academic community.

Through the need to integrate the COVID-19 theme into the scenarios of health education, specifically in the nursing area, and aiming to raise awareness and contribute to professional performance, as well as to stimulate individual, community prevention and intensification of strategies to cope with the pandemic, it became relevant that the course developed addressed this theme.

Although important, there is a challenge to put into practice the proposal, since, in times of COVID-19, the tensions arising from the uncertain future, together with difficulties in accessing the Internet and home environment often innocuous to concentration for the studies, instill concerns about the best possibilities of offering a short course that may provide satisfactory performance of students.

Nevertheless, such challenges are necessary to support a problem-solving sense in master's students, allowing cultivating their criticality and preparing for the future "being a professor", which can still be permeated by the repercussions of the pandemic.

Thus, the objective was to report the experience of master's students from the Academic Master's Course in Nursing of the Regional University of Cariri (URCA), in the construction and tutoring of a course in the DL modality entitled "Epidemiological, clinical, preventive and social aspects of COVID-19".

2. Study context

The pandemic caused by COVID-19 is a larger public health problem that presents aggressively, taking the lives not only of the elderly, initially considered as the main risk group, but also of children, young people and adults, who have also been affected by the disease.

In view of the problem, the measures of isolation and social distance adopted by all countries, through legislative instruments, have an impact on the economy of these countries, reflecting on the stoppage of different services and activities, including educational and teaching activities [12].

In this sense, as the need for social distancing increases, the need for information about the new coronavirus and its impacts on society also intensify. It is noteworthy that most information is obtained through digital means and can contribute to prevent the spread of the virus and reduce the exposure of the population and health professionals to the pathology.

Thus, the dissemination of information on the pandemic occurs through digital technologies and virtual teaching platforms, which is in use in basic and higher education, as pointed out in the study by Ferreira, Branchi and Sugahara [13], who highlight that teaching with the use of remote resources must be organized, considering the characteristics, the content of the subjects, as well as the use of instructional resources; which predisposes the professor to diversify his/her teaching methodological strategies [13].

It is noteworthy that the teaching process offered on virtual platforms is interspersed both by synchronous (real-time) classes and by asynchronous classes (recorded classes), allowing the display and sending of material through technological platforms. It is worth mentioning the modality of personalized distance learning, with individual attention to students through a type of tutoring [14].

However, although in pandemic times the provision of distance learning is stimulated, it is important to consider social vulnerabilities, which impact difficulties in access to social services, such as education, through limitations of internet access, technologies and environment unfavorable to the teaching-learning process [15]. It is also worth mentioning the overload of teaching work, resulting from the increased online workload that follows challenges still faced to adapt to the new model of teaching, learning and evaluation [16].

In addition to the aforementioned challenges, it is also important to consider the potential of remote education, such as the possibility of innovating in educational strategies based on digital technologies [17]. As long as it is implemented fairly and valuing the organization of the appropriate content and platforms, it is possible to present itself as a timely strategy for the current scenario.

The teaching and learning process in the remote environment must involve stimulation, development of critical skills and reflective competences, which can integrate elements and level the pedagogical proposal to the needs and contributions regarding the teaching role and the dissemination of knowledge on issues of a social, collective and educational nature [13].

In view of this, this short course was guided by the need to convey information about the new coronavirus and its impacts to nursing students, as well as to contribute as a master's program in coping with the pandemic, which was added to the stimulation of teaching roles in students.

3. Methodology

3.1 Design

This is a descriptive study, of the experience-report type, resulting from the elaboration and development of a short course on COVID-19, offered in the Distance Learning (DL) modality by *stricto sensu* postgraduate students, destined to undergraduate nursing students.

3.2 Methods

The construction of the short course occurred as part of the evaluation activities of the Higher Education Methodology (HEM) course of the Academic Master's Program in Nursing of the Regional University of Cariri (URCA), from April to June 2020.

The discipline aimed to contribute to the development of teaching skills in students, encouraging the active participation of students in the production of knowledge, understanding of methodological theoretical bases on teaching practice and intensifying the capacities of content production, virtual environment organization and tutoring. The proposal was to divide into teams with five master's students for the development of three short courses, with the offer of 20 places each.

For the preparation of the short course, initially, the teaching plan was constructed, guided by the professors of the discipline through the sequence of contents worked in remote classes, based on the literature pertinent to the theme and specific orientation of the groups. In the plenary presentation, professors and students were able to suggest changes, corrections and referrals to be observed by the three teams.

3.3 Ethical issues

As an experience report, this study does not require approval by the Research Ethics Committee. However, it is worth mentioning that, referring to the preparation and implementation of the short course, conducts were followed, which did not imply constraints or harm to the students. Moreover, the experience was carefully described, following the precepts of anonymity and confidentiality of the participants' identities and personal information.

4. Results

In a meeting scheduled to discuss and define the theme of the short course, taking into account the pandemic scenario and the need for training of nursing students (future health professionals) for professional practice, contributing not only to the care quality, but also to biosafety, the theme chosen focused on epidemiological, preventive and social clinical aspects of COVID-19.

Thus, considering that the pandemic exposed several aspects for health care, not only the biologicist aspect was conceptualized, but also the perspective of health social determinants was integrated in the theme, which led to a process of previous reading to stimulate reflections, being essential for personal and professional deconstruction of the master's students, providing self-learning and inciting, during classes, the criticality of the students.

To guide the construction of the short course, a teaching plan was elaborated that allowed both the self-learning of the students, as well as the organization of competencies, contents, use of resources, materials and complementary training strategies. It is emphasized the initial difficulty experienced by the team in the elaboration of the teaching plan and by the inexperience with the process; condition duly provided by the follow-up and teaching guidelines and by the in-depth studies on the subject.

The elaborated teaching plan led the entire development of the short course, focusing on the elaboration of learning objectives and competencies, conducting the entire process of content construction and preparation of evaluative activities.

Thus, the short course was entitled "Epidemiological, clinical, preventive and social aspects of COVID-19" and divided into four modules, namely: I) Epidemiological Aspects of COVID-19; II) Clinical Aspects of COVID-19; III) Guidelines and Prevention Measures of COVID-19 and IV) Social Aspects of the COVID-19 Pandemic; with a course load of five hours each module, totaling 20 hours and at the time, limiting to 20 applications for the students of the nursing undergraduate course, published on social networks.

The general objective of the short course was to address the epidemiological, clinical, preventive and social aspects of COVID-19 based on the principles of learning, educational skills and cognitive, procedural and attitude domains according to Bloom taxonomy. The desired competence was the ability to understand the theoretical and conceptual principles related to COVID-19, information on epidemiological aspects, clinical approach, guidance on preventive and coping measures, as well as reflections on social aspe0cts of the health context.

The process of construction of its content took place through the research and in-depth reading of articles, handbooks and protocols of the World Health Organization, the Ministry of Health and the Health Department of the State of

Ceará, seeking to extract contents necessary for the students' training process and their adaptation to educational strategies, compiling them in an easy-to-understand didactic language, which required reading and rereading the matrices of content and adequacy of the material produced for the short course.

The material produced concerns the slides that contained abstracts of the main points addressed in the handbooks, protocols and articles, as well as images, gifs and videos to illustrate the various contents. The students understand the adoption of slides as reading guides, requiring subsequent access to the complete documents for students to study. The integration of visual resources was seen as fundamental to boost the short course, due to the impossibility of practical activities in the DL model, such as the exposure of the correct technique for hand hygiene and wearing/ removal of Personal Protective Equipment (PPE).

Regarding the challenges of contemporary learning, in addition to the preparation of contents, it is necessary to adapt methodologies and value the integration of students to their own learning process. Thus, acting as students (in the master's degree) and at the same time as facilitators (in the short course), it was possible to experience the educational and evaluative processes that permeate learning.

The digital setting of the course occurred through a Virtual Learning Environment (VLE) of the Google Classroom platform, where 75% of this occurred through web conference and 25% through recorded classes, available at the virtual environment. A group was also created in the WhatsApp application to welcome and answer the doubts of the students, which facilitated the work of the tutors by allowing interaction with the students, currently hindered by social distancing.

The short course was mostly taught online through the Google Meet app. In both the online form and the recorded class, the texts were made available for prior reading in the Virtual Learning Environment (VLE) platform and, after each module, the slides of the contents taught were made available, aiming to provide the guiding points for future theoretical deepening in the cited references.

Moreover, aiming to ensure the reading of the materials in a timely manner, the short course occurred in two weeks, providing the interval of one to two days between one module and another, envisioning to offer timely time to solve the activities of each content.

The strategies for addressing the subjects ranged from dialogued exposure to the discussion of articles in plenary sessions, participation in group dynamics with brain storm and elaboration of word cloud, which were perceived by the master's students as essential strategies to stimulate the participation of synchronous activities.

These strategies aimed at facilitating learning, given the current scenario of extreme mechanization of content due to the pandemic, which considered to stimulate the greater participation of students through reflective educational approaches, aimed at a perspective of content integrated to the sanitary and social context, resulting from the conjuncture generated by the COVID-19.

To assess competencies, the activities chosen were multiple choice questions, dissertation evaluation, form with questions of subjective answers elaborated in Google Forms and evaluation of the participation of the students in the discussions.

The students were evaluated for attendance, frequency and delivery of evaluation activities, in which the approval criterion included participation in at least three modules and a minimum score of seven total points. Moreover, for each activity, evaluation criteria were established according to active participation in the classes offered and the discussions of the themes taught.

Module I obtained the highest percentage of participants and predominance of grades above average (7.0); in modules II and III, despite having 85% participation, varied scores were graded, some above and others below the established average;

in module IV, the participation was 65% of the students and despite scoring equal to or higher than the average, the tutors worried about the possibility of failures.

Regarding this concern, there were difficulties in performing the course registered by the students in a spreadsheet elaborated by the tutors and that converge with the deficit of their attendance. On the first day, only 18 people participated, among which only 12 completed the last module. On the frequency, 10 students actively participated (100%), seven were present in three modules (75%) and three attended only 25% of the short course. Concerning the number of approved by grade, 12 students obtained a score higher than seven and eight did not reach the required grade for approval.

In the students' perspective about self-assessment, the short course was successful, in relation to the content, disposition and organization of the materials and preparation of the tutors. However, it is appropriate to highlight that, at the times established for the tutorial or online classes, students faced some obstacles, such as technical problems with communication devices and personal reasons, which hindered the completion of the short course.

In general, the goals established and defined in the teaching plan were achieved, however, some challenges were identified along the route, especially in relation to the interactivity impaired by distancing, which directly affected the reflection of being a student in times of COVID-19. The challenges are necessary to identify weaknesses, potentialities and value the successes and modify the educational proposal.

The performance in teaching goes beyond the production of content. The students were able to glimpse, early, the teaching role and acquired confidence and autonomy over the teaching process, conquering throughout this growth and professional development.

5. Discussion

DL teaching has been growing considerably in Brazil and in the world, being fundamental in educational inclusion, although challenges are present in this type of teaching. According to a study by Santos and Santos [18], conducted with students of the social work course, these point to self-discipline to access classes and activities as the main difficulty, requiring conciliation with work, with difficulties in conducting their own teaching and lack of stimulus.

In the different teaching scenarios, digital information and communication technologies, until the present date of confirmation of the COVID-19 pandemic, were only used as complementary and alternative resources to pedagogical practice. However, during the pandemic, they were established as essential tools in the mediation of teaching and learning processes [12].

The current health situation throws additional challenges to access these tools concerning digital inclusion and reinforces the importance that its supply is not limited to contextual impositions, but rather to the contributions that DL can have in the educational context, contributing to the dissemination of knowledge. Furthermore, they help improving the quality of information and combating and/or coping with false news, as intended in the aforementioned short course [19].

Thus, planning stands out as an essential step for the success in the offer and application of the short course, considering that it not only directs its organization, but also anchors the construction of the content, which is greatly enhanced when the work is stratified as a team, whose organizers share their differentiated skills in the construction of a common purpose [20].

It is worth mentioning that the planning considered that the outbreak of the pandemic surprised the whole society with increasingly alarming numbers of contagion and death [21], which required/requires social support to flatten the curves of infections, such as the real need for professional qualification in health, in its broadest contexts, from academia to professional action on the subject.

In this perspective, the nursing student stands out, who, since graduation, is stimulated to the process of health promotion [22], which, during the pandemic, is indispensable, for both the co-responsibility of those students in adhering to the prevention of contagion as the active sensitization of family members and social circle. And possibly, future action at the frontline of combat and confrontation, since Ordinance no. 356 of March 20, 2020, authorizes students from the last year of health courses to work in areas compatible with the specific internships and practices of the course, in the current context of the COVID-19 pandemic [23]. Thus, the short course instilled theoretical components essential to critical social action in the stabilization of the contagion curve and relevant orientations.

Even with the proper planning, the undergraduate nursing student aims to overcome the theoretical dimension through practical experience, which is not possible in the DL model, often discouraging the student's active participation.

Nevertheless, online teaching has proven to be an excellent strategy to consolidate pre-existing or acquired knowledge throughout semesters, taking into account health training processes based on an analogy of three mathematical operations: the division in the sense of sharing experiences and knowledge; the sum of consensual thoughts and efforts for health improvements; and the multiplication in the approach that knowledge should be extended to multiple individuals and their social roles [24].

Thus, in the experience of the master's students, they considered their role as people in the community who should use social responsibility and consider the triad of reverse protection, in which their self-protection against the new coronavirus means others' protection, which, in turn, means their self-protection [25]. Furthermore, aiming to overcome the limiting perspective of information transfer, the short course aimed to stimulate awareness in the student as a social being, who will soon become more integrated into the professional field of nursing, and perhaps will still face the COVID-19 pandemic or others that may arise.

Therefore, the virtual learning environment, which allows DL to occur, should consider such prerogatives that stimulate participation, exchange of experiences and self-learning, thus requiring the elaboration of strategies, such as virtual groups, that facilitate the approximation and formation of bonds between tutors-students, aiming at the elaboration of a harmonious environment that stimulates the student's participation, fleeing the methods imposed by the traditional education [17–26].

Thus, in addition to an environment organized in Google Classroom, there was the WhatsApp group, contributing to the resignification of the student who, as the protagonist agent of the own learning, must have spaces for dialog, discussion of doubts and even criticisms that allow readjusting teaching [27]. Moreover, it is noteworthy that social networks have stood out in the pandemic, whose effect of approaching and strengthening personal relationships potentiated even more [28], which converges to a dialogical relationship between the tutor-student dyad, essential in collective work [29].

It is also noteworthy that the DL model allows an important flexibilization for the organization of the student's time [18], which was considered as a strategy, since synchronous and asynchronous classes were compiled, which were systematized considering an adequate interval of time between one module and another, so that the student had the opportunity to reconcile the activities to his/her routine.

The student's routine should be considered in the DL, since the learning is a continuous construction, which requires adequate time to achieve theoretical deepening, reflections about readings and proper execution of activities [26, 30].

The scope of such aspects becomes essential for the construction of criticality in the student [23]. Furthermore, critical sense was stimulated through the integration of the contents of the modules, breaking with the limitation of fragmented contents and considering the expanded concept of health [31].

In relation to this expanded concept of health, it is worth mentioning that the social aspects have great prominence. as well as the adoption of active methodology, through multiple strategies used, which promote dynamism, strengthen the relationship with the student [32] and allow their adequacy over time, because people learn in different ways and a single approach would not bring success [33].

Furthermore, the active methodologies aim at the students' incentive and autonomy, which was intended in the short course, considering knowledge, previous readings and encouraging active participation by multiple strategies. However, it is emphasized that the DL model brings with it challenges to student-professor interactivity, since the student's attention becomes increasingly difficult to be apprehended, with no possibility of body readings that corroborate for changes in behavior and methods, when these translate restlessness [34]. Such challenges sometimes compromise active participation, sometimes encourage the facilitator to recognize even more the importance of the protagonist action of the student, which should be encouraged through the adoption of active learning methodologies.

Some authors already bring that remote education can be significant since allied to active methods, centered on the participation of the student [35]. It is worth mentioning that in Brazil the active methodologies are based on the theoretical precepts of Paulo Freire and on the critical-social progressive pedagogical trend of contents, which aims at the formation of an autonomous professional, capable of solving problems based on previous knowledge of the reality where he/she lives [36].

Thus, for the construction of the short course, the pandemic context was considered, its mental impacts and access to digital media to understand the student's reality previously and adapt the content, as well as to design activities that would rescue their experience during this period and put them in problem situations related to COVID-19, in which, based on their previous knowledge and shared in the short course, they could reach a critical resolution.

The use of active methodologies in distance learning has repercussions on the way in which the student experiences learning, through the resignification of his/her way of learning, fostering his/her autonomy and the development of critical, reflective and analytical thinking. And it is in this context that distance learning and active methodologies are interconnected, through the offer of strategies that establish greater flexibility of time and space for students, and that consequently also enable professors to develop classes on digital platforms, with the same quality as traditional face-to-face meetings [37].

The content produced must follow criteria that lead to the acquisition of materials that significantly meet the students' needs and the course load, stimulating them to the participation [38]. Such precepts are expressed in the short course when discussing the judgment about the need to compile the vast scientific content in a didactic language, which can be considered as a challenge, because there is a fine line between making didactic content and escaping its essence, which shows the need for the producer's neutrality [39–40].

Regarding the students' evaluation, the short course envisioned the transcendence to traditional evaluative methods, through an integration of objective, dissertation and participatory activities, which break with the focus on accumulated and decorative knowledge, working in a perspective of reconstruction of knowledge for the development of competencies [26].

Nevertheless, this transcendence is shown to be a challenge, mainly due to the culture of traditional education, which crystallized and still resonates in ready responses [41], which may partly justify the failure of eight students. This is due to the fact that, instead of "ready-made" answers, students were assessed for their criticality when analyzing multiple choice questions, when discussing argumentative responses to the dissertation assessment and when taking a reflective position during the discussions.

Moreover, some fears that plague professors in the in-person teaching are intensified in the DL model, especially concerning the possibility of copying the work of colleagues and from various sources [42]. Thus, the intention was to minimize such fear, not only by the integration of dissertation and participation activities, but mainly, by the use of assessment criteria; the learner is then encouraged to express his/her critical position before a given situation [42].

It is worth highlighting yet another concern evidenced in virtual learning environments, such as the interaction between professors and students decreased due to the resources needed to access remote education not being available to everyone due to social inequalities [43]. Many students in Brazil do not have access to quality computers, mobile phones or the Internet, which was evidenced by the Departments of Education of states and municipalities at the current time of pandemic [44].

In addition, physical and family environments unfavorable to the teaching and learning process are also a present reality that hinders the permanence and concentration of the student in classes [45]. Thus, the relationships established between those who teach and those who learn are being reproduced in a deficient way and fragmented due to physical limitations [46].

Thus, the strategies of content approach and diversified evaluation are essential, especially in the current scenario, which emblematically presents the fluidity of phenomena. This is due to the pandemic having surprised the whole society, lacking innovative strategies to cope, not only in the health field, but also in the field of education.

Such difficulties are manifested by students and relate to sociodemographic aspects for access and permanence in a virtual environment, given the obstacles caused by the limitation of access to the internet network, often of low quality, in addition to overloading of teaching, work and domestic activities, which overlap [47].

Moreover, the low adaptation of students to technological resources and remote modality, due to the low interaction with other colleagues and professors, besides the fact that students have become responsible for their own learning, can contribute to dissatisfaction with this new teaching model [48, 49]. However, it is noteworthy that the short course in question was well evaluated by the students, which may be associated with the fact that it was taught in a short period of time.

Taking into account that the competencies required in tutoring are associated with the cognitive dimension, in which mastery of the contents addressed is expected; with the technical scope, from which one must have the ability to handle the tools of the course; pedagogical aspects, which provide for guidance and follow-up of the students; and the communicative domain, in which tutors must maintain a dialogical relationship with the student [47], a satisfactory experience was perceived for the mutual construction of knowledge between students and tutors responsible, as well as the development of skills of the master's students for a future teaching practice.

The prominent role of tutoring in DL is highlighted, through the humanization of a popularly mechanized teaching, and contributing to the student's constant encouragement, which weakens the barriers concerning the distancing of individuals and enables mutual learning [44], which, in this experience, was essential, by contributing to the critical sense necessary in the current health crisis, as well as in the training process at the *stricto sensu* level.

Thus, the prior preparation of the students for the elaboration of teaching and evaluation skills and strategies, as well as for the teaching of tutoring was quite valid, both to experience some challenges, as well as to acquire new skills for interactive moments and evaluation actions.

6. Conclusions

The Covid-19 pandemic brought with it the emergence of a new teaching configuration, which should occur at distance, but maintaining the ideological assumptions of face-to-face teaching, especially concerning the active participation of the student in his/her teaching process. In this context, the experience of constructing the teaching plan and tutoring of the course was positive for the students' teaching learning, since the contact with formative and teaching-learning processes based on the role and the ways of learning significantly enable new experiences, especially with this new format of teaching.

The collective and articulated construction between students and professors of the course had been crucial to achieve the proposed objectives, because the constant monitoring and discussion of ideas provided organization, strategy and autonomy during the moment of construction of the short course, conditions that are essential for the student's good development.

Thus, qualification courses in the nursing area consist of strategies of great relevance concerning the training and qualification of professionals and students. In this context, the use of technologies related to methods such as active learning can be considered a good option, considering that the educational method permeates daily transformations and improvements.

Thus, it is noteworthy that the construction, tutoring, as well as the recognition of the potentialities and difficulties of the process, helped formulating and applying, always based on objectives centered on the perspective of the student and tutor, which corresponds to an innovative experience in the context of didactic and teaching practices.

Conflict of interest

The authors declare no conflict of interest.

Author details

Beatriz De Castro Magalhães[1], Adriana Vieira Nobre[1], Rachel Cardoso De Almeida[1], Laís Barreto De Brito Gonçalves[1], Liz Marjorie Batista De Freitas Leite[2], Maria Do Socorro Vieira Lopes[1], Jucier Gonçalves Júnior[3]*, Evanira Rodrigues Maia[1] and Grayce Alencar Albuquerque[1]

1 Departament of Nursing, Universidade Regional do Cariri (URCA), Crato, Brazil

2 Departament of Hepatology, Escola Paulista de Medicina-Universidade Federal de São Paulo (UNIFESP), São Paulo, Brazil

3 Departament of Internal Medicine, Division of Rheumathology, Universidade de São Paulo (USP), São Paulo, Brazil

*Address all correspondence to: juciergjunior@hotmail.com

References

[1] Barros ADSX. Expansão da educação superior no Brasil: limites e possibilidades. Educação & Sociedade. 2015; 36 (131): 361-390. http://dx.doi.org/10.1590/ES0101-7330201596208

[2] Moreira LKR, Moreira LR, Soares MG. Educação Superior no Brasil: discussões e reflexões. Educação Por Escrito. 2018; 9(1): 134-150. https://doi.org/10.15448/2179-8435.1.29594

[3] Carvalho, A. A. A constituição da educação básica no brasil: os modos de conceber e praticar a cultura escolar no século XX. Cadernos de História da Educação. 2012; 11(2).

[4] Novoa A. Professores: Imagens do futuro presente. Lisboa: educa, 2009.

[5] Silva HD, Reis VN. Desenhos de estudos experimentais e quase-experimentais: definições e desafios na pesquisa em enfermagem. Journal of Nursing UFPE. 2016; 10(6): 2230-2241. http://dx.doi-org.ez152.periodicos.capes.gov.br/10.5205/reuol.9199-80250-1-SM1006201639

[6] Freitas MDFQD, Souza J. Pensar a formação e a pesquisa na pós-graduação stricto sensu. Educar em Revista. 2018; 34(71): 9-18. https://doi.org/10.1590/0104-4060.62549

[7] Nogueira Filho O, Corrêia GB, Reame L, Pereira T. Ensino a distância na Educação Básica frente à pandemia da Covid-19. Nota Técnica. 2020 abril [citado em 01 de novembro de 2020]; 1(1). Disponível em: https://www.todospelaeducacao.org.br/_uploads/_posts/425.pdf

[8] Costa R, Lino MM, Souza AIJD, Lorenzini E, Fernandes GCM, Brehmer LCDF, et al. Nursing teaching in covid-19 times: how to reinvent it in this context?. Texto & Contexto-Enfermagem. 2020; 29:e20200202. http://dx.doi.org/10.1590/1980-265x-tce-2020-0002-0002

[9] Folha de Pernambuco. 51% dos lares do Nordeste seguem sem internet. 2018. Consulta: 20 agosto de 2020. Disponível em: https://www.folhape.com.br/economia/51-dos-lares-no-nordeste-seguem-sem-internet/75915/

[10] Dias É, Pinto FCF. A Educação e a Covid-19. Ensaio: Avaliação e Políticas Públicas em Educação. 2020; 28(108): 545-554. https://doi.org/10.1590/s0104-40362019002801080001

[11] Ausubel DP. The acquisition and retention of knowledge: A cognitive view. Kluwer Academic Publishers: Lisboa, 1.Ed. dois mil.

[12] Alves, L. Educação remota: entre a ilusão e a realidade. Interfaces Científicas-Educação. 2020; 8(3), 348-365.

[13] Ferreira DHL., Branchi BA, Sugahara CR. Processo de ensino e aprendizagem no contexto das aulas e atividades remotas no Ensino Superior em tempo da pandemia Covid-19. Revista práxis. 2020; 12 (1 sup): sp.

[14] de Souza KR, dos Santos GB, dos Santos Rodrigues AM, Felix EG, Gomes L, da Rocha GL, Peixoto, RB. Trabalho remoto, saúde docente e greve virtual em cenário de pandemia. Trabalho, Educação e Saúde. 2021; 19.

[15] Figueiredo Santos JA. Covid-19, causas fundamentais, classe social e território. Trabalho, Educação e Saúde, 2020; 18(3): e00280112.

[16] Santos GMRF, Silva ME, Belmonte BR. COVID-19: emergency remote teaching and university professors' mental health. Rev. Bras. Saude Mater. 2021; Infant. [Internet].

2021 Feb [cited 2021 May 20]; 21 (Suppl 1): 237-243.

[17] Rocha FSM, Loss T, Almeida BLC, Motta MS, Kalinke MA. O Uso de Tecnologias Digitais no Processo de Ensino durante a Pandemia da Covid-19. Interacções. 2020; 16(55):58-82.

[18] Santos CP, Santos S. Desafios do ensino em EAD. Maiêutica serviço social. 2013; 1(1). https://publicacao.uniasselvi.com.br/index.php/SES_EaD/article/view/604/272

[19] Ornell F, Schuch JB, Sordi AO, Kessler FHPP. "Pandemic fear" and COVID-19: mental health burden and strategies. Brazilian Journal of Psychiatry. 2020; 42(3):232-235. http://dx.doi.org/10.1590/1516-4446-2020-0008

[20] Brasil. Referenciais de qualidade para educação superior a distância. Secretaria de Educação a Distância. Ministério da Educação. 2007. Consulta: 30 de outubro de 2020. Disponível em: http://portal.mec.gov.br/seed/arquivos/pdf/legislacao/refead1.pdf

[21] World Health Organization. Situations reports coronavírus disease (COVID – 19). 2020.

[22] Pereira FGF, Caetano JA, Moreira JF, Ataíde MBC. Health education practices in the training of nursing Undergraduates. Cogitare Enfermagem. 2015; 20(2):332-7. http://dx.doi.org/10.5380/ce.v20i2.39767

[23] Brasil. Ministério da Educação. Diário Oficial da União. Portaria n° 356 de 20 de março de 202. Dispõe sobre a atuação dos alunos dos cursos da área de saúde no combate à pandemia do COVID-19 (coronavírus). 2020. Consulta: 16 de agosto de 2020. Disponível em: https://www.in.gov.br/en/web/dou/-/portaria-n-356-de-20-de-marco-de-2020-249090908

[24] Ribeiro IL, Medeiros Júnior A. Graduação em saúde, uma reflexão sobre ensino-aprendizado. Trabalho, Educação e Saúde. 2016; 14(1):33-53. https://doi.org/10.1590/1981-7746-sip00099

[25] Cruz EDA. Facing coronavirus – the triad of reverse protection: by protecting myself, i protect the other by protecting the other, i protect myself. Cogitare Enfermagem. 2020; 25: e73708. http://dx.doi.org/10.5380/ce.v25i0.73708

[26] Souza TES, Menezes AHN. Avaliação em educação a distância: concepções e possibilidades. Revista de Educação do Vale do São Francisco-REVASF. 2015;4(6): 158-170. https://www.periodicos.univasf.edu.br/index.php/revasf/article/view/275/170

[27] Paiva MRF, Parente JRF, Brandão IR, Queiroz AHB. Metodologias ativas de ensino-aprendizagem: revisão integrativa. SANARE-Revista de Políticas Públicas. 2016;15(2). https://sanare.emnuvens.com.br/sanare/article/view/1049/595

[28] Manca S. Snapping, pinning, likingortexting: Investigating social media in higher education beyond Facebook. The Internet and Higher Education. 2020; 44:100707. https://doi.org/10.1016/j.iheduc.2019.100707

[29] Lara EMDO, Lima VV, Mendes JD, Ribeiro ECO, Padilha RDQ. The teacher in active methodologies and the nuances between teaching and learning: challenges and possibilities. Interface-Comunicação, Saúde, Educação. 2019;23: e180393. https://doi.org/10.1590/Interface.180393

[30] Franzoi MAH, Cauduro FLF. Participation of nursing students in the covid-19 Pandemic. Cogitare Enfermagem. 2020;25. http://dx.doi.org/10.5380/ce.v25i0.73491

[31] Mendonça ETD, Cotta RMM, Lelis VDP, Moreira TR, Carvalho Junior PM. Integração Intercampi no Ensino: Desenvolvendo Competências do Profissionalismo. Revista Brasileira de Educação Médica. 2016;40(3): 344-354. https://doi.org/10.1590/1981-52712015v40n3e00822015

[32] Pereira FC, Lopes TDAM. Como preparar conteúdo para EAD. Revista Aprendizagem em EAD. 2019;8(1). https://bdtd.ucb.br/index.php/raead/article/viewFile/10443/6443

[33] Masetto MT. Competência pedagógica do professor universitário. 2 ed. São Paulo: Summus editorial; dois mil e doze.

[34] Xiao C, Li Y. Analysis on the Influence of the Epidemic on the Education in China. International Conference on Big Data and Informatization Education (ICBDIE). 2020:143-147. https://americanethnologist.org/features/collections/covid-19-and-student-focusedconcerns-threats-and-possibilities/analysis-on-the-influence-of-epidemic-oneducation-in-china

[35] Dosea GS, do Rosário RWS, Silva EA, Firmino LR, dos Santos Oliveira AM. Métodos ativos de aprendizagem no ensino online: a opinião de universitários durante a pandemia de COVID-19. Interfaces Científicas-Educação. 2020; 10(1): 137-148.

[36] Palmeira RL, da Silva AAR, Ribeiro WL. As metodologias ativas de ensino e aprendizagem em tempos de pandemia: a utilização dos recursos tecnológicos na Educação Superior. HOLOS. 2020; 5: 1-13.

[37] Berbel NAN. As metodologias ativas e a promoção da autonomia de estudantes. Semina: Ciências Sociais e Humanas. 2011;32(1):25-40. http://dx.doi.org/10.5433/1679-0383.2011v32n1p25

[38] Clementino A. Planejamento pedagógico para cursos EAD. Kensky, Vani Moreira. Design instrucional para cursos on-line. São Paulo: Editora Senac. 2015.

[39] Filatro A, Cairo S. Produção de conteúdos educacionais. São Paulo: Saraiva. 2015.

[40] Diesel A, Baldez ALS, Martins, SN. Os princípios das metodologias ativas de ensino: uma abordagem teórica. Revista Thema. 2017;14(1):268-288. https://doi.org/10.15536/thema.14.2017.268-288.404

[41] Nunes RC. A avaliação em educação a distância é inovadora? Uma reflexão. Estudos em Avaliação Educacional. 2012;23(52): 274-299. http://dx.doi.org/10.18222/eae235220121940

[42] Morais Neto ACD, Tagnin LH, Araújo ACD, Sousa MIO, Barra BGA., Hercowitz A. Ensino em Saúde LGBT na Pandemia da Covid-19: Oportunidades e Vulnerabilidades. Revista Brasileira de Educação Médica. 2020; 44.

[43] Charczuk SB. Sustentar a transferência no ensino remoto: docência em temposde pandemia.Educ. Real. 2020; 45(4) e109145.

[44] Dias E, Pinto FCF. A Educação e a Covid-19. Ensaio: aval. pol. públ. educ. 2020; 28 (108).

[45] Digner IS, Deina M, Zantut L, Dall'Oglio LM, Sfredo LR. Os desafios do ensino em saúde nos tempos de pandemia por Covid-19: uma revisão integrativa. Espaço para Saúde. 2020; 21(2): 68-79.

[46] Neves VNS, de Assis Valdegil D, do Nascimento Sabino R. Ensino remoto emergencial durante a pandemia de COVID-19 no Brasil: estado da arte. Práticas Educativas, Memórias e Oralidades-Rev. Pemo. 2021; 3(2), e325271-e325271.43

[47] Mattar J, Rodrigues L, Martins M, Czeszak W, Graciani J. Competências e funções dos tutores online em educação a distância. Educação em Revista. 2020;36. https://doi.org/10.1590/0102-469821743944 Warmling D, Boell JEW, Costa VT, Peres GM, Faust SB, Bolsoni CC, et al. Aproximando saberes e experiências à distância: relato da tutoria de um curso de especialização. Revista de Salud Pública. 2018;20: 132-137. http://dx.doi.org/10.15446/rsap.v20n1.64480

[48] Basso SEO, Santos RO, Oliveira DHI, Mertizig PLL, Costa MLF. EaD, currículo e hegemonia: o necessário debate. Revista em Rede. 2020; 7(1): 225-241.

[49] Cunha LFF, Souza AS, da Silva AP. O ensino remoto no brasil em tempos de pandemia: diálogos acerca da qualidade e do direito e acesso à educação. Revista com censo: estudos educacionais do distrito federal. 2020; 7 (3): 27-37.

Section 4

Impact of the COVID-19 Pandemic

Chapter 12

Impact of COVID-19 on Dental Education

Isla Camilla Carvalho Laureano, Alidianne Fábia Cabral Cavalcanti and Alessandro Leite Cavalcanti

Abstract

The COVID-19 pandemic has brought impacts and changes on dental education around the world. People who are in close contact with the COVID-19 patients, including students and teaching staff, are at increased risk of contamination, as they work close to the oral cavity of patients in direct contact with salivary fluids and in closed environment. In addition, social isolation and distancing measures have been adopted by governments, with severe restrictions on dental education. At this moment, students should have the teaching and experience for adequate dental practice, dental educators should provide solutions to resume dental education remotely to ensure the well-being of students, employees and teaching staff. This chapter discusses the impact of the COVID-19 on dental education and the role of emergency remote education in the continuity of face-to-face classes and preclinical and clinical education, in addition to addressing the challenges and the Brazilian reality of teaching-service-community activities.

Keywords: COVID-19, dental education, emergency remote teaching, online learning, distance education, dentistry, Brazil

1. Introduction

The pandemic imposed by Coronavirus, in addition to economic, social and health problems, also affected the educational sector, so that in order to comply with determinations imposed by the government agencies of each country, there was a temporary interruption in the teaching activities of undergraduate and graduate courses in all areas of knowledge, including Dentistry [1], since classroom classes - theoretical, preclinical (laboratory) and clinical - were interrupted as a measure of social isolation.

The teaching and learning of dental practice differs from other undergraduate courses in the health and social care disciplines, as dentistry students perform irreversible procedures on patients under the supervision of clinical professors, who assume indirect responsibility for the work of these students [2]. The Dentistry course has large load of practical activities, so it became a great challenge to carry out clinical activities, since teachers and students are isolated at home without access to dental equipment. One of the greatest challenges in dental education was the interruption of direct patient care, which is a key component of the dental curriculum [3]. This fact resulted in the extension of study terms, and deferral of exams and graduation dates [4].

In order to safeguard the health of students and following the government social distancing rule, teachers and patients, universities were forced to take different measures to ensure the continuity of education. Didactic courses, hands-on workshops, presentations and seminars have transitioned to online instructions in most institutions [5]. In the last few months, emergency remote education became the only option to guarantee the continuity of higher education learning [3]. While online learning is carefully planned and resourced, emergency remote education was quickly constructed with minimal time and resources, as a temporary measure during the crisis [6]. As a way to continue offering remote distance learning, teachers and students had to accept this new reality and adopted new learning technologies. Therefore, adapting to these changes in the curriculum and assessment methods in a short period of time was a challenge not only for teachers and academicians, but also for university directors. However, many educators had never delivered sessions in online environments, which required them to acquire an extensive set of skills over a short period of time [7].

Due to the new normal situation, in many universities, offering preclinical education in the traditional format with synchronous feedback (SFB) was not possible during the pandemic [8]. In several countries, including Brazil, students begin preclinical practice (laboratory) in the third or fourth semester of the course. Although different clinical dental care simulators have been developed and yielded satisfying results, they are insufficient in educational institutions, are not portable, do not cover all areas of dentistry and are very expensive and unaffordable in large scale [9].

Most graduate dental education activities were ceased during the early stages of the pandemic [9]. Face-to-face education was also affected, as was the development of epidemiological, clinical and laboratory research. Researchers, whose studies involved collecting clinical data from patients, had their research abruptly stopped, without being sure when they could resume this stage. Therefore, the serious educational losses and the quality of research developed are also aspects to be carefully analyzed.

Online learning is the use of internet and some other important technologies to develop materials for educational purposes, instructional delivery and program management [10]. With regard to emergency remote education, when compared to traditional teaching methods, there are some advantages such as the theoretical material made available to students can be easily updated and quickly accessed. However, for it to be effective, team development, assessment strategies and technological elements must be well planned and standardized [3].

The training of dentistry students is dynamic and complex, as it involves many factors, such as the curriculum structure of the course, the quality of physical facilities of the educational institution, the number of hours devoted to the development of preclinical and clinical activities, internships developed in health services, the teaching methods used by teachers, among others. Therefore, the interruption of all these activities due to the COVID-19 pandemic may impact the student's education. Therefore, the responsibilities of educators include not only providing adequate theoretical teaching and consistent with the best scientific evidence in force, but also ensuring that students are able and qualified to perform clinical procedures with different degrees of complexity for the correct professional practice.

In light of the above, this chapter discusses the impact of the COVID-19 pandemic on dental education and the role of emergency remote education in the continuity of classes through the various types of methodologies and available digital platforms. There are also possibilities for the continuation of preclinical and clinical teaching, and advantages and limitations of the adoption of this new model of education through experiences of dentistry educators and students from different countries. Some alternatives for the evaluation of students, the guidelines recommended by competent bodies to control the dissemination of COVID-19 in the resumption of face-to-face dental education activities and the Brazilian panorama of teaching-service-community integration activities has also been discussed.

2. Methods

This is a bibliographic search conducted through the analysis of articles indexed until April 2021 in PubMed (U.S. National Institutes of Health's National Library of Medicine), Web of Science (Clarivate Analytics) and Scopus (Elsevier) databases. For the study, the search keywords used were "Dental Education" AND "Dentistry" AND "COVID-19".

Articles eligible for this chapter were publications that presented data and suggestions about emergency remote teaching in continuing the dental educational process in terms of theoretical, preclinical and clinical education. The analysis of studies was independently carried out by two researchers (ALC and ICCL) through a previous reading of the titles and abstracts of the found references. The selected articles were accessed in their entirety, being read and evaluated. At the end of the analysis, differences were discussed. In lack of consensus, a third researcher (AFCC) decided to include or exclude the article.

Furthermore, this review listed the main international and Brazilian guidelines for providing clinical education and commented Brazilian panorama on teaching-service-community integration. Data were descriptively presented.

3. From face-to-face teaching to the use of digital platforms: a new model for dental education

Due to the COVID-19 pandemic, emergency remote education was temporarily adopted [6] as well as "teleodontology" [11]. The latter term, in addition to referring to remote counseling and diagnosis using technologies, can be used in the form of web-based self-instruction, which allows students the ability to control their learning, or interactive videoconference, in which patient information is transmitted live, with or without the presence of the patient, allowing immediate feedback and review of cases at the students' pace [12]. This type of learning is a distance education modality that uses electronic devices to promote learning, making use of information and communication technologies (ICTs) [13].

Among so many interrupted activities, patient care, research continuity and scientific meetings stand out; in addition, changes in academic calendars, with the inclusion of extra semesters and postponement of the entry of new students [14, 15]. In this context, the current challenges of dental education are to ensure that students have the training and experience necessary to guarantee competence for the dental practice and that educators have solutions to resume distance dental education, ensuring the well-being of employees, students and teachers.

The Bachelor's degree in Dentistry ranges from four [16] to six years of formal education [17], and, in general, it is divided into preclinical and clinical years [16]. In the preclinical years, students mostly learn basic science subjects, with practice in laboratories, where they practice on mannequins and teeth. In the clinical years, students mainly have activities with patients, under the supervision of teachers [16].

Usually, classes are physically assisted by students and are an essential component of dental education [11]. With emergency remote education, several types of methodologies are available, which consist of synchronous teaching - students and teachers meet in real time, and asynchronous, which does not require students and teachers to be online at the same time, through the use of digital platforms [18]. These methodologies include video classes, flipped classroom, case studies, discussions, problem based-learning (PBL) [19, 20], among others.

In the synchronous method, the advantages are live interaction and immediate reaction; in the asynchronous method, the user can control the learning pace and review the material several times whenever necessary [12]; in the flipped classroom method, students need to have prior knowledge of the subject, and in PBL approaches, students develop critical thinking [20].

There are several platforms for conducting emergency remote education, such as Zoom®, G Suite®, Skype®, Moodle®, Microsoft Teams®, Jitsi®, WebEx®, Instagram®, Facebook®, WhatsApp®, Telegram® and YouTube® [21, 22]. For the use of these technologies, adequate training of the teaching staff must be carried out [20], as this change in teaching methodology can be of difficult adaptation for these individuals, and students must be familiar with these tools [21].

A recent systematic review identified that the Zoom® platform was the preferred one among interviewees in studies included in this research [23]. Zoom® offers videoconferencing services for up to 1000 participants, with several possibilities, such as recordings, transcriptions, screen sharing, sending and receiving of files and chatting [24].

The Google Classroom® and Google Meet® compose the G Suite® platform. The first is a free tool for the management and evaluation of students, while the second allows connection and communication through video calls, using a computer or mobile device, which can be recorded and shared [25]. Skype® allows communication by voice and video calls with up to 100 people, sending of messages, screen sharing, meeting recordings of up to 24 hours and offers call captions in ten languages and chats in more than 60 languages in real time, for different devices [26]. Moodle® is a learning platform that provides a unique system to create personalized education environments, trusted by institutions around the world, in addition to being easy to use and free of cost [27]. In Moodle®, it is possible to send didactic material, post videos, conduct discussion forums, tasks, assessments and organize communication with students [22].

Microsoft Teams® is a platform that brings together conversations, content and applications, offers the creation of online classrooms, tasks, synchronous meetings, with recordings and screen sharing, in addition to enabling the use of a digital notebook for storing texts, images, notes, documents, links, voices, videos and others, allowing teachers to create personalized learning environments [28].

Likewise, Jitsi® [29] and WebEx® [30] are free voice, video conference and messaging software, with screen sharing, which allow meetings of up to 100 participants; however, they have paid plans with more advantages. Other social media platforms, such as Instagram® and YouTube®, are also used as teaching alternatives through "lives", which can be discussed on WhatsApp® [22].

4. Preclinical teaching

Preclinical teaching includes laboratory learning for the practice of human and dental anatomy [31], use of the optical microscope to observe histological sections [18], radiographic image interpretation exercises [32], simulation models in typodont, after demonstration performed by teachers [18, 21], among others.

However, these activities have been suspended in many countries due to social distancing [21, 31].

Alternatives that apply technology in laboratory activities have been described [19, 31, 33] and suggested [32, 34] in some studies. Education using virtual anatomy was the solution for the practice of anatomy [31]. Virtual microscopy helped in the practical learning of oral histology and histopathology, in which conventional sections were digitized and shared on online platforms - synchronous and asynchronous formats - allowing observation similar to optical microscope [19, 33], with structures illustrated and marked in detail [19]. There is also the possibility to carry out radiology interpretation activities through social networks [32].

There are technological teaching tools that allow the development of preclinical skills, which use virtual reality, augmented reality, and haptic technology [35], such as Simodont®, PerioSim®, Forsslund and Individual Dental Education Assistant (IDEA) simulators attached to a stand PHANToM omni [4]. Virtual reality refers to simulation generated by computer graphics with virtual sense of reality [36]. Augmented reality is the integration of real and virtual environments [37]. Haptic technology allows the tactile sensation when interacting with computer generated objects [38]. These technologies can overcome the disadvantages of typodont practice, because with these devices, it is not possible to calibrate the evaluation process due to the focus on the result of the activity, and there is strong dependence on the subjective evaluation of the teacher [35].

These technologies, if made portable, can simulate meetings with the patient and assist in the continuity of education and clinical evaluation during the COVID-19 pandemic and the "new normal", as they are versatile, immersive and accessible [18]. However, they have many disadvantages, as they are generally very expensive, require training [35], are not portable and, therefore, cannot be used at this time [20]. Thus, researchers proposed the use of a mannequin attached to the micromotor for students to carry out practical training at home through videoconferences [34].

In this context, a group of researchers has recently created a compact and portable teaching-learning resource, DenTeach, composed of an instructor workstation (DT-Performer), a student workstation (DT-Student), advanced wireless networking technology, and cloud-based data storage and retrieval [4]. The platform synchronizes the instructor's and student's operations with real-time video, audio, feel, and posture (VAFP). It was developed for use in teaching, shadowing, and practice modes. In the first, the student can perceive how the instructor is conducting the dental operation through the tactile feedback obtained from the dental tool on the instructor workstation [4]. In the second, the student can watch, feel and repeat the tasks alone, downloading the videos. Finally, students can use the system to perform tasks and have their dental performance skills automatically assessed in terms of key performance indices (KPIs). DenTeach has proven to be a useful system for educational and professional purposes, which can be used to train and educate students in remote clinics/laboratories [4].

5. Clinical teaching

With the pandemic, health organizations asked for caution about the clinical care of institutions due to the risks of procedures that generate aerosols, limited supplies of personal protective equipment (PPE) and difficulties in individual supervision of students [39]. Teleodontology can be used to assist students in clinical teaching. In some disciplines, patient data can be used and subsequently discussed [12].

PBL [2], case-based discussion [2, 22, 40] and virtual patients (VPs) [11, 22] used in the simulation of clinical cases, in interviews, in the analysis of ethical cases [41], to improve students' skills in decision making and diagnosis, are also alternatives that can develop clinical reasoning [22]. VPs are efficient, interactive, enable experience with rare cases and allow for the improvement of skills in a less intimidating environment [41]. In addition, virtual meetings between students and simulated patients (actors) can be held, representing clinical interaction [42].

Research carried out with students before and after teleodontology meetings using actors as patients found that most participants reported some level of discomfort before using this type of care and after, 23% still reported discomfort when leading remote care [42]. Therefore, teleodontology should be stimulated in higher education, so that students become more qualified and future professionals more experienced in providing guidance, thus avoiding unnecessary dislocations in this new world context.

In Brazil, teachers and course managers are encouraged to use this technology to improve their teaching activities [43], since the Federal Council of Dentistry (CFO), which regulates the practice of distance dentistry, prohibits the use of teleodontology by undergraduate students [44], which can be used in the following situations:

- Tele-education in health: synchronous or asynchronous meeting associated with information on preventing situations that may represent the need for urgent care.
- Telescreening: comprises anamnesis and initial screening, prior to scheduling dental care.
- Telemonitoring: assessment of the need for the patient's face-to-face return, with ongoing treatment.
- Teleinterconsultation: exchange of opinions between dental surgeons through technologies, with or without the presence of the patient, for the construction of the diagnosis or therapeutic assistance.
- Teleconsulting: communication, through technologies, between health professionals and managers for the exchange of information in order to clarify doubts, oral health actions and issues related to the work process.
- Second Formative Opinion: source of information originated from questions from teleconsultants and based on the best evidence and on relevant criteria of primary health care [43, 44].

However, remote strategies should not replace clinical practice with patients in the acquisition of skills inherent to dental training [3, 45]. Studies corroborate this information, in which the majority of Jordanian students considered that clinical training was the experience most affected by the pandemic and dental specialties most negatively affected were conservative dentistry (73.2%), followed by prosthodontics (69.4%) [3], and only 27.1% of American students reported good performance of their teachers in providing clinical experience during the lockdown [39].

Students suggest that it would be interesting to have review classes and practical teaching after the pandemic is under control [40]. In addition to all issues resulting from the sudden change in dental education, the psychological impact of this pandemic on students' mental well-being is another issue that should not be neglected, as it can influence their future practices [3].

6. Advantages and limitations of online education

Despite all the negative impact on dental education, this moment of transition can also generate opportunities with regard to the replacement of classes for online courses during the pandemic, which can be disseminated on the internet to a large number of students [21]. It was found that, for the teaching staff, emergency remote education helps to ensure learning and allows accessibility between students and teachers [40]. For students, it is comfortable, reduces costs, facilitates access to teaching materials [13, 40], given the chat option, timid students can be more participatory [18], and, both for students and teachers, emergency remote education modalities encourage a focus on the student [40], as they demand more responsibility and protagonism [19]. In online clinical teaching, the absence of the patient caused students to make mistakes, without compromising patient safety [2].

Reported difficulties included the limited knowledge of the teaching staff on technology, the availability and quality of students' connection to the internet [13, 23, 31], extra expenses for increasing internet franchise [13], inadequacy of some topics for the online version [23, 41], lack of development of clinical skills and communication with patients [2], lack of attention on the part of students [13, 31, 40], lack of motivation and lack of adequate books or study material in their homes [31], the intensive nature of resources, student misbehavior [40], time management difficulties [31] and lack of electronic devices, especially in middle- [41] and low-income countries [46].

A study with Indian students [31] found that most of them used smartphones for emergency remote education. However, the small dimension of the screen can impair the proper understanding of three-dimensional structures, as for example in anatomy [31].

As recommendations for emergency remote education, everyone involved in this process should be prepared for a paradigm shift, with the establishment of practices and initiatives to promote improvements [19], with improvement of the teaching staff, reduction in the cognitive load and stimuli related to interactivity [40].

7. Alternatives for student assessment

Student assessment is a mechanism by which learning outcomes are analyzed, comprising two main forms: formative and summative. The first assesses the learning process throughout the school term, provides feedback to students and assists in obtaining improvements. The summative assessment is carried out mainly at the end of the course and may include several methods, among them the Objective Structured Clinical Examination (OSCE) [35].

In this context, exams can be applied through Socrative [40], Kahoot [19, 40] and Moodle® [19]. Tools with quizzes, such as Kahoot, can stimulate interaction, and also provide the possibility of an immediate feedback from the teacher [19]. Google Forms® [31], the use of software that prevents cheating such as ExamSoft; online supervision, such as ProctorU, Honorlock, Respondus Monitor and Examity [20], remote supervision integrated with block browser - prevents students from searching the internet to find an answer during assessment [21] - using Eproctor [47] and real-time question platforms, such as the Mentimeter [48] can also be alternatives. Preclinical and case-based activities can be delivered as videos, with incorporated questions using platforms like EDpuzzle, which allows questions to be asked with instant feedback while students watch the video [20].

In many institutions, OSCE is considered to be an adequate tool for identifying the clinical competencies of undergraduate students. During the pandemic, it was necessary to adapt OSCE to the online environment - virtual OSCE (VOSCE). According to studies carried out in the United Kingdom [49] through Zoom, and in Finland [50] through Moodle, experiences of the evaluation process have been positive.

Even with all these possibilities, more than half of students consider that the online assessment is not a good method of evaluating the acquired knowledge [3]. Therefore, the combination of several evaluation methods can minimize dishonesty, recover possible negative results from internet connection failures and stimulate commitment and critical reflection.

8. Biosafety in the return to face-to-face activities

The resumption of face-to-face dental education activities depends on the pandemic situation of each country. Currently, some dentistry schools have returned to face-to-face education or are preparing to reopen after government decisions; therefore, recommendations for resuming face-to-face activities are necessary [45].

Guidelines recommended for the dental team by the World Health Organization (WHO) [51], by the Centers for Disease Control and Prevention (CDC) [52] and by the health agencies of countries to control the COVID-19 dissemination must be considered. The Brazilian Dental Education Association (ABENO) [43] and the Association for Dental Education, Asia Pacific (ADEAP) [53], in July 2020, published safety guidelines for dental education. Among them, recommendations for teaching in classroom, in laboratories and in clinical environments and biosafety protocols were addressed to ensure the safety of students, teachers, employees and patients [43, 53].

The main guidelines are: wash and sanitize hands, practice social and respiratory etiquette, check temperature, keep distancing, clean and decontaminate objects and surfaces, ensure the ventilation of environments, mandatory use of face masks, use full PPE during dental care, screening patients and offering mouthwash rinses containing effective antiseptics, choosing procedures that produce little or no aerosol and using manual instruments, and when possible, using high power suckers and absolute isolation and, preferably, work with 4 hands [43, 53].

9. Teaching-service-community integration: brazilian panorama

In Brazil, as well as in Europe [54], the scope of undergraduate dental education is defined by the Ministry of Education. In the Brazilian territory, the student's trajectory and the consequent training of dental surgeons are guided by the so-called "National Curriculum Guidelines", which are valid for the entire country, including public and private institutions [55].

The aforementioned directive provides that professionals have a generalist and humanistic profile, so that through critical and reflective performance, they can act at all levels of health care, providing improvements in the oral health conditions of the population. For this to occur, it is necessary to carry out internships, which correspond to a supervised educational act developed in the work environment [56] and should account for at least 20% of the total hours of the undergraduate Dentistry course and needs to be developed in an articulated manner and with increasing complexity throughout the training process [55].

In this formative path, there is interaction between higher education institutions and health services that make up the Unified Health System (SUS), which was created in 1988 [57] and, considering the many advances and setbacks, is considered the largest public health system in the world. Thus, in the perspective of SUS as the locus of learning and training agent, the Brazilian dental surgeon is trained. It means that the articulation between the health system and higher education institutions materializes in the insertion of students in the health care network [58] and in the implementation of the teaching-service-community integration [59].

Experiences based on the teaching-service-community integration are not exclusive to Brazilian dental education, since at the University of British Columbia, in Canada, students are inserted in the community context, a fact that allows them to understand the challenges faced by vulnerable segments of the population and actively reflect on experiences acquired [60].

But since March 2020, when WHO announced that COVID-19 had reached a pandemic state [61], dental education has taken on new shapes. Face-to-face education was completely interrupted and the impact on the training of professionals was overwhelming [21, 39], since teaching-service-community activities were discontinued, given the current sanitary situation and the impossibility of carrying out them remotely. It is possible to state that dentistry training faces serious challenges, something that in addition to Brazil can be extrapolated to other countries [21]. Students have experienced increasing levels of stress and feel that their clinical education has been impaired [39].

In Brazil, in the first weeks of the pandemic, the Ministry of Health recommended the suspension of elective oral health care and the maintenance of emergency care throughout the national territory [62]. The Ministry of Education, in turn, prohibited the substitution of face-to-face classes with classes in digital media when it came to professional practices, such as internships [63].

However, additional guidelines outlined months later, with the revocation of Ordinances No. 343, of March 17, 2020, that the application of the substitution of practical activities, in compliance with National Curriculum Guidelines, could include specific work plans, approved at institutional level dentistry courses and attached to the pedagogical project of the course [64].

The position of the Ministry of Education regarding the possibility of internships occurring in the distance education mode in Dentistry caused controversy and caused the Federal Council of Dentistry (CFO) to be strongly opposed to such guidance [65].

Due to the continuation of the pandemic scenario in the year 2021, the effects on students' knowledge and skills are difficult to assess and the consequences may be visible in the near future. For Gaudín et al. [54], less productive and efficient students are expected.

Undoubtedly, dentistry students face a global health crisis, whose direct reflection in their education is the closure of educational institutions and the challenges to practice and improve their clinical skills [39], whether in school clinics based in their own universities, or within the scope of public health services, a place where the technique is practiced and experiences are accumulated in the community. Therefore, dentistry students are unable to complete these requirements [14].

In the Brazilian context, the perspective in view of the epidemiological changes in states and municipalities, is the establishment of new parameters to guide and promote the gradual and responsible return of habitual activities. Thus, as this is a moment of transition, it is possible, in some places, to plan the return of elective care in different services and to expand the offer of care [62], as a consequence, there is the possibility, still without an expected date, of return to teaching-service-community activities, so important during the training of dentistry students.

10. Conclusion

The COVID-19 pandemic strongly impacted the development of theoretical, laboratory and practical activities in the student, teacher and university trinomial, so that higher education institutions adopted different teaching technologies to ensure the continuity of the teaching-learning process. Clinical practice and experiences in the teaching-service-community context were those most impacted by the temporary interruption and await new government and institutional guidelines for their resumption.

We highlight the need for more research in this area, to assist in decision-making by managers and institutions and in the adaptation of professors and students. Educational bodies should be encouraged to invest in infrastructure and training for new teaching modalities and to formulate institutional policies that generate diversified learning options, in order to reduce students' unequal access to very expensive technologies and quality internet, which can compromise the performance of remote activities. To return to face-to-face activities, large investments must be made in dental clinics and in the SUS, covering the new biosafety standards.

Conflict of interest

The authors report no conflicts of interest.

Author details

Isla Camilla Carvalho Laureano, Alidianne Fábia Cabral Cavalcanti and Alessandro Leite Cavalcanti*
State University of Paraíba, Campina Grande, Paraíba, Brazil

*Address all correspondence to: alessandrouepb@gmail.com

References

[1] United Nations Educational, Scientific and Cultural Organization. Education: from disruption to recovery [Internet]. 2020. Available from: https://en.unesco.org/covid19/education response [Accessed: 2020-04-16].

[2] Nasseripour M, Turner J, Rajadurai S, San Diego J, Quinn B, Bartlett A, et al. COVID 19 and dental education: transitioning from a well-established synchronous format and face to face teaching to an asynchronous format of dental clinical teaching and learning. J Med Educ Curric Dev. 2021;8:1-3. DOI: 10.1177/2382120521999667

[3] Hattar S, AlHadidi A, Sawair FA, Alraheam IA, El-Ma'aita A, Wahab FK. Impact of COVID-19 pandemic on dental education: online experience and practice expectations among dental students at the University of Jordan. BMC Med Educ. 2021;21(1):151. DOI: 10.1186/s12909-021-02584-0

[4] Cheng L, Kalvandi M, Mckinstry S, Maddahi A, Chaudhary A, Maddahi Y, et al. Application of DenTeach in remote dentistry teaching and learning during the COVID-19 pandemic: a case study. Front Robot AI. 2021;7:611424. DOI: 10.3389/frobt.2020.611424

[5] Wu DT, Wu KY, Nguyen TT, Tran SD. The impact of COVID-19 on dental education in North America—Where do we go next? Eur J Dent Educ. 2020;24(4):825-827. DOI: 10.1111/eje.12561

[6] Hodges CB, Moore S, Lockee BB, Trust T, Bond MA. The difference between emergency remote teaching and online learning. Educause Rev. 2020:1-14.

[7] Rad FA, Otaki F, Baqain Z, Zary N, Al-Halabi M. Rapid transition to distance learning due to COVID-19: Perceptions of postgraduate dental learners and instructors. PLoS One 2021;16(2):e0246584. DOI: 10.1371/journal.pone.0246584

[8] Puranik CP, Mack E, DeLapp J, de Peralta T. Digital preclinical education and assessment in pediatric dentistry during COVID pandemic. J Dent Educ. 2021;1-3. DOI: 10.1002/jdd.12595

[9] Thilakumara IP, Jayasinghe RM, Jayasinghe RD. Facing challenges of COVID-19 on dental education in Sri Lanka. J Multi Dent Res. 2021;6(2):75-80.

[10] Fry K. E-learning markets and providers: Some issues and prospects. Education+ Training 2001;43(4/5):233-9. DOI: 10.1108/EUM0000000005484

[11] Farooq I. Interpretive versus didactic learning approach towards oral biology: a student's perspective. J Coll Physicians Surg Pak. 2014;24(10):772-774. DOI: 10.2014/JCPSP.772774

[12] Chen JW, Hobdell MH, Dunn K, Johnson KA, Zhang J. Teledentistry and its use in dental education. J Am Dent Assoc. 2003;134(3):342-346. DOI: 10.14219/jada.archive.2003.0164

[13] Amir LR, Tanti I, Maharani DA, Wimardhani YS, Julia V, Sulijaya B, et al. Student perspective of classroom and distance learning during COVID-19 pandemic in the undergraduate dental study program Universitas Indonesia. BMC Med Educ. 2020;20(1):392. DOI: 10.1186/s12909-020-02312-0

[14] Desai BK. Clinical implications of the COVID-19 pandemic on dental education. J Dent Educ. 2020;84(5):512. DOI: 10.1002/jdd.12162

[15] Emami E. COVID-19: perspective of a dean of dentistry. JDR Clin Trans Res. 2020;5(3):211-213. DOI: 10.1177/2380084420929284

[16] American Dental Education Association. Dental School Curriculum [Internet]. 2021. Available from: https://www.adea.org/GoDental/Future_Dentists/Dental_school_curriculum.aspx [Accessed: 2021-04-12].

[17] Dalanon J, Matsuka Y. The Evolution of Dental Education in the Philippines. Health Prof Educ. 2018;5(3):172-176. DOI: 10.1016/j.hpe.2018.07.001

[18] Elangovan S, Mahrous A, Marchini L. Disruptions during a pandemic: Gaps identified and lessons learned. J Dent Educ. 2020;84(11):1270-1274. DOI: 10.1002/jdd.12236

[19] Spalding M, Rauen C, de Vasconcellos LMR, da Cruz Vegian MR, Miranda KC, Bressane A. Higher education challenges and possibilities: a Brazilian experience in times of COVID-19. Res Soc Dev. 2020;9(8):e534985970. DOI: 10.33448/rsd-v9i8.5970

[20] Iyer P, Aziz K, Ojcius DM. Impact of COVID-19 on dental education in the United States. J Dent Educ. 2020;84(6):718-722. DOI: 10.1002/jdd.12163

[21] Chang TY, Hong G, Paganelli C, Phantumvanit P, Chang WJ, Shieh YS, et al. Innovation of dental education during COVID-19 pandemic. J Dent Sci. 2021;16(1):15-20. DOI: 10.1016/j.jds.2020.07.011

[22] Machado RA, Bonan PRF, Perez DEDC, Martelli Júnior H. COVID-19 pandemic and the impact on dental education: discussing current and future perspectives. Braz Oral Res. 2020;34:e083. DOI: 10.1590/1807-3107bor-2020.vol34.0083

[23] Santos GNM, da Silva HEC, Leite AF, Mesquita CRM, Figueiredo PTS, Stefani CM, et al. The scope of dental education during COVID-19 pandemic: A systematic review. J Dent Educ. 2021. DOI: 10.1002/jdd.12587

[24] Zoom Video Communications, Inc. [Internet]. 2021. Available from: https://zoom.us/meetings [Accessed: 2021-04-12].

[25] Google for Education. Google Classroom. [Internet]. 2021. Available from: https://edu.google.com/products/classroom/ [Accessed: 2021-04-12].

[26] Microsoft. Skype. [Internet]. 2021. Available from: https://www.skype.com/pt-br/features/ [Accessed: 2021-04-12].

[27] Moodle. About Moodle [Internet]. 2020. Available from: https://docs.moodle.org/310/en/About_Moodle [Accessed: 2021-04-12].

[28] Microsoft. Educator Center. [Internet]. 2021. Available from: https://education.microsoft.com/pt-BR/resource/d5b62e3e [Accessed: 2021-04-12].

[29] 8x8, Inc. Jitsi. [Internet]. 2021. Available from: https://meet.jit.si/ [Accessed: 2021-04-12].

[30] Cisco. Webex. Pricing [Internet]. 2021. Available from: https://www.webex.com/pricing/index.html [Accessed: 2021-04-12].

[31] Singal A, Bansal A, Chaudhary P, Singh H, Patra A. Anatomy education of medical and dental students during COVID-19 pandemic: a reality check. Surg Radiol Anat. 2021;43(4):515-521. DOI: 10.1007/s00276-020-02615-3

[32] Pontual MLA, do Nascimento EHL, da Cruz Perez DE, Pontual AA, Ramos-Perez FM. Challenges in oral radiology teaching during COVID-19 pandemic. Dentomaxillofac Radiol. 2020;49(5):20200178. DOI: 10.1259/dmfr.20200178

[33] Zhong Y, Sun W, Zhang W, Liu L, Xu Y, Jiang Y. Application of remote online learning in oral histopathology teaching: an acute response to the COVID-19 pandemic. Res Sq. 2020. DOI: 10.21203/rs.3.rs-51823/v1

[34] Galibourg A, Maret D, Monsarrat P, Nasr K. Impact of COVID-19 on dental education: How could pre-clinical training be done at home? J Dent Educ. 2020;84(9):949. DOI: 10.1002/jdd.12360

[35] Khalaf K, El-Kishawi M, Mustafa S, Al Kawas S. Effectiveness of technology-enhanced teaching and assessment methods of undergraduate preclinical dental skills: a systematic review of randomized controlled clinical trials. BMC Med Educ. 2020;20(1):286. DOI: 10.1186/s12909-020-02211-4

[36] Haleem A, Javaid M, Khan IH. Virtual reality (VR) applications in dentistry: An innovative technology to embrace. Indian J Dent Res. 2020;31(4):666-667. DOI: 10.4103/ijdr.IJDR_501_19

[37] Huang TK, Yang CH, Hsieh YH, Wang JC, Hung CC. Augmented reality (AR) and virtual reality (VR) applied in dentistry. Kaohsiung J Med Sci. 2018;34(4):243-248. DOI: 10.1016/j.kjms.2018.01.009.

[38] Sreelakshmi M, Subash TD. Haptic Technology: A comprehensive review on its applications and future prospects. Materials Today: Proc. 2017;4(2, Part B):4182-7. DOI: 10.1016/j.matpr.2017.02.120

[39] Hung M, Licari FW, Hon ES, Lauren E, Su S, Birmingham WC, et al. In an era of uncertainty: Impact of COVID-19 on dental education. J Dent Educ. 2021;85(2):148-156. DOI: 10.1002/jdd.12404

[40] Mukhtar K, Javed K, Arooj M, Sethi A. Advantages, Limitations and Recommendations for online learning during COVID-19 pandemic era. Pak J Med Sci. 2020;36(COVID19-S4):S27-S31. DOI: 10.12669/pjms.36.COVID19-S4.2785

[41] Chavarría-Bolaños D, Gómez-Fernández A, Dittel-Jiménez C, Montero-Aguilar M. E-learning in dental schools in the times of COVID-19: a review and analysis of an educational resource in times of the COVID-19 pandemic. Odovtos-International J Dent Sci. 2020;22(3):69-86. DOI: 10.15517/ijds.2020.41813

[42] Patel SA, Halpin RM, Olson GW, Franklin A. Global pandemic and the rise of teledentistry. J Dent Educ. 2020. DOI: 10.1002/jdd.12355

[43] Pires FS, Fontanella V. Abeno consensus: biosafety in post-pandemic dental education on COVID-19. Porto Alegre: Brazilian Association of Dental Education, 2020. 86 p.

[44] Federal Council of Dentistry. Resolution 226/2020: CFO presents Clarification Guide on the practice of Dentistry at a distance [Internet]. 2020. https://website.cfo.org.br/resolucao-226-2020-cfo-apresenta-guia-de-esclarecimento-sobre-exercicio-da-odontologia-a-distancia/?doing_wp_cron=1619048002.8169128894805908203125 [Accessed: 2021-04-13].

[45] Gurgel BCV, Borges SB, Borges REA, Calderon PS. COVID-19: Perspectives for the management of dental care and education. J Appl Oral Sci. 2020;28:e20200358. DOI: 10.1590/1678-7757-2020-0358

[46] Tuladhar SL, Pradhan D, Parajuli U, Manandhar P, Subedi N. Study on the effectiveness of online classes for undergraduate medical and dental students of Gandaki Medical College during COVID 19 pandemic period in

Nepal. Orthod J Nepal. 2020;10(2):36-40. DOI: 10.3126/ojn.v10i2.31146

[47] Moore Z, Stallard J, Tittemore A, Lee JY. The COVID-19 pandemic: opportunity for integration of educational technology. J Dent Educ. 2020. DOI: 10.1002/jdd.12344

[48] Patterson K, Ritwik P, Kerins C, Adewumi A. Real-time measurement for effectiveness of novel educational endeavors during the COVID-19 pandemic. J Dent Educ. 2020. DOI: 10.1002/jdd.12363

[49] Donn J, Scott JA, Binnie V, Bell A. A pilot of a Virtual Objective Structured Clinical Examination in dental education. A response to COVID-19. Eur J Dent Educ. 2020. DOI: 10.1111/eje.12624

[50] Hytönen H, Näpänkangas R, Karaharju-Suvanto T, Eväsoja T, Kallio A, Kokkari A, Tuononen T, Lahti S. Modification of national OSCE due to COVID-19 - Implementation and students' feedback. Eur J Dent Educ. 2020. DOI: 10.1111/eje.12646

[51] World Health Organization. Considerations for the provision of essential oral health services in the context of COVID-19 [Internet]. 2020. Available from: https://www.who.int/publications/i/item/who-2019-nCoV-oral-health-2020.1 [Accessed: 2021-04-13].

[52] Centers for Disease Control and Prevention. Interim Infection Prevention and Control Guidance for Guidance for Dental Settings During the COVID-19 Response. [Internet]. 2020. Available from: https://www.cdc.gov/coronavirus/2019-ncov/hcp/dental-settings.html [Accessed: 2021-04-13].

[53] Association for Dental Education, Asia Pacific. Guideline for Dental Education under COVID-19 situation [Internet]. 2020. Available from: https://adeap.org/wp-content/uploads/2020/07/ [Accessed: 2021-04-13].

[54] Gaudin A, Arbab-Chirani R, Pérez F. Effect of COVID-19 on Dental Education and Practice in France. Front Dent Med. 2020;1:5. DOI: 10.3389/fdmed.2020.00005

[55] Brazil. National Council of Education Chamber of Higher Education resolution CNE / CES 3, of February 19, 2002. Institutes National Curricular Guidelines for the Undergraduate Dentistry Course. [Internet]. 2002. Available from: https://portal.mec.gov.br/cne/arquivos/pdf/CES032002.pdf [Accessed: 2021-04-18].

[56] Brazil. Law No. 11,788, of September 25, 2008. Provides for the internship of students; changes the wording of art. 428 of the Consolidation of Labor Laws - CLT, approved by Decree-Law No. 5,452, of May 1, 1943, and Law 9,394, of December 20, 1996; repeals Laws 6,494, of December 7, 1977, and 8,859, of March 23, 1994, the sole paragraph of art. 82 of Law No. 9,394, of December 20, 1996, and art. 6th of Provisional Measure No. 2,164-41, of August 24, 2001; and makes other arrangements. [Internet]. 2008. Available from: https://www.planalto.gov.br/ccivil_03/_Ato2007-2010/2008/Lei/L11788.htm [Accessed: 2021-04-18].

[57] Brazil. Constitution. Constitution of the Federative Republic of Brazil. Brasília, DF: Federal Senate; 1988.

[58] Brazil. Ordinance No. 4,279, of December 30, 2010. Establishes guidelines for the organization of the Health Care Network within the scope of the Unified Health System (SUS). [Internet]. 2010. Available from: https://bvsms.saude.gov.br/bvs/saudelegis/gm/2010/prt4279_30_12_2010.html [Accessed: 2021-04-18].

[59] Forte FDS, Pontes AA, Morais HGF, Barbosa AS, Nétto OBS, Barros NF.

Teaching-service-community integration in Dentistry: a cultural study. Interface (Botucatu). 2020;24:e200166 DOI: 10.1590/Interface.200166

[60] Brondani MA. Teaching social responsibility through community service-learning in predoctoral dental education. J Dent Educ. 2012;76(5): 609-619.

[61] World Health Organization. WHO characterizes COVID-19 as a pandemic [Internet]. 2020. Available from: https://www.paho.org/pt/news/11-3-2020-who-characterizes-covid-19-pandemic [Accessed: 2021-04-18].

[62] Brazil. Ministry of Health. Health Surveillance Secretariat. Secretariat of Primary Health Care. Guide to guidelines for dental care in the context of Covid-19. Brasília, DF, 2020. [Internet]. 2020. Available from: https://www.gov.br/saude/pt-br/media/pdf/2020/novembro/17/17_12_guia-de-orientacaoes-para-atencao-odontologica-no-contexto-da-covid-19.pdf [Accessed: 2021-04-18].

[63] Brazil. Ordinance No. 343, of March 17, 2020. Provides for the substitution of face-to-face classes with classes in digital media while the pandemic situation of the new coronavirus - Covid-19 lasts. [Internet]. 2020. Available from: https://www.in.gov.br/en/web/dou/-/portaria-n-343-de-17-de-marco-de-2020-248564376 [Accessed: 2021-04-18].

[64] Brazil. Ordinance No. 544, of June 16, 2020. Provides for the replacement of face-to-face classes with classes in digital media, while the pandemic situation of the new coronavirus - Covid-19 lasts, and revokes MEC Ordinances No. 343, of March 17 2020, n° 345, of March 19, 2020, and n° 473, of May 12, 2020. [Internet]. 2020. Available from: https://www.in.gov.br/en/web/dou/-/portaria-n-544-de-16-de-junho-de-2020-261924872 [Accessed: 2021-04-18].

[65] Federal Council of Dentistry. CFO officiates Ministry of Education and seeks in court to prevent internship in distance education in Dentistry [Internet]. 2020. Available from: https://website.cfo.org.br/cfo-oficia-ministerio-da-educacao-e-busca-na-justica-impedir-estagio-na-modalidade-ead-em-odontologia/ [Accessed: 2021-04-18].

Chapter 13

Together Apart during the COVID-19 Pandemic: Assessing Students' Readiness for Online Assessments Using an E-Learning System

Glenda H.E. Gay

Abstract

Electronic learning (e-learning) is an indispensable management system that supports face-to-face, blended, or fully online courses. In January 2020, 258 students in a second-year management course at a regional university were evaluated on their preparedness for online lectures via e-learning. However, by mid-semester, the COVID-19 pandemic halted face-to-face teaching, pushed final assessments to an online modality, and forced some governments to quickly repatriate their students. This chapter evaluates students' level of e-learning readiness (e-readiness) and whether it had any effect on their performance in the final assessment. The results show that six percent of the cohort had returned to their home country, six percent had no privacy to take their final online assessments, while 31% depended on Wi-Fi. However, although two-thirds of the cohort preferred the online modality, only a third had acceptable levels of e-readiness. E-ready students felt the disruption in their study routine most, while those who were not e-ready found more time to study after the curfew restrictions were in place. E-ready students attempted their final online assessment earlier than those who were not yet e-ready, but the two groups had similar assessment grades. Evaluating students' level of e-readiness is vital in providing support for those who have challenges with online learning.

Keywords: higher education and E-learning, E-learning, E-learning and assessment, e-learning readiness, e-readiness, COVID-19

1. Introduction

The spread of SARS-CoV-2 disease (COVID-19) has affected citizens globally, including the Caribbean region and its academic community. This pandemic has triggered the implementation of strict protocols including 'physical distancing' in an attempt to reduce interpersonal contact. For educational institutions, their protocols were intended to lessen the spread of the virus to clusters of students in classrooms and complex networks of social groups often found on a campus [1]. The abrupt cessation of face-to-face classes to prevent further community spread has therefore forced an urgent shift to fully online teaching and learning via the use of e-learning systems (ELSs). Indeed, while online education has been expanding at a rate faster than traditional campus-based programs [2], there is no doubt that the pandemic has heightened the focus on the use of ELSs and online learning [3].

The brief time required to transition to online learning using an ELS has revealed some shortcomings for instructors and students. These include the unknown level of their preparedness for the ELS, inadequate training to quickly adapt to the online learning environment [3], limited or unstable internet connectivity, or an inability to afford the necessary technology such as a laptop [4, 5]. Irrespective of these challenges, the use of ELSs has become an integral part of higher education institutions (HEIs) [6].

This chapter evaluates the effect of e-learning on a cohort of students at a leading Caribbean higher education institution. Data was captured at the start of the semester, and after its temporary closure because of the COVID-19 pandemic. This research focuses on answering three questions:

- What is the level of e-readiness for this group of management students at a leading Caribbean higher education institution?
- How does students' level of e-readiness differ according to key personal demographics (i.e. age, gender) and academic-related factors (i.e. access to Wi-Fi, study time and private space) in the sample?
- To what extent has students' level of e-readiness impacted their ability to complete online final assessments?

The next section provides a comparison of face-to-face, online, and blended learning, as well as review of e-learning and e-learning readiness. This is followed by the context and methodology. The results section evaluates students' level of e-learning readiness (e-readiness), and their ability to adapt to online learning to complete their studies. Finally, this chapter assesses how students may have been affected by the digital divide and measures implemented to ensure a level playing field for all in preparation for their final online assessments.

1.1 Face-to-face, online, and blended learning

The critical questions today regarding fully face-to-face, online, and blended learning involve the conditions and strategies that promote student engagement, satisfaction, and retention [7]. Studies on student satisfaction have been inconsistent where results may be impacted by variables other than the method of course delivery. However, the value of teaching presence was significant among all three learning modalities in guiding students through their course of study [8].

Students in traditional face-to-face courses have the benefit of in-person interaction where they could be influenced and more motivated to submit assignments, resulting in greater chances of completing the course [9]. However, even though students may be advocates of technology, many of them are seemingly unwilling to forgo the face-to-face learning experience [4]. Students have a tendency to be more satisfied with a traditional course, when compared with students' satisfaction in online courses [8].

Online learning, as an alternative to traditional face-to-face learning, takes place partially or entirely over the Internet [10]. It encourages synchronous and asynchronous participation, but more so, it provides the potential for increased enrolment through access to a wider range of students. However, online learning involves a dependence on technology, an expectation of preparedness for the online learning environment, adequate online communication skills, and a predisposition for independent learning [5, 11, 12]. Although most students could easily adapt to the technology associated with online learning, those who are not adequately prepared for this type of experience tend to have challenges with critical thinking, independent learning and time management [12]. Students in strictly online courses tend to be more self-motivated since the onus is on them to be self-disciplined in order to complete the course. It is therefore not surprising that time management and motivation were found to positively influence their final exam grade [13]. However, feeling a sense of isolation and loneliness are often reported by students in online courses [12].

A meta-analysis and literature review of 176 studies on students in HEIs conducted between 1996 and 2008 compared the effectiveness of face-to-face and online instruction [10]. Their findings showed that students had slightly better exam grades with the online course and suggested that there is support for online learning as a replacement for face-to-face instruction. However, online and face-to-face learning differed in terms of the length of time students reserved for their studying. A more recent literature review of 104 studies between 2014 and 2019 focused on university students in online courses with respect to factors on course design, student support, faculty pedagogy, student engagement, and student success [7]. Their findings showed that for face-to-face courses, increased interaction with course content was associated with better exam grades and increased student satisfaction. For online courses, faculty feedback was paramount, but factors such as previous academic success, self-motivation, family support, workload management, and technology savviness were key for positive course outcomes and increased student satisfaction.

Blended learning, refers to the integration of traditional classroom methods with various online instructional technologies to improve teaching [11, 14]. While it is believed to be using the best elements of the two methods of learning, HEIs are increasingly using blended learning as a complement to, but not a replacement for traditional forms of learning [7]. This is because of the need to maintain the classroom experience as much as possible, which is difficult to mirror behind the structure of an ELS [15]. Higher education students seem to prefer blended learning which is supported by reduced attrition and improved examination marks [9, 14]. However, mature students were noted to drop out from courses more readily than younger students [9, 12, 14].

A study that compared blended and online learning methods regarding learning outcomes, reported that students were able to access online support more easily for courses in blended learning than online learning. However, the workload and difficulty level in online learning environments were believed to be more challenging for them, even though there was no significant difference noted regarding their final scores [16]. Students' learning strategies [7], e-readiness [5, 17, 18] and levels of motivation [11, 13] were also noted to have a significant effect on both the learning process and learning outcomes.

1.2 E-learning

Electronic learning (e-learning) is defined as the use of technology (e.g., computer or electronic device) to provide learning material including tutorials, simulations, case- or game-based learning modules [19]. It is a system that promotes online learning by storing, processing, and distributing teaching materials. It also supports interaction and communication in the context of teaching and learning [6, 12]. However, it primarily aimed at fostering students' independence in order to take responsibility for their learning, and thus encouraging them to play a more active role in their learning [11, 19]. In doing so, e-learning has changed the way learning takes place through a student's experience and perception of studying, and has become the chosen method in higher education [20].

Academic preparedness is known to play a key role in a student's desire to persist in his or her current program [21]. However, although reliance on ELSs has become an integral part of HEIs, as shown by consistently increasing enrolments in online learning over a 14-year span [2], many students entering university know little about what preparation is required for becoming capable to study via an ELS. That is, students must now 'learn how to learn, how to study, and how to solve problems' using this type of modality [18]. The lack of readiness or preparation for the ELS has contributed to higher attrition rates for students in blended or online courses than for traditional face-to-face courses [12]. Two studies reported on the implementation of a mandatory online orientation for students at registration. Students were allowed multiple attempts to successfully pass the orientation, before they could be given access to the online or blended course [22, 23]. Both studies reported that the students were generally better prepared for and more confident with their courses, with higher retention rates. The importance of e-learning therefore mandates that students' preparation for an ELS be assessed in order to provide training or support [24].

1.3 Student e-learning readiness

E-learning readiness (e-readiness) was originally developed to assess the digital divide between developed and developing countries, organisations, or individuals [25]. In an educational context, it refers to the digital divide between students' competence and confidence in using electronic devices for online communication, their preferences in using technology tools, and their ability to be involved in self-directed learning [12]. It also captures the potential experience of users of an ELS [18, 24]. Students' readiness for online learning is also reported to have a positive impact on their successful course performance [16]. Students' level of e-readiness has therefore become one of the core factors in evaluating success with ELSs [4, 7, 18]. Notably, self-directed learning and student motivation were found to be significant for their e-readiness [26, 27]. However, attributes such as gender, university, or courses, do not seem to show any effect on student e-readiness [17, 18, 24, 28]. More so, whether it is technical competence, self-directed learning, motivation for learning or online communications skills, there was no significant difference between gender and the attitudes and behaviours in these dimensions [28]. However, [17] found that students in the second year of a three-year degree programme were more computer and Internet savvy than students in the first or third year. More so, third year students had better study habits than students at levels one or two.

Since students' career choices and opportunities depend on completion of their studies, it is important that students' e-readiness be evaluated to ensure that it is not a hindrance towards their success [18]. This evaluation could assess students' ability to work around any technological challenges, adapt to collaborative learning and training, as well as determine their motivation for synchronous and asynchronous self-paced learning [24]. A benchmark of student's abilities would be an indication of which aspects of their skills need to be improved to meet at least the minimum competencies required for the ELS [5].

The level of students' e-readiness uses specific criteria to establish a baseline value for student success in an online course. It is not used to force students into using the ELS per se, but rather to confirm that they are prepared for and receptive to the ELS [29]. Its purpose is to differentiate those students with substantial readiness for the online course from those who exhibit deficiencies across various categories. Students with deficiencies can be provided with support or pre-course training to give them the necessary tools and skills for working in the online environment. The categories generally evaluate students communicative and collaborative skills, meta-cognitive skills, technology availability and skills, cognitive skills, and self-directed learning [18]. Most categories are grouped into students' technical readiness, study habits, and online learning preference based on research by [29]. These three categories will be used in this study, and are described in more detail.

1.3.1 Technical readiness

Technical readiness evaluates students' possession of and access to technology, such as devices with appropriate software, access to the Internet and stable network connectivity [5]. Studies have reported poor internet connectivity as one of the biggest technical readiness challenges for students. However, even with students' extensive use of digital devices, there is still a gap between technology use for entertainment and technology required for the ELS [17]. Successful learning outcomes in online courses require strong digital literacy skills, which suggests that students' readiness to use the ELS has some influence on academic achievement [18]. An orientation to the ELS prior to starting a course has shown to benefit students by providing hands-on exercises using tools that they would should be familiar with, as well as helping to rectify any technology issues without added pressure of assignment deadlines [23]. Therefore, students who are proficient with using computers to access the ELS, can comfortably use new technologies with stable Internet access, are also proficient in this category [29].

1.3.2 Study habits

Study habits involve students' interaction with the course content, rather than engaging with the instructor or other students. Routinely working through the content allows students to become familiar with getting information from the ELS [26]. Having good study habits therefore fosters the ability to effectively navigate the content during the semester. Students who successfully work through a course on their own tend to be more suited to the online learning environment. This includes the necessary writing skills and ability to collaborate online. Students therefore who are not savvy with online communication will be hindered during an online course [8, 17, 18].

1.3.3 Preference for online learning

Students' preference for online learning reflects their reliance on the ELS for the duration of their course [4, 27]. Thus, it is important that they have attributes that are suitable for blended or online learning [29]. These attributes include being highly motivated and self-confident [30], engaging in self-directed learning [17], and having an ability to interact with their peers using the ELS [26].

2. Context of the study

Students at a Caribbean university rely on an ELS to access their course work which also serves as the central hub for the submission and management of assignments. Generally, students use their own laptops or mobile devices, but desktop computers are also available in five computer laboratories. There is also a stable network connectivity on the campus that students use to access the ELS. Classes are mostly scheduled between 8 am and 9 pm during the week. In recent years, students' dependence on the ELS has escalated, based on instructor training to use the ELS, but more so because of the ever-increasing number of working students who are challenged to physically attend face-to-face lectures during the day. However, final examinations are traditionally conducted at the end of each semester in a face-to-face environment on the campus.

A second-year core management course is offered each semester in a blended format. Course topics are revealed weekly via the ELS, supported by tutorial sessions in the computer laboratories. At the beginning of the January 2020 semester, as part of the orientation activities, 258 students were invited to complete an anonymous survey. It sought to determine their level of e-readiness regarding their technical preparedness, study skills and motivation for using the ELS. However, six weeks later, at mid-semester, the SARS-CoV-2 (COVID-19) pandemic had reached the region and the campus community, resulting in a 24-hour curfew and country-wide lockdown. This halted face-to-face teaching, forcing some students to immediately return to their home country. Final examinations were redefined as final assessments and placed online via the ELS. With students off campus and even spread across the region, a second anonymous survey was posted at week seven via the ELS to garner additional information in preparation for their final online assessment.

Traditionally, students complete their examinations scheduled in specific rooms under supervision. Since students were now completing their final assessment in an online environment, the integrity of the process required a different approach. Therefore, the format of the online assessment and its scheduling was a major consideration in catering to courses with over 150 students.

3. Survey instruments and exam creation

The two anonymous surveys were created using tools in the ELS. Purposive sampling was used since, according to [31], only the students in this course would have been able to provide the desired information that impacted their assessments. The instructor used the information to make informed decisions that supported these students' needs in order to successfully complete the topics and assessments for the course. The responses were used to collectively determine whether students' access to stable network connectivity remained, and whether their access to technology, Internet, study habits, or predisposition for working online had any influence on their final online assessment.

The first survey comprised 18-items that captured students' level of e-readiness, while the second five-item survey was created to obtain information such as their location off-campus and network connectivity. Both surveys were reviewed by two experienced instructors and pilot-tested before revealing to students. The survey instruments both captured other demographic data such as students' gender, age range, and year level.

3.1 Survey at the start of semester

This 18-item e-readiness survey was adapted from [29] and used as a framework for evaluating the students' level of e-readiness. It captured responses on three categories and used a five-point Likert-type scale, ranging from "1 = strongly-disagree" to "5 = strongly-agree". The three categories are described in more detail below:

The technical readiness (TR) category captured responses on students' technology literacy and device setup. The items included questions that asked students whether their devices comprised specific software applications required for the course, as well as whether they had a dedicated network connection, access to the Internet, or knew how to contact the IT Services help desk;

The study habits (SH) category captured responses on students' study environment, including whether they had a private space in which to focus on their course work.

The online learning preference (OL) category captured responses that related to students' routine and preferences. Items required responses on students' ability to study alone and meet assignment deadlines, as well as their preference for the structure of a classroom environment.

3.2 Survey at midsemester

The second survey comprised five items that asked students about their geographical location, technology in their possession, stability of their network connectivity that would allow them to logon to the ELS from their location, as well as their perception of their study and time management skills.

3.3 Online assessment creation

Due to the large number of students in the course, an online quiz format was thought to be the best option, where higher-order multi-choice, short-answer items, and essays were created. The online assessment was worth 60 marks and comprised two sections. Section one contained 15 multiple-choice items that addressed the eight topics taught in the course. The items were randomly selected from a question bank of about 200 questions that were categorised by topic. Each student was therefore shown one or two items randomly selected from each topic.

Section two was based on a case study where three questions were randomly selected from a larger group of questions. To do this about 80 short-answer and essay-type items were created, based on the eight topics, ensuring the same or similar level of difficulty and mark allocation. A set of questions, each worth 15 marks, was then designed from these groups of items.

4. Methodology

4.1 Surveys

Both surveys were created in the ELS and set to receive anonymous responses, therefore no identifying information for any student was captured. As a survey was completed, it was assigned a uniquely generated ELS number which on download, provided the ability to merge the raw data from both surveys for statistical analysis. The first survey was distributed during the first week of registration for the course and remained opened for two weeks until the add/drop course deadline. Its purpose was to obtain as many responses as possible during the early weeks of the course. The second survey was distributed at week seven after the lockdown and remained open for three weeks. Completed responses from both surveys were selected for the final data set, which was then cleaned and analysed using the software application Statistical Package for the Social Science (SPSS) version 22.0.

The characteristics of an e-ready student were identified by the items that had the highest mean in the technical competence, study habits, and online learning preference categories. Items with the lowest mean in the same categories denoted challenges for students who would not be adequately prepared for the ELS [5, 17, 29]. To determine the overall level of e-readiness of this cohort, the average score of *all* three e-readiness scales was calculated. The cohort was rated as satisfactory if this average score was at least four out of a maximum of five points [29]. Furthermore, each student's level of e-readiness was also calculated, and reported as satisfactory if the average of the ratings in *each* of the three categories for that student was at least four out of a maximum of five points [29].

This study used a quantitative approach, where students' e-readiness was used as an independent variable. Chi-square tests were used to determine if there was a significant difference between the two e-readiness groups, their readiness characteristics, and their access to computers. A set of independent samples t-tests were used to determine whether there were any significant differences between the two e-readiness groups and their demographics, access to stable connectivity, and ability to manage study time. A paired samples t-test was used to determine if there was significant difference between students' ability to have a private place with adequate uninterrupted time before and after the lockdown.

4.2 Final online assessment

The final online assessment comprising randomly selected multiple-choice, short-answer and essay items was duplicated four times. Students were also randomly placed into four groups and allocated to one of the assessments. **Figure 1** shows the layout of the final assessments on the course page. Each assessment was visible for 24-hours, and was set so that students could only see the assessment to which they were assigned from midnight to midnight on the following day. However, students were given a duration of one and one-half hours to attempt all questions once they accessed the assessment, and were restricted to one attempt. Once a student started the assessment, a timer started a countdown. The format was also set to be sequential in progression, so that a previously completed item could not be viewed. This arrangement and duration were intended to deter cheating and reduce any chance to search for answers.

In order to understand if there was any difference between students' level of e-readiness and the time they started the exam, the time stamp for these logs were first analysed. Any log that showed a start time between midnight

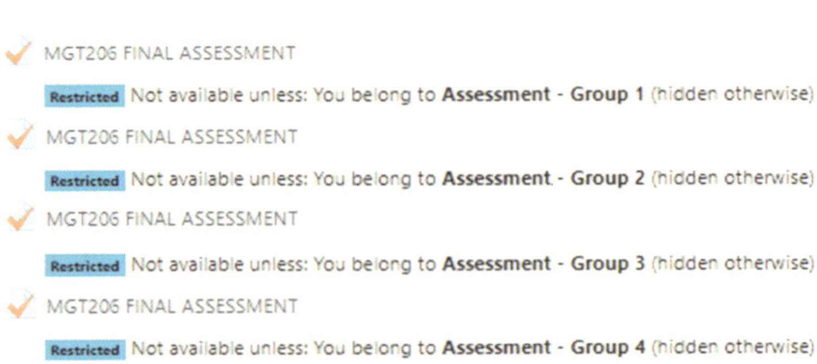

Figure 1.
Screenshot of final assessment, showing how they were set to give each student the impression that they were accessing the same assessment.

and 8 am was assigned a value of one; the value of two was assigned to the time frame between 8:01 am and 10 am, a value of 3 was assigned to the 10:01 am and 12 noon time frame, and so on, with the value 9 assigned to the 10:01 pm to midnight time frame. The smaller values therefore reflected the earlier times that students started the examination while the higher values indicated a later start time. A set of independent samples t-test were used to determine whether there were any significant differences between the two e-readiness groups and the time of day that they completed their assessment, as well as their final assessment grades.

5. Results

The surveys were distributed to 258 students with 252 (97.7%) completed responses received from the first survey and 233 (90.3%) completed responses from the second survey. This resulted in 228 (88.4%) completed responses from students who responded to both surveys. **Table 1** shows that around three-quarters of the cohort were female, in their second year of their degree programme, representing a median age range of 29 years or younger.

Cronbach's alpha tested the internal consistency of the e-readiness items using 0.7 as an acceptable value for a reliable construct [28, 31]. The instrument was deemed to be reliable since the alpha coefficient for the composite scale was 0.92, while the three scales ranged between 0.71 and 0.86 (**Table 2**). Correlations among

		(228)
Category	**Variables**	**N (%)**
Gender	Male	53 (23.2)
	Female	175 (76.8)
Age range	29 or under	185 (81.1)
	30–39	30 (13.2)
	40–49	7 (3.10)
	50–59	6 (2.60)
Year level	First Year	48 (21.1)
	Second Year	150 (65.8)
	Third Year	30 (13.2)
Home country	Local	215 (94.3)
	In Region	13 (5.70)

Table 1.
Demographics of respondents.

E-readiness	**Reliability**	**M (SD)**
Technical readiness (TR)	0.86	4.27 (0.80)
Study habits (SH)	0.71	3.96 (0.83)
Online learning preference (OL)	0.72	3.77 (0.79)
Average	**0.92**	**4.00 (0.72)**

Table 2.
Reliability of the three e-readiness categories.

the three variables were positively and significantly correlated to each other, with a p value <0.01. All constructs had strong correlations of above .60 with each other, ranging from .635 to .773.

Pearson correlation analysis was used to examine whether any association existed between the students' level of e-readiness and demographic variables. None existed for gender $\chi(1) = -.019$, $p = .775$); age range ($\chi(1) = .303$, $p = .069$) or year level ($\chi(1) = .714$, $p = -.024$).

5.1 Characteristics of student e-readiness

The highest means of the three e-readiness items defined an e-ready student as one who routinely communicates with persons using electronic technologies, has access to the Internet for substantial periods of time, perhaps 45 minutes or so, at least 3 times a week, and is eager to try new technologies and applications. In contrast, students who did not meet the threshold scores for e-readiness had characteristics that involved lack of access to software applications required for the course, and a preference for attending a traditional class on the campus, possibly in order to receive immediate verbal feedback during this type of instruction. A comparison of means for the characteristics that depict a student who is deemed to be e-ready or not e-ready is shown in **Table 3**.

E-readiness characteristics	
E-ready	**M (SD)**
Has access to the Internet for substantial periods of time, perhaps 45 minutes or so, at least 3 times a week (TR).	4.54 (1.03)
Routinely communicates with others using electronic technology (SH)	4.50 (1.02)
Is eager to try new technologies and applications (OL)	4.18 (1.11)
Not e-ready	**M (SD)**
Does not have access to software applications required for the course (TR)	4.00 (1.18)
Prefers to come to campus to attend a traditional class (SH)	3.51 (1.26)
Is uncomfortable waiting for written feedback and prefers receiving immediate verbal feedback (OL)	3.41 (1.16)

Table 3.
Characteristics of students who are e-ready or not yet e-ready.

5.2 Students' level of e-readiness

The average of the three categories for the cohort was calculated as 4.0 out a maximum of 5 (80%), indicating that the cohort had met the minimum requirement to be deemed prepared for engaging in the ELS. The high score for the technical readiness category, however, could have offset the lower scores in the study habits and learning predisposition categories. To derive a better understanding of how these students had met or surpassed the required minimum score, each student's level of e-readiness was then calculated. A student was considered to be e-ready if four or more points in each of the three e-readiness scales were achieved. The results showed that only 78 (34.2%) students were deemed to be e-ready, while 150 (65.8%) exhibited deficiencies in one or more categories.

Three independent samples t-test were run to determine if there was a significant difference between students who were deemed e-ready and those not yet e-ready in terms of their technical readiness, study habits, and online learning predisposition (**Table 4**). The results showed that for technical readiness, there was

Variable	E-readiness benchmark	Number of students (N)	Mean (M)	Standard deviation (SD)	t	df	p
Technical readiness	Not yet e-ready	150	4.02	0.866	−9.69	194.71	.000
	e-ready	78	4.76	0.263			
Study habits	Not yet e-ready	150	3.64	0.830	−12.13	213.28	.000
	e-ready	78	4.58	0.322			
Preference for online learning	Not yet e-ready	150	3.39	0.687	−13.17	225.81	.000
	e-ready	78	4.49	0.345			

Table 4.
Differences between students who were deemed e-ready and those who were not yet e-ready in relation to technical readiness, study habits and learning preferences.

a significant difference between students who were deemed e-ready (M = 4.76, SD = 0.263), (t (194.71) = −9.69, $p < 0.05$) and those who were not yet e-ready (M = 4.02, SD = 0.866). Thus, students who were deemed to be e-ready had significantly higher technical readiness than those who were not. For their online study habits, the results found that there also was a significant difference between e-ready students (M = 4.58, SD = 0.322), (t (213.28) = −12.13, $p < 0.05$) and those who were deemed not yet e-ready (M = 3.64, SD = 0.830). That is, e-ready students also had significantly better online study habits than those who were not. The results for their online learning predisposition found a significant difference between e-ready students (M = 4.49, SD = 0.345), (t (225.81) = −13.71, $p < 0.05$) and those who were deemed not yet e-ready (M = 3.39, SD = 0.687). Again, e-ready students had significantly higher preferences for online learning than those who were not yet e-ready.

5.2.1 Further analysis of non-e-ready students

This section focuses on the 65.8% (150) of the students who were not classified as e-ready. **Table 5** examines the extent of the deficiencies exhibited by these students on the three categories. Of the 31.3% (47) in this sub-group who experienced technical challenges, 70.2% (33) were female and 89.4% (42) were 29 years old or younger. For the 58.7% (88) who exhibited unsatisfactory study habits, 79.5% (70) were female with 82.9% (73) in the 29 years or younger age group. The highest number of students, 84.7% (127) showed deficiencies in the online learning predisposition category, with a similar trend of 77.1% (98) female with 81.1% (103) in the 29 years or younger age group. In each category, over 70% were females and over 80% were 29 years or younger [32].

Number of students with deficiency in...	Total number not e-ready (150)	Age group 29 or younger	Gender (Females)
Technical readiness	47 (31.3%)	42 / 47 (89.4%)	33 / 47 (70.2%)
Study habits	88 (58.7%)	73 / 88 (82.9%)	70 / 88 (79.5%)
Preference for online learning	127 (84.7%)	103 / 127 (81.1%)	98 / 127 (77.1%)

Table 5.
Analysis of students who were not deemed to be e-ready (n = 150).

Further analysis of the 150 students who were not deemed to be e-ready revealed that while 48% (72) were deficient in any one category, 29.3% (44) had deficiencies in two categories, and 22.7% (34) were found to be deficient in all three categories. These details are displayed in **Table 6**.

E-readiness deficiencies	Students	%
Deficiency in one category	72	48.0
Deficiency in two categories	44	29.3
Deficiency in all categories	34	22.7
Total	150	100.0

Table 6.
Number of students with deficiencies in one or more categories (i.e. technical readiness, study habits, or online learning predisposition) (n = 150).

5.3 Mid- semester shutdown

With the arrival of COVID-19 in the country at mid-March 2020, and subsequent remote teaching in order to complete courses and bring an end to the semester, the second anonymous survey garnered responses from students on whether they might have been affected by the digital divide, change in study habits or interruption in the move to fully online learning.

5.3.1 Devices and network connectivity

Students were asked to identify the type(s) of computer or mobile device that they used to access the ELS from their geographical location, as well as the stability of their Internet connectivity. Most students had remained in the country, while 13 (5.7%) had travelled back to their home country. **Table 7** shows that while most

	Individually e-ready	Not e-ready	Total
	78 (34.2%)	150 (65.8%)	228
Location after shutdown			
In campus country	72 (92.3%)	143 (95.3%)	215 (94.2%)
Outside of campus country but in the Caribbean	6 (7.7%)	7 (4.7%)	13 (5.70%)
Access to one set of technology			
Laptop	24 (30.7%)	63 (42.0%)	87 (38.1%)
Desktop	4 (5.1%)	2 (1.3%)	6 (2.7%)
Mobile device (iPad, phone)	1 (1.3%)	9 (6.0%)	10 (4.4%)
Stability of Network			
Always	53 (35.3%)	33 (42.3%)	86 (37.7%)
Sometimes	45 (30.0%)	22 (28.2%)	67 (29.4%)
Rarely	4 (2.7%)	1 (1.3%)	5 (2.2%)
Depend on Wi-Fi only	48 (32.0%)	22 (28.2%)	70 (30.7%)

Table 7.
Students' location, access to technology and stable connectivity.

students had a laptop computer, 10 had access to only a mobile device. Those 10 students indicated that they only had an iPad or mobile phone in their possession. Nine of these students were (6.0%) deemed not to be e-ready.

A chi-square test for independence was run to determine if there was a significant difference between students who are deemed to be e-ready and those not yet e-ready in relation to their access to a desktop computer, laptop PC or Mac, or other mobile device. The results indicated that there was no significant difference in the proportion of students who were e-ready from those who were not yet e-ready with regard to their access to a laptop or Mac, $X^2(1, 227) = .549$, $p > 0.05$, access to a desktop, $X^2(1, 227) = .418$, $p > 0.05$, and access to another mobile device $X^2(1, 227) = .816$, $p > 0.05$. This suggests that e-ready students did not differ significantly in their access to online learning devices than those who were not yet e-ready.

An independent samples t-test was run to determine if there was a significant difference between students who were deemed e-ready and those not yet e-ready in terms of the frequency of the stability of their Internet connection. A Likert scale from 1 to 4 indicated whether the frequency of the connection was always, sometimes, or rarely stable or whether there was dependence on Wi-Fi. The test found that there was no significant difference between students who were deemed e-ready ($M = 2.85$, $SD = 1.25$), ($t(226) = -9.12$, $p > 0.05$) and those who were not yet e-ready ($M = 2.69$, $SD = 1.25$) (**Table 8**). Therefore, students who were deemed e-ready had as stable a connection as those who were not yet e-ready.

Variable	E-readiness benchmark	Number of students (N)	Mean (M)	Standard deviation (SD)	t	df	p
Stable connectivity	E-ready	78	2.85	1.25	−.912	226	.363
	Not yet e-ready	150	2.69	1.25			

Table 8.
Independent samples t-test determined that there was no significant difference between students who were deemed e-ready and those who were not yet e-ready regarding the stability of their internet connection.

5.3.2 Time management

Students were now dispersed from the campus environs, dependent on their own technology and access to consistent network connectivity. Based on the significant number of students who had poor study habits, and concerns about online learning, an independent samples t-test was run to determine if there was a significant difference between students who were deemed e-ready and those not yet e-ready in terms of their ability to manage their study time. A Likert scale from 1 that indicated that they believed they were able to successfully manage their time to 4 indicating an inability to manage study time at all. The test found that there was a significant difference between students who were deemed e-ready (M 3.40, $SD = 0.706$), ($t(226) = -2.378$, $p < 0.05$) and those who were not yet e-ready ($M = 3.18$, $SD = 0.650$) (**Table 9**). Therefore, students who were deemed e-ready had significantly better time management skills than those who were not yet e-ready.

5.3.3 Private space, and adequate time for studying

Based on the previous results, it was important to further assess the extent to which students' rhythm of the semester was disrupted by the campus' lockdown

Variable	E-readiness benchmark	Number of participants (N)	Mean (M)	Standard deviation (SD)	t	df	p
Time management	E-ready	78	3.40	0.706	−2.378	226	.018
	Not yet E-ready	150	3.18	0.649			

Table 9.
Independent samples t-test determined students who were deemed e-ready had significantly better time management skills than those who were not yet e-ready.

and subsequent move to online learning via the ELS. Therefore, having a private place at home or work, and having adequate uninterrupted time to study were assessed based on whether the e-readiness of both groups of students.

5.3.3.1 E-ready students

A paired samples t-test was run to determine if there was a significant difference between e-ready students having a private place at home or work they could use for extended periods before and after the lockdown. The results revealed that students who were e-ready had access to such a place significantly more so before the lockdown ($M = 4.85$, $SD = 0.40$), than after ($M = 4.26$, $SD = 0.95$), ($t(77) = 5.082$, $p < 0.05$).

A paired samples t-test was also run to determine if there was significant difference between e-ready students having adequate time that would be uninterrupted in which they could work on their online courses before and after the lockdown. The results revealed that students had adequate uninterrupted time significantly more so before the lockdown ($M = 4.71$, $SD = 0.51$), than after ($M = 4.32$, $SD = 0.86$), ($t(77) = 3.243$, $p < 0.05$). Thus, these results indicate that students' access to these conditions significantly decreased after the lockdown. **Table 10** shows the results of these two conditions.

E-ready	Number of students (N)	Mean (M)	Standard deviation (SD)	t	df	p
Private place before	78	4.85	0.397	5.082	77	.000
Private place after		4.26	0.946			
Study-time before	78	4.71	0.512	3.243	77	.002
Study-time after		4.32	0.860			

Table 10.
A paired samples t-test showed that there was less privacy to study and also less time to study after the COVID-19 lockdown.

5.3.3.2 Students not deemed to be e-ready

A paired samples t-test was run to determine if there was significant difference between students who were not yet e-ready having a private place at home or work that they could use for extended periods before and after the lockdown. The results revealed that these students had similar access to such a place before the lockdown ($M = 3.93$, $SD = 1.28$), and after ($M = 3.78$, $SD = 1.00$), as there was no significant difference ($t(149) = 1.271$, $p > 0.05$). Therefore, students indicated that their access to such an environment, or lack thereof, did not change.

A paired samples t-test was run to determine if there was significant difference between students who were not yet e-ready having adequate time that would be uninterrupted in which they could work on their online courses before and after the lockdown. The results revealed that students had less uninterrupted time to work before the lockdown (M = 3.57, SD = 1.24), than after (M = 4.06, SD = 0.84), (t (149) = −4.368, p < 0.05). **Table 11** shows the results of the t-test.

Not e-ready	Number of students (N)	Mean (M)	Standard deviation (SD)	t	df	p
Private place before	150	3.93	1.278	1.271	149	.206
Private place after		3.78	1.001			
Study-time before	150	3.57	1.239	−4.368	149	.000
Study-time after		4.06	0.837			

Table 11.
A paired samples t-test showed that there was no change in a private place to study but more time to study after the lockdown.

5.4 Preparing for and taking the final online assessment

An independent samples t-test was then run to determine if there was a significant difference between students who were deemed e-ready and those not yet e-ready, regarding the time they started the final online assessment. The test found that there was a significant difference between students who were deemed e-ready (M = 4.38, SD = 2.17), (t (225) = 2.153, p < 0.05) and those who were not yet e-ready (M = 5.01, SD = 2.05) (see **Table 12**). Therefore, e-ready students started their online assessment earlier than those who were not yet e-ready.

	E-readiness benchmark	Number of participants (N)	Mean (M)	Standard deviation (SD)	t	df	p
Time student started exam	e-ready	78	4.38	2.170	2.153	225	.032
	Not yet e-ready	150	5.01	2.047			

Table 12.
An independent samples t-test determined that e-ready students started their online examination earlier than those who were not yet e-ready.

5.5 Final course results

An independent samples t-test was run to determine if there was a significant difference between e-ready students and those not yet e-ready in relation to their final grade. The test found that there was no significant difference between e-ready students (M = 39.41, SD = 6.10), (t (225) = −0.308, p > 0.05) and those who were not yet e-ready (M = 39.14, SD = 6.33) (**Table 13**). Therefore, both groups of students had similar final grades.

The final assessment results for the cohort are shown in **Table 14**. Most of the e-ready students performed slightly better in the A-to A+ range. However, students who were not deemed to be e-ready performed slightly better in the B- to B+ and C to C+ range. Three students who were not deemed to be e-ready failed or were absent for the final examination.

	E-readiness benchmark	Number of participants (N)	Mean (M)	Standard deviation (SD)	t	df	p
Final grade	e-ready	78	39.41	6.100	−.308	225	.758
	Not yet e-ready	150	39.14	6.332			

Table 13.
Independent samples t-test to determine whether there was a significant difference between e-ready students and those not yet e-ready in relation to their final grade.

Grade	E-ready N (%)	Not e-ready N (%)	Total N (%)
A- to A	33 (42.3)	53 (35.3)	86 (37.7)
B- to B+	39 (50)	77 (51.3)	116 (50.9)
C to C+	6 (7.7)	17 (11.3)	23 (10.1)
Failed	0 (0)	2 (1.3)	2 (0.9)
Absent	0 (0)	1 (0.7)	1 (0.4)
Total	78 (34.2)	150 (65.8)	228 (100)

Table 14.
Comparison of examination results for students who were e-ready and not e-ready.

6. Discussion

The demographic data of this cohort was representative of other studies with the majority female students, in the 29 years or younger age range, who were at level 2 of their studies [4, 5, 17, 27]. Analyses on student characteristics and their level of e-readiness of this cohort, resulted in no significant differences among demographics such as age or gender with any of the e-readiness variables as reported in other research by [17, 18, 27].

6.1 Characteristics of student e-readiness

The characteristics of e-ready students identified in this study were shown to be similar to those in other studies, especially with having a natural inclination towards adapting to new technologies [4, 5, 27]. Characteristics of students who did not meet the criteria for e-readiness were also similar to those who preferred the face-to-face component of blended courses [21]. These students who suffer from technology challenges or require immediate verbal feedback highlight resistance towards changing their study habits and learning preferences in order to interact with an ELS [4, 5]. Those students who can easily access help desk support in face-to-face or blended courses, may be reluctant to switch to an online format if the course places high value on course assignments and outcomes. The dependence on technology for assistance and support may negatively impact their preference for an online course [11].

6.2 Students' level of e-readiness

The results revealed that about a third of the students were deemed to be e-ready, while about two-thirds showed deficiencies in one or more e-readiness categories. Other studies reported comparable results with similar cohorts, especially where e-ready students were found to be technologically savvy and had acquired some computer literacy skills [4, 5, 17]. However, for those with deficiencies, challenges still exist in adapting their learning lifestyle and study habits towards working with an ELS [5, 17].

Providing students with an orientation in the use of the ELS for students might still be useful, in spite of their general lack of interest in what may appear to be another course or workshop [5, 22, 23]. Providing a compulsory orientation to the ELS prior to enrolment in their courses could give students an opportunity to become more comfortable with the ELS. Hands-on exercises that involve interacting with technology tools that they will be using in their course, along with time to resolve any potential technology barriers can be beneficial without the added anxiety associated with coursework or grades. In this study, while an orientation activity was available for this cohort of students as part of the introductory tasks, it did not specifically focus on training for the ELS. As noted by [17], since most students were in the second year of their studies, it could have been assumed that they would have had the requisite knowledge or expertise at this level of their studies.

Further analyses of students' level of e-readiness or lack thereof, showed that e-ready students had significantly higher technical readiness, significantly better online study habits, and significantly higher preferences for online learning than those who were not yet e-ready. This is supported by other studies that indicated that students who take responsibility for their learning and have good study habits are suited for working in the ELS [18].

In contrast, a drill down of the data to evaluate the extent of deficiencies exhibited by students on the three measures also support studies where students tend to rate highest in the technical readiness scales but lowest in the self-directed or learning predisposition scales [5, 17, 18]. One consideration is that students could be distracted by other online activities while learning online, thus impacting their study habits [4, 17].

In this study, of the 150 students who were not deemed to be e-ready, 48% (72) were deficient in any one category, and 52% (78) who were deficient in two or three categories is cause for concern. The sudden move to online learning might not have given these students time to adapt or seek additional resources in order to become prepared for the change to online assessment. Although students are mostly exposed to and possess basic technological skills, significant challenges remain in adapting their lifestyle and learning to interacting with an ELS [32]. One such challenge that is frustrating for students involves lack of help desk assistance when facing technical problems while learning online [8].

Furthermore, 22.7% (34) students were deficient in all three categories and would be at a distinct disadvantage based on their inability to effectively use the technology, with poor study habits and a preference for the face-to-face environment. These results are comparable to another study that reported 25.1% of its sample in a blended cohort and 22.3% in an online cohort who had similar deficiencies in multiple categories [5]. Even though these numbers are small, all students should be given the resources and support for a fair chance at successfully completing their course of study. Students with technical deficiencies, are encouraged to visit the campus IT service desk with software and hardware issues to receive technical assistance. They could also visit one of the six computer laboratories on the campus to work on their assignments. However, with a stay-at-home order, this would have compounded the situation for these students.

The other two deficiencies - study habits and online learning predisposition categories - were beyond the expertise of the course facilitator to directly support the students' needs. However, in an effort to provide guidance to these students, hyperlinks and information on the university's student services were shared during scheduled weekly lectures and posted on the ELS. These services include useful information and scheduled appointments to discuss study habits and academic support, whether in an online or face-to-face setting.

6.3 Mid- semester shutdown

6.3.1 Devices and network connectivity

Regarding the type(s) of computer or mobile devices that students used to access the ELS from their geographical location, as well as the stability of their Internet connectivity while most students had a laptop computer, it was concerning that of the 10 students who had access to only a mobile device, nine (6.0%) of them were not deemed to be e-ready. Those students indicated that they only had an iPad or mobile phone in their possession. The fact that 10 (4.4%) students relied on an iPad or mobile phone, while 70 (30.7%) students depended on Wi-Fi were causes for concern regarding their continued access and ability to manipulate content in the ELS for the final online assessment. While these numbers were small, it was imperative that those caught in the digital divide were also given a fair chance to complete their courses. Fortunately, some internet service providers quickly offered to assist students by delivering laptops to those who required them for the duration of the assessment period [33, 34].

Based on these contributions, the chi-square test determined there was no significant difference in the proportion of e-ready students and not yet e-ready students regarding access to a laptop PC or Mac, or other mobile device, as well as the frequency of the stability of their internet connection. That is, e-ready students did not differ significantly in their access to online learning devices than those who were not yet e-ready. Also, students who were deemed e-ready had as stable a connection as those who were not yet e-ready. These results differ from [17], who reported that 80% of their respondents had challenges with poor connectivity.

6.3.2 Time management

E-ready students were found to have significantly better time management skills than those who were not yet e-ready. These results seem to be realistic since students who have good study skills are reported to be more organised and manage their time better [26]. However, for those students who were not deemed to be e-ready, the results are supported by [17] who noted that lack of self-directed learning or motivation for learning, were major challenges for this category of student since it is reflected in poor study habits and therefore poor time management skills. In this study, it is unknown whether any students had sought assistance from the Office of Student Services before the curfew. Nevertheless, one could argue that they would probably not have had enough time to successfully follow through with any interventions before the disruption. More so, students employed in security, medical and other essential services, would most likely have seen an increase in their workload. This could have negatively impacted their ability to successfully manage their study time.

6.3.3 Private space, and adequate time for studying

The results indicated that students who were deemed to be e-ready had less privacy and less time to study after the lockdown. These results highlighted the impact of the COVID-19 pandemic on this group of e-ready students. A similar study reported that this category of student typically has high expectations for themselves regarding their own study schedules and could manage their time well [17]. Additionally, as noted by [27] in their research, more than 60% of those students studied at home during COVID-19, compared to 94.3% of the students in this study. E-ready students who are seemingly disciplined could have previously used a private space such as the library on campus or one of the six computer laboratories to spend time on their assignments. However, with the lockdown in place, this would have resulted in restricted access to the campus library, possible distractions from other family members, or having to reduce the time spent online in order to allow another family member to use the computer or laptop. These factors could have disrupted an otherwise scheduled study routine.

For students who were not deemed to be e-ready, the results showed that while access to a private place for study time remained the same before and after the lockdown, it appears that they had more time to study after lockdown. This seems to have worked for the benefit of this group of students, since the country was under lockdown for over four weeks. While the lack of privacy remained during the lockdown, perhaps the importance of studying for final assessments or the confinement to one location could have created some personal and perhaps family structure with time required to dedicate to their studying.

6.4 Preparing for and taking the final online assessment

The results showed that e-ready students started their final online assessment earlier than those who were not yet e-ready. One could suggest that students who were not yet e-ready may still have lacked confidence with working in the online environment, which could have contributed to their delay in starting the online assessment. They could also have used the available time to study further, thus waiting until the last moment to take the online assessment. In contrast, students who were e-ready could have had the confidence to complete the assessment early in order to study for other assessments.

6.5 Final course results

This study found that both groups of students had similar final grades. This result is supported by [9] who reported no significant differences in the final scores, and [16] who showed that the format of instructional delivery may not have an effect on students' learning outcomes. However as suggested by [9, 10, 14], blended learning activities provided in this course prior to the lockdown may have had some influence on the students' final marks.

Based on these final results, one could suggest that the course content could have been accessible to all students. Additionally, the scheduling of the final assessment and questions could be considered to be as fair as in the opportunity given to students to select their time to take the assessment, and duration to complete the required questions. More so, students who were not deemed to be e-ready could have benefitted from the additional time taken before starting the assessment, while those who were e-ready could have suffered from the disruption in their study routine. Nevertheless, most of the e-ready students performed slightly better in the A-to A+ range. Students who were not deemed to be e-ready performed slightly better in the B- to B+ and C to C+ range. Three students who were not deemed to be e-ready failed or were absent for the final assessment.

7. Conclusions

This study has shown that for this cohort of students, only about a third were deemed to be e-ready. They displayed significantly higher technical readiness, significantly better online study habits, and significantly higher preferences for online learning than those who were not yet e-ready. As confirmed by [4], it should not be assumed that all students have access to a laptop and a quiet study space. Those who relied on visiting the library and using computer labs on the campus could have been especially disadvantaged by the lockdown if they did not have access to technology, adequate space and time to study while under the lockdown. Fortunately, both categories of students had about the same access to online learning devices and stable connectivity. Further, private companies and certain university services had arranged for students in the digital divide to receive laptops for the duration of the lockdown.

For e-ready students, the impact of the lockdown was felt most by a disruption in their study routine. This is supported by [13, 26] who found that time management was a necessary factor in positively influencing a student's final grade. The findings in this study also revealed that e-ready students had less privacy and less time to study after the lockdown. However, for those who were not yet e-ready, while there was no change in their private space for study, they found more time to study after the lockdown.

It may seem that e-ready students are more disciplined and would therefore spend more time in a quiet space with little to no disruption. However, students who are not yet e-ready are known to prefer a classroom environment. The scheduled class time each week could have provided a welcomed routine and maybe force some time management skills for the duration of the lecture. The lockdown, however, could have possibly mimicked some of that environment for those students which now became a place of learning and a space for learning. The findings by [13, 17] suggest that in this case, the forced time at home to study could have been a silver lining for this category of student. One could only wonder to what extent this change impacted their study routine and time management skills because of other influences beyond their control.

The results showed 31% of the students had technical challenges, over 60% had issues with study habits and over 80% had weaknesses with working in the online environment. Further analyses are required to determine if those who were borderline e-ready could have slipped below the benchmark after the lockdown. Perhaps, a post-survey reassessment of students' level of e-readiness could have highlighted the plight of those on that e-readiness boundary.

The results also revealed that students' level of e-readiness has some influence on when their take their online assessment via an ELS. It also impacts their final assessment results based on their self-discipline, study routine and study habits, as supported by other studies [26, 29]. Similar to [10], students had slightly better exam grades, since in this study, e-ready students performed slightly better in the A-to A+ range while those not e-ready performed slightly better in the B- to B+ and C to C+ range.

8. Recommendations

While the Office of Student Services remained available for academic support using online consultations during the lockdown, their extensive services seem not be known to the wider student body. If the e-readiness evaluation is implemented, then students, who were deemed to be not yet e-ready could initially benefit from these resources. At the beginning of each semester assistance on improving their study habits, or perhaps information on building a study schedule could be provided in order to give them a good chance to excel during the semester. For students in this course, the recommendation for visits to student services during the early weeks of the semester could have made a positive impact on those who were not deemed to be e-ready. However, it is not known if any students made appointments and more importantly if they did, whether they followed through with their sessions and changed any practices.

It is further recommended that during the initial weeks of every semester, officers of student services schedule visits or join courses, whether face-to-face or online, to introduce students to various types of academic support, and share information or quick tips. Instructors could also place links and 'information bits' on course pages to bring awareness to these services so that students are informed about the range of support services. Furthermore, supported by findings of this study and those of [12, 19], it is strongly recommended that prior to the start of their courses, students complete an ELS orientation inclusive of an e-readiness assessment, even if it is a self-evaluation. This assessment, also supported by [21, 22], would provide an initial baseline and also highlight any e-readiness deficiencies that require additional support or ELS training. Over subsequent semesters of re-evaluation, students could monitor changes from previous semesters and pinpoint the type of assistance they may need before the start of the semester. It is hoped that a different type of self-awareness towards evaluating their own proficiency would develop when working via the ELS. The end result could possibly be seen in increased student satisfaction, and overall improvement of student outcomes which is ultimately important for university administrators, instructors, and indeed the students.

Thanks

Sincere appreciation and admiration to the students in this course and across the globe who persisted in the midst of COVID-19 pandemic to complete their online assessments.

Author details

Glenda H.E. Gay
The University of the West Indies at Cave Hill, Bridgetown, Barbados

*Address all correspondence to: glenda.gay@cavehill.uwi.edu

References

[1] Weeden KA, Cornwell B. The small-world network of college classes: Implications for epidemic spread on a university campus. Sociological Science. 2020;7: 222-241.

[2] Seaman JE, Allen IE, Seaman J. Grade increase: Tracking distance education in the United States. Babson Park, MA: Babson Survey Research Group, LLC; 2018.

[3] Rashid S, Yadav SS. Impact of Covid-19 pandemic on higher education and research. Indian Journal of Human Development. 2020. DOI: https://doi.org/10.1177/0973703020946700.

[4] Adams D, Sumintono B, Mohamed A, Noor NSM. Elearning readiness among students of diverse backgrounds in a leading Mayalsian higher education institution. Malaysian Journal of Learning and Instruction. 2018;15(2):227-256.

[5] Gay G. Fixing the 'Ready' in e-learning readiness. In: Sinecen M, editor. Trends in E-learning. Trends in E-learning. London: InTech Open; 2018. p. 22. DOI: 10.5772/intechopen.74287

[6] Chang C-L, Fang M. E-Learning and online instructions of higher education during the 2019 novel coronavirus diseases (COVID-19) epidemic. ICCASIT 2020 Journal of Physics: Conference Series: IOP Publishing; 2020.

[7] Lockman AS, Schirmer BR. Online instruction in higher education: Promising, research-based, and evidence-based practices. Journal of Education and e-Learning Research. 2020;7(2):130-152.

[8] Young S, Duncan HE. Online and face-to-face teaching: How do student ratings differ? MERLOT Journal of Online Learning and Teaching. 2014;10(1):70-79.

[9] Burns K, Duncan M, Sweeney DC, North JW. A longitudinal comparison of course delivery modes of an introductory information systems course and their impact on a subsequent information systems course. MERLOT Journal of Online Learning and Teaching. 2013;9(4):453-467.

[10] Means B, Toyama Y, Murphy R, Bakia M, Jones K. Evaluation of evidence-based practices in online learning: A meta-analysis and review of online-learning studies2010 Nov 12, 2014 [cited 2014 Nov 12]. Available from: https://www2.ed.gov/rschstat/eval/tech/evidence-based-practices/finalreport.pdf.

[11] Keskin S, Yurdugül H. Factors affecting students' preferences for online and blended learning: Motivational vs. cognitive European Journal of Open, Distance and E-Learning. 2019. DOI: 10.2478/eurodl-2019-0011.

[12] Parkes M, Stein S, Reading C. Student preparedness for university e-learning environments. The Internet and Higher Education. 2015;25(1):1-10.

[13] Broadbent J. Comparing online and blended learner's self-regulated learning strategies and academic performance. The Internet and Higher Education. 2017;33:24-32. DOI: https://doi.org/10.1016/j.iheduc.2017.01.004.

[14] López-Pérez MV, Pérez-López MC, Rodríguez-Ariza L. Blended learning in higher education: Students' perceptions and their relation to outcomes. Computers & Education. 2011;56:818-826.

[15] Murphy MPA. COVID-19 and emergency eLearning: Consequences of the securitization of higher education for post-pandemic

pedagogy. Contemporary Security Policy. 2020;41(3):492-505. DOI: 10.1080/13523260.2020.1761749.

[16] Lim DH, Morris ML. Learner and instructional factors influencing learning outcomes within a blended learning environment. Educational Technology & Society. 2009;12(4):282-293.

[17] Chung E, Noor NM, Mathew VN. Are you ready? An assessment of online learning readiness among university students. International Journal of Academic Research in Progressive Education and Development. 2020;9(1):301-317. DOI: 10.6007/IJARPED/v9-i1/7128.

[18] Rasouli A, Rahbania Z, Attaran M. Students' readiness for E-learning application in higher education. Malaysian Online Journal of Educational Technology. 2016;4(3):51-64.

[19] Wargadinata W, Maimunah I, Dewi E, Rofiq Z. Student's responses on learning in the early COVID-19 pandemic. Journal of education and teacher training. 2020;5(1):141-153.

[20] Garrison D, Anderson T. E-learning in the 21st century: E-learning framework for research and practice. London: Routledge/Falmer; 2003.

[21] Stoebe A, Grebing R. The effect of new student orientations on the retention of online students. Online Journal of Distance Learning Administration. 2020;23(2).

[22] Taylor JM, Dunn M, Winn SK. Innovative orientation leads to improved success in online courses. Online Learning. 2015;19(4):1-9.

[23] Jones KR. Developing and Implementing a Mandatory Online Student Orientation. Journal of Asynchronous Learning Networks. 2013;17(1):43-45.

[24] Hashim H, Tasir Z, editors. E-Learning readiness: A literature review. 2014 international conference on teaching and learning in computing and engineering (LaTiCE); 2014; Kuching: IEEE.

[25] Hung W-H, Chang L-M, Lin C-P, Hsiao C-H. E-readiness of website acceptance and implementation in SMEs. Computers in Human Behavior. 2014;40:44-55.

[26] Kaymak ZD, Horzum MB. Relationship between Online Learning Readiness and Structure and Interaction of Online Learning Students. Kuram ve Uygulamada Egitim Bilimleri. 2013;13(3):1792-1797.

[27] Chung E, Subramaniam G, Dass LC. Online learning readiness among university students in Malaysia amidst Covid-19. Asian Journal of University Education. 2020;16(2):46-58. DOI: https://doi.org/10.24191/ajue.v16i2.10294.

[28] Hung ML, Chou C, Chen CH, Own ZY. Learner readiness for online learning: Scale development and student perceptions. Computers & Education. 2010;55(3):1080-1090.

[29] Holsapple CW, Lee-Post A. Defining, assessing, and promoting e-learning success: An information systems perspective. Decision Sciences Journal of Innovative Education. 2006;4(1):67-85.

[30] Baturay M, Yukselturk E. The role of online education preferences on student achievement. Turkish Online Journal of Distance Education. 2015;16(3):1-10.

[31] Sekaran U. Research methods for business: A skill-building approach. New York: John Wiley & Sons; 2003.

[32] Mandernach BJ, Mason T, Forrest KD, Hackathorn J. Faculty

views on the appropriateness of teaching undergraduate psychology courses online. Teaching of Psychology. 2012;39(3):203-208. DOI: 10.1177/0098628312450437.

[33] Flow providing connections for students. May 1, 2020 [cited 2020 October 19]. Available from: https://barbadostoday.bb/2020/05/01/flow-providing-connections-for-students/,UWI

[34] Mona to distribute over 500 tablets to students in need. Loop News [Internet]. 27 April, 2020. Available from: https://www.loopjamaica.com/content/uwi-mona-distribute-over-500-tablets-needy-students.

Chapter 14

Transnational Education and E-Learning during a Pandemic: Challenges, Opportunities, and Future

Atm S. Alam, Ling Ma, Andy Watson, Vindya Wijeratne and Michael Chai

Abstract

Higher education institutions are globally facing unprecedented disruptive trends, which have rapidly changed the landscape of global higher education due to the COVID-19 pandemic. While transnational education (TNE) is increasingly becoming popular as a provision for internationally recognised education at the doorstep of students, the temporary shift from traditional classroom teaching and learning (T&L) to remote online T&L caused by the COVID-19 pandemic has been challenging for all stakeholders to provide the similar student experience as previously. Regarding TNE programmes, the emergency replacement of traditional classrooms with virtual ones has also raised significant challenges of both equity and pedagogy. However, given the current crisis in higher education, TNE can be a cornerstone in rebuilding the post-COVID-19 international education system. This chapter explores the challenges faced by the TNE programmes based on a systematic literature review and information gathered informally from various stakeholders and discusses the opportunities and future impacts in teaching, learning, and student support as the post-COVID-19 educational landscape emerges. It also provides an insight into how a sustainable transnational learning community can be developed for the quality and sustainability of international higher education in this new decade.

Keywords: transnational education, higher education, COVID-19, student experience, blended learning, mixed-mode learning, e-learning, remote online education

1. Introduction

The current COVID-19 pandemic has shaken almost all sectors including the education sector, and it has caused unprecedented disruption to education systems worldwide, resulting in the closure of schools, colleges and universities in most countries. The closure of educational institutions nationally was essential to prevent the spread of the virus using social distancing. To limit the spread of the virus and render the continuation of education, the predominant model used for education delivery is remote online teaching and learning (T&L), which is considered the best path forward. The government also recognises the increasing importance of online T&L in this dynamic world [1]. It was suddenly necessary to transform all educational activities ranging from in-class teaching and learning activities to assessments into online-based. As a result, the COVID-19 pandemic has changed the overall global education landscape and strengthened the visionary idea that education should not be limited by where or how you learn, what matters is that you learn from anywhere, at any time. In this situation, technologies are playing a key role in this, thanks to recent technological advancement. As a result, universities have started to develop blended learning approach, making use of key technologies, to prepare themselves to survive and flourish together for the continuity of education even in emergencies.

As information and communication technologies (ICT) have kept advancing, online education has become more feasible technologically, economically, and operationally [2]. Henceforth, the T&L approaches are continually kept changing, and online education has been adopted globally by institutions as an accepted teaching and learning form [2, 3]. However, a common perception about delivering online education is that the quality of online education is perceived as not equal to the traditional face-to-face classroom-based education.

During the COVID-19 pandemic, there are in fact as many as nearly 1.6 billion learners in more than 190 countries across the globe affected by the closures of educational institutions at the national level, representing approximately 90% of the global student population [4]. Additionally, it has been reported that there is a decline in the number of international students in many popular studies abroad countries. For example, new international student enrolment has dropped significantly, reporting a 43% decrease in the US in Fall 2020, according to the Institute of International Education (IIE) [5]. On the other hand, transnational education (TNE) is an emerging area of scholarship with a growing number of both students and providers moving across national borders to deliver higher education programmes. A similar situation (the closure of host institutions) also happened to most TNE programmes, especially TNE programmes in those countries, which were disrupted right at the beginning of the pandemic and had to close their activities. As a result, the pedagogic activities in TNE have rapidly been transformed into online education or remote online T&L due to the travel restrictions, thanks to the recent advancement of educational tools and technologies. Although most TNE providers had forced exceptionally swift adaptations of remote online T&L, the virtualisation of the TNE programmes, however, raised significant issues of both equity and pedagogy.

Due to the length of the COVID-19 pandemic, online education or a combination of online and traditional education (blended) is today an integral part of education and learning across the world. A growing number of colleges and universities have been implementing and adopting such approaches. Likewise, the perception of the online education quality mentioned earlier is changing and COVID-19 while being a hazard to humanity has evolved institutions to invest in online education [6]. Moreover, online education has proven to be valid and useful for many students during the COVID-19 pandemic that is opening up a new era - the revolution of online education.

Despite the current transformation of education systems and the challenges faced, the TNE programmes can still be a cornerstone in rebuilding the post-COVID-19 international education system. Therefore, this chapter firstly provides the concept and models of TNE programmes describing their pros and cons, as well as discusses the challenges faced by the TNE programmes during the COVID-19 pandemic and the opportunities created due to the replacement of traditional classrooms into the remote online T&L (restructuring the education system). In this chapter, authors have shared their experience on how their TNE students experience remote online education and cope with COVID-together with the benefits/challenges of remote learning for TNE students. Furthermore, this chapter provides future barriers and envisions of the future (post-COVID-19) of transnational higher education.

2. Methodological perspective and approach

This chapter presents a review of the scholarly and grey literature on transnational education and e-learning with a special emphasis being put on COVID-19. The commentary and discussion are structured around objectives, perspectives, and experiences of key stakeholders of TNE facing challenges and taking measures during the COVID-19. As such, a systematic approach was used to identify 57 peer-reviewed articles from 2010 to 2021. Of which, only 19 articles were published before the COVID-19 pandemic and these articles are mainly reviewed for compiling the introduction of TNE and the related information while the remaining articles are mainly focusing on the challenges and opportunities created around TNE and e-learning as well as the good practices adopted by different stakeholders.

To complete the review, we searched the Web of Science, and Google Scholar for literature using the keywords "transnational education," "e-learning," "COVID-19 pandemic," "online education," and "blended learning." We focused our search on peer-reviewed journal articles from 2010 to 2020. Theoretical studies, editorials, and non-peer-reviewed literature were excluded from the review. Additionally, we explored recent reports and guidelines produced by local governments and local higher education regulatory bodies for quality assurance of top TNE host and foreign countries. The inclusion criteria for e-learning and online education were mainly related to transnational or cross-border higher education. On the other hand, blended learning covers a broad range of learning approaches and is often used as an umbrella term to capture an assortment of blends or is placed on a spectrum ranging from more face-to-face instruction to more technology-assisted instructions. There are three categories of blended learning in terms of i) low-impact blends, where extra activities are added to an existing course; ii) medium-impact blends in which activities in an existing course are replaced; and iii) high-impact blends in which a blended course is designed from scratch [7]. In this review, the inclusion criteria for selecting articles on blended learning were those studies that were conducted in blended learning environments with reducing face-to-face instruction or replacing face-to-face instructional activities with remote online learning, which are mainly the case for transnational education during the pandemic.

After screening and excluding articles, 59 articles were finalised for the systematic literature review based on the above-mentioned criteria. Moreover, several good practices for mitigating some concerns for TNE and online learning (e-learning) are highlighted based T&L related discussions and meetings throughout the academic years 2019–2020 and 2020–2021.

3. Overview of transnational education (TNE)

Exports of education have significantly grown over the last two decades. This is achieved through developing sophisticated and successful approaches to the provision of higher education internationally to many students, who are located outside of the countries of higher education institutions (HEIs) that are awarding the degree. These approaches can be an array of collaborative arrangements with degree-awarding institutions from major education-exporting countries [8]. Traditionally, those students would have travelled to foreign countries to study for an international qualification and are now pursuing foreign degrees in their home or neighbouring countries at local institutions. This form of award-bearing educational provisioning by an HEI in one country to students based in another country is termed as ***transnational education*** (TNE) or sometimes as ***cross-border education***. The range and number of TNE activities, such as remote campuses and joint degree programmes, continue to grow rapidly to address international customer demand, especially in higher education [8].

3.1 Definition of TNE

Among many definitions and interpretations of TNE, according to the UNESCO/Council of Europe Code of Good Practice in the Provision of Transnational Education, "*TNE refers to study programs or educational services in which the learners are located in a country different from the one where the awarding institution is based*" [9]. In other words, TNE is education delivery from institutions in one country to students in another. Usually, students do not cross national borders or move to the country of degree-awarding HEI to undertake study at an overseas institution. Instead of students moving to foreign countries, the programmes move to the students in their home countries [10]. Moreover, besides the host country's domestic students taking TNE programmes, students taking TNE programs including expatriate students living in the host country and international students travelling to the TNE host country especially for taking a TNE program [10]. Therefore, the definition of TNE can be generalised as:

> *TNE is all types of higher education programmes in which students based in country B study for a degree from a university in country A.*

Sending/Foreign TNE country: TNE students get a degree award from a foreign institution and the country, in which the awarding institution is based, is called the Sending or Foreign TNE country.

Host/Receiving TNE country: The country, where TNE students take the TNE program to achieve a foreign degree is called the host or receiving TNE country, and the institutions in that country are called host institutions.

The delivery of such an education is often done through joint degrees or partnerships with overseas host institutions, branch campuses or online courses with qualifications. In recent years, many countries have engaged in TNE, and there has been an unprecedented growth of predominantly Western foreign universities delivering education throughout Asia, the Middle East, and Africa [11–13]. The UK, US, Australia, Germany, and France are the leading exporters of TNE or sending countries providing the TNE programmes [14]. On the other hand, China, UAE, Malaysia, Singapore, and Qatar are the leading host countries studying hundreds of thousands of students for a TNE programme [14, 15]. Based on the data available from different sources [14, 16], **Figure 1** illustrates the top host and sending countries for TNE activities including some emergent destination countries.

While most TNE programmes provide education at the undergraduate level under different modes of TNE with engineering, technology, maths, medical science, and computing being the principal subjects of study, the post-graduate level TNE programmes are also getting popular [16].

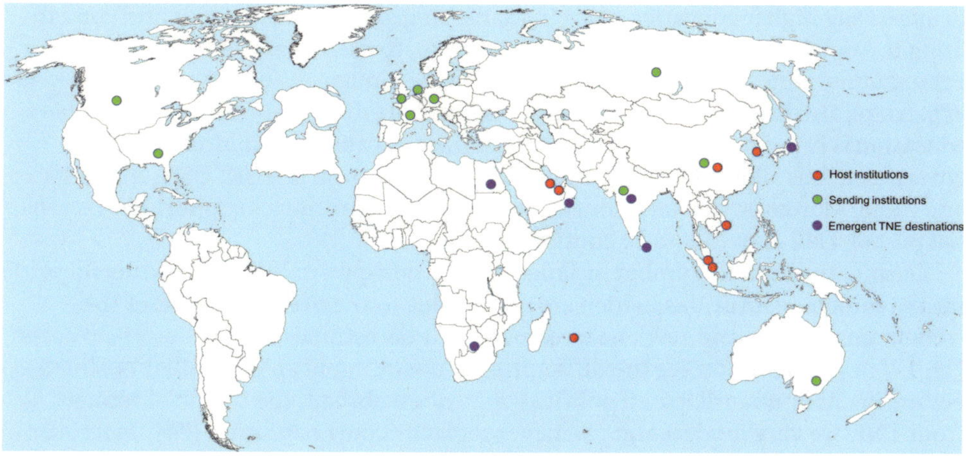

Figure 1.
A list of top transnational higher education sending, host and emergent destinations.

4. Benefits and criticisms of TNE

TNE mainly consists of three main stakeholder groups, namely students, partner institutions (both host and foreign) and governments [17]. An appropriate setting of a TNE programme can be considered as a win-win option for all those three main stakeholder groups. For many students, getting a degree in popular study destinations such as the UK, US, and Australia sounds like an enriching and exciting experience. However, they are expensive and not everyone can afford them. Achieving an international degree by studying in the home country via the TNE route at a considerably lower cost is a lucrative option. Students can get the learning experience of international standards (i.e., exposed to pedagogies from Europe, the US, Australia or wherever the awarding institution is based) receiving quality international education without having to go overseas. Besides paying much lower tuition fees, which are often much higher if studying at the foreign institution directly, students also save their travel and accommodation costs [18]. In addition to developing a deep conceptual understanding of the content of the subject of study, students are often taught by using innovative teaching and learning practices exploring state-of-the-art technologies. Moreover, they are usually assessed by exams and their participation in discussion and group projects that allow them to gain valuable soft skills such as communication and teamwork [19, 20].

Moreover, studying abroad is a challenge - an introduction to a new culture and an emotional roller coaster at times when your daily routine, culture, and the attitudes of people around you are no longer familiar [21]. In some cases, culture shock[1] can resemble or trigger study abroad depression. In the case of TNE, students often face culture shock less and they will be able to concentrate more on their studies. However, it should not discourage students to stop studying abroad due to the concern of culture shock as there are hundreds of ways and guidelines available to overcome cultural shock while studying abroad [21–23]. It is also equally beneficial for both home and foreign institutions that TNE programmes can easily gain revenue streams with relatively little risk or effort. On the other hand, authors in [13] have highlighted that host country governments have found TNE as a potential contributor

[1] The process of recognising, understanding, and adapting to a new culture is called culture shock.

to increasing higher education capacity, satisfying skilled labour needs and contributing to knowledge creation and innovation (e.g., to create an "Education Hub"). For example, almost 90% of the population in the United Arab Emirates (UAE) is an expatriate, also known as non-Emiratis who cannot enter public universities, where education is free. To fulfil the demand from their expatriates' children, the UAE government has allowed foreign universities, mainly from the UK, USA, Australia and India. Moreover, it is mentioned that the host government's support is an essential part of TNE activities to be continued [24].

Despite the limited number of failed and/or non-profitable TNE partnerships for the foreign institutions, which are mainly due to the overestimation of the student enrolments and revenue streams, the underestimation of the start-up costs [13, 17] or failure to foresee the difficulties of operating in an unfamiliar business environment or unanticipated political opposition abroad, the financial returns from TNE are very modest and can never replace export education [24]. Moreover, many awarding TNE institutions are often expanding their operation in multiple host countries and multiple institutions in the same host country while they are also moving into new, larger, purpose-built campuses in the case of International Branch Campuses (IBC) (will discuss later). It is not only all about financial gain for the institutions, which is important for its expansion and sustainability but also to enhance their prestige, legitimacy and educational quality helping themselves in building a global brand. Additionally, some institutions see TNE engagement as other ways to enhance their research, knowledge capacity and cultural understanding (Knight, 2006 and [17]).

Even though the TNE programmes are becoming a popular way of achieving foreign degrees, there are some criticisms of TNE concerning the student experience and satisfaction from the TNE. It is expected that TNE is to provide identical programmes as the awarding institution to preserve its reputation [25]. However, there is a concern among many students and/or some host governments that TNE programmes are unlikely to be delivered by the core faculty of the awarding institutions, so the quality of such TNE programmes may not be the absolute equivalence to the one on the campus of the awarding (foreign) university [26]. For example, concerns about the quality of some TNE provisions in China by UK universities led to the Ministry of Education abruptly cancelling the licences of many HEIs and calling off many partnerships that were under development [24].

Moreover, it is also highlighted based on a TNE tutor survey [25] that it was advocated for the need to tailor the curriculum to the culture and context resulting in not all the content being necessarily transnationally transportable. Other most prominent concerns are related to misalignment between home and branch campus, replicating diversity and quality of the student body, mirroring forms of cultural imperialism, lack of data to drive decision-making, organisational culture and policies, and the ability to adapt to the "new" local context [27].

4.1 Common forms of TNE

Under the concept of TNE as defined earlier, academic institutions are collaborating to jointly teach students or solely providing TNE (with no direct relationship with a local HEI) to teach students who are benefitting from quality teaching locally without needing to travel abroad. The TNE programmes and activities can be delivered through a wide variety of forms or modes ranging from remote campuses to joint degree programmes with institutions sharing best practices on a global scale. There are mainly two major categories of TNE [10], namely *collaborative TNE provision*, under which foreign institutions have a local collaborative partner from the host country for the delivery of the academic programs, and *independent TNE provision* (stand-alone), under which no institutions from the host country are normally involved in the process of the design or delivery of the academic program.

Under these two categories, there is a wide variety of concepts and modes of operation in transnational education. They include but are not limited to online and distance learning, joint and dual degree programmes, fly-in faculty for short courses or international branch campuses. Based on the literature survey, the followings are the common forms of TNE that are widely adopted around the world and summarised in **Table 1**:

1. **Twinning and Articulation:** This is a systematic recognition by an institution (say, *A*) of specified study at an institution (say, *B*) in another country as partial credit towards a program at institution *A*. This approach allows students to experience the campus of the foreign institution by physically studying at the foreign campus of the awarding university for some time upon agreement of the TNE arrangement. Often, the study period is split between partner institutions and the study in the foreign country could be involved either as a compulsory period of study or as an optional part of the programme [16]. For example, students registered with the overseas partner can have a guaranteed entry into a UK-validated programme if they achieve an agreed level of performance in their studies with the overseas partner [16].

2. **International Franchising and Degree Validation Agreement:** This is a contractual agreement between institutions from different countries based on licence and/or mutual recognition. In this model, an institution (franchiser) in a foreign country approves an institution (franchisee) in the host country to provide one or more of the foreign institution's programs to students in the local institution. Often the home university retains authority for setting and marking assessments and examinations. While franchising is a financially inexpensive way of penetrating a new market, problems often arise if the home university and the joint venture partner, usually a private for-profit college, have divergent objectives (e.g., academic quality versus profit maximising) [28]. Under the franchising arrangement, new trends are evolving from individually franchised programmes to the development of new private independent universities in a host country that primarily offer franchised academic programmes from different foreign providers [12].

Types of TNE/categories	Independent TNE provision	Collaborative TNE provision
Twinning and articulation	No	Yes
International franchising and degree validation	Yes	No
International branch campus (IBC)	Yes	No
Joint/Dual/Multiple degree	No	Yes
Co-founded/Joint institutions*	No	Yes
Distance/Online delivery	Yes	No
Progression agreement/Sequential degrees	No	Yes
Course-to-course credit transfer	No	Yes

**May also be independent in the sense that there may not be any relationship with a local institution from the host country, but only with multiple institutions from foreign countries [10].*

Table 1.
Types and categories of popular TNE formats.

In the validation model popularised by UK universities, this is just a variation of franchising that the curriculum for a degree is designed by the awarding institution in the foreign country and taught in the home university. The recognition of the degree and the quality of the degree are tested by the awarding institution. In other words, validation is a variation of franchising, where instead of the home university developing and licencing the curriculum, the curriculum is developed by the foreign partner and, through an institutional accreditation process, is deemed to be equivalent to that of the home university, thus allowing the partner to offer the university's degrees.

3. **International Branch Campus (IBC):** International branch campuses and flying-faculty models are also part of the broad set of TNE engagement models. In this case, campuses are often set up by a specific foreign higher education institution in another country to provide its education to local students in that country. The awarding (foreign) institution has some degree of responsibility for the overall strategy and quality assurance of the branch campus [13]. The branch has basic infrastructure such as a library, an open-access computer lab and dining facilities, and overall, students at the branch have a similar experience to students at the home campus [13]. They may be either fixed or temporary. This is similar to international franchising, but the franchisee is a campus of the franchiser. Among others, China, UAE, Malaysia, Singapore, and Qatar are the major transnational higher education hubs hosting most IBCs [17]. While the rate of IBC establishment has slowed due to many factors (e.g., difficulty to attain student recruitment targets leading to financial loss), the demand for IBCs is still there in some parts of the world and over 306 IBCs are operating around the world including newly opened IBCs in Morocco, Mexico and Indonesia in the last year [29]. For showing an overall picture of IBC development globally, **Table 2** summarises some statistics based on literature.

Attributes	Remarks	Reference
The overall number of students enrolment in majority IBCs	Usually, <1000 students	[17]
Major drivers for IBC development	• For seeking to establish an education hub • For generating foreign exchange (financial gain) • For producing skilled labour and employment • For projecting soft power • For enhancing research, knowledge capacity and culturing understanding • For enhancing institutional prestige, educational quality and for establishing a global brand (increase global status and reputation)	[17, 24]
Unsuccessful IBC cases and lessons learned	• University of East London closed its IBC in Cyprus after recruiting only 17 students in its first year of operation • University of Wolverhampton closed its IBC in Mauritius within 3 years (only 140 students enrolled) • University of Aberystwyth closed after 2 years of its IBC operation in Mauritius (only 106 students enrolled) All these cases were unsuccessful due to an underestimation of the set-up costs and overestimation of the student enrolment.	[17]

Table 2.
Some attributes of IBCs.

4. **Joint or Dual or Multiple Degree:** This is one of the most popular modes of TNE engagement with offering one or dual or multiple qualifications. In the Joint Degree programme, one academic qualification is offered with badges of both sending and host HEIs on the certificate while two separate qualification certificates are provided individually for each HEI for the Double Degree case, which is quite popular nowadays. Additionally, Multiple Degree Programmes offer at least three qualification certificates.

5. **Co-founded or Joint Institutions:** This is relatively a new form of TNE is an interesting alternative to the IBC model co-founded by multiple universities from different countries [10].

6. **Distance Delivery:** Distance education is another form of the TNE landscape, where local host country support is being provided to distance education students [10]. those distance education programmes that are delivered—through satellites, computers, correspondence, or other technological means—across national boundaries.

4.2 Delivery modes of teaching and learning materials

While there are numerous TNE formats discussed in the previous section, the delivery of T&L materials can be varied for the same TNE format at different institutions. Depending on the TNE formats, some TNE programmes feature a blend of online and face-to-face delivery of teaching and learning materials, and others consist of wholly online or face-to-face delivery or a combination of both these modes at different ratios [16]. For example, some Joint Degree programmes offer in-person delivery of T&L materials and in this case, faculties from both foreign and host institutions are directly involved in the T&L delivery. Sometimes foreign institutions recruit their staff based on the host country only (i.e., their faculties live in the host country during the whole term) or at the foreign institution and send them to the host country for only T&L delivery (flying faculty). The teaching and learning delivery can be in the Block teaching style, where lectures, tutorials and other forms of teaching are provided in an intensive block, sometimes as short as 1 week and student learning is compressed, typically with students studying only one course at a time. Alternatively, they can be spread over, e.g., 15 weeks of student learning and assessment (the conventional to the delivery of a full-time course of study in the UK).

4.3 Key elements in developing a TNE

Over the last decade, there has been an evolution in the development of new forms of TNE programmes. TNE is growing rapidly and getting widely accepted as well as becoming a popular way of acquiring international educational awards. In the TNE development process, many new elements related to higher education have emerged and are continuing to emerge. Examples of such key elements are new actors, new partnerships, new modes of delivery and new regulations [10]. The TNE modes discussed above are being developed based on defining and agreeing upon the key elements, i.e., the type of qualification TNE students get, mode of delivery, faculty arrangement, curriculum development, accreditation and so on, which are elaborately discussed in [10] and interested readers are referred to in this article [10].

4.4 Growth of TNE in the UK and around the world

The UK offers world-class education with a global reputation and a strong presence in global markets. Currently, the UK is the second largest provider of international education with a 10% share of the global market. When it comes to exporting the UK education expertise abroad, there is a strong demand all over the world for the quality of British education products and services. For example, the British Educational Suppliers Association (BESA) identified that China is one of such markets worth $500 billion, with $677 million spent on EdTech each year[2]. The UK dominates the provision of TNE around the world, especially in those countries that aspire to be regional education hubs. For example, Malaysia relies heavily on transnational education to meet the high demand for tertiary places which local public universities could not adequately meet [15]. The main reason for this is the quality and acceptability of British education around the world (e.g., a competitive employability advantage and an international outlook). It is also believed that a UK TNE provides valuable cultural capital in the forms of knowledge, skills, dispositions, and qualification. On the other hand, UK TNE programmes are commonly marketed as cost-effective for students who could not study wholly overseas but still seek a UK education and its associated benefits [15]. Most UK TNE programmes are usually offered as similar to those offered at the main (foreign) institution in the UK in terms of, e.g., course content, academic standards and qualification awarded.

Statistically, the UK is one of the leading exporters of TNE with 164 UK higher education providers reported 432,500 students studying through TNE in 2019/20, which decreased by 234,315 students (−35.2%), which is largely due to an increasingly competitive market, a developing local higher education sector in the host countries and changes in local regulations, and increased by 22 UK higher education providers (+15.5%) as compared to the corresponding data in 2018–2019 [30] (source: HESA[3]). As compared to the number of international students enrolled in the UK in the same year, there were ~ 1.4 times higher and ~ 1.22 lower UK TNE students, respectively. The number of UK TNE students and the number of UK TNE providers over academic

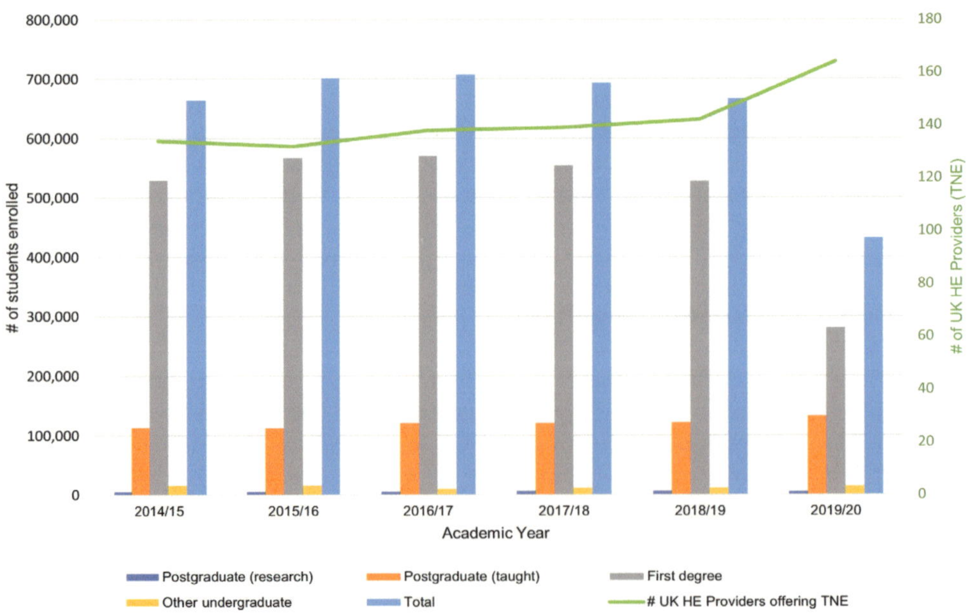

Figure 2.
Transnational students studying wholly overseas for a UK higher education qualification in 2019/20 (note: Only showing countries with over 1000 transnational students).

[2] www.great.gov.uk
[3] https://www.hesa.ac.uk/

years 2014/15 to 2019/20 is illustrated in **Figure 2**. It is found that there is an increasing trend of the number of UK HE providers involved in TNE programmes even though the total number of UK TNE students has started declining from the academic year 2016/17, which is mainly on the undergraduate programmes. However, there is a slow gain in the number of UK TNE students in the postgraduate (taught) programmes.

Australia also maintains a well-established reputation as an education exporter and many Australian providers operate in several countries offering quality higher education through different TNE arrangements. **Figure 3** shows the number of students studying a TNE course with Australian Providers at a campus outside of Australia in major markets, and it can be seen that Singapore, Malaysia and China are the three markets studying the largest number of enrolled students in 2018 [11]. Besides these markets shown in **Figure 3**, there are other potential markets (e.g., Sri Lanka, Vietnam, and India) identified for significant growth.

TNE is rapidly evolving with rapidly changing its scope and scale and emerging partnership models, modes of delivery, and regulations. Likewise, the changing nature of TNE partnerships has also been noticed in Australian Providers over a couple of decades. For example, in China, there are 150 Chinese-Australian programmes at the Bachelor level and above since the first Chinese-Australian

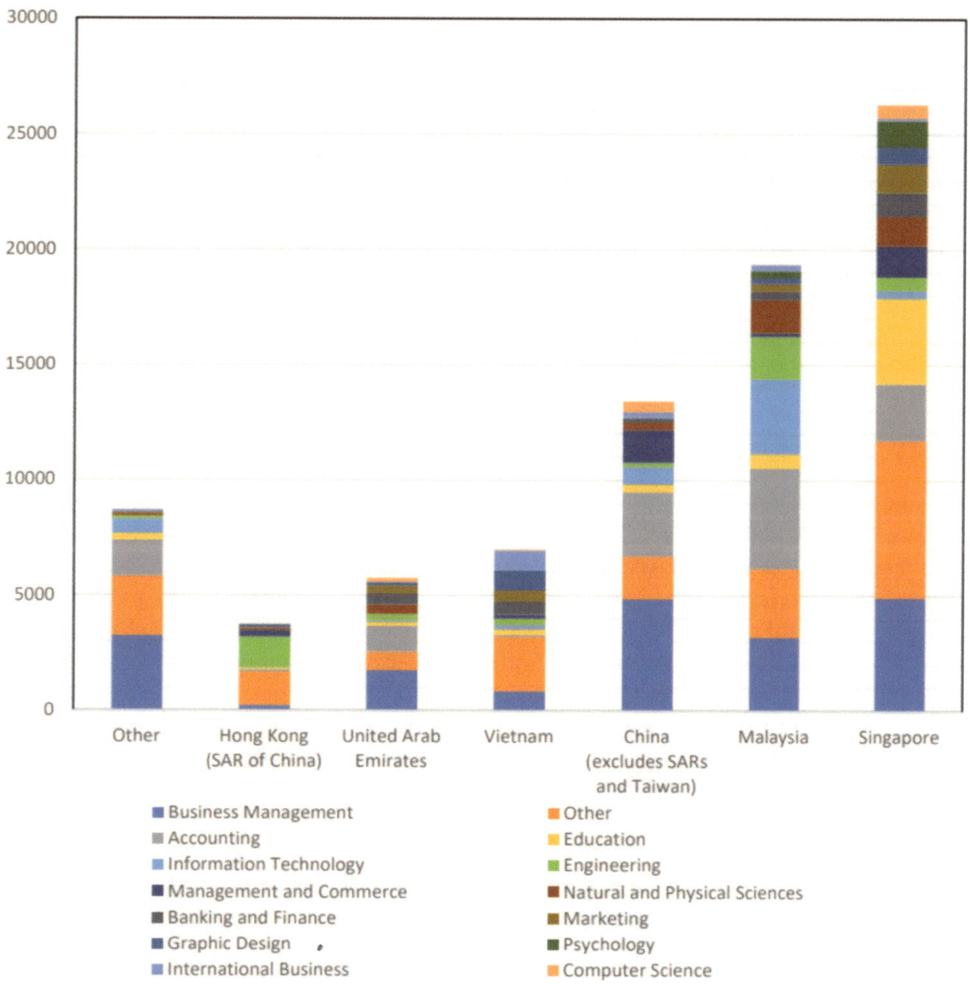

Figure 3.
TNE students at an offshore campus in major markets in 2018 [11].

programmes that were first approved in 1994, with Australia being the third-largest partner country behind the UK and the US [11]. Based on consultations and surveys undertaken by a study in [11], all Australian TNE programmes are managed by individual providers that employ their specific approaches and TNE partnerships and delivery models are in a state of constant evolution. IBCs, which provide greater control over quality and standards at the cost of larger investment and risking sustainability, are the most preferred TNE models for most Australian TNE providers, and as a consequence, at least six Australian IBCs in different markets have been closed.

4.5 Main issues of TNE partnerships: regulatory and quality assurance

TNE implies the crossing of cultural, linguistic, legislative as well as national and often intercontinental borders. In most cases, the rapidly growing economies such as the Middle East and Asia are often the target regions for the TNE partnerships, where the linguistic, cultural, political and legislative environments are completely different from those of the exporting universities that are mainly from the North [28]. Therefore, it is extremely complex to adapt and harmonise different systems working with different keys and different reference points.

Additionally, there is no TNE benchmark or general legal framework, which could harmonise the different educational structures and values of TNE institutions and qualifications. Therefore, TNE partnerships must comply with the legal requirements of both foreign and host countries and show standards of good practice. Regarding the TNE policy, practice and regulatory aspects, many host countries are imposing new restrictions. For example, authors in [11] have also found that "providers are most concerned about a lot of the sovereign issues, and by that, I mean how they're dealing with governments and the rules in different countries and navigating that can be quite complex". However, this brings the benefits of having excellent super- or extra-national universities that might find difficulties to expand their study courses outside the national boundaries, whilst some non-recognised and fraudulent institutions (the so-called "degree mills") can operate in different national contexts at the same time.

5. TNE and the COVID-19 pandemic

Since early 2020, the spread of the novel coronavirus COVID-19 has started to cause a significant impact in many sectors across the world, and the education sector is not an exception, which has led to profound changes in the education sector. After declaring COVID-19 as a pandemic on 30 January 2020 by the Director-General of the World Health Organisation (WHO) [31], many governments around the world had taken pandemic precautionary measures such as social distancing to prevent the spread of the COVID-19 virus. Within weeks, it has led to the unprecedented health and socio-economic crisis, which we live in and which will mark our times for long, and has severely impacted the entire education sector around the world [3]. Notably, all levels of education have been stopped by the closure of schools, colleges and universities from the respective local government. For example, the Chinese government first announced or implemented school and universities closure and asked to take all forms of education online for the entire nation, and shortly after, many other governments also announced the same. This is the first time the world has ever seen the digital pedagogical revolution. Many countries also imposed strict travel restrictions and locked down entire cities resulting in significant impacts on education. One of the measures adopted by most countries for the continuation of education is to switch from traditional classes into remote online formats. Likewise, most TNE programmes regardless of their format also decided to transform the traditional teaching and learning activities into remote online education [32]. It was a rapid transition of education delivery involving pedagogic transformation, technology adoption in teaching and learning, and so on [33–35].

While international student mobility has been severely disrupted by COVID-19, TNE is not as vulnerable to travel restrictions and closed borders due to its nature. Therefore, TNE is in a better position to continue to accommodate the demand for international qualifications by adjusting some parameters, either as a short-term 'holding pattern' or as a rapidly growing business model for the post-pandemic world.

Even though there were some criticisms about the quality of transnational education regardless of the partnership models and delivery modes, the merits of TNE is now visible in the event of the COVID-19 pandemic that many students, who originally planned to travel abroad for a foreign degree, are now decide to study from their home country. This is due to governments being forced to impose international or domestic travel restrictions, worry about health and well-being in a foreign country, families being in financial hardship during the pandemic so worry about sending their children abroad to high-cost countries and so on [36]. In such cases, TNE is an alternative option for students wanting to achieve a foreign degree at an affordable cost. Moreover, it has also been noticed from many Alumni statistics of TNE graduates that employers value the TNE experiences in a positive way. Therefore, the opportunity to achieve a foreign degree via the TNE partnerships route is becoming more attractive and popular [37].

As for the TNE programmes in China, there was uncertainty before the start of the new semester in 2020 due to the fast spreading of the virus and it became apparent in mid-February 2020 that a plan B option is required. Also, most academics took it seriously and started to prepare for online teaching and learning [38]. In the end, universities rapidly transferred the onsite teaching to online [39]. A similar situation happened in other TNE host countries when the virus was progressively moving to other countries such as Malaysia, Vietnam, Thailand, Korea, Singapore, the Middle East, etc. Some foreign institutions took extra measures in terms of rearrangement of the course delivery (e.g., blended), curriculum (e.g., changing the weight of coursework and examination), removal (or switching) of in-laboratory activities (into, e.g., computer-based activities) and so on.

With the COVID-19 pandemic and recent developments around the world, both parents and students are concerned about safety and well-being and no longer feel that it is safe to travel and settle in another country. While many students have had their plans to study abroad, they defer and/or cancel their plans to study abroad at the last minute due to fears and uncertainties over COVID-19. Moreover, some students have decided to remain in their home country while enrolled in overseas universities studying remotely and/or to take admission at a host institution for the foreign degree via TNE programs. However, the time difference between, for example, the US and Singapore, put off many students thinking that the lessons would be held from 8 pm to 6 am [37].

6. TNE and online learning (e-learning)

The COVID-19 pandemic has opened the puzzle to test the preparedness of HEIs of how universities deal with a crisis for the continuation of essential teaching activities such as delivering courses, sharing lectures in real-time and running video-based international tutorials [40]. Many problems in TNE have been created by the closure of universities and the imposed travel restrictions, such as interruption of student learning and engagement, review and internal evaluation or continuous assessment, recruitment of teaching staff, maintaining of the academic calendar and admission processes in the next session, etc. (Rathe & Sarkar, 2020). The easiest and fastest way to keep the educational activities going is by switching to an online format. It is often referred to as online learning or online education or remote online teaching and learning.

Online education has been there for many years, but it is not an "off-the-shelf" process for most universities and goes far beyond the digitalisation of on-campus material and activities. Instead, it requires careful planning and a substantial amount of resources including a high workload for staff, and any economies of scale will only be realised in certain courses and the long term [41]. Otherwise, the risk of diminishing the student learning experience and education quality may arise.

Over the last almost 2 years, the growth and broader adoption of online education have been enormous and there is an acceptance of replacing parts of the regular provision (such as lectures) among academics. While the in-person interaction in the traditional classroom is an invaluable and irreplaceable component of teaching and learning, there has been a greater change in the perception of key stakeholders including regulators, higher education providers, academics, students, and families when it comes to the value of online education [41].

We have witnessed over the past two years that remote online teaching and learning have been adopted and recognised by most countries' institutions even though some of those countries have not formally recognised online education in the past [42]. The COVID-19 pandemic has not only proved the acceptability and the efficacy of online teaching and learning but also there is greater flexibility in terms of course content, conducting the assessment, engaging learners or delivery permitted by both the host country and foreign country institutions. Hence, COVID-19 while being a hazard to humanity, has a greater impact on evolving institutions to invest in online learning.

6.1 The implication of a rapid change and education quality

Where the original delivery model involves students physically attending a campus or other study location, the providers, awarding bodies and students are needed to adopt different forms of delivery. The location of the students will also influence any revisions to the mode of delivery. In some countries, a certain amount of in-person or on-campus delivery has been able to continue. This has resulted in some blended or dual delivery where on-campus activity is combined with the provision of materials and staff contact through digital means. For example, models which involved flying faculty visiting from the UK have, for the most part, moved to online rather than in-person delivery due to travel restrictions. Models which include local tutor support, such as staff located in a branch campus or TNE partner staff, in some cases have been able to continue depending on the local government requirements for managing COVID-19.

Authors in [42] have highlighted and recommended an important aspect that any retrospective changes that had to happen suddenly, should be submitted for approval by professional, statutory, or regulatory bodies, such as collaborative framework documents, annual activity agreements, operational delivery plans and so on. It is also important that the decision-making process on the changes involves key professional services such as IT and library services, given the need to ensure continued access to learning resources [42, 43].

6.2 Some tips for remote online learning (e-learning)

This is the first time the world has ever seen a rapid transition from face-to-face learning to remote online learning. In many cases, this happened with little advanced support or guidance, and as a result, not everyone made a smooth transition to teaching this way. While the basis of teaching such as content, pedagogy and assessment remain the same as the centre of successful teaching for both face-to-face and remote online learning, the forms of teaching and learning interactions may change. With technologies, students and teachers have found innovative ways to connect and interact with each other allowing them to move beyond substitution and redefine learning. When teaching online, this is as, or even more, important. Therefore, it is important to consider incorporating tools and techniques with careful planning on content, pedagogy and assessment and intentional use of online technologies that help teachers and students connect giving the best learning experience. In this section, a list of good practices has been identified for online teaching and learning in the context of TNE based on experiences (mostly coming from discussion and teaching-related meetings, e.g., weekly Teaching Hub):

- **Managing your technology:** Use multiple monitors, if possible, turn off your computer's notifications (the worst is getting email/calendar/slack/ etc. notifications in the middle of lecture), i.e., close or disable interruptive notifications. Since online learning involves technologies, it is important to start any session early, e.g., checking the connections, audio, video, etc. to avoid unexpected situations.

- **Speaking:** When you deliver lectures and if you use a microphone, it is better to keep the microphone further from your mouth and speak louder so that it does not amplify the sound of your breath giving you more confidence.

- **Holding students' attention/Better clarifications of terminologies:** Learning achievement is greatly influenced by individual learners' tendencies together with communication and interaction with others [44]. For example, students can get demotivated so easily in any synchronous live session. To hold students' attention, a live lecture can start with a show and tell while making a short video for asynchronous learning. Moreover, unfamiliar terminology can de-motivate students and it is always better and/or more engaging for students if lecturers describe complex terminologies and problems with examples. It is recommended to use readable font sizes (classroom projectors/monitors vary classroom to classroom), to maximise the chance that everyone in the classroom can read the slides.

- **Synchronous vs asynchronous teaching and learning:** It proved to be good practice to provide lecture notes/slides in PDF formats before a scheduled class, then short pre-recorded videos of the lecture notes made available to students asynchronously. These would be followed by synchronous live sessions that should not be a repetition of lecture slides, but should instead complement these by explaining concepts in more detail, giving illustrative examples, and supplying tasks for the students to engage with. The use of Q&A slides, such as Mentimeter, and short quizzes should be encouraged. Depending on cultural sensitivities, questions from students could be posted anonymously. On the other hand, the use of practical tasks for students to undertake in live synchronous sessions, where relevant, encourages student engagement.

  Although the physical presence of the teacher in the classroom is not possible, the use of Teaching Assistants in the classroom during live synchronous sessions "in loco teacher" helps to smooth the transition between the teacher's delivery and the student engagement.

- **Interactivity in asynchronous teaching and learning:** Supporting student engagement is one of the key challenges for designing asynchronous learning, but asynchronous activities can still be highly interactive and engaging experiences. It is important to stress that lecturer's engagement and visibility are also hugely important for student engagement, as are opportunities for students to work together and collaborate. For example, discussion forums are a common asynchronous activity, and they enable students and teachers to come together asynchronously to discuss, share information, exchange ideas, give feedback and collaborate with the following added benefits:

  - Offering inclusive teaching methods as students who feel less able to participate in face-to-face group discussions may feel more confident in contributing.

  - Allowing students time to reflect and consider before they respond to others.

  - Enabling students to give and receive peer feedback on their work or ideas.

  - Allowing students to lead to collaborative learning experiences and collaborative constructions of meaning.

  - Forums can be wholly open, or students can be divided into groups.

- **Increase students' engagement/Get real-time feedback from students:** Many tools allow lecturers to encourage and facilitate even more "lean forward" behaviours and more interaction with and among students. For example, one can use online platforms (e.g., Mentimeter) to get real-time input and a sense of students' experience, comprehension, and reactions ("reading the classroom") anonymously from students. Some best practices on improving students' engagement are:

  - Spend some time at the beginning of the lecture to identify students' questions about the material.

  - Use polls and other interactive technologies to get a sense of students' experience, comprehension, and reactions ("reading the room").

  - Open the floor with the help of interactive technologies to a general discussion of particular questions

  - Create small groups via breakout rooms for having peer discussion using platforms like Zoom, MS Teams, etc. and/or other opportunities for student collaboration using tools like Google Docs, Miro, etc.

- **Online quizzes:** Quizzes are an excellent way of engaging students, and they can offer students the chance to self-assess their progress, and/or act as a tool for lecturers to review their learning. Correct answers and feedback can be pre-programmed so that students automatically receive the answers and the reasons why they were incorrect if they get a question wrong.

- The tools can be used by students to ask questions about a recorded lecture, a reading, or following a synchronous webinar discussion. Quizzes can be a good way to review learning at the end of a topic or week. If any of module summative assessment takes the form of multiple-choice questions or similar then quizzes also offer students the opportunity to practice for this.

6.3 The role of HEIs

It is needless to say that COVID-19 is causing a great deal of ongoing stress and disruption to all our lives. The universities have also been trying to ensure that students' academic progression and achievement are not disadvantaged by the current crisis. Therefore, the first and foremost task for HEIs is to take extra precautions to keep students safe. It makes emergency preparedness plans for the continuation of learning by transforming face-to-face learning into online mode. This requires a lot of effort from the institution's point of view ranging from the change/mitigation of policies and procedures (e.g., teaching, learning, assessments, etc.) to the adaptation of new (often unknown) teaching and learning methods and technologies, which may result in unexpected outcomes. For example, the unexpected shutdown of the computer servers of the online learning platform due to a large number of users [45]. Moreover, some online education platforms have good features such as breakout for small group discussion while others may lack such important features. Most universities had to change their assessment policies - specifically, adopting an alternative assessment and relaxing or mitigating Extenuating Circumstances (EC) (e.g., students can self-certify for EC, automatic approval, etc.). The alternative assessment adopted can be varied from university to university and here are some common assessment formats: take-home exams, online proctor exams, long-period online exams, i.e., answering the paper within the normal exam time, but students can submit their answers within the allocated long hours window, etc. There are also other measures taken by HEIs such as communications and compliance that universities offer frequent communications for COVID-19 guidance and measures to enable students to continue to engage effectively with learning and assessment. Therefore, HEIs must have alternative plans (Plan B/Plan C) for any unexpected issues in advance and students must also be well informed about those plans with proper instructions.

6.4 The role of regulatory bodies and agencies

Quality assurance and regulation of TNE have become an important element for both host and foreign institutions to ensure the quality of TNE programmes in an acceptable standard. Most TNE host countries have regulatory bodies and established procedures for assuring quality [13]. For example, the Malaysian Qualification Framework (MQF) implemented by the Malaysian Qualification Agency (MQA) is used as a basis for quality assurance of higher education in Malaysia as a host country while the quality of UK TNE is demonstrated through independent evaluation by the Quality Assurance Agency for Higher Education (QAA) [46]. While foreign countries are encouraging and helping their universities to expand their TNE activities, many countries have also started monitoring those TNE activities to project their higher education reputation [28]. For example, the UK's QAA has been conducting in-country audits of UK TNE operations since 2009 across a range of countries[4]. It is believed that the export success of UK higher education is critically dependent on explicit and visible confirmation of rigorous internal quality assurance, external quality evaluation and careful regulation. The method for the quality evaluation and enhancement of

[4] https://www.qaa.ac.uk/international/transnational-education

UK transnational education was commissioned by Universities UK (UUK) and GuildHE, and the Quality Evaluation and Enhancement of UK Transnational Higher Education Provision (QE-TNE) demonstrates the commitment of UK higher education to deliver high-quality TNE experiences for students [46].

7. Challenges and opportunities of TNE

Education sectors have seen a dramatic digital revolution in recent years due to the COVID-19 pandemic putting universities in change and innovation mode. Over the course, individuals from all stakeholders (regulators, higher education providers, academics, students, and families) have faced several challenges, and one of the great challenges in TNE programmes is, in most cases, the rapid change in the delivery mode, which completely relies on technologies [47], and adjusting with the technology is a challenging task for both students and teachers. In this section, several challenges that are faced by TNE stakeholders are identified and briefly explained below.

7.1 Technological challenges and adjustment

In recent years, there is a significant advancement of educational tools and platforms, thanks to the fast technological advancement, that are readily available to adopt within a short time. For example, cloud-based teleconferencing with video platforms includes Zoom, Microsoft Teams, Blackboard Collaborate, etc. Since TNE students and staff require to engage with remote online education from home via educational tools and platforms, there can be significant challenges for both students [43, 48] and staff if a high-speed and uninterrupted internet connection is not accessible. Overall, this is a common problem for any remote online education resulting in a serious concern for the education providers to ensure the inclusive education provision. It was found [32] that many TNE students have limited access to a suitable internet connection and their learning experience is unequal.

7.2 Student expectation and support

TNE students are often used to a particular delivery mode, and significant changes are being made, which are essential tasks during the shift to online education, causing disruption to student learning [49]. Therefore, the measures taken by the institution and/or any changes must be communicated frequently with students and additional support must be ensured so that the learning outcomes can be achieved, and student expectations are met. It is even more important than usual that providers engage with students to ensure that any changes to delivery and assessment are communicated.

7.3 Different time zones and well-being

During the pandemic, most students travelled back home due to the closure of universities, and it was important for the best interest of students' physical and mental wellbeing resulting in students being started attending online learning activities in different time zones. This was an important issue to consider before transforming traditional face-to-face learning into remote online learning. For example, it is not possible to deliver most learning activities in synchronous mode like in normal circumstances [35]. There are many ways [50] to blend the traditional face-to-face learning activities in the remote online format and many universities have adopted a blended approach consisting of synchronous and asynchronous modes of delivery.

7.4 Learning and inequality

Authors in [51] have compiled many relevant kinds of literature to identify the learning gaps due to several factors. There is much evidence that learning loss can be severe during the COVID-19 crisis exacerbating educational inequality [52] as according to the "faucet theory" [53]. Similarly, COVID-19 and the closure of universities may not affect students equally. In the case of remote online education, many TNE students have limited access to necessary technical equipment, a suitable broadband service, or perhaps facilities such as a quiet room with a desk and a computer.

One of many important challenges for the sudden forced switch to online education is learning and inequality. The fact is that not all households are equally prepared to move on to online education with a personal device and a stable Internet connection as necessary requirements not to fall behind. These factors have made the digital divide between those who can meet the new basic needs of the contemporary world and those who cannot, which is wider than ever. Such access inequalities are established on attributes of the individual (e.g., technology skills), contextualised social realities (e.g., gender discrimination), and economic circumstances (e.g. the ability to afford relevant technologies) [40]. Given this mixed situation, personalised blended learning that takes these factors into account is the ideal compromise for a post-pandemic society.

7.5 Addendum to the TNE partnership agreement if required

Depending on the TNE partnership agreement and delivery models, there might be some legal bindings in terms of changing the delivery modes though most TNE programmes have already adapted an alternative delivery model during the COVID-19 pandemic. The rapid temporary change in the delivery mode for any TNE arrangement was required for the continuation of education. However, an important advisable comment was made by authors in Green et al. [42] that TNE partners should review the terms of the overarching legal agreement and any operational agreement, which articulates the roles and responsibilities between both partners: firstly, to check whether these formal agreements allow any changes in the delivery mode or not; secondly, to introduce addendums to the agreements in line with their usual approval processes for permitting the necessary changes adhering to any emergency regulations (e.g., COVID-19). The emergency regulations can be adapted for their operating agreements as a consistent plan in the shorter term, and this may require substantial adjustments in terms of teaching, learning, assessment, student support as well as adapting and accessing technologies.

7.6 Spaces for wellbeing (impacts of student and staff wellbeing)

There is an increasing pressure to perform well academically and to sustain in an increasingly competitive environment contributing to suboptimal wellbeing [54]. Higher education students also have to cope with a new learning environment due to the COVID-19 pandemic, and the dramatic shift in the learning environment is the biggest contributor to poor wellbeing for students. A lack of physical contact with academic staff, coupled with their reduced capacity associated with the technological shift, has put students under increased pressure to meet deadlines without the typical access to support that they would normally experience (Zhai and Du, 2020).

New research conducted by Pearson and Wonkhe suggests that an emphasis should be given on improving online learning, which will have the most direct impact on students' future wellbeing, engagement, and motivation [55]. It is suggested that it is not only about the result of students being at home and the concerns over Covid-19, but also the way that universities have managed interactions and online learning has increased their anxiety and harmed their wellbeing [55].

7.7 Opportunities

COVID-19 has tested the capability of the current education systems and challenged us in many ways. With the forced adoption of new ways of delivering teaching and learning, COVID-19 is also showing us the value of online education and the effectiveness of technology-assisted learning. It brings confidence and resilience to the education system, which has gained the capacity to deal with any future emergencies. The blended and/or mixed-mode learning approach is considered a viable model for the future of education. Therefore, it is the ideal way to prepare students, who are employable, locally and globally, for a world where knowledge is not a fixed set of facts.

8. Future of HE and TNE

Education is a core aspect of the United Nations (UN) Sustainable Development Goals (SDGs), and is considered essential to their success (UN, online). Likewise, transnational education (TNE) plays an important role for SDG 4 (i.e., "Ensure inclusive and equitable quality education and promote lifelong learning opportunities for all.") in the pursuit of sustainable development.

Before COVID-19, online learning was often considered as an afterthought, or an optional extra and face-to-face education has always been the norm for university programs. However, like many other sectors that have evolved to support remote workers and colleagues working from home, many universities have reconsidered their use of technologies to do the same, offering a truly blended approach to learning, to survive. In today's world during COVID-19, education is not limited by where or how you learn, what matters is that you continue to learn regardless of the pandemic. As such, universities around the globe have developed and adopted blended learning approaches to learning, making use of technologies, thanks to the recent advancement of computer science, information technology, computing, telecommunications, and other technological sectors.

Now, the questions about the post-COVID landscape of the higher education sector - What would be the teaching and learning delivery model when face-to-face teaching resumes? Whether going back to what it was before or will a new delivery model be introduced? Is a higher education revolution on the way due to COVID-19? What should universities be doing to minimise similar risks in the future, and what will that future look like for higher education? [56]. There has already been a lot of effort and investments placed for the adoption of the new education model and there is also a growing discussion ongoing about the future post-COVID-19 model of higher education whether it is to review their course structure and content, a fundamental revision of strategic priorities, a redesign of universities' core activities and so on [41, 57]. It is speculated by experts [58] that a post-pandemic recession will accelerate the latest shift away from high-cost study destinations towards more affordable locations nearer to students' home countries. This means the TNE programmes, which often cost less fees as compared to the fees required to pay in the West for the same programme, would particularly be attractive to those from low- and middle-income countries. Since most TNE programmes include the face-to-face element of TNE provision, which is essential to many students, it may be more appropriate to implement the mixed-mode education provision as a future pandemic-proof TNE solution with investing in online technologies and the development of online pedagogies. It is now clear that online pathways to overseas degrees are likely to expand, primarily in the form of blended learning at branch campuses and partner institutions [58].

While it will take another year to fully grasp the impact of the pandemic on international enrolments in traditional destinations, the short-term impact appears not to have been as bad as was first feared. An audience poll during a recent Times Higher Education session on international recruitment, for instance, found that international demand for UK university places has dipped by less than 25 per cent while most TNE programmes are overwhelmingly receiving students. What is clear is that universities need to consider more holistically their role as global social enterprises with their key remit being to address sustainability and employability challenges [41].

9. Conclusions

With efforts to prevent the spread of COVID-19, the global education system including transitional education (TNE) has been transformed with online education becoming the primary means of instruction. However, there are several challenges to be faced. The technological challenges are mainly related to the unreliable Internet connections for thousands of students and staff being simultaneously connected and the lack of digital devices for many students. This chapter presented a detailed discussion about COVID-19 and its impact on transitional education. It may be too early to say how students and teachers will cope with online learning and what future impacts it will have in terms of, e.g., student employability. All stakeholders such as academics, students and their families, enterprises, experts, universities and Policymakers should collaborate closely to develop accessible and inclusive learning environments, educational resources and tools are additionally able to maintain the sociality, inclusiveness and accessibility of education. At the same time, it will strengthen the capacity of universities in terms of preparedness for future emergencies. Moreover, future research will further analyse students' perspectives, assessment, student experiences, and employability for graduates in COVID-19 and compare them across different TNE models and delivery modes, to provide a more comprehensive view and more detailed results.

Author details

Atm S. Alam*, Ling Ma, Andy Watson, Vindya Wijeratne and Michael Chai
School of Electronic Engineering and Computer Science, Queen Mary University of London, London, United Kingdom

*Address all correspondence to: a.alam@qmul.ac.uk

References

[1] Dhawan S. Online learning: A panacea in the time of COVID-19 crisis. Journal of Educational Technology Systems. 2020;**49**(1):5-22

[2] Palvia S, Aeron P, Gupta P, Mahapatra D, Parida R, Rosner R, Sindhi S. Online Education: Worldwide Status, Challenges, Trends, and Implications. UK: Taylor & Francis Online; 2018

[3] Marinoni G, Van't Land H, Jensen T. The impact of Covid-19 on higher education around the world. In: IAU Global Survey Report. France: International Association of Universities; 2020

[4] UN. "Goal 4: Sustainable Development Knowledge Platform". USA: United Nations; 2020. Available from: https://sdgs.un.org/goals/goal4 [Accessed: 9 March 2021].

[5] Baer J, Martel M. Fall 2020 International Student Enrollment Snapshot. USA: Institute of International Education (IIE):[сайт]; 2020. November

[6] Mukhtar K, Javed K, Arooj M, Sethi A. Advantages, Limitations and Recommendations for online learning during COVID-19 pandemic era. Pakistan Journal of Medical Sciences. 2020;**36**(COVID19-S4):S27

[7] Alammary A, Sheard J, Carbone A. Blended learning in higher education: Three different design approaches. Australasian Journal of Educational Technology. 2014;**30**(4):440-454

[8] Clark N. Understanding transnational education, its growth and implications. World Education News and Reviews. 2012;**1**:1-9

[9] UNESCO/Council of Europe. Code of good practice in the provision of transnational education. Riga: UNESCO/Council of Europe; 2001

[10] Knight J. Transnational education remodeled: Toward a common TNE framework and definitions. Journal of Studies in International Education. 2016;**20**(1):34-47

[11] Croucher G, Elliott K, Locke W, Yencken E. Australia's Higher Education Delivery Offshore and Online–Trends, Barriers and Opportunities. Australia: Melbourne Centre for the Study of Higher Education; 2020

[12] Knight J. International programme and provider mobility (IPPM) in selected African countries. In: A Mapping Study of IPPM National Policies, Regulations and Activities. UK: British Council; 2019. pp. 1-60

[13] Wilkins S, Juusola K. The Benefits and Drawbacks of Transnational Higher Education: Myths and Realities. Australian Universities' Review. 2018;**60**(2):68-76

[14] Jisc and Internet2. "Transnational Education (TNE) Data Report." UK: Jisc; 2018

[15] Sin IL, Leung MW, Waters JL. Degrees of value: Comparing the contextual complexities of UK transnational education in Malaysia and Hong Kong. Compare: A Journal of Comparative and International Education. 2019;**49**(1):132-148

[16] Mellors-Bourne R, Fielden J, Kemp N, Middlehurst R, Woodfield, S. The Value of Transnational Education to the UK. UK: UK Government; 2014

[17] Wilkins S. Two decades of international branch campus development, 2000-2020: A review. International Journal of Educational Management. 2020

[18] Tremblay K. Internationalisation: Shaping strategies in the national context. International Organisations Research Journal. 2010;**5**(3):110-169

[19] Mellors-Bourne R, Jones E, Woodfield S. Transnational Education and Employability Development. York, UK: Higher Education Academy; 2015

[20] Mellors-Bourne R. The wider benefits of Transnational Education to the UK. In: Social Science in Government. UK: UK Government; 2017. pp. 1-80

[21] Schmitt M. How to Deal with Culture Shock while Studying Abroad. Go Overseas. USA: Go Overseas; 2015. Retrieved from: https://www.gooverseas.com/blog/how-to-deal-with-culture-shock-while-studying-abroad

[22] Tompson A. Survive Culture Shock While Studying Abroad Off-the-Beaten-Path. USA: Go Abroad; 2020. Retrieved from: https://www.goabroad.com/articles/study-abroad/surviving-culture-shock-while-studying-abroad-off-the-beaten-path

[23] UKCISA. Facing Cultural Shock. UK: UK Council for International Student Affairs; 2018. Retrieved from: https://www.ukcisa.org.uk/information--advice/preparation-and-arrival/facing-culture-shock

[24] Healey NM. The end of transnational education? The view from the UK. Perspectives: Policy and Practice in Higher Education. 2020;**24**(3):102-112

[25] Magne PJ, Poverjuc O, Heffernan T. Pedagogies across borders: perspectives from teaching staff and students engaged with transnational programmes in Hong Kong. Practice and Evidence of the Scholarship of Teaching and Learning in Higher Education. 2017;**12**(1):45-62

[26] Mercado S, Gibson L. The Key Elements of Transnational Education (TNE). Amsterdam: European Association for International Education; 2013

[27] Wilkins S, Stephens Balakrishnan M, Huisman J. Student satisfaction and student perceptions of quality at international branch campuses in the United Arab Emirates. Journal of Higher Education Policy and Management. 2012;**34**(5):543-556

[28] Healey NM. The challenges of managing transnational education partnerships: The views of 'home-based'managers versus 'in-country'managers. Transnational Education: Oversexed, Oversold and Over There? 2018;**55**(3):276

[29] Cross-Border Education Research Team (CBERT) (2020). C-BERT International Campus Listing. [Data originally collected by Kevin Kinser and Jason E. Lane]. USA: C-BERT; Retrieved on 19 August 2021, Available from: http://cbert.org/resources-data/intl-campus/. Albany, NY: Author

[30] Wake D, Ryan G. The Scale of UK Higher Education Transnational Education 2018-19. UK: Universities UK; 2020. Available from: https://www.universitiesuk.ac.uk/policy-and-analysis/reports/Pages/The-Scale-of-UK-Higher-Education-Transnational-Education-2017-18.aspx

[31] WHO. Statement on the Second Meeting of the International Health Regulations (2005) Emergency Committee Regarding the Outbreak of Novel Coronavirus (2019-nCoV). Switzerland: World Health Organisation; 2020. Retrieved from: https://www.who.int/news/item/30-01-2020-statement-on-the-second-meeting-of-the-international-health-regulations-(2005)-emergency-committee-regarding-the-outbreak-of-novel-coronavirus-(2019-ncov) [Accessed: 2 March 2021]

[32] Alam AS, Lau E, Oh C, Chai KK. An Alternative laboratory assessment approach for multimedia modules in a transnational education (TNE) programme during COVID-19. In 2020 Transnational Engineering Education using Technology (TREET) (pp. 1-4). New York, USA: IEEE; 2020

[33] Demuyakor J. Coronavirus (COVID-19) and online learning in higher institutions of education: A survey of the perceptions of Ghanaian international students in China. Online Journal of Communication and Media Technologies. 2020;**10**(3):1-9

[34] Oyedotun TD. Sudden change of pedagogy in education driven by COVID-19: Perspectives and evaluation from a developing country. Research in Globalization. 2020;**2**:100029

[35] Vollbrecht PJ, Porter-Stransky KA, Lackey-Cornelison WL. Lessons learned while creating an effective emergency remote learning environment for students during the COVID-19 pandemic. Advances in Physiology Education. 2020;**44**(4):722-725

[36] Lane JE, Borgos J, Schueller J, Dey S, Kinser K, Zipf S. What is the Future for International Branch Campuses? UK: University World News; 2021. Retrieved 19 August 2021, from https://www.universityworldnews.com/post.php?story=2021031012405285

[37] Oh T. Students in S'pore defer, cancel plans to study abroad due to fears, uncertainties over Covid-19. In: Singapore Today. Singapore: Singapore Today; 2020. Retrieved from: https://www.todayonline.com/singapore/students-spore-defer-cancel-plans-study-abroad-due-fears-uncertainties-over-covid-19

[38] Peters MA, Wang H, Ogunniran MO, Huang Y, Green B, Chunga JO, et al. China's internationalized higher education during Covid-19: Collective student autoethnography. Postdigital Science and Education. 2020;**2**:968-988

[39] Aristovnik A, Keržič D, Ravšelj D, Tomaževič N, Umek L. Impacts of the COVID-19 pandemic on life of higher education students: A global perspective. Sustainability (Switzerland). 2020;**12**(20):1-34

[40] Shohel MMC, Ashrafuzzaman M, Ahsan MS, Mahmud A, Alam AS. Education in emergencies, inequities, and the digital divide: Strategies for supporting teachers and students in higher education in Bangladesh. In: Handbook of Research on Inequities in Online Education During Global Crises. USA: Pennsylvania: IGI Global; 2021. pp. 529-553

[41] Tsiligiris V. Towards a Global Delivery Model for International Higher Education. UK: University World News; 2020. Retrieved on 20/08/2021 and from https://www.universityworldnews.com/post.php?story=2020082111264620

[42] Green B, Glautier D, Haddleton F, King M, MacKinlay A, McLaughlin M, Shaw C. Effective Practice in UK Transnational Education during the COVID-19 Pandemic. UK: QAA; 2020

[43] Clune A. Using technology to cope with Covid-19 on (Or off) campus. In: Wonkhe. Vol. 13. UK: Wonkhe Ltd.; 2020, March, Available from: https://wonkhe.com/blogs/using-technology-to-cope-with-covid-19-on-or-off-campus/ [Accessed: 4 June 2020]

[44] Islam M, Kim DA, Kwon M. A comparison of two forms of instruction: Pre-recorded video lectures vs. live ZOOM lectures for education in the business management field. Sustainability. 2020;**12**(19):8149

[45] Bao W. COVID-19 and online teaching in higher education: A case study of Peking University. Human Behavior and Emerging Technologies. 2020;**2**(2):113-115

[46] QAA. The Quality Evaluation and Enhancement of UK Transnational Higher Education Provision 2021-22 to 2025-2. UK: QAA; 2021

[47] Lederman D. Evaluating teaching during the pandemic. In: Inside Higher Ed. Vol. 8. USA: Inside Higher Ed.; 2020 April, Available from: https://www.insidehighered.com/digital-learning/article/2020/04/08/many-colleges-are-abandoning-or-downgrading-student-evaluations [Accessed: 4 June 2020]

[48] Owusu-Agyeman Y, Amoakohene G. Student engagement and perceived gains in transnational education in Ghana. International Journal of Comparative Education and Development. 2021;**23**: 297-316

[49] Coman C, Țîru LG, Meseșan-Schmitz L, Stanciu C, Bularca MC. Online teaching and learning in higher education during the coronavirus pandemic: Students' perspective. Sustainability. USA: C-BERT; 2020;**12**(24):10367

[50] Clow D. What should universities do to prepare for COVID-19 coronavirus? In: Wonkhe. Vol. 2. UK: Wonkhe Ltd.; 2020, March, Available from: https://wonkhe.com/blogs/what-should-universities-do-to-prepare-for-covid-19-coronavirus/ [Accessed: 4 June 2020]

[51] Di Pietro G, Biagi F, Costa P, Karpiński Z, Mazza J. The Likely Impact of COVID-19 on Education: Reflections Based on the Existing Literature and Recent International Datasets. Vol. 30275. Luxembourg: Publications Office of the European Union; 2020

[52] Downey DB, Yoon A, Martin E. Schools and inequality: Implications from seasonal comparison research. In: Handbook of the Sociology of Education in the 21st Century. Cham: Springer; 2018. pp. 55-70

[53] Entwisle DR, Alexander KL, Olson LS. Keep the faucet flowing summer learning and home environment. American Educator. 2001;**25**(3):10-15

[54] Burns D, Dagnall N, Holt M. Assessing the impact of the Covid-19 pandemic on student wellbeing at universities in the UK: a conceptual analysis. In: Frontiers in Education. Vol. 5. Switzerland: Frontiers Media; 2020

[55] Jackson A. The Expectation Gap: Students' Experience of Learning During Covid-19 and Their Expectations for Next Year. UK: Wonkhe Ltd.; 2020

[56] Thompson F. Revolutionizing Universities: The Blended Learning Approach. USA: eLearning Industry; 2020. Available from: https://elearningindustry.com/revolutionising-universities-blended-learning-approach. [Accessed from: 7 March 2021]

[57] Simamora RM. The challenges of online learning during the COVID-19 pandemic: An essay analysis of performing arts education studies. Studies in Learning and Teaching. 2020;**1**(2):86-103

[58] Ilieva J, Pilsbury D. Transnational Education Will Resist the Post-Pandemic Recruitment Crunch. UK: Times Higher Education; 2021